AN ILLUSTRATED ENCYCLOPAEDIA

OF TRADITIONAL

SYMBOLS

More than 23 symbols, all of them discussed and explained in this
book, are in this illustration from *Microcosmos Hypochondriacus*, a
17th-century alchemical text. Besides the familiar symbols, such
as SUN, TRIANGLE, EAGLE, LION, DOVE and LAMB, the picture also
contains the PEACOCK, PELICAN, FORGE, CADUCEUS, GOOSE, SHIP and
many other symbolic allusions to the transformative steps and
processes of alchemy.

AN ILLUSTRATED ENCYCLOPAEDIA OF TRADITIONAL SYMBOLS

J.C.COOPER

with 210 illustrations

THAMES AND HUDSON

*Filmset in Great Britain by Keyspools Ltd, Golborne, Lancs.
Printed and bound in Great Britain
by Butler & Tanner Ltd, Frome*

Contents

Introduction

7

Acknowledgments

9

THE ENCYCLOPEDIA

10

Glossary

201

Bibliography

203

In memoriam
Vincent Morse Cooper

Introduction

The study of symbolism is not mere erudition; it concerns man's knowledge of himself. Symbolism is an instrument of knowledge and the most ancient and fundamental method of expression, one which reveals aspects of reality which escape other modes of expression.

Although the full portent of the symbol cannot be captured and imprisoned within the confines of any encyclopaedia or written word, there exists, nevertheless, a large body of symbolism which has become traditional over the ages and which constitutes an international language transcending the normal limits of communication. Furthermore, whereas it is impossible to limit the symbol to mere meaning and definition, it is possible to provide, or indicate, a point of departure for a voyage of exploration, a two-way journey, or quest, of mind and spirit, of inner depth and outer height, the immanent and the transcendent, the horizontal and the vertical planes. Symbolic usage, mediate in itself, can lead to the immediate and to direct apprehension.

Symbolism is not only international, it also stretches over the ages; it has 'the virtue of containing within a few conventional lines the thought of the ages and the dreams of the race. It kindles our imagination and leads us to realms of wordless thought' (Lin Yu-tang). This thought is not that of the individual ego; the symbol cannot be created artificially or invented for some purely personal interpretation or whim: it goes beyond the individual to the universal and is innate in the life of the spirit. It is the external, or lower, expression of the higher truth which is symbolized, and is a means of communicating realities which might otherwise be either obscured by the limitations of language or too complex for adequate expression. Thus the symbol can never be a mere form, as is the sign, nor can it be understood except in the context of its religious, cultural or metaphysical background, the soil from which it grew. The symbol is a key to a realm greater than itself and greater than the man who employs it. As Coleridge said, 'A symbol ... always partakes of the Reality which it renders intelligible; and while it enunciates the whole, abides itself as a living part of that Unity of which it is the representative.'

The symbol does not merely equate; it must reveal some essential part of the subject to be understood; it contains the vast ever-expanding realm of possibilities and makes possible the perception of fundamental relationships between seemingly diverse forms or appearances.

Strictly speaking, the symbol differs from the emblem and allegory in that it expresses, or crystallizes, some aspect or direct experience of life and truth and thus leads beyond itself. On the other hand the frontiers between the territories governed by these close relations can be so ill-defined that one can lead to the other and provide a bridge by which it is possible to cross and re-cross from one to the other. Although the symbol captures and integrates abstractions and places them in their effective context, it can also be effective on more than one level at the same time; the emblem, or attribute, usually portrays something concrete, but can, in turn, embody some symbolic quality; thus attributes and emblems of divinities may also be symbols of the cosmos, its laws and functions. Here a large measure of syncretism occurs. A symbol need not arise from any one source, but can adapt or respond to different ages, religions, cults and civilizations. Exclusiveness is a primitive and immature characteristic; the symbol is inclusive and expansive, and there may be many and diverse applications of the same symbol which can become ambivalent or polyvalent in accordance with its subsidiary connections. A symbol may also have both an esoteric and exoteric meaning, so that the most obvious and usual interpretation is not necessarily complete and can be merely a half-truth: it may both reveal and conceal.

Much of symbolism directly concerns the dramatic interplay and interaction of the opposing forces in the dualistic world of manifestation, their conflicting but also complementary and compensating characteristics, and their final union, symbolized by the androgyne or the sacred marriage. These are expressions of the unity of life which is the central point of all traditional symbolism. As the Tree of Life, axial, unifying and either evergreen or perpetually renewed, stands at the centre of Paradise and the spring at its roots gives rise to the Rivers of Life, so man's thought and aspiration, embodied in the myth and symbol, centre on unity and life.

Traditional symbolism assumes that the celestial is primordial and that the terrestrial is but a reflection or image of it: the higher contains the meaning of the lower. The celestial is not only primordial but eternal, and confers on the symbol that undying power which has remained effective over the ages and continues so to the extent that it evokes the sense of the sacred and leads to a power beyond itself.

Symbolism is basic to the human mind; to ignore it is to suffer a serious deficiency; it is fundamental to thinking, and the perfect symbol should satisfy every aspect of man – his spirit, intellect and emotions. All religious rites have a symbolic significance and quality without the understanding of which they become empty and 'superstitious'. In ceremonial there is a wide symbolism of attitude and posture, such as the *mudras* and postures of supplication or submission, of direction assumed in prayer and worship, of sound and movement – all profoundly meaningful and interwoven in the fabric of human nature and needs. As Dean Inge says of symbols: 'Indifference to them is not, as many have supposed, a sign of enlightenment and spirituality. It is, in fact, an unhealthy symptom.' Mircea Eliade sees in the recovery of symbolism the chance to 'rescue modern man from his cultural provincialism and, above all, from his historical and existentialist relativism'.

The pattern adopted in this Encyclopaedia is first to present the generalized or universal acceptance of the interpretation of a symbol, then to particularize its diverse applications in varying traditions, cultural and geographic. Where no tradition is specified it is indicative of an accepted meaning wherever that particular symbol occurs.

Finally, no encyclopaedia of symbolism can ever hope to be complete; the symbol is living and ever-expanding.

Acknowledgments

My debt to all the authors whose books are listed in the Bibliography is very evident.

I also take this opportunity of expressing my sincere thanks to the County Library service, in particular for help provided by the Preston, Carlisle and Ulverston branches, whose indefatigable and highly efficient efforts were instrumental in tracing and supplying a great variety of books of reference, many of them rare and otherwise unobtainable. This efficiency was always combined with unfailing patience and courtesy. My thanks are especially due to Miss B. Henderson of the Preston Library and Miss B. Adams of the Ulverston Branch. My thanks are also due to the University of Lancaster for the use of their Reference Library.

A See ALPHA.

Ablutions Purification; initiation. *Alchemic*: In the *Magnum Opus* the soul is purified by washing, and the change takes place from black to grey to white. *Buddhist*: Ablutions at the initiation of a monk represent the washing away of the past as a layman. *Christian*: Innocence; the *lavabo*, the washing of the priest's hands, signifies: 'I will wash mine hands in innocency.' *Islamic*: An important rite; the return of man to primordial purity.

Abnormality Ambivalent, but generally anything abnormal contains magic possibilities or powers, often chthonic. Bringers of luck, such as hunchbacks and dwarfs, have positive powers; on the other hand, the cross-eyed are unlucky, as is the abnormality of a crowing hen, cock-crow at night or the scream of the owl in daylight, or an out-of-season flower.

Abyss Ambivalent, as both the profundity of the depth and as abasement and inferiority. The watery abyss is the primordial source of the universe; the Mother Goddess; the underworld. In Gnostic symbolism it is Supreme Being, the author of the Aeons.

Acacia In Mediterranean countries it represents life; immortality; platonic love; retirement. As having both white and red flowers it denotes life and death, death and rebirth. Its thorns are the horns of the crescent moon. *Christian*: Immortality; a moral life. One tradition suggests that the crown of thorns was made of acacia with the dual purpose of mocking and using the sacred Hebrew wood. *Egyptian*: Solar; rebirth; immortality; initiation; innocence. Emblem of Neith. *Hebrew*: The Shittah Tree, the sacred wood of the Tabernacle. Immortality; a moral life; innocence. It is also funerary, mourning.

Acanthus In Mediterranean countries it is life; immortality; the horns of the lunar crescent; veneration of the arts. In Christianity the thorns represent pain, sin and its punishment.

Aconite *Graeco-Roman*: Crime; the poison of words; coolness; sacred to Saturn; grew where the saliva of Cerberus fell; a witch flower.

Acorn A Scandinavian and Celtic symbol of life, fecundity and immortality; sacred to Thor; the androgynous.

Adder *Christian*: Evil; one of the four aspects of the devil according to St Augustine. The deaf adder depicts sinners who close their ears to the voice of the doctrine and words of life.

Aegis Protection; preservation; fecundity. The aegis was worn, while the shield was carried. It is an attribute of Zeus/Jupiter and was made from the skin of the goat which suckled Zeus Dictynnos; also an emblem of Athene/Minerva and the Egyptian Bast, worn by Achilles; see also SHIELD.

Aerolite Revelation; descent of the spirit; celestial messages; heavenly vestments.

Agate See JEWELS.

Agriculture Symbolized by the Corn Goddess with ears of wheat, also by the plough, cornucopia and budding branch.

Alb *Christian*. A sacrificial vestment; the white garment in which Christ was clothed by Herod; its white linen represents purity and chastity, as the celebrant says 'make me white'.

Albatross Typifies long, tireless flight and distant oceans; forecasts bad weather and high winds. It can embody the soul of a dead sailor, hence killing it is unlucky.

Alcohol *Alchemic*: The *aqua vitae* as both fire and water; the conjunction of opposites; the *coincidentia oppositorum*; the male and female, active and passive both in a state of creation and destruction.

Alder Associated with death and with the smith's fire and the power of evaporation. *Celtic*: The fairy tree; divination, resurrection. *Greek*: Emblem of Pan. Associated with Spring and fire festivals.

Alloy Marriage; the union of male and female, fire and water.

Almond Virginity; the self-productive; the yoni; conjugal happiness. It is also the *vesica piscis* which, in art, often surrounds virgin Queens of Heaven; the MANDORLA (q.v.). As the first flower of the year the blossom is 'the Awakener', hence it depicts watchfulness; it also represents sweetness, charm and delicacy. *Chinese*: Feminine beauty, fortitude in sorrow, watchfulness. *Christian*: Divine favour and approval. The purity of the Virgin. *Hebrew*: 'Skeked' – to waken and watch. *Iranian*: The Tree of Heaven. *Phrygian*: The father of all things: Spring. It is associated with the birth of Attis, the almond having sprung from the male genitalia of the androgynous Cybele.

Aloe Bitterness, but also integrity and wisdom. Sacred to Zeus/Jupiter.

Alpha The beginning; the First Principle from which all things proceed. Alpha and omega represent the totality, the beginning and the end; like the Hindu AUM (see OM) they symbolize the entire range of sounds, also infinity. A and Ω are sometimes portrayed by the eagle and owl, day and night, and in Christianity they appear with the cross and the Chi-Rho (see LABARUM).

Alsirat See BRIDGE.

Altar The divine presence; the sacrifice; reunion with the deity by means of sacrifice; integration; thanksgiving. Its situation at the East end of the temple, cathedral or church represents the position of worship towards the sun and in the direction of paradise. Being in the shape of a tomb symbolizes the passage from death to life and from time to eternity. The steps up to the altar are ritual ascent. Stone altars, or bethels (see STONE), signify the indestructibility and everlasting duration of the divinity, associated often with the Tree as the complementary aspect of change and renewal. *Aztec.* The cylindrical solar stone was used for both sacrificial and astronomical purposes. *Buddhist.* The centre of devotion is a shrine rather than an altar, although the latter may be applied where it serves to carry images, books, sacred objects and offerings to the Buddha, but the idea of an instituted rite as sacrifice is absent. *Christian:* The altar represents both the tomb and the resurrection, death transformed into life, the sacrifice of Christ in the Eucharist and Christ as the Sun of Righteousness. The wood is the cross, the stone the rock of Calvary and the raised altar is both ascension and Christ's suffering on a hill. The rails are the division from the Holy of Holies where only the High Priest may enter. The three or seven steps to the altar symbolize the Trinity or the seven gifts of the Holy Spirit; the linen cloth on the altar is the winding-sheet and the brocaded cloth is the glory of the royal throne. *Hebrew:* The Altar of Perfumes is 'the operation of grace for the elements' (Philo). *Hindu:* The Vedic Fire Altar takes on the vertical symbolism of a world centre, it is an *imago mundi* and the creation of the world: 'the uttermost end of the earth' (*Rig Veda*). The clay from which it is built is the earth, the waters for mixing are the primordial waters, the lateral walls are either the atmosphere or the surrounding ocean. The altar is based on three circular, perforated bricks or stones symbolizing the three worlds superimposed and also representing Agni, Vaya and Aditya, the lights of the world; the lowest stone is the Vedic fire of Agni; the middle stone the intermediate world, and the highest stone is the 'eye' or opening heavenwards; the continuous space in the centre is both a passage for the ascending fire and a way to the higher world, passing from death to immortality, from darkness to light. The fire altar is also the year and time materialized; the 360 bricks are the days of the year. The sacrifice on the altar restores original unity and being orientated towards the East and the sunrise symbolizes an ever-new beginning.

Amaranth A fabulous everlasting flower symbolizing immortality; faith; fidelity; constancy in love. In China a red amaranth was offered to the lunar hare at the Moon Festival.

In his *Vision of the Blessed Gabriele*, Crivelli encloses the Virgin and Child in an **almond**-shaped VESICA PISCIS, formed by the two intersecting circles symbolic of each of the holy persons' all-perfection.

The **altar** as a symbol of sacrifice was used as a printer's device or trademark by Christian Egenolff of Frankfurt in the 1540's.

Amber The golden transparency of the sun; congealed light. In China it is courage, 'the soul of the tiger'. Gives magic strength, helps the dead. Sacred to Apollo/Helios. Freya's tears for Svipdag fell as amber.

Amice *Christian*: The linen cloth with which Christ was blindfolded in the Praetorium; the helmet of a soldier of Christ.

Ampulla *Christian*: Signified having made the pilgrimage to Canterbury.

Anadem See GARLAND.

Anchor Hope; steadfastness; stability; tranquillity. The Foul Anchor can also symbolize a boat and mast, in which case it takes on the significance of the union between the feminine, protective lunar boat and the masculine, phallic pole or mast. In Egypt this symbolism was further strengthened by coiling the serpent of life round the mast. Anchor with Dolphin: the anchor is slowness and the dolphin depicts speed, hence the two together represent the happy medium or 'hasten slowly'. *Christian*: Salvation; steadfastness (Heb. 6, 19); the true faith. Emblem of SS Clement and Nicholas of Myra. The anchor with the dolphin is also used to depict Christ on the cross. In early Christian art the anchor was used as a disguised form of the cross as hope. In notably sea-faring nations the anchor is also a symbol of safety, security and good luck.

Androgyne Primordial perfection; wholeness; the *coincidentia oppositorum*; the unconditioned state; autonomy; paradise regained; the reunion of the primordial male–female forces; the union of heaven and earth, king and queen, the two becoming the One, the all-father, all-mother. In Alchemy the Great Work is the producing of the perfect androgyne, mankind restored to wholeness. It is symbolized by the male–female figure or the two-faced head of king and queen, or the red man and his white wife. Symbols of this state of unity among the gods are: the androgynous Zervain, Persian God of Limitless Time; in Greek mythology Chaos and Erebus are neuter, Zeus and Heracles are often dressed as women; in Cyprus there is the bearded Aphrodite; Dionysos has feminine features; the Chinese God of Night and Day is androgynous and the perfection of the androgyne is also represented by the yin-yang symbol and by the yin-yang 'Spiritually Endowed Creatures', the Dragon, Phoenix and *Ky-lin* which can all be yin or yang or both. In Hinduism there is the shakta-shakti and certain divinities, notably Siva, are depicted as physically half-male, half-female. Shamanism and initiation ceremonies use TRANSVESTISM (q.v.); Baal and Astarte are androgynes; early 'Midrashim' show Adam as androgynous, and in Plato's *Symposium* man was originally bisexual. Other androgynous symbols are: the

lotus, palm tree, cross, arrow, anchor, dot-in-circle, transvestism, serpent, scarabaeus, bearded women. Before the Great Mother, the Primordial Mother, the *Tellus Mater*, was a-sexual or androgynous.

Anemone Abandonment; sorrow. *Christian*: Sorrow; the passion of Christ, the red spot on the flower is His blood, the triple leaf is the Trinity. *Greek*: Sorrow; death. Attribute of Venus and Hermes, also the blood of Adonis who died on a bed of anemones.

Angels Messengers of God; intermediaries between God and man, heaven and this world; powers of the invisible world; enlightenment. There are nine choirs of angels: Seraphim, Cherubim, Thrones, Dominions, Virtues, Powers, Principalities, Archangels, Angels. The Angiris of Hinduism are also messengers between gods and men. In Islamic symbolism eight angels stand round the throne of Allah, representing the cardinal and intermediate points. Angelic symbols are: flaming swords, trumpets, sceptres, thuribles, musical instruments, the lily.

Anger Symbolized by a flaming torch; a wild boar; striking with a spear, thunderbolt or lightning; rending garments.

Angling *Chinese*: The art of ruling: 'An unskilled angler will catch no fish; a tactless ruler will not win over the people.' *Christian*: Bringing converts into the Church; the Apostles as 'fishers of men'.

Animals Instinctual life; fertility and teeming life; the instinctual and emotional urges which must be transcended before man can enter spiritual realms; passive participation; animal nature in man: 'We can find no animal without some likeness to man'. Theriomorphism is explained by Porphyry thus: 'Under the semblance of animals the Egyptians worship the universal power which the gods have revealed in the various forms of living nature.' Friendship with animals and ability to communicate with them symbolizes the restoration of, and re-entry into, the paradisal state, the Golden Age. Animals accompanying or helping man on quests depict the different aspects of his own nature, or the instinctive and intuitive forces of nature as distinct from the intellect, will and reason. Animals which must be slain or tamed, in myth and legend, are man's animal instincts brought under control. Combat between man and animal can have a prophylactic significance. Wearing animal skins or masks reproduces the paradisal state of understanding and speech between man and animals; it also means access to animal and instinctual wisdom. Funerary animals, such as a lion or dog with prey in its paws, represent all-devouring death. Solar-with-lunar pairs of animals, e.g. lion and unicorn, boar or bull and bear, depict the two contending powers of the universe, positive and negative, male and female, but some animals are interchangeable as solar or lunar, according to circumstances, such as the boar and bear. Among the Maoris, animals are 'the ancestral people'. A Mother Goddess is usually the Lady of the Beasts. Siva in his aspect of Pasupati is Lord of the Beasts and statues of these deities appear with cult animals.

Ankh An Egyptian symbol of life; the universe; all life both human and divine; the key of knowledge of the mysteries and hidden wisdom; power; authority; covenant. The ankh is formed of the combined male and female symbols of Osiris and Isis, the union of the two generative principles, of heaven and earth. It also signifies immortality, 'Life to come', 'Time that is to come'. It has also been suggested as a Tree of Life form, or that the oval may have been eternity and the cross extension in length and breadth, that is to say from infinity to space, or it may have been the sun rising above the horizon. Maat, Goddess of Truth, holds the ankh in her hand.

Anointing Consecration; that which is made sacred or set apart; prosperity; joy; an infusion of divine grace.

Anonymity In iconography, notably Hindu, anonymity can symbolize loss of identity, hence absorption into the divine.

Ant Industriousness. *Chinese*: 'The righteous insect'; orderliness; virtue; patriotism; subordination. *Greek*: Attribute of Ceres. *Hindu*: The transitoriness of existence.

Antelope *African Bushmen*: The divinity can appear in the form of an antelope. *Asia Minor and Europe*: A lunar animal, associated with the Great Mother. *Egyptian*: Sacrificed to Set, but can also represent Osiris and Horus as opponents of Set. *Heraldic*: Fierceness; strength; dangerousness. It is depicted as having the head of the heraldic tiger, the body of a stag, tail of unicorn, and with tusks on its nose. *Hindu*: Emblem of Siva; Soma and Chandra have chariots drawn by antelopes; Pavana, god of winds, rides an antelope. *Sumero-Semitic*: A form of Ea and Marduk. Ea-Oannes is 'the antelope of the subterranean ocean', 'the antelope of Apsu', 'the antelope of creation'. The dragon aspect of the antelope may also be assumed by the bull, buffalo or cow. The lunar antelope is sacred to Astarte.

Antlers Attribute of the Horned God and of the Sumerian Ea and Marduk, antlers may be incorporated with Ea's fish or goat-fish body. Antlers denote fertility in nature and fecundity in man and animals; supernatural power; power over nature. The ten-point antler is the mark of the shaman.

Mylius' 17th-century alchemical treatise, *Philosophia Reformata*, illustrates the **androgyne**, the united male and female principles whose reunion was considered the purpose and end of alchemy and, indeed, of human endeavour.

The **angel** Gabriel, messenger and herald of God, blowing his trumpet of announcement: from a 14th-century Islamic miniature.

The priest is offering up a figure of Maat, goddess of Truth and World Order, who holds the **ankh** in her hand.

Anvil Forging the universe; the primordial furnace; the earth; matter; together the hammer and anvil are the male–female formative forces of nature, the active and passive, positive and negative; an attribute of all storm, thunder and smith gods such as Hephaestos, Vulcan, Thor, etc. In Christianity the anvil is an emblem of SS Adrian and Eloy. Juno is sometimes depicted in mid-air with anvils on her feet, when she symbolizes the element of air.

Ape *Chinese*: Mischievousness; conceit; mimicry. *Christian*: Malice; cunning; lust; sin; unseemliness; levity; luxury; Satan; those who pervert the Word; idolatry. An ape in chains is sin overcome; and an ape with an apple in its mouth depicts the Fall. *Hindu*: Benevolence; gentleness; emblem of the monkey-god Hanuman.

Apple Fertility; love; joyousness; knowledge; wisdom; divination; luxury; but also deceitfulness and death. The apple was the forbidden fruit of the Golden Age. As round it represents totality and unity, as opposed to the multiplicity of the pomegranate, and as the fruit of the Tree of Life given by Iduma to the gods. Eris threw the golden apple of discord among the Gods. As the apples of the Hesperides and the fruit of Freya's garden, it symbolizes immortality. Offering an apple is a declaration of love. Like the orange, as fertility, the apple blossom is used for brides. *Celtic*: The Silver Bough. It has magic and chthonic powers; the fruit of the Otherworld; fertility; marriage. Halloween, an apple festival, is associated with the death of the old year. *Chinese*: Peace and concord. *Christian*: Ambivalent as evil (Latin *malum*) and the fruit of temptation and sin of the Fall, but depicted with Christ or the Virgin Mary it is the New Adam and salvation. An ape with an apple in its mouth depicts the Fall. *Greek*: Sacred to Venus as love and desire; a bridal symbol and offering; the 'apple of discord' was given to Venus by Paris. Apple branches are an attribute of Nemesis and Artemis and used in the rites of Diana; also awarded as a prize in the Sun-bridegroom race as was the olive branch at the Moon-virgin race. The apple of Dionysos was the quince. The apple tree was associated with health and immortality; sacred to Apollo. Apple blossom: a Chinese symbol of peace and beauty.

Apricot As self-fertilizing, the androgyne. *Chinese*: Death; timidity.

Apron Craftsmanship; fertility; it also covers sexuality. *Chinese*: The apron was part of the sacrificial regalia from the time of the Emperor Yu; it symbolized innocence and the bond of friendship; it also divides the body in half into the upper and nobler and lower and baser parts.

Aquamarine See JEWELS.

Aquarius See ZODIAC.

Arc Takes on the symbolism of the circle as dynamic, moving life and growth.

Arch The vault of the sky; also the yoni. Passing through an arch in initiation ceremonies is being born again, leaving behind the old nature. In Graeco-Roman symbolism it represents the sky god Zeus/Jupiter and in Rome the triumphal arch was used for military victory.

Archangels One of the orders of ANGELS (q.v.). Michael, messenger of divine judgment, is depicted as a warrior with a sword; Gabriel, messenger of divine mercy, holds a lily at the Annunciation; Raphael, divine healing and guardianship, is a pilgrim with a staff and gourd; Uriel, the fire of God, prophecy and wisdom, holds a scroll and book; Chamuel; the seer of God; Jophiel, the beauty of God; Zadiel, the justice of God. In Islam there are four archangels who inhabit the Heavens beneath the Throne.

Archer See ARROW.

Aries See ZODIAC.

Ark A moon and sea symbol. The ark is usually portrayed as crescent-shaped; the feminine principle; bearer of life; the womb; regeneration; the ship of destiny; a vehicle for carrying and transmitting the life principle; preservation. The ark on the waters is the earth swimming in the ocean of space. The ark with the rainbow represents the two powers of the lower and upper waters which together complete the One and mark universal regeneration. The ark and the flood, an almost universal myth, takes two forms of symbolism, one, as in Hinduism, where the ark, built by Satyavrata at the command of Manu, carried the seeds of life, and the other, as in the Old Testament, where Noah built an ark at Jahveh's order, carried men and animals. Both contain the elements of life, continuity and stability. The ark itself was supposed to have been constructed to the proportions of man's body and to symbolize the microcosm. *Christian*: The ark represents the Church in which man should be saved, safely riding the waters of life; the pure and impure animals in it symbolized saints and sinners. It is also Christ, saviour of mankind; the Virgin Mary as the bearer of Christ; and is the nave of the Church in architectural symbolism. St Thomas Aquinas said the Ark of the Covenant denoted Christ, the gold overlay was his wisdom and charity, the golden vase his soul, Aaron's rod his priestly dignity and the Tables of the Law his office as lawgiver. For St Bonaventura it was the Eucharist and for St Ambrose it signified Our Lady in whom was enclosed the heir of the law. *Egyptian*: The ark of Isis is the womb of the Mother, the life-bearer. *Hebrew*: The Ark of the Covenant signified the Divine Presence, the place of God, the most sacred symbol in the Hebrew religion. It was made of incorruptible wood and covered with gold, representing the beneficent power. Philo equates the ark with the Intelligence, as opposed to the table with the twelve loaves as the sensible and manifest world. *Sumero-Semitic*: The ark, as the symbolic ship, appears frequently in Chaldea.

Arm Arms upraised denote supplication, prayer, surrender. The many arms of gods and goddesses in Hindu and Buddhist iconography depict compassionate aid, and, carrying various symbols, the different powers and operations of universal nature, also the particular functions of the deity. The two arms are Sophia and Dynamis: wisdom and action. In Christianity the arm of the Lord is the instrument of sovereign power, God's will. In the Trinity the arm represents the Father. It can also symbolize vengeance. The upraised arms of the orant can depict piety or, on funerary art, the soul of the person. One raised arm is a gesture of bearing witness or of taking an oath.

Armour Chivalry; protection. In Christianity it is used as a symbol of protection against evil (Eph. 6. 11 ff.).

Arrow The piercing, masculine principle; penetration; phallic; lightning; rain; fecundity; virility; power; war. A flight of arrows symbolizes ascent to the celestial. Arrows loosed from a bow represent the consequences of actions which cannot be recalled or revoked. The arrow, as with the lance and sword, is a solar symbol depicting the sun's rays, also the attribute of the warrior. An arrow piercing a serpent is the sun's rays piercing the dark clouds of the humid principle. The broad arrow (the fleur-de-lis) denotes royal property. *Amerindian*: The sun's rays. *Christian*: Martyrdom; suffering; the nails of the cross; emblem of SS Christina, Edmund, Giles, Sebastian, Ursula. *Egyptian*: Two crossed arrows on a shield are an emblem of Neith as warrior goddess. *Greek*: Apollo's arrows are the sun's rays which can be both beneficent and fertilizing or scorching and harmful. The arrows of Eros are the piercing darts of love. A heart pierced by an arrow is union. Arrows are an attribute of Diana as light. Homer uses arrows as symbols of pain and disease, shot at mankind by the gods, especially Apollo. *Hindu*: Attribute of Rudra, god of earth, lightning and storms, killing men and animals, causing pain and trouble, but also bringing fertility and healing rain. Attribute of Indra as sky god; his arrows are both the sun's rays and lightning. *Islamic*: The wrath and punishment of God inflicted on his enemies. *Mithraic*: Emblem of Mithras as god of light: *Shamanistic*. The feathered arrow represents the bird-flight to heaven; transcending the earthly state.

Artemisia *Amerindian*: The feminine, lunar, nocturnal life principle with the chrysotham-

An 18th-century Masonic **apron**, used as an item of ritual apparel, has for its central decoration the pelican in her piety, perhaps in allusion to every Freemason's pledge to do good works.

Each **arm** of Siva Nataraja, Lord of the Dance, has its own symbolism: the upper right holds the drum of creative rhythm, balanced by the flame of destruction in the upper left; the lower right hand performs a gesture of reassuring benediction, while the lower left promises release from suffering.

nus as the masculine, solar, day principle. *Chinese*: Dignity; it is one of the Eight Precious Things. *Greek*: Sacred to Artemis.

Ascension Transcendence; the break through to a new ontological plane and transcending the merely human state; the way to Reality and the Absolute; reintegration; the soul's union with the divinity; uplifting the soul; the passage from earth to heaven, from darkness to light; freedom. Ascension frequently follows a descent into the underworld and symbols of ascent are used for the regaining of Paradise, since to find spiritual freedom and enlightenment is not only to attain the centre but also to transcend earthly limitations.

Ash The Scandinavian sacred Cosmic Tree, the YGGDRASIL (q.v.); also sacred to Zeus/Jupiter. The ash also typifies adaptability, prudence, modesty. It is associated with the blood of Ouranos' castration. Meliae were ash-nymphs.

Asherah Semitic symbolic trees associated with the feminine aspect of the divinity, especially Ashtoreth or Astarte, usually represented as a votive wooden column; also suggested as phallic or an emblem of a tree god.

Ashes The transitoriness of human life; the perishable human body; mortality. With sackcloth they denote abject humiliation and sorrow; penitence. In some rituals they have a purifying power.

Ashlar *Egyptian*: The material to be worked upon to achieve perfection through creative activity; the rough ashlar is unregenerate man, the perfect ashlar is the spiritual and perfected man.

Asp *Christian*: Evil; venom. *Egyptian*: Solar; royalty; dominion and power. *Greek*: Protective and benevolent power.

Aspen Fear; uncertainty; lamenting.

Asperges Purification; holiness; the expulsion of evil powers.

Asphodel *Graeco–Roman*: Paradise; the Isles of the Blest, the Elysian Fields, hence, later, a funerary emblem of death and regret, associated with cemeteries and ruins. Emblem of Persephone and Dionysos. Associated with the Virgin Mary.

Ass Humility; patience; peace; stupidity; obstinacy; lewdness; fertility. An ass's head was also regarded as a source of fertility. As a beast of burden the ass can typify the poor. *Christian*: Christ's nativity; the flight into Egypt; the entry into Jerusalem. It was also used to depict the Jews and the Synagogue and has Satanic connotations. Emblem of St Germanus. *Egyptian*: Emblem of Set in his typhonic aspect;

inert power; evil. *Greek*: Sloth; infatuation. Sacred to Dionysos and Typhon as a brutish aspect. Sacred to Priapus as the procreative principle; also sacred to Cronos/Saturn. Silenus is sometimes depicted as riding on an ass. *Hebrew*: Stubbornness. Kings, prophets and judges rode on white asses. *Hindu*: Asses drew the celestial chariot of Ravana when he abducted Sita. *Sassanian*: The three-legged ass is purity and a power against evil; it is also lunar as the three phases of the moon.

Aster *Chinese*: Beauty; charm; humility; elegance. *Greek*: Love; sacred to Aphrodite.

Aureole See NIMBUS.

Aurochs The symbolic animal of the Assyrian–Sumerian Bel or Enil, ruler of heaven, earth and fate.

Axe Solar emblem of the sky gods; power; thunder; fecundity of the rain of the sky gods; conquest of error; sacrifice; a support, stay or help.
  The double axe is suggested as the sacred union of the sky god and earth goddess; thunder and lightning. *African*: The double axe of the Yoruba is the magic power and thunderbolt of the storm god. *Buddhist*: Severs the round of birth and death. *Celtic*: Indicates a divine being, chief or warrior. *Chinese*: Justice; judgment; authority; punishment; the sacrificial axe is the death of the sensual, unillumined man. *Christian*: Martyrdom; destruction. Emblem of SS John the Baptist, Matthew, Mathias, Proclus. *Egyptian*: A solar symbol. *Greek*: Emblem of Zeus; also an aniconic form of Tenedos Dionysos. *Hindu*: Attribute of the fire god Agni, together with wood and bellows. Vishnu holds an axe with which he cuts down the tree of Samsara, the dualistic tree of Knowledge. *Minoan*: The origin of the double axe of Crete is uncertain. Presumably it symbolized sovereignty and the power and presence of the deity; it has been suggested that in Crete it was not so much a symbol as a direct aniconic image of the deity and was invested with supernatural power. Emblem of Zeus Labrayndeus as god of thunder and lightning, also of the Mother as huntress. *Oceanic*: An axe symbolizing the human form was thought to have divine power. *Scandinavian*: Accompanies a divine being, chief or warrior. *Sumero-Semitic*: Emblem of Tammuz. The Hittite axe and double axe is an attribute of Teshub, sun god and Lord of Heaven, and symbolizes sovereignty.

Axis The Cosmic Axis is the central point of time and space; the supreme support of all things; that round which all things revolve; the norm; the essence of all existence. Symbolized by the Cosmic Tree; sacred mountains; the celestial ray; pillar; pole; staff; spindle; spear; lance; dart; rod; the thread of the umbilical cord; the axle of the chariot; nails; key; etc.

Azalea Transitoriness; the ephemeral. *Chinese*: Feminine grace; great abilities. Also a tragic flower which grew from the tears of blood shed by a boy turned into a cuckoo by a cruel stepmother.

Ba *Egyptian*: The soul, depicted as a bird, or human-headed bird.

Baboon *Egyptian*: 'Hailer of the Dawn'; with uplifted hands it denoted wisdom saluting the rising sun and represents the gods Thoth and Hapi.

Badger *Chinese*: A lunar, yin animal typifying the supernatural powers; also mischief and playfulness. *European*: Clumsiness, a weather prophet. The steed of Avarice. *Japanese*: Supernatural powers; a *fata morgana* and a producer of *ignes fatui*.

Baetylic Stones/Bethels See STONES.

Bag Secrecy; containing; hiding; the winds; Aeolus has a bag of winds. The bag of the Celtic sea-god Manannan contained all the treasures in the world.

Balance Justice; impartiality; judgment; man's merits and demerits weighed. The equilibrium of all opposites and complementaries; Nemesis; the ANDROGYNE (q.v.). For *Libra* see ZODIAC.

Baldacchino Spiritual and temporal authority.

Ball The ball can symbolize either the sun or the moon and ball games are connected with solar and lunar festivals and rites. They are symbolic of the power of the gods in hurling globes, meteorites and stars across the skies. Golden balls are an attribute of the Harpies; also an emblem of St Nicholas of Myra.

Balm/Balsam Love; sympathy; rejuvenation.

Bamboo Gracefulness; constancy; yielding but enduring strength; pliability; good breeding; lasting friendship; longevity and hardy old age (it is always green); also the perfect man who bows before the storm but rises again. *Chinese*: Longevity; filial piety; the winter season, with the plum and pine one of the Three Friends of Winter; an emblem of Buddha; the scholar-gentleman who is upright in bearing but has an inner emptiness and humility. The seven-knotted bamboo denotes the seven degrees of initiation and invocation. Bamboo and sparrow together depict friendship; the bamboo with the crane is long life and happiness. *Japanese*: Devotion; truthfulness.

A 16th-century Cretan icon of Christ's entry into Jerusalem shows him riding on an **ass**, symbol of lowliness contrasting with his later claim to be King of the Jews.

Minoan Great Mother goddess holding the double **axe**, a phallic representation of her parthenogenetic fertility.

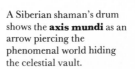

A Siberian shaman's drum shows the **axis mundi** as an arrow piercing the phenomenal world hiding the celestial vault.

Banner Conquest; victory; the standard of a king or prince, providing a rallying point in battle. *Buddhist*: Hoisting the Dharma Banner proclaims the Supreme Law. *Christian*: Victory. The banner with the cross, or labarum, is victory over sin, death or persecution. Emblem of SS Ansana, George of Cappadocia, Julian, Reparata, Ursula, Wenceslas. *Hindu*: 'Ketu', the banner of India, is a ray of light, a shining forth; manifestation; victory over darkness.

Baptism Initiation; death and rebirth; regeneration; renewal; dying to the titanic nature of man and being born again of water, fire, or wind, into the divine. Baptism represents regression into the undifferentiated; the dissolution of form and reintegration with the pre-formal; crossing the sea of life; re-emergence from the water is rebirth and resurrection. By fire symbolizes the purging and burning away of dross. By wind, winnowing away the chaff. It is a rite of passage, emerging from the darkness of the womb to the outer light, hence the passage of the soul from matter to spirit. See also IMMERSION.

Barley All grain is a symbol of renewal of life, resurrection and fertility. Barley sown on the body of Osiris sprouted and was 'new life after death'. 'Beds of Osiris' were barley grown on wet cloth or in a receptacle and placed on tombs; or images of Osiris were made from earth and barley and their growing symbolized his resurrection and the return of Spring to the land. Barley heads were used in the Greek Mysteries to depict fertility and fruitfulness. Associated with Kore/Demeter and the White Goddess. See also CORN.

Basil An apotropaic herb used at funerals and rites of the dead.

Basilisk See FABULOUS BEASTS.

Basket Baskets are attributes of the Seasons and symbolize offerings of first fruits; fertility and sanctity; also the feminine containing principle. A full basket is full fruition; abundance; the first fruits. In funerary art it indicates the fruition of immortality. Spilling of the basket portrays the end of the season of fruitfulness. Being contained in a basket depicts rebirth or escape from death. Baskets of bread signify a sacramental meal. *Buddhist*: The Tripitaka, the 'three baskets', are the Buddhist canon: the Vinaya or discipline basket; the Dhamma or Sutta, the sermon or discourse basket; and the Abhidhamma, or exposition basket. *Chinese*: A basket of flowers is longevity; fruitful old age. *Egyptian*: Attribute of Bast, the cat-headed goddess. *Greek*: A basket covered with ivy indicates the Dionysian mysteries and is also an emblem of Ceres. The *liknon* was a basket used in the Mysteries to contain fruit and a covered phallus, symbols of Dionysian fertility and the powers of life and death.

Bat *African*: Ambivalent as perspicacity, but also darkness and obscurity. *Alchemic*: As a double nature of bird and mouse it can represent the androgyne. *Amerindian*: A rain-bringer. *Buddhism*: Darkened understanding. *Chinese*: A yin animal as nocturnal, but as a homophone of happiness, *fu*, it becomes happiness and good luck, wealth, longevity, peace. A pair of bats indicates good wishes and is an emblem of Shou-hsing, god of longevity; a group of five bats represents the five blessings of health, wealth, long life, peace and happiness. *Christian*: 'The bird of the Devil', an incarnation of the Prince of Darkness. Satan is depicted with bat's wings. As a hybrid of bird and rat it is duplicity and hypocrisy; as haunting ruins and lonely places it is melancholy. *European*: Associated with black magic and witchcraft; wisdom; cunning; revenge. *Hebrew*: Impurity; idolatry. *Japanese*: Unhappy restlessness; a chaotic state.

Bathing See ABLUTIONS.

Baton Authority. In Amerindian symbolism it is equated with punishment and pain.

Bay Renewal of life; immortality; takes on the symbolism of the LAUREL (q.v.). *Chinese*: Victory; literary eminence. *Roman*: Resurrection; renewal; glory and honour; emblem of Apollo.

Beacon Warning; communication.

Beads A circle of beads depicts continuity, perpetuity and endless duration. See ROSARY.

Bean Immortality; transmogrification; magic power; phallic. *Roman*: Sacred to Silvanus. *Teutonic*: Eroticism; sexual pleasure.

Bear Resurrection (as emerging from its winter cave of hibernation with its new-born cub in Spring); new life, hence initiation and its association with rites of passage. In hero myths the bear is solar; in inundation myths it becomes lunar and is also lunar when associated with moon goddesses such as Artemis and Diana. It is the emblem of the Kingdom of Persia and of Russia. *Alchemic*: The *nigredo* of the *prima materia*. *Amerindian*: Supernatural power; strength; fortitude; the whirlwind. *Celtic*: A lunar power; attribute of the goddess of Berne. *Chinese*: Bravery; strength. *Christian*: The Devil; evil; cruelty; greed; carnal appetite. Bear cubs were thought to have been born amorphous and so were taken to represent the transforming, regenerating power of Christianity over the heathen. Emblem of SS Blandina, Gall, Florentinus, Maximus. The fight of David with the bear symbolizes the conflict between Christ and the Devil. *Greek*: Sacred to the lunar goddesses Artemis and Diana and an attribute of Atalanta and Euphemia. Girls taking part in the rites of Artemis were called 'bears', wore yellow robes and imitated bears. Diana turned

Callisto into a bear. *Japanese*: Benevolence; wisdom; strength. A culture hero and divine messenger among the Ainu. *Scandinavian and Teutonic*: Sacred to Thor. The she-bear Atla is the feminine principle and the he-bear Atli the masculine. *Shamanistic*: A messenger of the forest spirits.

Beard Strength; virility; sovereignty; manhood in the West; old age in the East. The beard of sky gods such as Zeus/Jupiter is variously interpreted as the rays of the sun descending on earth, or as fertilizing rain. Goddesses with beards, such as Ashtoreth and Venus Mylitta, symbolize dual sex, the ANDROGYNE (q.v.).

Beasts See FABULOUS BEASTS.

Beating Beating breasts or thighs is an expression of anguish, grief or repentance. Beating the forehead depicts grief, shame or wonder. See also FLOGGING.

Beaver Industriousness, 'working like a beaver'. In Christianity it represents chastity, the ascetic, since it was thought to castrate itself if pursued. Vigilance; peacefulness.

Bee Immortality; rebirth; industry; order; purity; a soul. Bees were believed to be parthenogenic and so signified virginity and chastity. They carry a heavenly import, and honey is the offering to supreme deities. Bees often represent the stars and are also winged messengers carrying news to the spirit world; 'telling the bees' of a death, or important event, is to send a message to the next world or to the spirits. Bees are messengers of oak and thunder gods. As carved on tombs they signify immortality. *Celtic*: Secret wisdom coming from the other world. *Chinese*: Industry; thrift. *Christian*: Diligence; good order; purity; chaste virgins; courage; economy; prudence; co-operation; sweetness; religious eloquence; the ordered and pious community 'who produce posterity, rejoice in offspring yet retain their virginity' (*Exultet Roll*); the virginity of Mary, the producer of Christ who is symbolized by the honey. The bee, regarded as never sleeping, is Christian vigilance and zeal. Flying in the air, it is the soul entering the Kingdom of Heaven. The bee also symbolizes the Christian with the hive as the Church. Emblem of SS Ambrose and Bernard of Clairvaux. *Egyptian*: The 'giver of life', therefore birth, death and resurrection; industry; chastity; harmonious living; royalty. Emblem of the Pharaoh of Lower Egypt. The tears of Ra, falling to the ground, became working bees. *Essenes*: 'King bees' were priestly officials. *Greek*: Industry; prosperity; immortality (the souls of the departed may enter bees); purity; Demeter was 'the pure Mother Bee'. The Great Mother was also known as the Queen Bee and her priestesses were *Melissae*, the Bees; she was also represented by the lion and bees in Greek art. The Pythian

The 12th-century Winchester Psalter illustrates the **baptism** of Jesus by John the Baptist, while an angel waits, holding a garment symbolizing Jesus' 'new life' through baptism.

Moulded shape of the god Osiris, from Tutankhamun's tomb. When the young Pharaoh was buried, this was filled with Nile mud in which seeds of **barley** were pressed. Sprouting, they symbolized resurrection.

This 5th-century BC coin of Ephesus shows a queen **bee**, emblem of the city and also of the Great Mother, whose priestesses were called *melissae*, bees.

priestess at Delphi was the Delphic Bee. The officiants at Eleusis were Bees. Bees were bestowers of eloquence and song, the 'birds of the Muses'. The appearance of a bee denoted the arrival of a stranger. As an emblem of Demeter, Cybele and Diana, the bee was lunar and virgin. Pan and Priapus were protectors and keepers of bees. The Cretan Zeus was born in the cave of bees and fed by them; they are also an attribute of the Ephesian Artemis; bees fly round Cupid, who was stung by a bee. *Hindu*: A bee on a lotus is a symbol of Vishnu; blue bees on the forehead represent Krishna, also the Ether; a bee surmounting a triangle is Siva, Madheri, 'the suave one'; bees as sweet pain compose the bow-string of Kama, god of love, and a train of bees follows at his back. The bee is also depicted with the lion. Soma, the moon, was called a bee. *Islamic*: The faithful; intelligence; wisdom; harmlessness. Bees 'benefit fruit blossoms, practise useful things, work in the daytime, do not eat food gathered by others, dislike dirt and bad smells, and obey their ruler; they dislike the darkness of indiscretion, the clouds of doubt, the storm of revolt, the smoke of the prohibited, the water of superfluity, the fire of lust' (Ibn al-Athir). *Mithraic*: The soul; the vital principle springing from the bull as connected with the bull-ox-bone-bee. Bees and oxen, as sexless, were regarded as androgynous. The bee with the caduceus represents Mercury, shepherd of souls, the bee symbolizing the soul. *Roman*: Swarms of bees denote misfortune. The headless bee with the headless frog averts the evil eye. A staff topped with a beehive is an emblem of Mellonia and Nantosvelta (Roman–Germanic). According to Virgil the bee is 'the breath of life'; Porphyry equates it with justice and sobriety, and Seneca with the monarchy.

Beech Tree Prosperity; divination. Sacred to Zeus. Emblem of Denmark.

Beehive Eloquence, 'honeyed words'; an ordered community. See also BEES and HIVE. In Greece the beehive was often used as the shape of a tomb, suggesting immortality.

Beetle See SCARAB.

Behemoth See FABULOUS BEASTS.

Bell Consecration; the motion of the elements; a charm against the powers of destruction. The swinging of the bell represents the extremes of good and evil, death and immortality; its shape is the vault of heaven. Small bells sounding in the breeze symbolize the sweet sounds of Paradise. The ringing of a bell can be either a summons or a warning. *Buddhist*: The pure sound of the doctrine of perfect wisdom. In Tantric Buddhism the bell is the feminine principle with the *dorje* as the masculine. *Chinese*: Respect; veneration; obedience; faithful ministers; meritorious warriors; it averts the evil eye

and wards off evil spirits. The ritual bell symbolizes harmony between man and heaven. *Christian*: The sanctus bell announces the presence of Christ at the mass. Church bells call and encourage the faithful, put evil spirits to flight and quell storms. The hollow of the bell is the mouth of the preacher, the clapper is his tongue. *Graeco-Roman*: Bells were attached to figures of Priapus and used in Bacchic rites as associated with phalli. *Hebrew*: Vestments; bells with pomegranates are the Quintessence, with the pomegranates as the four elements, on the Ephod. They are also suggested as symbolizing thunder and lightning. Bells also signified virginity as they were worn until marriage (Isa. 3, 16). *Hindu*: Rank, dignity. The Bull of Nandi is always depicted with a bell round his neck, or a chain. As the yoni the bell denotes virginity. *Teutonic*: The hawk-bell is a symbol of nobility.

Belly In the West symbolic of gross appetite; in the Orient a seat of life. The belly of a whale, monster, or big fish is equated with Hell, Sheol and Hades, the descent to the underworld; cosmic night; the embryonic state of being; death and rebirth; regression to the womb and being born again; returning to the pre-manifest; the end of time; acquiring esoteric or sacred knowledge in initiatory death and resurrection. The hero, emerging from this state, has often lost his hair, symbolizing the hairlessness of the newborn. In Alchemy the darkness of the belly is the transforming laboratory. The fat belly of the Chinese god of wealth and the Hindu Ganesha is gluttony, hence prosperity. The belly is also a vital centre. In Japan the belly is regarded as the centre of the body, *Hara*, the seat of life, hence *Harakiri*, to strike at the life-centre.

Belt Binding to power or office; dedication; fulfilment; victory; virtue; strength; the belt of Thor doubled his strength.

Beryl See JEWELS.

Bethel/Baetyl See STONES.

Birch Tree Fertility; light; protects against witches and drives out evil spirits, hence the birching of felons and lunatics. *Scandinavian and Teutonic*: Sacred to Thor, Donar and Frigga. The last battle in the world will be fought round a birch tree. *Shamanistic*: The birch is the Cosmic Tree of shamanism, and the shaman ascends the seven or nine notches of the tree trunk or birch pole, symbolizing the ascent through the planetary spheres to the Supreme Spirit. Emblem of Estonia.

Birds Transcendence; the soul; a spirit; divine manifestation; spirits of the air; spirits of the dead; ascent to heaven; ability to communicate with gods or to enter into a higher state of consciousness; thought; imagination. Large birds are often identified with solar, thunder and wind gods, and their tongues are lightning. Birds are a feature of tree symbolism: the divine power descends into the tree or on to its symbol, a pillar.

Two birds in a tree, sometimes one dark and one light, are dualism, darkness and light, night and day, the unmanifest and the manifest, the two hemispheres. Birds often appear in the branches of the Tree of Life with the serpent at its foot; this combination is a union of air and fire, but the bird and serpent in conflict are solar and chthonic powers at war. Fabulous birds also depict the celestial realms and powers opposing the chthonic serpent. Birds frequently accompany the Hero on his quest or in slaying the dragon, giving him secret advice ('a little bird told me'), and he understands the language of birds. This ability symbolizes heavenly communication or the help of celestial powers, such as angels. A bird on a pillar is the union of spirit and matter, or a symbol of a sun god. A cage of birds represents the mind, according to Plato. Flocks of birds are magic or supernatural powers connected with gods or heroes. Birds' claws portray the Harpies as symbolic of the dark, destructive aspect of the Great Mother. *Alchemic*: Two contending birds are the dual nature of Mercurius, the philosophical mercury, the *nous*; this can also be depicted by birds flying upwards and downwards. *Buddhist*: A bird is a symbol of the Lord Buddha; it also signifies auspiciousness. *Celtic*: Ambivalent as both divinity and the happy otherworld, or as magic power and malevolence, as with the raven and wren. The Tuatha can appear as birds of brilliant plumage and be linked together with golden chains when presaging an important event. Birds are also messengers of the gods. *Chinese*: Most birds, but especially the cock, crane and peacock, are solar, yang, symbolizing longevity and good fortune. *Christian*: Winged souls; the spiritual; souls in Paradise. The Christ Child is often depicted holding a bird. *Egyptian*: The human-headed bird represents the power of the soul to leave the body at will. The bird Bennu incarnates the soul of Osiris and is sometimes equated with the PHOENIX (q.v.); it is the creative principle, producer of the Cosmic Egg. At death the soul, the Ka, leaves the body in the shape of a bird. *Hindu*: Intelligence, 'Intelligence is the swiftest of birds' (*Rig Veda*); 'He who understands has wings' (*Pancavimca Brahmanan*). Garuda is the bird of life, the sky, the sun, victory; it is creator and destroyer of all, a vehicle of Vishnu and sometimes equated with the phoenix. *Islamic*: The souls of the faithful living on the Tree of Life. Souls of infidels enter birds of prey. *Japanese*: (Shinto) The creative principle. *Maori*: The Bird Man is the divinity, the all-seeing, all-wise; strength and valour. *Scandinavian*: The spirit freed from the body; wisdom; see RAVEN. *Shamanistic*: Ascent to heaven; mediumistic and magical journeying; bird robes and feathers are worn by shamans in their rites; dressed as a bird the soul can take

This 18th-century Chinese **bell** of green jade has its power to ward off evil reinforced by the protective DRAGONS carved on its side and the central TRIGRAMS.

On a 13th-century BC Egyptian papyrus, the Ba, the **bird** of the soul, hovers over a mummy before beginning its flight to the afterlife.

The **birds** on this 19th-century Arapaho Indian Ghost Dance costume represent the spirits of guidance and strengthening which the dancers hoped to contact in their ritual.

wings. *Taoist*: The three-legged red crow is the solar, yang, principle; it lives in the sun and can also symbolize the Great Triad, the three great powers of the cosmos, Heaven, Earth, Man. See also COCK, EAGLE, PHOENIX, RAVEN, etc.

Bit and Bridle Control; endurance; forbearance; temperance. In Christian art the bit and bridle can accompany the figure of Temperance.

Black See COLOURS.

Blackbird *Christian*: Temptations of the flesh (its alluring song and black plumage). In St Benedict's temptation the devil appears as a blackbird.

Blindness, blindfolding Ignorance; sin; dereliction of duty; failure to see the light and the right path; the undiscerning; the irrational ('blind fury'). To blindfold or 'hoodwink' depicts deception, leading astray. In Buddhism the blind old woman in the Round of Existence symbolizes the absence of knowledge, the blindness of ignorance leading to death. Blindfolded Cupid depicts the blindness of secular love. In Christian art the synagogue is represented as blindfolded.

Blood The life principle; the soul; strength; the rejuvenating force, hence blood sacrifice. The red, solar energy. Blood and wine are interchangeable symbols. Blood and water are associated as complementaries in Chinese symbolism as representing the yang and the yin principles. In Christian symbolism blood and water at the crucifixion are the life of the body and the life of the spirit. Stepping over blood confers fertility: in the Middle East brides stepped over the blood of a sacrificed sheep. Tyrian purple, 'the highest glory' (Pliny), was the colour of congealed blood, also the 'blood of purple hue'. (Homer). Drinking blood is usually symbolic of enmity, but it can also absorb the power of the foe and so render him harmless after death.

Blue See COLOURS.

Bo Tree The *Ficus religiosa*. Perfection; contemplation; meditation. Sacred to Buddha as the tree under which he attained enlightenment.

Boar Ambivalent as both solar and lunar; as solar the boar is the masculine principle, but when white it becomes lunar and is also feminine as the watery principle and a dweller in the swamps. It is also intrepidity, lust, gluttony. *Celtic*: A sacred animal; the supernatural; prophecy; magic; warfare; protection of warriors; hospitality. It is associated with gods and magic powers and with the tree, wheel, ravens and the human head, and was sacrificed to Derga. The sacrificial fire was the

Boar of the Woods. The boar's head symbolizes health and preservation from danger, the power of the life-force, the vitality contained in the head, hence abundance and good luck for the coming year. The boar and bear together represent spiritual authority and temporal power. *Chinese*: The wealth of the forests; a white boar is lunar. *Christian*: Brutality; ferocious anger; evil; the sins of the flesh; cruel princes and rulers. *Druidic*: Druids called themselves 'Boars', probably as solitaries, withdrawn into the forest. *Egyptian*: Evil; an attribute of Set in his typhonic aspect when he swallows the eye of the God of the Day. *Graeco–Roman*: Sacred to Ares/Mars; destruction and strife. It also symbolizes Winter as killing Adonis and Attis who represent the power of the sun. The boar which slew Adonis was sacrificed to Aphrodite. The killing of the Boar of Calydon was the slaying of Winter with the coming of the solar power in Spring. The boar is an attribute of Demeter and Atalanta. Heracles captured the wild boar of Erymanthus. *Hebrew*: The enemy of Israel, destroying the vine. *Heraldic*: One of the four heraldic animals of venery. *Hindu*: Varahi, the third incarnation of Vishnu, or Parjapati, who, in the form of a boar, saved the earth from the waters of chaos and was the first tiller of the soil. The boar also represents Vajravrahi, goddess of dawn and Queen of Heaven, as the sow, source of life and fertility. *Iranian*: The 'shining boar' is associated with the sun in the *Zendavesta*. *Japanese*: The white boar is the moon; courage; conquest and all warrior qualities. *Mycenaean*: Warriors wore a boar's tusk helmet. *Scandinavian and Teutonic*: Fertility; the harvest; a storm animal; funerary; sacrificed to Frey at Yule; sacred to Woden/Odin, Frey and Freyja, who ride boars. Boar masks and helmets put warriors under the protection of Frey and Freyja. The golden bristles of Frey's boar, Gulliburstin, are the sun's rays. *Siberian*: Courage; steadfastness; conquest; all warrior qualities. *Sumero–Semitic*: The winged boar slew Tammuz; the boar can be a messenger of the gods.

Boat See SHIP.

Bonds Symbolized by all things that bind or ensnare: ropes, cords, fetters, manacles, knots, nooses, halters, snares, nets, chains, threads, etc. These are all attributes of 'gods who bind' and funerary gods who hold powers of binding and loosing, life and death, who are also judges of the dead, binding and ensnaring the guilty and freeing the just. Binding and loosing is also the transmuting of chaos into cosmos, of conflict into law and order. The lunar Great Mothers, who are all spinners (see also SPIDER) and weavers and binders, represent fate, time, limitation, the inescapable ('bound' to happen) and are possessed of mysterious, magic and spellbinding powers.

Nets, knots, etc., like the powers of the divinities of binding and loosing, are ambivalent, being symbolic of either preventing illness or causing it, bringing death or saving from it; they protect at nuptial rites or prevent consummation of the marriage, hinder or help at childbirth and represent the negative and positive, the malefic or beneficent, attack or defence; they bind man to his fate, his existential situation, yet provide a line of communication with the creator and the divine, binding him to his past but giving him a link with the weaver of destiny, restricting but also uniting. Bonds and binding also symbolize submission, slavery, vassalage, prisoners. The silver cord binds the soul to the body during life and is broken, to release the soul, at death. Naval and military cords, stripes, braids, sashes of orders, chains, etc., are also symbols of binding to office. *Buddhist*: Ropes, cords, represent the binding of offenders. Yama, god of the dead, is a god who binds. *Chinese*: Pau-hi is a god of winds and nets. *Christian*: The bonds of sin and death. God ultimately binds and casts out Satan. *Greek*: Ouranos binds his rivals and is also destiny, and there are the fetters of Cronos as time; the Fates all weave and ensnare. *Hebrew*: Jahveh has snares of death and nets to punish the sinners. *Hindu*: The noose symbolizes knowledge and intellectual power, the force which seizes and holds firm; but it also depicts death. Varuna, 'master of bonds', is a magical binder and carries a rope round his shoulders to bind sinners. The rope also symbolizes the sins by which men bind themselves to ignorance. Varuna is lunar and the non-manifest, imprisoning and binding the waters of chaos. Vritra and Nirrti are also magical binders and 'masters of bonds'. Indra releases the waters and has power to bind and loose. Yama holds the bonds of death and carries a rope. *Iranian*: Ahriman, lord of lies, the power of darkness, holds a snare. *Japanese*: The rope is an attribute of Fudo-Myoo and is held in the left hand to bind those who oppose the Buddha. *Oceanic*: Vaerua and Akaanga are gods of nets and cords and bind the dead. *Roman*: Saturn is fettered except during the Saturnalia, when chaos is let loose. *Scandinavian*: Woden/Odin is a magical 'god of the ropes'. *Sumero–Semitic*: In Babylon the rope or bond represented the cosmic principle uniting all things and the law which supports and holds all things together. Tammuz is 'lord of snares'; Marduk a master binder, with noose, snares and net; Shamash is armed with snares and cord; Ea binds by magic; Nisaba binds the demons of illness; Enil and his wife Ninkhursaq are lunar divinities who catch the guilty with nets; Ninurta is 'lord of the encompassing net'. *Teutonic*: The ceremonial binding of kings was practised.

Bones The indestructible life principle; the essential; resurrection, but also mortality and the transitory; destruction of the bones is often supposed to preclude resurrection.

Bonfire Strengthening the power of the sun,

On this allegorical representation of a synagogue (from Strasbourg cathedral) the blindfold symbolizes **blindness**, the spiritual blindness of the Jews' inability to 'see' the truth of Christ's teaching.

The crucified Christ's **blood** is caught by an angel in Giovanni Bellini's painting 'The Blood of the Redeemer', dramatically symbolizing the force and energy of that 'vital fluid'.

These Scandinavian warriors wear **boar** helmets to place themselves under the protection of Frey and Freyja.

especially at the solstices, encouraging the powers of light and good.

Book The universe, the *liber mundi* and *liber vitae*. The open book depicts the book of life, learning and the spirit of wisdom, revelation and the wisdom of the scriptures. The book is connected with tree symbolism and the Tree and Book can represent the whole cosmos. In Grail symbolism the book can also typify the Quest, in this case for the lost Word. *Buddhist*: Perfection of wisdom, language and expression. Tara has the book of illuminating wisdom resting on the lotus of spiritual flowering. *Chinese*: Scholarship. The leaves of the book are the leaves of the Cosmic Tree, symbolizing all beings in the universe, the 'ten thousand things'. The book is one of the Eight Precious Things of Chinese Buddhism. *Christian*: Books are the Apostles teaching the nations. Emblem of SS Augustine and Cyprian. Christ is often portrayed holding a book. *Islamic*: 'The universe is a vast book' (ibn Arabi). The book, with the pen, is creative substance, static being, while the pen is the creative principle. The Sacred Book is the Name of God; truth; mercy.

Bottle A womb symbol; the principle of containing and enclosure. In Buddhism it is the womb of the Buddha nature. In Christianity it represents salvation and is an emblem of St James the Great.

Bough/Branch Related to TREE symbolism (q.v.). The Tree of Life and fertility can be depicted by a branch, hence it was a bridal symbol; boughs on houses and 'bringing home the may', the hawthorn branch on May 1, was a Spring fertility rite. The Golden Bough is the link between this world and the next; the passport to the heavenly world; initiation; the magic wand; it enabled Aeneas to pass through the underworld and survive. The priest of Diana's sacred grove on Lake Nemi won his office by killing his predecessor with the Golden Bough. The Silver Bough, the apple, is the link between this world and the fairy world, Tir-nan-og. Breaking the bough means the death of a king. The bough is also related to the symbolism of the wand, pole and oar. *Celtic*: Renewal of youth. *Druidic*: The golden bough is the MISTLETOE (q.v.). *Hebrew*: The sacred wood of the acacia is sometimes referred to as the golden bough.

Boundary See THRESHOLD.

Bow Symbolically it is both masculine and feminine: masculine as prowess and dispatching the masculine arrow; feminine as the crescent moon. *Buddhist*: Will power; the bow is the mind which dispatches the arrows of the five senses. *Chinese*: The bow and arrow together are fertility, offspring; drawing the bow is masculine prowess. *Christian*: Worldly power (Jer. 49, 35). *Graeco–Roman*: The bow of Artemis/

Diana is the crescent moon. Bows and arrows are attributes of Apollo, Eros, Artemis and Diana, bow and quiver an attribute of the giant hunter Orion. *Hindu*: Will power (as Buddhism above). The bowstring of Kama, god of love, is composed of bees as 'sweet pain'. *Islamic*: The power of God. The grip of the bow in the middle, uniting both parts, is the union of Allah with Mohammed. *Sumero–Semitic*: The weapon of Ishtar/Inanna as war goddesses. *Taoism*: The bow and arrow symbolize the Tao which brings down the high, raises the low, takes away excess and supplies needs.

Bowels See INTESTINES.

Bower The feminine principle; shelter; protection. In Christianity it is a symbol of the Virgin Mary.

Bowl A bowl of water represents the feminine, receptive principle and fertility. The almsbowl signifies aloofness from life; renunciation; the surrender of the ego. *Buddhist*: The almsbowl is an attribute of the monk or *bhikkhu*. The seven small bowls of water on a shrine represent the seven offerings for an honoured guest: water for drinking, water for washing, flowers, incense, lamps, perfume, food. *Hindu*: The bowl is an attribute of Ganesha.

Box The feminine principle of containing; enclosure; the womb. The box bush, as evergreen, is immortality, youth, vigour, vitality, perpetuity.

Bread Life; the food of the body and the soul; the visible and manifest life. It is also a symbol of union as having many grains in one substance and when broken and shared represents shared and united life. Sacramental bread is usually in small round form, or a larger loaf is broken and shared out; it is often marked with a cross, as in Mithraic, Sumero–Semitic and Christian rites. Bread and wine: the wine is the divine ecstasy and the bread is the visible manifestation of the spirit which dies and rises again; man and divinity united; the balanced product of man's skill and efforts in agriculture; the masculine wine with the feminine bread; the combination of the liquid and the solid which can represent the androgyne. Bread and wine were often a feature of funeral feasts or graveside ceremonies. The breaking of bread signifies the death of the victim of sacrifice; also sharing and communion. *Christian*: The sustainer of life; God's providence; Christ, 'the bread of life' (John 6, 35); the 'body of Christ' (Luke 22, 19). Bread and wine denote the two natures of Christ, the body and blood of Christ in the eucharistic meal. *Sumero-Semitic*: Breaking bread was providing food for the souls of the dead; communion. The bread and water of immortal life were kept in heaven by Anu.

Breaking Breaking in pieces (of lunar deities,

dying gods, or man at initiation) symbolizes the lunar division into parts; the new moon is the emblem of these deities, and is death and rebirth and the many arising from the One. Breaking a glass typifies the transitoriness of human happiness. Breaking a tablet is the dissolution of a contract or partnership or rescinding a debt. Breaking an object intended for the dead 'kills' the object and releases its soul so that the dead can take it to the next world. See also DISMEMBERMENT.

Breastplate Protection; preservation. An attribute of Athene/Minerva. The Hebrew breastplate, in the middle of the ephod, is a Cosmic Centre.

Breasts Motherhood; nourishment; protection; love; the nourishing aspect of the Great Mother. Many-breasted goddesses depict nourishment; abundance; fertility. The bared breast is humility; grief; repentance; penitence. Beating the breast signifies grief; repentance.

Breath Life; the soul; life-giving power; the *spiritus mundi*; the power of the spirit; also the transient, insubstantial and elusive. The intaking and outgoing of the breath symbolize the alternating rhythm of life and death, manifestation and reabsorption in the universe. In Christianity insufflation, the breathing or blowing upon a person or thing, signified the influence of the Holy Spirit and the expelling of evil spirits.

Bridge Communication between heaven and earth, one realm and another; uniting man with the divinity. In rites of PASSAGE (q.v.) it is the transition from one plane to another; the passage to reality. In the primordial state, in the Golden Age, man could cross at will, as there was no death; the bridge is now crossed only at death, or in mystical states, or in initiation ceremonies, or by solar heroes. In crossing the perilous bridge man proves he is a spirit and returns to the lost Paradise. The bridge between this world and the next can also be symbolized by the rainbow, the celestial dragon and the celestial serpent. It is also associated with the Strait Gate and the ladder which has sword rungs, etc. The two banks of the river to be crossed by the bridge represent the two worlds of mortals and death, immortals and life; the bridge is the passage from death to immortality, from the unreal to the real.

Narrow bridges, razor-edged and sword bridges, etc. represent the slender separation between opposites, spacelessness in the realm of the supernatural, and ways which are inaccessible to ordinary physical experience and the senses, ways which can be attained by transcending the physical by mind and spirit, as in the Upanishads and in Holy Grail legends: 'A sharp edge of a razor, hard to traverse, a difficult path' (*Upanishads*). The Islamic bridge is 'narrower than a hair'. Lightness and swiftness,

Christ Pantocrator holds the closed **book** of life and destiny in this 11th-century Greek mosaic.

The many **breasts** of the 1st-century AD Artemis of the Ephesians symbolize the virgin goddess's abundant and ever-available fertility and succour.

symbolic of wisdom and intelligence, enable man to cross quickly and safely, while the heavy, ignorant and stupid break the bridge and fall down to hell or to demons and monsters waiting below, representing sin and ignorance. The Bridge Perilous is also the way to enlightenment, victory over death and division in the realm of differentiation. The river can also be crossed by a boat, raft or ford. The Iranian Cinvat Bridge separates the two worlds and must be crossed by the soul; it leads to the Mount of Judgment and is guarded by two dogs. Bridge symbolism also includes man as mediator, the central or axial position between heaven and earth, hence the Hierophant and the Roman Pontifex.

Bridle Restraint; control. Attribute of Nemesis and Fortuna. Sometimes depicted in Christian art with Temperance.

Broom See BRUSH.

Broom Plant *European*: Humility; zeal.

Brothers Brothers at enmity are the conflicting powers of light and darkness, dryness and humidity; also the nomadic and agricultural ways of life. They are often associated with founding the first city and are frequently represented as pairs of opposites, such as Ormuzd and Ahriman, Vritra and Indra, Osiris and Set, Romulus and Remus, Cain and Abel. In South Eastern European folklore, God and Satan were brothers. These symbolize the necessity of opposites in the dualistic realm of manifestation. See also TWINS.

Brown See COLOURS.

Brush *Chinese*: Wisdom, insight; brushing away worries and difficulties. *Japanese*: The broom made of grass and used at the Spring ritual represents purification.

Bucentaur See FABULOUS BEASTS.

Buckle Protection; self-defence. *Egyptian*: The buckle of Isis, or her girdle, is the protection of Isis; strength; power; the blood of Isis which guaranteed her favour and that of her son Horus.

Buddhist Symbols The Eight Emblems of Good Augury are the conch, umbrella, canopy, mystic knot, fish, lotus, vase, Wheel of the Law. Other symbols are the scroll, axe, goad, spear, rope, begging-bowl, sacrificial cup, fan, bow and arrow, incense burner, rosary, fly-whisk, cock-and-sun, hare-and-moon, musical instruments, calabash or gourd. The emblems on the footprint of Buddha are the swastika, wheel, conch, fish, vajra, crown, vase.

Buffalo *Amerindian*: The buffalo or bison portrays supernatural power; strength; forti-

tude; the whirlwind. *Buddhist*: Yama, god of the dead, is sometimes buffalo- or bull-headed. *Taoist*: Lao Tzu rides a buffalo or ox and was riding a green buffalo when he disappeared in the West. Riding a buffalo is mastery over man's animal nature. The buffalo sometimes takes the place of the ox in the 'Ten Ox-herding Pictures', in which the buffalo, as unregenerate nature, starts as wholly black and, during the process of taming, is gradually depicted as becoming whiter until in the tenth picture he has disappeared completely.

Bull Ambivalent; usually the bull is the masculine principle in nature; the solar generative force sacred to all sky gods; fecundity; male procreative strength; royalty; the king; but it also symbolizes the earth and the humid power of nature, when it becomes lunar and is ridden by moon goddesses such as Astarte and Europa and then signifies the taming of the masculine and animal nature. Riding a bull, or bulls drawing a chariot, is also a solar-warrior attribute connected with sky, storm and solar gods; the roaring of the bull represents thunder, rain and fertility.

Embodying the procreative power, it is associated with the fertilizing forces of the sun, rain, storm, thunder and lightning and hence with both the dry and humid principles. Sky and weather gods as the bull appear from the earliest records and the goddess is frequently depicted with them as consort. The bull sacrifice and Taurobolium occur in the worship of Attis and Mithra and in ancient New Year festivals. Bull symbolism is common among all Sumerian and Semitic cults. The bull-man is usually a guardian who protects a centre, or treasure, or doors; he wards off evil and is apotropaic. A bull's head (the most important part since it contains the vital principle) signifies sacrifice and death. The slaying of the bull at the New Year is the death of Winter and the birth of the creative life-force. *Buddhist*: The bull is the moral self, the ego, and is an attribute of Yama, god of the dead, who is sometimes bull or buffalo-headed. *Celtic*: Bull gods are divine power and strength. With the Druids the bull is the sun and the cow the earth. *Chinese*: One of the animals of the Twelve Terrestrial Branches. *Christian*: Brute force; emblem of St Eustace, martyred in a brass bull, and of St Thecla. *Egyptian*: The bull Apis was an avatar of Osiris and 'the second life and servant of Ptah'. It was also worshipped under the form of Mnves or Merwer and was sacred to the solar Ra who, as the Bull of Heaven, daily impregnated the sky goddess Nut. Neb, the earth god, was also the bull of the sky goddess. The thigh of the bull was the phallic leg of Set as fertility, strength and the North Pole. *Greek*: Attribute of Zeus as sky god, also of Dionysos who was horned and sometimes bull-headed when manifesting as the male principle. Sacred to Poseidon, whose wine-bearers at Ephesus were 'bulls'. As the humid power the bull was an attribute of Aphrodite.

Hebrew: Jahveh is the 'Bull of Israel', thus it is the might of Jahveh. *Hindu*: Strength; speed; fertility; the reproductive power of nature. The bull Nandin is a vehicle of Siva, guardian of the West, who rides a bull. It is an attribute of Agni, 'the Mighty Bull', and a form of Indra in his fertile aspect. The bull is also the vital breath of Aditi, the all-embracing. The power conferred by Soma is frequently equated with that of the bull. Rudra unites with the cow-goddess. *Iranian*: The soul of the world; its generative power is associated with the moon and rain clouds in fertility. The bull was the first created animal and was slain by Ahriman; from the soul of the bull came the germ of all later creation. *Minoan*: The Great God. The bull was sacrificed to the earth and earthquake god: 'In bulls does the Earth-Shaker delight' (Homer). In some societies the bull was thought to cause earthquakes by tossing the earth on its horns and its roaring was heard. In Crete he appears to represent the reproductive force in nature. *Mithraic*: The solar god; the bull sacrifice was the central ceremony in Mithraism. It also represented victory over man's animal nature and life through death. The bull and lion together symbolize death. *Roman*: Attribute of Jupiter as sky god; sacrificed to Mars; attribute of Venus and Europa as moon deities; Europa, as the dawn, is carried across the sky by the solar bull. *Scandinavian*: Attribute of Thor and sacred to Freyja. *Sumero-Semitic*: The celestial bull ploughed the great furrow of the sky. Ramman, Asshur and Adad, who ride on bulls, are 'bulls of heaven'; Marduk, or Merodach, is identified with Gudibir, the 'bull of light'. The sun, Enil or Enki, is the 'savage bull of the sky and earth'; Sin, a lunar god, also takes the form of a bull; Teshub, the Hittite sun god, takes the form of a bull; it is an aspect of Ea as lord of magic and is often depicted in Sumerian art as holding door-posts; the Syrian and Phoenician Baal or Bel, a solar god of fertility of the soil and flocks, was symbolized by the bull; the Accadian 'directing bull' begins the zodiacal year. Winged bulls are guardian spirits. *Zodiacal*: The bull, Taurus, is a sun symbol and the creative resurgence of Spring.

Bullroarer Represents thunder and wind and is an evocation of the deity; it was used in Dionysian mystery rites, in the Stone Age civilizations and in initiation and rain-making ceremonies among Australian aboriginals. With the Amerindians it is an evocation of the Great Spirit; the outward sign of the tribal All-Father.

Burning Bush Divine manifestation; the presence of God. The burning bush becomes the Cosmic Tree in Vedic fire symbolism of Agni.

Buttercup *Graeco-Roman*. Mockery; spite; madness; emblem of Ares/Mars.

Butterfly The soul; immortality. As changing from the mundane caterpillar, through the state

Lao Tzu rides a **buffalo**, symbolizing his final triumph over his animal nature, on his last journey, to 'the West', in this 17th-century Chinese bronze.

The ancient Cretan **bull**-dancers, like the one on this Minoan onyx seal, simultaneously yielded to and challenged the power of the Great God, the 'Earth Shaker', symbolized by the bull.

From Mycenae, about 1500 BC, comes this **butterfly** motif, representing the Great Mother: like her, the butterfly contains within itself all its previous incarnations and the promise of future generations. The shape echoes the Minoan double AXE.

of dissolution, to the celestial winged creature, it is rebirth, resurrection. Also, like the double-headed axe, a symbol of the Great Goddess. *Celtic*: The soul; fire. *Chinese*: Immortality; abundant leisure; joy. The butterfly with the chrysanthemum portrays beauty in old age; with the plum it is longevity. *Christian*: Resurrection; its stages of development are life, death and resurrection. Sometimes shown in the hand of the Christ Child. *Greek*: Immortality; the soul; the psyche; also Psyche in Greek art. *Japanese*: A vain woman; a geisha; a fickle lover. A pair of butterflies is conjugal happiness; a white butterfly is a spirit of the dead. *Maori*: The soul.

Buttons Chinese ceremonial robes have large buttons symbolizing the sun and moon and small buttons as the stars.

Caduceus The wings symbolize transcendence, the air; the wand is power; the double serpent is the opposites in dualism, ultimately to be united; they are also the two serpents of healing and poison, illness and health, they are hermetic and homoeopathic, 'nature can overcome nature', the complementary nature of the two forces operative in the universe and the union of the sexes. They represent the powers of binding and loosing, good and evil, fire and water, ascending and descending, also equilibrium, wisdom and fertility. In Alchemy they are the male sulphur and the female quicksilver, the power of transformation; sleeping and waking; the *solve et coagula* of the Great Work; the synthesis of opposites and the transcendent function of mediation between the upper and lower realms.

The wand, or herald's staff, is the *axis mundi*, up and down which all mediator-messenger gods travel between heaven and earth. The caduceus is carried by messengers as a symbol of peace and protection and is pre-eminently their attribute. The Egyptian Anubis, the Graeco-Roman Hermes/Mercury (in whose hands it also depicts health and youthfulness), the Phoenician Baal, and sometimes Isis and Ishtar all carry it. It is 'the golden rod, three-petalled, of happiness and wealth' (Homer), and is also suggested as the staff supporting the sun and moon symbols. The caduceus can also be represented as a globe surmounted by horns, a Phoenician and Hittite solar symbol. It is also found in India. It is the astronomical symbol of Hermes/Mercury.

Cakes Sacrificial cakes, or buns, marked with the cross, symbolize the round of the moon and its four quarters.

Calabash or Gourd *Amerindian*: The female breast; nourishment. *Chinese*: In Chinese Alchemy the calabash, as a gourd, is the cosmos in miniature; the creative power of nature; the original unity of the primordial parents. The double gourd is the united yin and yang.

Calf In sacrifice the calf is the offering without blemish, hence, in Christian iconography, it can represent Christ. In Vedic symbolism it is the mind of Aditi, with the bull as the vital breath of Aditi, the All-Embracing.

Calumet The Amerindian Pipe of Peace also symbolizes reconciliation; conciliation; humility; sacrifice and purification; the integration of the individual with the Totality, becoming one with the fire of the Great Spirit. The round bowl of the pipe is the centre of the universe, the heart; the smoke symbolically transports to heaven; the canal of the pipe is the spinal column and the channel the vital spirit.

Camel *Christian*: Temperance; royalty; dignity; obedience; stamina; associated with the Magi and with John the Baptist who was clothed in camel's hair. Also, as kneeling to receive its burden, it depicts humility and docility. *Iranian*: The camel is associated with the dragon-serpent. *Roman*: The personification of Arabia on coins.

Camellia Steadfastness. *Chinese*: Beauty; health; physical and mental strength. *Japanese*: Sudden death.

Camphor The senses which, like camphor, should burn themselves out with no residue.

Cancer See ZODIAC.

Candle Light in the darkness of life; illumination; the vitalizing power of the sun; also the uncertainty of life as easily extinguished; evanescence. Candles lit at death illuminate its darkness and represent the light in the world to come; they are a feature of Catholic and most Oriental funeral rites. *Christian*: The divine light shining in the world; Christ as the light of the world; spiritual joy; Christ risen from the dead in the light of transfiguration; the pious lit with love. Candles on either side of the cross on the altar are the dual nature of Christ, human and divine. In Eastern Orthodox Christianity three joined candles depict the Holy Trinity and two joined candles the dual nature of Christ. See also PASCHAL TAPER and TENEBRAE. *Hebrew*: The Mosaic seven-branched candlestick, the Menorah, indicates the divine presence (candles of fat are sacred to Jahveh); the stem of the candlestick is suggested as the Cosmic Tree and an *axis mundi*. Josephus says that the seven branches are the sun, moon and planets, also the seven days of the week, the seven stars of Ursa Major and the seven cycles or forces in the world. According to Philo, the Menorah represents the operation of grace for all things celestial. In Qabalism the three candles, or candlesticks, are wisdom, strength and beauty.

Cannibalism Eating the flesh is to absorb the vital power of the person eaten.

Canoe A lunar barque; the crescent moon. In Maori symbolism it is the Mother of the Race.

Canopic Jars *Egyptian*: The protection of the four gods of the dead, represented by the heads of the baboon, jackal, hawk and man, placed at the four corners of the tomb.

Canopy Royalty; sovereign power. *Buddhist*: The Sacred Tree of Enlightenment; one of the Eight Auspicious Signs. A white canopy is the pure mind embracing the Dharma and protecting human beings. *Chinese*: Royalty; sovereign power; protection. *Hindu*: Spiritual and temporal power, a square canopy for priests and circular for kings.

Cap Nobility; freedom (slaves went bareheaded). *Graeco-Roman*: The conical caps of the Dioscuri are the two halves of Leda's egg from which they were born, and also represent the two hemispheres. *Hebrew*: The blue ritual cap of the vestments depicts the heavens. *Shamanistic*: The cap of power is one of the chief symbols of the shaman. *Teutonic*: Nobility; power; the 'Tarn-kappe' or 'Nebel-kappe'. See also PHRYGIAN CAP.

Cap and Bells See FOOL.

Capricorn See ZODIAC and FABULOUS BEASTS.

Carbuncle *Christian*: A symbol of Christ's passion and sacrifice; a cross with five carbuncles on it portrays the five wounds.

Cardinal Points See DIRECTIONS OF SPACE,

Cards Playing cards. The fifty-two cards in the pack symbolize the weeks of the year, the thirteen cards in each suit are the thirteen lunar months of the year, the four suits represent the four worlds, elements, directions of space, winds, seasons, castes, corners of the temple, etc.

Two red suits indicate the warm seasons and powers of light; two black are the cold seasons and powers of darkness. All four designs on the cards are life symbols: the spade, a leaf, the Cosmic Tree; the heart, the life centre and world centre; the diamond, or lozenge, the feminine principle; the club, the trefoil or masculine principle. The Ace is the Monad; the King, the spirit, essence, father; the Queen, the soul, the personality, mother; the Knave, the ego, energies, the messenger. Together the King-Queen-Knave form the spiritual Triad. The Joker is the fifth element, the non-material world, the quintessence of the Alchemists and the ether of the Hindus. *Spades*, or swords, are penetrating intellect; the circle or the sphere; daring; action; expression; air; matter in gaseous form; the astral world; the thunderbolt; death. The King is the earth king, Saturn,

The **caduceus** held by Mercury in this 15th-century alchemical illustration symbolizes the harmonious and healing union of opposites, of which Mercury himself is the ideal embodiment.

The seven **candles** of the Hebrew Menorah symbolize the sun, moon and principal planets shining in the darkness of chaos and life's uncertainty, as in this 12th-century Bible.

Pluto, David. The Queen is war, the flash of lightning, Pallas Athene, Neith. The Knave represents Mercury, Aesculapius. *Hearts*, or cups, are knowledge; mind; the creative and formal world; the creative waters; matter in liquid form; the chalice; the silver crescent. The King is the water king, Poseidon/Neptune, Charlemagne. The Queen, love, roses, Hathor, Sekhet, Semiramis, Venus, Helen. The Knave, Mars, god of war and agriculture, Parasurama. *Diamonds*, coins or lozenges, are the world of the senses; material earth; physical form; provisions; money; solid matter; the cube or square. The King is the fire king, Caesar, the arrow-head. The Queen, fire and fuel, Nephthys, Persephone. The Knave, the warrior. *Clubs*, sceptres or wands, are the will; fire; matter in combustion; ideas; radiant energy; the archetypal world; the triangle or pyramid. The King is the sky king Zeus/Jupiter, Alexander the Great, King Arthur. The Queen, queen of the air, Hera/Juno, Argine. The Knave, Apollo, Aeneas, Lancelot.

Carnation The red carnation depicts admiration, marriage, passionate love; the pink represents the tears of the Virgin Mary, hence motherhood; the white is pure love and the yellow, rejection.

Carnival See ORGY.

Carp *Chinese*: Literary eminence; perseverance in struggle against difficulties; courage. The carp is said to 'leap the Dragon Gate' by perseverance and become a dragon, hence the successful scholar in the literary examinations is 'a carp that has leapt the Dragon Gate'. Twin carp signify the union of lovers. *Japanese*: An emblem of the Samurai as courage; dignity; resignation to fate; endurance; good fortune. It also symbolizes love as a homophone of carp.

Cask The feminine, receptive, enclosing principle. A bottomless cask signifies senseless and wasted labour.

Cassia *Chinese*: Immortality; a Tree of Life in Paradise; a tree in the moon; good fortune; rise to greatness.

Castanets *Taoist*: The two contending powers of the universe; emblem of Ts'ao Kuo-chu, one of the eight Taoist genii or immortals.

Caste Symbolized by the square, it is the pattern of the universe; the pairs of opposites; the four cardinal points which, in turn, are connected with the four seasons, elements and emblematic colours. Brahmans, the sacerdotal, are equated with the polar region, Winter and the North; Kshatriyas, the royal and warrior, with the rising sun, Spring and the solar East; Vaishyas, trade and agriculture, with the setting sun (i.e. that which is past the zenith or 'twice-born'), Summer and the South; Sudras,

servants, with darkness, obscurity, Autumn and the West.

Castle Shares the symbolism of the enclosure and of the walled and defended city and represents the difficult to obtain; spiritual testing. It usually holds some treasure or imprisoned person and is inhabited by a monster or wicked person who must be overcome to obtain the treasure or release the imprisoned, which depicts the treasure of esoteric knowledge or spiritual attainment. BRIDGE symbolism (q.v.) is also involved in crossing the moat to the castle.

Castration The death of the fertility of a god or hero; a life sacrifice; cutting the grain is castration as is the sun in eclipse when it enters the realm of the moon goddess. From the blood of the castrated Ouranos/Cronos sprang the Erinyes, the Gigantes and the Meliae and, falling on the sea-foam, it gave birth to Aphrodite/Venus. The Barley King and Oak King were ritually castrated at the end of their reigns. Set was emasculated by Horus. Symbols of castration are the scythe and sickle, and lameness.

Cat Its eyes being variable, the cat symbolizes the varying power of the sun and the waxing and waning of the moon and the splendour of the night; it also denotes stealth; desire; liberty. As black it is lunar, evil and death; it is only in modern times that a black cat has been taken to signify good luck. *Amerindian*: The wild cat portrays stealth. *Celtic*: Chthonic powers; funerary. *Chinese*: A yin animal as nocturnal; powers of evil; powers of transformation. A strange cat is unfavourable change; a black cat, misfortune, illness. *Christian*: Satan; darkness; lust; laziness. *Egyptian*: Lunar; sacred to Set as darkness; as lunar the cat can also be an attribute of Isis and of Bast, the moon; it represents pregnant women as the moon makes the seed grow in the womb. *Graeco-Roman*: Attribute of the lunar Diana. The goddess of liberty has a cat at her feet. *Japanese*: Powers of transformation; peaceful repose. *Scandinavian*: Attribute of Freyja, whose chariot is drawn by cats. *Witchcraft*: A familiar and disguise of witches; the black cat as the witches' familiar is evil and ill luck. Cats and dogs as witches' familiars are rain-makers.

Cauldron Nourishment; sustenance; abundance; fertility; the feminine receptive and nourishing principle. The magic cauldron is fecundity and the feminine power of transformation; life and death; renewal and rebirth. It can also be equated with the Grail. The witches' cauldron signifies magic spells. *Celtic*: Abundance; inexhaustible sustenance (as with the cornucopia); powers of resuscitation; the reproductive earth powers; rebirth; restoring warriors to life. The magic cauldron of Keridwen has three powers of inexhaustibility, regeneration, inspiration. Attribute of Bran and Dagda. *Christian*: Emblem of SS Fausta, Felicitas, John, Vitus. *Scandinavian*: 'The Roaring Cauldron' is the source of all rivers.

Cave 'A symbol of the universe' (Porphyry); an omphalos; the world centre; the heart; the place of union of the Self and the ego; the meeting place of the divine and the human, hence all dying gods and saviours are born in caves; inner esoteric knowledge; that which is hidden; a place of initiation and the second birth. The cave is also the feminine principle, the womb of Mother Earth and her sheltering aspect; it is both a place of burial and rebirth, of mystery, increase and renewal, from which man emerges and to which he returns at death in the stone sepulchre; this emergence associates the cave with the Cosmic Egg. The cave is closely related to the symbolism of the HEART (q.v.) as the spiritual and initiatory centre of both the macrocosm and the microcosm; both the cave and the heart are symbolized by the feminine, downward-pointing triangle. The mountain is the masculine principle, the visible and external, and is represented by the upward-pointing triangle, while the cave within the mountain is the feminine, hidden and closed; both are cosmic centres. The cave, being part of the mountain, shares its axial symbolism.

Initiation ceremonies most frequently took place in a cave as symbolic of the underworld and the sepulchre where death took place prior to rebirth and illumination. As a place of initiation it was also a secret place, the entrance to which was hidden from the profane by a labyrinth or dangerous passage, often guarded by some monster or supernatural person, and entry could only be gained by overcoming the opposing force. Entering the cave is also re-entry into the womb of Mother Earth, as with cave burials. Passing through the cave represents a change of state, also achieved by overcoming dangerous powers. The cave is often the place of the sacred marriage between heaven and earth, king and queen, etc., the *hieros gamos*. *Amerindian*: The worlds are symbolized by a series of caves one above the other. *Celtic*: The way of entrance to the otherworld. *Chinese*: The cave is the feminine, yin principle, with the mountain as the yang. *Hindu*: The heart; the centre; the 'cave of the heart' is the dwelling place of Atma. *Mithraic*: Worship and initiation took place in a cave in which there were flowers and springs in honour of Mithras, Father and Creator of All; the cave reproduced in miniature the universe he had created. *Platonic*: The world in its obscurity and illusion.

Cedar Strength; nobility; incorruptibility. Emblem of Lebanon. *Christian*: Majesty, stateliness; beauty; Christ (Ezek. 17,22). *Hebrew*: The sacred wood of Solomon's Temple. *Sumerian*: The Cosmic Tree; the Tree of Life; it possessed magical properties and was sacred to Tammuz.

To the ancient Egyptians, a **cat** mummy like this one from Abydos symbolized the abiding protection and favour of Isis, Mother Goddess, and Bast, the moon goddess who was herself cat-headed.

The Gundestrup **cauldron**, decorated with scenes of commerce between gods and men, is a tangible symbol of the divine powers of destruction and regeneration within the same vessel.

Censer Offering prayer to the divinity. *Christian*: Prayer rising to God (Ps. 141, 2). Emblem of SS Laurence, Maurus, Stephen. See also INCENSE.

Centaur Man's lower nature, the animal nature combined with his higher nature of human virtue and judgment; the savage and benign aspects of nature and the conflict between these opposites. The HORSE (q.v.) depicts virile solar power and is the mount of the directing spirit of the man; this is a combination of blind power and guiding spirit. *Christian*: Sensuality; passions; adultery; brute force; man torn between good and evil, animal and spiritual nature; the heretic; an incarnation of the devil. The bow and arrows are the fiery darts of evil. *Greek*: The centaur Chiron, who taught Achilles, personified wisdom. Centaurs sometimes accompany Dionysos/Bacchus.

Centre Totality; wholeness; absolute reality; pure being; the origin of all existence; unmanifest being; the world axis; the pole; the point around which everything revolves; Paradise; the potential; the point containing the totality of all possibilities; sacred space; a break in space and the point of intercommunication between the three worlds, transcending time and space; an axis uniting the cosmos both vertically and horizontally; the intersection of macrocosm and microcosm; cosmic order; the 'Pivot of the Law'; the point of resolution and reconciliation where all opposites disappear; the Eternal Now; the 'point quiescent'; the 'unmoved mover' of Aristotle. The centre is also the point of origin of departure and the point of return; all emerges from it, revolves round it and returns to it in the two complementary movements, the centrifugal and centripetal, also symbolized by outbreathing and inbreathing and by the circulation of the blood from the heart centre. Moving from the centre to the circumference is the journey into manifestation and multiplicity, while the journey back is to the spiritual centre, unity, the One. It is also the point from which space is produced, from which motion emanates and form arises, both the point of expansion and of contraction in drawing multiplicity back to unity, to harmony, knowledge and illumination.

The sun represents the centre of the universe, as the heart, the 'inner place', is the centre of man. There is a symbolic centre, or kingdom, in every domain: the sun, or gold, among metals; a jewel among stones; the lotus, lily or rose in plants; the lion among animals; the eagle in birds; the dolphin among fishes and man among all living creatures; the hearth in the home and the altar in the temple or church. The fixity of the centre symbolizes eternity and perfect simultaneity. Any central projection, such as the central boss in an ancient metal mirror, or the oculus in a dome, marks the Sun Door or Gate of Heaven, the apex of the universe and the upper end of the world axis, a point of communication between heaven and earth; this symbolism is found in many oriental traditions and was once common in Christianity. Symbols of the centre are the pillar, Cosmic Tree, Sacred Mountain, heart, fire altar, the spring or well of life, the hearth, spiral, labyrinth, pyramid, or any sacred space. On the cross the central point is sometimes shown as a jewel or flower. *Amerindian*: The Great Spirit, which is the centre, but is also everywhere. *Buddhist*: Pure Being; enlightenment; Nirvana. *Chinese*: Perfect peace; divine immanence; stillness; being at one with the will of Heaven; the 'Pivot of the Law' (Chuang Tzu); the invariable mean. *Hebrew*: The Shekinah, the central presence of God; the Holy Place; the Inward Palace where God dwells; the One; the beginning of existence; thought. *Hindu*: Pure Being; unity; Ishvara; the place of the unconditioned, Brahman, 'the dark source of all light'; the point beyond time; the Inner Witness. The chakras are the symbolic spiritual centres of the body. *Islamic*: The Point; the 'Divine Abode'; the 'Divine Station' of harmony, equilibrium and order; the secret centre; the incommunicable; the 'eye of the heart'. *Taoist*: The Tao; Pure Being; 'nought but infinity, which is neither this nor that' (Chuang Tzu).

Cerberus See FABULOUS BEASTS.

Chain Ambivalent as office, dignity and unity, but also bondage and slavery. Chains of office, e.g. mayor, mandarin, etc., bind to office, function and power. The links of the chain symbolize communication and marriage. In Buddhism the links bind man to continued phenomenal existence. In Christianity chains are the emblem of SS Balbina and Leonard. In Islam the Chain of Being is the hierarchical order of things in the universe. See also BONDS.

Chakra A spiritual and psychic centre in the being, symbolized by the lotus and the wheel. When the centre is awakened the lotus opens and revolves; the lotuses of the different centres have a different number of petals.

Chalcedony See JEWELS.

Chalice The source of inexhaustible sustenance; abundance. It is associated with the symbolism of the heart, containing the life-blood which, in the chalice, is represented by wine, wine and blood having the same portent; it is also connected with the GRAIL (q.v.). *Celtic*: Marriage. *Christian*: The blood of Christ and the New Testament (Mark 14, 23/4); the cup of salvation; the Eucharist; faith. Emblem of SS Barbara, Thomas Aquinas, Bonaventura. See also CUP.

Chameleon The element of air (it was supposed to be nourished by the wind). In

Christianity it depicts Satan taking different guises to deceive mankind. In some African tribes it is a rain-bringer.

Chariot The human body-vehicle, with the horse as the solar, spiritual vehicle. Chariots drawn by white or golden horses, or sometimes by gryphons, are attributes of sky gods who drive the sun-chariot across the sky. Fiery chariots are ascent to heaven by the spirit, or by divinities or holy people. Victors or heroes are often depicted driving chariots; these are then a battle symbol. The qualities and intentions of the driver are symbolized by the team driven, e.g. white horses are spirituality, purity, or solar, while Freyja's chariot drawn by cats is lunar and magical. The driver depicts the mind, intelligence or spirit directing the body. The two wheels are heaven and earth. *Celtic*: Flidass, goddess of venery and wild things, has a chariot drawn by deer. The solar chariot is sometimes drawn by a white swan or swans. *Buddhist*: The sun chariot is the Great Vehicle. *Christian*: The chariot, cart, wain, or ark, is the Church as a vehicle to convey the faithful to heaven; its two wheels are desire and will, charity and prudence, according to Dante. *Graeco-Roman*: The vehicle of all sun gods, driving the solar white horses who, as either the solar or humid principle, convey the sun and moon across the sky, e.g. Apollo as solar and Poseidon's white horses as the watery element. Chariot and horses are also warlike attributes of the war god Ares/Mars. Cybele drives a chariot drawn by lions; Tritons, blowing conch shells, draw the chariot of Poseidon; Sabazios drives a sun chariot. Jupiter Dolichenus drives a yoke of bulls. Doves draw the chariot of Venus, stags of Diana, peacocks of Juno, dogs of Hephaestos/Vulcan, eagles of Zeus/Jupiter, goats or leopards of Dionysos/Bacchus and Eros/Cupid, and black horses the chariot of Pluto. *Hindu*: The 'vehicle' of the being in manifestation; the charioteer is the Self which directs the horses, as symbolized by Krishna who drives, but is not involved in the fighting or action around him; the horses are the physical life-forces; the reins the intelligence and the will of the driver; the axle is the world axis and the two wheels are heaven and earth joined by the axis; their revolutions are cycles of manifestation. Savitri drives a chariot with luminous horses; Soma has the three-wheeled lunar chariot drawn by the pied antelope or ten white horses; the Asvins, twin powers, drive a three-wheeled chariot; Ushas, Dawn, drives a chariot with cows or red horses; Indra rides in a golden chariot; Siva drives a chariot drawn by lunar gazelles or antelopes. *Iranian*: The chariot of the Magi is drawn by four chargers symbolizing the elements and consecrated to their four gods. Anahita, a fertility goddess, had a chariot drawn by four white horses – wind, rain, cloud, hail. She appears with Mithra. *Scandinavian and Teutonic*: Thor's chariot is drawn by solar rams or goats; Freyja's by lunar cats.

Against a background of the three nails of the Crucifixion, the angels in this 15th-century miniature support the **chalice** of Christ's blood, whose size alludes to the abundance of mercy, salvation and redemption.

An ancient Scandinavian sun-**chariot** combines the symbolism of the horse as animal, earthly, with that of the celestial and spiritual solar disk.

Charity In Christian art Charity is depicted as a woman either surrounded by children or, more usually, nursing a child or suckling it; she often holds a heart or a flower. Other symbols of charity are the heart, lamb, the pelican feeding its young from its own blood, or a person receiving or nursing children; also Christ's seamless robe.

Chasuble *Christian*: Christ's seamless robe, representing charity. The cross on the back is the cross carried to Calvary and the Y of Christ's arms on the cross; the stripe on the front is the pillar of scourging; covering other vestments portrays the protection of charity; it is also the purple robe of royalty put on the 'King of the Jews'.

Chequers The diversity of dualism in the manifest world; light and darkness, day and night etc. For chequer-board see CHESS.

Cherry As bearing flowers before its leaves the cherry tree symbolizes man born naked into the world without possessions and as he also returns to the earth. *Chinese*: The blossom is Spring; hope; youth; virility; feminine beauty; the feminine principle. *Christian*: A fruit of Paradise and the blessed; good works; sweetness; often depicted with the Christ Child. *Japanese*: Prosperity; riches; a flower emblem of Japan.

Cherubim 'The cherubim are winged creatures, but the form of them does not resemble that of any living creature seen by man' (Josephus). They signify the presence of divinity and are guardians of the sacred and of the threshold. As TETRAMORPHS (q.v.) cherubim are the quaternary of elemental powers guarding the centre of Paradise which is inaccessible to unregenerate man. They combine the bull (Taurus), lion (Leo), eagle (Scorpio), and man (Aquarius), symbolizing the four elements, the four corners of the earth and, in Christianity, the four Evangelists. After the Seraphim they are the highest of the nine orders of angels. In heraldry a cherub is depicted as a child's head (purity and innocence) between a pair of wings (spiritual nature). Jahveh is 'enthroned upon the cherubim' (1 Sam. 4, 4). The throne of the Temple of Jerusalem in the Holy of Holies was flanked by two cherubim and the throne was formed by their wings.

Chess The royal game of life; the conflict between the spiritual powers of light and darkness; devas and asuras; angels and demons struggling for domination of the world; existence as a field of action of opposing powers and forces; manifestation and re-absorption. The black and white, or red and white, chequer-board symbolizes the alternating pull of all fundamental dualities and complements in manifestation, the negative and positive; night and day; sun and moon; male and female; obscurity and clarity; the light and dark of the moon; time and space etc., also the criss-cross pattern of life alternating between good and bad, fortune and misfortune. The sixty-four squares are the mandala of Siva in his transforming aspect and are based on the fourfold symbolism of the 8 × 8, the fundamental form of a temple or city, denoting the cosmos in all its possibilities together with the forces at work in the universe and in man; it thus implies cosmic perfection. The Indian circular chessboard typifies Infinity and the Round of Birth and Death; each game is an epoch, and putting away the pieces symbolizes a period of non-manifestation. The movement of the pieces is the realization of all possibilities in this world and in individual man in manifestation. The choice of movement is free but is responsible for setting in motion an inescapable series of effects; both free will and destiny are involved; the spirit is Truth and in it man is free; outside it he is the slave of destiny.

The *King* is the sun; the heart; the forces of law and order; his moves are limited by manifestation. The *Queen*, or Vizier, is the spirit, the Mover at Will, the moon. The *Bishop*, or Elephant, represents rulers of the spiritual world and his move is based on the triangle; moving on the white squares denotes the intellectual, positive way, and on the red or black squares the devotional way, the *via negativa*; the diagonal movement signifies the existential and feminine, ruled by Jupiter. The *Rook*, Castle, or Chariot, is the temporal power, the rulers of this world; the move is based on the square, which symbolizes matter and the earth, while the axial movement, cutting across colours, denotes the virile and masculine and is ruled by Saturn. The *Knight*, the initiate, uses both the intellectual and devotional way, but without the power of the spirit; the jump of the Knight's move represents the jump of intuition, also the left-hand path. It is also suggested that it has military and chivalric associations with initiatory orders of the Templars, etc., and is a 'WANDERER' (q.v.) or 'knight errant'; it is ruled by Mars. *Pawns* are ordinary man, attempting to cross the board, through the seven grades of initiation, to reach the eighth square, the goal of the initiate. To attain the eighth state is Paradise Regained, realization, enlightenment, becoming a Mover at Will. Pawns are ruled by Venus and Mercury, the pair of lovers.

In Arabic–Spanish chess the checkmate (*shah mat*) is not necessarily the death of the King, but he is dishonoured or defeated and deposed. The Castle or Rook (Spanish *roque*) is the dreaded Roc, encountered by Sinbad; but it is also the word for a chariot, hence the straight move. The Bishop (Spanish *el alfil*, Arabic *al-fil*, the elephant) appears as the elephant as in Eastern chessmen; there is no Queen, but a Counsellor who could move one square diagonally, though for the first move he could jump to the third square, either diagonally or straight. (The Fers of Chaucer; Arabic *al-firzan*.) The board varied from sixty-four squares to one hundred and there was also a double game played on a 16 × 12 square board. Grand, or Great, Chess had a hundred and forty-four squares and there were twelve pieces and twelve pawns; a Gryphon stood next to the King, then a Cockatrice, Giraffe, Unicorn, Lion, Rook.

Chestnut *Christian*: Virtue, chastity, surrounded by thorns but untouched by them; victory over temptation.

Child/Children The embodiment of potentialities; possibilities of the future; simplicity; innocence. The child, or son, also symbolizes a higher transformation of the individuality, the self transmuted and reborn into perfection. Children, usually little boys, depict the seasons: Winter wrapped in a cloak; Spring with flowers and leaves; Summer with ears of corn; Autumn with fruit. Children are embryonic in the Great Mother, controller of the Great Waters, hence, in legend, children are brought by fishers such as the stork, or water-dwellers as the frog, or are born of Mother Earth, under a bush or in a cave. In Egyptian iconography a child sucking a finger is the infant Horus, a symbol mistaken by the Greeks and adopted by them as representing silence. In Alchemy a crowned child symbolizes the Philosophers' Stone. In Christianity a child on the back or shoulders depicts St Christopher; a child in arms St Vincent de Paul; the Christ Child in arms St Anthony of Padua; a woman suckling a child is a Christian symbol of Charity.

Chimera See FABULOUS BEASTS.

Chimney A chimney or any opening in a roof of a temple, tepee, tent, etc. represents the passage of escape to the heavens; the solar gateway; escape from the temporal to the eternal, from space to the unconfined. Santa Claus coming down the chimney symbolizes gifts brought direct from heaven to earth instead of through the earthly gateway or door.

Chi-Rho See LABARUM.

Chisel In sacred architecture the chisel is the active, masculine principle in relationship with the passive and feminine. With the hammer and mallet it symbolizes will, discrimination, distinction; it is the determining of the form of the feminine *prima materia* by the sharp, male, shaping instrument. It also signifies education; distinctive knowledge in initiation; cutting away errors.

Chörten See STUPA.

Christmas Tree The evergreen tree is the Winter Solstice; the New Year and a fresh beginning. It is the tree of rebirth and immortality, the Tree of Paradise of lights and gifts, shining by night. Each light is a soul and the lights also represent the sun, moon and stars shining in the branches of the Cosmic Tree. The

Andrea del Sarto's **Charity**, with its obvious similarity to a Madonna and Child group, underlines the traditional and universal equation between charity and maternal love, sustenance and care.

In this 13th-century Spanish illustration of 'a Christian and a Muslim playing **chess**', the artist has naïvely but pointedly drawn in the game's symbolic representation of opposing forces meeting and contending within a single and restricted field of action.

pine tree, sacred to Attis, Atargatis, Cybele, was hung with gold and silver ornaments, bells, etc., with the sacred bird in the branches and sacrificial gifts underneath; the tree was afterwards burnt. The Yuletide tree (q.v.) was the fir, sacred to Woden/Odin.

Chrysalis Metamorphosis; change.

Chrysanthemum *Chinese*: Autumn; retirement; ease; cool splendour; scholarship; joviality; harvest; wealth; longevity; that which survives (the cold). *Japanese*: Longevity; happiness; a flower emblem of Japan.

Chrysothamnus *Amerindian*: The masculine, solar, day, life-principle, with the Artemisia as the feminine, lunar and nocturnal.

Churning Creation; in Hinduism, e.g., the churning of the waters with the *axis mundi* produced creation; or the primordial waters can be churned with a phallic symbol, such as the spear.

Cicada The demon of light and darkness; the cyclic periods of light and darkness. *Chinese*: Resurrection; immortality; eternal youth; happiness; restraint of cupidity and vice. Jade cicadas were placed in the mouth of the dead to ensure immortality. *Greek*: Immortality (the cicada was supposed to be bloodless and live on dew); sacred to Apollo and an emblem of Tithonus who obtained immortality but not eternal youth and so grew older and feebler until he turned into a cicada.

Cinnabar *Alchemic*: The 'living gold', product of the generative interaction of Sulphur and Quicksilver, the masculine and feminine principles, the hard and the volatile, hot and cold, upon each other in the Great Work.

Circle A universal symbol. Totality; wholeness; simultaneity; original perfection; roundness is sacred as the most natural shape; the self-contained; the Self; the unmanifest; the infinite; eternity; time enclosing space, but also timelessness as having no beginning or end, and spacelessness as having no above or below; as circular and spherical it is the abolition of time and space, but also signifies recurrence. It is celestial unity; solar cycles; all cyclic movement; dynamism; endless movement; completion; fulfilment; God: 'God is a circle whose centre is everywhere and circumference is nowhere' (Hermes Trismegistus). As the sun it is masculine power, but as the soul or psyche and as the encircling waters it is the feminine maternal principle; also the circular or 'infinite' symbolizes the feminine as opposed to the 'bound', straight, masculine, paternal creative power. The circle also depicts the Precious Pearl, or the Pearl of Great Price (see PEARL). Small circles on sacrificial vessels often represent the sacrificial wafer, cake or bread. The circle is

typified by the number 10 (see NUMBERS) which has one as the centre and nine as the number of the circumference. The circle is the formation of nomadic tents and encampments, symbolizing the dynamic and endlessly moving as opposed to the square of houses, plots and cities of agricultural and sedentary people. Certain flowers, notably the lotus, lily and rose, are associated with the circle and share much of its meaning.

A circle with a dot at its centre depicts a complete cycle and cyclic perfection, the resolution of all possibilities in existence; in Astrology it portrays the sun; in Alchemy it is the sun and gold; it is also a symbol of all sun gods. Concentric circles are both solar and lunar; the sky; the heavens; different states or degrees in manifest existence. Three concentric circles signify past, present and future, the three spheres of earth, air and water, the worlds of heaven, earth and hell, the phases of the moon, the rising, noon and setting sun; also the dynamics of the reconciliation of opposites. The circle with the square is heaven and earth; integration; the *conjunctio*; they presuppose each other as time and space. Squaring the circle is the transformation of the spherical form of the sky and the heavens into the rectangular form of the earth in a sacred building, temple or church, bringing heaven down to earth, uniting the four elements and returning to primordial simplicity in unity; the octagon is the halfway stage in squaring the circle. The lower half of the semi-circle is the Lower Waters and the ark and the upper half is the Upper Waters and the rainbow. Together they are completion; the Cosmic Egg; the completion of a cycle of manifestation.

The winged circle represents the Primordial Cosmic Pair, the creative sky and the fertile earth; power from heaven; the sun god and solar power (see also DISK). Twin circles are the male and female; love and knowledge; the Dioscuri. Triple circles and three interlocking circles depict the Triad; the indissoluble unity of the three persons of a trinity; life, movement, the dynamic in tension. Four circles as a cross, linked by a central circle, are wisdom, fear, knowledge, hope. The sevenfold solar circle symbolizes the All-Knower; perfection; the seven heavens. *Alchemic*: Circle with a dot in the centre is the sun; gold. *Amerindian*: The circle radiating outward and inward, as the FEATHERED SUN (q.v.) is a symbol of the universe. Camp circles and the circular tepees are a pattern of the cosmos with the North side as the heavens and the South side as the earth. *Astrology*: Circle with central point is the sun symbol. *Buddhist*: The circle is the ROUND OF EXISTENCE (q.v.), enclosing all in the phenomenal world. Three circles in triangular form are the Three Jewels. In Zen the empty circle is enlightenment. *Chinese*: The circle is the heavens with the square as the earth, as in the old cash; the circle with the square at the centre depicts the union of heaven and earth, yin and

yang and, by analogy, the perfect man. The
circle is also the moving heavens which revolve
round the unmoving square of the earth.
Christian: The Church Universal. Three
concentric or interlocking circles depict the
Trinity. Two concentric circles signify intellect
and will, according to Dante. Twin circles, as
love and knowledge, represent Christ, also his
dual nature. *Egyptian*: The winged circle is the
rising sun, Ra, and resurrection (see DISK).
Greek: (Orphism) The circle of Ouroboros
round the Cosmic Egg was called Cronos and
was defined by Pythagoras as the psyche of the
universe. Cronos was mated to Necessity, also
circling the universe, hence Time and Fate were
both circles. *Hindu*: The Round of Existence in
the phenomenal world. The flaming circle is a
symbol of Prakriti, 'that which evolves,
produces, brings forth'. *Islamic*: The dome; the
vault of heaven; divine light. *Platonic*: 'The
moving image of an unmoving eternity.' *Sumero-
Semitic*: The winged circle is an aniconic symbol
of solar gods; divinity; solar power. *Taoist*: A
circle with a point at the centre represents the
supreme power, the Tao; the circle is also the
Precious Pearl (see PEARL).

The circle enclosing the cross denoted
Paradise and its four rivers rising from the
centre, the Tree of Life, and flowing in the four
cardinal directions; enclosing the double cross it
is the 'Rose of the Winds', the four cardinal and
four intermediate directions. It is also the
Cosmic Solar Wheel, 'the vivifying principle
that animates the universe' (Proclus); the four
quarters of the earth; the four divisions of the
cosmic cycle; the four seasons of the year and
the ages of man, etc. The solar wheel-cross is
always a symbol of good fortune and of change.
The circle surmounting the cross is the union of
male and female principles of life, both human
and divine; is found in Egypt (as the Ankh),
Syria, Phoenicia, in temples of Serapis, in China
and Tibet, Lapland, Sweden and Denmark; it is
also a symbol of Venus in astrology. The North
American Indian lodge cross inscribed in the
circle symbolizes sacred space and is a Cosmic
Centre. The four directions of space in the
celestial circle are the totality comprising the
Great Spirit. In Mexican symbolism the peyotl,
the cactus which gives the draught of
immortality, grows at the point of intersection of
the cross and the circle. Some Byzantine
churches are based on five circles, or glories,
placed in the form of a cross and surmounted by
the circles of corresponding domes. A Christian
church frequently forms a cross inside the circle
of the churchyard.

Circumambulation Fixes the axis of the
world in a particular sacred place such as a
temple or church; it also represents the relation
and harmony of motion and stillness, the
manifest and the Supreme Reality; it defines a
boundary between the sacred and the profane;
it is also an imitation of the path of the sun.
Making a ritual circuit was also associated with

An engraving after the fresco by Piero di Puccio
(*c.* 1400) in the Campo Santo, Pisa, shows the **circle**
as the basis of the astrological scheme. Nine outer
circles representing the nine orders of angel surround
the planetary circles with the elemental world at the
centre. The whole cosmos is held in the hands of
God.

The great earth **circle** enclosing the medieval
cathedral city of Old Sarum is uterine in form,
reinforcing the symbolism inherent in 'Mother
Church' as creative and regenerative.

the revolving of the Great Bear which indicated and controlled the seasons. The Hindu and Buddhist circumambulation of a sacred object (*Pradakshina*), keeping the object always on the right hand, is symbolic of circling the world, the All, contained in the Self; it is a pilgrimage to find the Self. In Islam the seven circuits of the Ka'aba, made by the pilgrim anticlockwise, represent the seven attributes of God.

Circumcision Initiation; dedication; purity; a rite of religious or tribal membership.

Circumference Limitation; the world in manifestation; enclosure; rotation; movement. It is represented by the number 9 (see NUMBERS).

Citadel Protection; the guarded; the defended; the sheltering and enclosing aspect of the feminine.

Cithern *Greek*: The universe, with its shape as the heavens and earth and its strings as the planes. Attribute of Apollo and Terpsichore.

Citron *Buddhist*: One of the 'Three Blessed Fruits' of China, with the peach and pomegranate; the 'fingered' citron is the shape of the hand of Buddha. *Hebrew and Roman*: Love, the ornament of the bridal chamber.

Climbing See LADDERS.

Cloak Ambivalent as both a symbol of dignity and position but also as a disguise, withdrawal and obscurity; darkness; the secretive; dissimulation. In magic it is invisibility. The cloak, as opposed to the tunic, hides man's true nature, while the tunic reveals the true man. A dark cloak can signify protection. *Christian*: Emblem of SS Alban and Martin, who have the cloak on the ground; of St Hyacinth, floating on the sea; of St Raymond, used as a sail. The Devil often wears a black cloak. *Greek*: The cloak of *epheboi* was of mourning colour, black or dun, at initiation ceremonies, symbolizing the death of the child and the birth of manhood. *Hindu*: Indra wears a blue rain-cloak. See also MANTLE.

Clouds The sky, air, evanescence, rain or a celestial condition, e.g. when an angel or person is depicted standing on a cloud or a divine hand appears from a cloud. A cloud of light denotes a theophany. Living 'under a cloud' is disgrace. *Amerindian*: Fertility. *Chinese*: Fertility; the Dragon of the Clouds; the blessing of rain; good works; visible breath, the life-force. Clouds which release the reviving rain are also compassion since they cover and protect all living things. *Christian*: The unseen God, veiling the sky; clouds also veil God, as with the cloud on Mt Sinai and the pillar of cloud. A hand, or hands, emerging from a cloud is divine omnipotence. *Greek*: Clouds are the flocks of Apollo. *Scandinavian*: The steeds of the Valkyrie are clouds.

Clover Divine Triads; the three-fold aspect of life as body, soul and spirit. *Chinese*: Summer. *Christian*: The Trinity; emblem of St Patrick in Ireland.

Clown See FOOL.

Club Great strength; phallic. *Celtic*: The weapon of Dagda as lord of life and death; great strength and appetite; also an attribute of the Gallic Sucellos, 'the great striker' or 'good striker'. *Christian*: The betrayal of Christ and an emblem of SS James the Less and Jude. *Graeco-Roman*: Attribute of Heracles/Hercules and of Melpomene. *Semitic*: 'The crusher and grinder of the world'; attribute of Baal and Ninurta; corresponds in symbolism to the thunderbolt as used by sky gods.

Cobra See SERPENT.

Cock A solar bird, attribute of sun gods except in Scandinavian and Celtic symbolism. The masculine principle; the Bird of Fame; supremacy; courage; vigilance; the dawn. Two cocks fighting depict the battle of life. The black cock is an agent of the Devil. *Buddhist*: The cock, with the pig and snake, are at the centre of the Round of Existence, with the cock as carnal passion and pride. *Celtic*: Chthonic; an attribute of gods of the underworld. *Chinese*: The yang principle; courage; benevolence; valour; faithfulness. The red cock is the original form of the sun and protects against fire; the white cock protects against ghosts. The cock is the tenth symbolic animal of the Twelve Terrestrial Branches. With a crown on its head it portrays the literary spirit; with spurs it is a warlike character. A cock with a hen in a garden indicates the pleasures of rural life. In some Chinese initiation ceremonies a white cock is killed to signify the death of the old life and the purity of the new. A homophone equates 'cock' and 'fortunate', hence it is used in funerary rites to ward off the powers of evil spirits. The cock represents sunset in China; aggressive, it is a war symbol; astrologically it is October, when preparations for war were undertaken; it is the Pleiades. *Christian*: Greets the dawn of the sun of Christ in the East; Christ putting to flight the powers of evil and darkness; vigilance, hence used as a weathervane turning in all directions to watch for powers of evil; the gilded, solar cock guards the steeple through the hours of darkness when the bells are silent. It also signifies liberality as supposed to share its food with the hens, and represents preachers to the faithful, telling of the coming of the dawn of Christ; it depicts 'the souls of the just awaiting the dawn' (Bede). As connected with Christ's passion it is resurrection; as associated with St Peter it is human weakness and repentance. Cocks fighting are Christians striving for Christ. The cock and the lion are often portrayed in opposition. *Egyptian*: Vigilance; foresight. *Gnostic*: The cock with an ear of corn in its beak depicts vigilance producing plenty. *Graeco-Roman*: Vigilance; pugnacity. Sacred to Apollo, Aesculapius, Ares, Mercury, Priapus, Athene; associated with Persephone in Spring as the renewal of life; also sacred to Attis as Spring fertility. Sacrificed to Lares. *Hebrew*: Fertility; the cock and hen are associated with the bridal couple. *Heraldry*: Both soldierly courage and religious aspiration. *Iranian*: A kingly bird, frequently mounted on sceptres. *Japanese*: A Shinto symbol, standing on the drum which summons people to prayer in the temple. *Mithraic*: Sacred to Mithras as a sun god. *Scandinavian*: The bird of the underworld; its crowing wakes the heroes of Valhalla for the last great battle. *Sumerian*: Nergal is sometimes depicted as a cock-headed god.

Cockatrice In Christianity it is the Devil poisoning mankind. See also FABULOUS BEASTS.

Cocoon The potential power of the wind; magic power. The place of birth of a soul as a butterfly; the soul surrounded and protected.

Coffer/Coffin Takes on the same symbolism as the sepulchre where dying gods and saviours were laid, the *regressus ad uterum*; the mystic womb of the second birth, hence redemption, resurrection, salvation.

Collar With the chain of office and the necklace, the collar signifies office and dignity, but also slavery and servitude. *Celtic*: The collar, or torc, is an attribute of Cernunnos. *Egyptian*: An emblem of Isis; also represents the power of her son Horus.

Colours Colour symbolizes the differentiated, the manifest; diversity; the affirmation of light. Colours which give back light, e.g. orange, yellow, red, are active, warm, advancing; those which absorb light, e.g. blue, violet, are passive, cold, retreating, while green synthesizes the two divisions. Black and white represent negative and positive and all opposites. Light and dark colours used in contrast symbolize the materialization of light. God, as light, is the source of colour.
  BLACK Primordial darkness; the non-manifest; the Void; evil; the darkness of death; shame; despair; destruction; corruption; grief; sadness; humiliation; renunciation; gravity; constancy. Black also signifies Time, hard, pitiless and irrational and is associated with the dark aspect of the Great Mother, especially as Kali who is *Kala*, Time, and with Black Virgins. Black or blue-black is the colour of chaos. In the Occident black is connected with mourning and with the sinister aspect of witchcraft, black magic and black arts. It is the colour of Cronos/Saturn (also as Time) and the number 8. *Alchemic*: The absence of colour; the first stage of the Great Work; dissolution; fermentation; the sinister; descent into hell. *Amerindian*: The North; mourning; night, as opposed to the red

The **clouds** worked into the lacquer of a 13th-century Chinese box represent the care and protection intended for the treasures contained within the box, whose eight sides are an omen and symbol of good luck.

The **cock**, symbol of St Peter's denial of Christ, but also of his vigilance as first Pope, decorates an early Christian sarcophagus.

of day. *Buddhist*: The darkness of bondage. *Chinese*: The North; yin; Winter; water; the Tortoise among the Four Spiritually Endowed Animals. *Christian*: The Prince of Darkness; Hell; death; sorrow; mourning; humiliation; spiritual darkness; despair; corruption; evil arts. It is the colour used for masses for the dead and Good Friday. *Egyptian*: Rebirth and resurrection. *Hebrew (Qabalism)*: Understanding; the Kingdom. *Heraldic*: Prudence; wisdom. *Hindu*: The *tamas*; sensual and downward movement; Time, the dark aspect of Kali and Durga. *Mayan*: Death of an enemy.

BLUE Truth; the Intellect; revelation; wisdom; loyalty; fidelity; constancy; chastity; chaste affections; spotless reputation; magnanimity; prudence; piety; peace; contemplation; coolness. Blue is the colour of the great deep, the feminine principle of the waters; as sky-blue it is the colour of the Great Mother, Queen of Heaven and of all sky gods or sky powers, such as the Azure Dragon. It is also the Void; primordial simplicity and infinite space which, being empty, can contain everything. It is also a lunar colour. *Amerindian*: The sky; peace. *Buddhist*: The coolness of the heavens above and the waters below; the wisdom of the Dharma-Dhatu. *Celtic and Druidic*: A bard or poet. *Chinese*: The heavens; clouds; the Azure Dragon of the East; Spring; wood. *Christian*: Heaven; heavenly truth; eternity; faith; fidelity; the colour of the Virgin Mary as Queen of Heaven. *Gnostic*: Baptism by water. *Graeco-Roman*: Attribute of Zeus/Jupiter and Hera/Juno as sky deities, also the colour of Venus. *Hebrew (Qabalism)*: Mercy. *Hindu*: The blue rain-cloak of Indra. *Mayan*: Defeat of an enemy.

BROWN The earth. *Chinese*: The colour of the Sung dynasty. *Christian*: Spiritual death; death to the world (as worn by religious communities); renunciation; penitence; degradation. *Hindu*: The Northern region.

GOLD The sun; divine power; the splendour of enlightenment; immortality; God as uncreated light; the highest value; the stuff of life; fire; radiance; glory; endurance; the masculine principle. The gold of the sun symbolizes all sun gods, the corn goddesses and gods and the ripeness of the harvest. The golden cord of Zeus draws all things to him; for Homer it is the link between heaven and earth; for Plato, the sun and reason. Gold and silver, sun and moon, are the two aspects of the same cosmic reality. *Alchemic*: The 'essence' of the sun; the earthly sun; congealed light; durability; the equilibrium of all metallic properties. Turning base metal into gold is the transmutation of the soul; regaining the primordial purity of human nature. *Amerindian*: The West. *Celtic*: Fire. *Egyptian*: The sun god Ra; the golden corn. *Hindu*: Life, light; truth; immortality; the seed; the fire of Agni.

GREEN Ambivalent as both life and death in the vernal green of life and the livid green of death; also as youth, hope and gladness but equally change, transitoriness and jealousy. Compounded of blue and yellow, heaven and earth combined, green forms the mystic colour; it also combines the cold blue light of the intellect with the emotional warmth of the yellow sun to produce the wisdom of equality, hope, renewal of life and resurrection. As the colour of Venus and Mercury, the pair of lovers, green is Spring; reproduction; gladness; confidence; Nature; Paradise; abundance; prosperity; peace. As unripeness it is symbolic of inexperience, hence folly, and naïvety. It is associated with the number 5 and is the fairy colour. Green changing to gold is the young corn god, the green lion, or the green man, before turning into the gold of the ripe corn. The Green Knight denotes death as impartiality and represents treason as slaying youth and beauty. A green flag signifies a wreck at sea. *Alchemic*: The Green Lion or Green Dragon is the beginning of the Great Work; the young corn god; growth; hope. *Buddhist*: Vernal green is life; pale green depicts the kingdom of death, a corpse and everything pertaining to the realm of the dead. *Celtic*: Tir-nan-og; the Green Isle; the colour of Bridgit, the earth goddess. *Chinese*: Green takes the same symbolism as blue, with which it is interchangeable in the Blue or Green Dragon, Spring, the East, wood and also water. Green is the colour of the Ming dynasty. *Christian*: Vernal green is immortality; hope; the growth of the Holy Spirit in man; life; triumph over death and Spring over Winter. It is also initiation; good works, and in medieval times it became the colour of the Trinity, Epiphany and St John the Evangelist. Pale green is equated with Satan, evil and death. *Egyptian*: Osiris symbolizes the unripe green corn which turns into the gold of the sun god Ra. *Hebrew (Qabalism)*: Victory. *Hindu*: As Buddhism. *Islamic*: Green is the sacred colour.

GREY The neutral; mourning; depression; ashes; humility; penitence. *Christian*: Death of the body and immortality of the soul; hence the colour worn by religious communities. *Hebrew (Qabalism)*: Wisdom. *Heraldic*: Tribulation.

ORANGE Flame; fire; luxury. *Chinese and Japanese*: Love; happiness; symbolized by the 'fingered citron'. *Hebrew (Qabalism)*: Splendour.

PURPLE Royalty; imperial and sacerdotal power; pomp; pride; truth; justice; temperance; the colour for ritual services of underworld divinities. Tyrian purple, 'the highest glory' (Pliny) was the colour of congealed blood, also the 'blood of purple hue' (Homer) *Aztec and Inca*: Majesty; sovereignty. *Christian*: Royal and sacerdotal power; God the Father; truth; humility; penitence. The colour for Lent and Advent. *Roman*: The colour of Jupiter.

RED The zenith of colour; represents the sun and all war gods. It is the masculine, active principle; fire; the sun; royalty; love; joy; festivity; passion; ardour; energy; ferocity; sexual excitement; the bridal torch or fire; health; strength; also blood; blood-lust; blood-guiltiness; anger; vengeance; martyrdom; fortitude; faith; magnanimity. It can also be the colour of the desert and calamity. Staining or painting red depicts renewal of life. Red with white is death; red with white and black represent the three stages of initiation. Gods are often painted red to denote supernatural power, sacredness, or solar power. *Alchemic*: Man, the masculine principle, the Red Lion or Red Dragon; the sun; sulphur; gold; the zenith point of colour; the third stage of the Great Work, the *servus rubens*. *Amerindian*: Joy; fertility; the red of the day as opposed to the black of night. *Aztec*: Fertility, as blood colour; but also the desert; evil; calamity. *Buddhist*: Activity; creativity; life. *Celtic*: Death, the red horseman; disaster. *Chinese*: The sun; the phoenix; fire; Summer; the South; joy; happiness; the luckiest of all colours. *Christian*: Christ's passion; the blood shed on Calvary; the fire of Pentecost; zeal in faith; love; power; dignity; priestly power; intrepidity; the colour of cardinals' robes as soldiers of the Pope. Red is also the colour of martyrdom and cruelty. Saints' days are written in red, hence 'red letter days'. It is the colour of Whitsuntide and the feasts of martyrs. Red with white denotes the Devil; Purgatory; death. *Greek*: The active masculine principle as opposed to the purple, royal and passive principle. It is the colour of Phoebus as solar and Ares as war, also of Priapus known as the Red God. *Hebrew (Qabalism)*: Severity. *Hindu*: Activity; creativity; energy of life; the *rajas* as expansion in manifestation; the South. *Maya*: Victory; success. *Oceanic*: Divinity and nobility. *Roman*: Divinity. Gods' faces were often painted red. The colour of Apollo as solar and Mars as war. *Semitic*: The sun god Baal/Bel.

SILVER The moon; the feminine principle; virginity. Gold and silver are the two aspects of the same cosmic reality. *Alchemic*: Luna, 'the affections purified'.

VIOLET Intelligence; knowledge; religious devotion; sanctity; sobriety; humility; penitence; sorrow; temperance; nostalgia; grief; mourning; old age. *Christian*: Sacerdotal rule and authority; truth; fasting; sadness; obscurity; penitence. The colour of St Mary Magdalene. *Hebrew (Qabalism)*: Foundation. *Roman*: The colour of Jupiter.

WHITE The undifferentiated; transcendent perfection; simplicity; light; sun; air; illumination; purity; innocence; chastity; holiness; sacredness; redemption; spiritual authority. A white robe indicates purity, chastity or the triumph of the spirit over the flesh; it is worn in mourning in the Orient and was used as such in ancient Greece and Rome. White is associated with both life and love, death and burial. In marriage it symbolizes death to the old life and birth into the new, while in death it represents birth into the new life beyond. A woman robed in white also carries the love-life-death connotations, as with the Delphic Aphrodite of the Tombs, the Scandinavian Freyja or Frigg and the Teutonic Hel/Freya, 'the Beloved', goddess of death. White with black and red

Black is the colour associated with mourning and death in the Christian world. This funeral scene is from the Grimani Breviary, 1480–1520.

In other times and other cultures, **white** symbolizes sorrow. This vase painting by the Kleophrades painter, about 480 BC, shows a dead youth lying in state, attended by white-clad mourners.

depicts the three stages of initiation. White with red is death. The white flag denotes surrender, truce, friendship, goodwill. *Alchemic*: The *femina alba*, the White Lily, is woman, the feminine principle, the moon, silver, quicksilver, the purity of undivided light and the second stage of the Great Work. *Amerindian*: Sacredness; the East. *Aztec*: The dying sun; night. *Buddhist*: Self-mastery; redemption; the White Tara, the highest spiritual transformation through womanhood, 'she who leads out beyond the darkness of bondage', the Mother of all Buddhas. *Celtic*: The terrestrial goddess. *Chinese*: The White Tiger; the West; Autumn; metal; mourning. *Christian*: The purified soul; joy; purity; virginity; innocence; the holy life; light; integrity. White is worn at all sacraments: baptism, confirmation, first communion, marriage, death. It is the colour of saints not suffering martyrdom and of virgin saints and of Easter, Christmas, Epiphany and Ascension. White with red is the Devil, Purgatory, death. *Druidic*: Worn by priests and at baptism. *Egyptian*: White with green depicts joy. *Greek*: Mourning, love, life and death. *Hebrew*: Joy (Eccl. 9, 8); Cleansing (Isa. 1, 18). *Qabalism*: the Crown. *Hindu*: Pure consciousness; self-illumination; light; *sattva* – upward movement; manifestation; the East. *Maori*: Truce; surrender. *Mayan*: Peace; health. *Roman*: Worn on propitious occasions but also for mourning.

YELLOW Ambivalent, light or golden yellow is solar; the light of the sun; intellect; intuition; faith and goodness. Dark yellow denotes treachery; treason; jealousy; ambition; avarice; secrecy; betrayal; faithlessness. A flag of yellow or yellow and black signifies quarantine. A yellow cross denoted the plague. *Amerindian*: The setting sun; the West. *Buddhist*: Saffron, the robe of the monk, symbolizes renunciation, desirelessness; humility. *Chinese*: The Earth; the Centre; metal; the lunar hare; the Ch'ing Dynasty. *Christian*: As golden, sacredness; divinity; revealed truth; 'the Robe of Glory'; used for feasts of Confessors. As dull yellow, treachery; deceit; the Jews; heretics; Judas Iscariot. *Hebrew (Qabalism)*: Beauty. *Hindu*: Golden yellow; light; life; truth; immortality; the West.

Comb Fertility; rain; the rays of the sun; entanglement; music. Attribute of Venus, mermaids and sirens.

Comet The coming of calamity, war, fire or pestilence; or can be a messenger of the sun gods.

Compasses Unerring and impartial justice; the perfect figure of the circle with the central point, the source of life. With the square, the compasses define the limits and the bounds of rectitude. In sacred architecture the compasses represent transcendent knowledge; the archetype controlling all works; the nagivator. *Chinese*: Right conduct. An attribute of Fo-hi,

whose sister, Niu-kua, holds the square; together they are the male and female principles, the yin-yang harmony. *Greek*: With the globe, an attribute of Urania.

Conch Its convolutions are variously suggested as the rising and setting sun, the lunar spiral, or the waters. It also shares the symbolism of the SHELL (q.v.). *Buddhist*: The voice of Buddha preaching the Law; oratory; learning; sound; victory over *samsara*; one of the Eight Symbols of Good Augury. The white conch depicts temporal power. *Chinese*: Royalty; a prosperous voyage. *Graeco-Roman*: The emblem of Poseidon/Neptune and Triton; tritons blow conch shells while drawing the chariot of Poseidon. *Hindu*: Sacred to Vishnu as lord of the waters. From the conch issued the primordial creative word OM, which is the Word made manifest. *Islamic*: The ear which hears the divine Word. *Mayan*: The conch appears frequently in Maya symbolism associated with the waters.

Cone (Pine.) Phallic; fecundity; good fortune. An attribute of Dionysos and called 'the heart of Bacchus'; also an emblem of Sabazios, Serapis, Cybele, Astarte at Byblus and Artemis in Pamphylia. The white cone is an emblem of Aphrodite. The conical head-dress was worn by Sumerian and Egyptian kings and priests. Bastius says that the pine cone and spinning top have the same symbolism of a vortex or spiral whorl, that is to say the great generative and creative force.

Convolvulus Clinging; humility; uncertainty; insinuation. *Chinese*: Love and marriage; dependence; dawn; transitoriness.

Coral The sea-tree of the Mother Goddess; the moon, giver of life; the fertility of the waters. It is apotropaic. *Chinese*: Longevity; promotion. *Greek*: The growth from the blood of Medusa.

Cord The life of the individual, broken at death. The silver cord holds the soul to the body during incarnation. The Golden Cord of Zeus is that on which the universe hangs, it is the 'rope of heaven' on which all things 'depend' or are threaded. Plato speaks of 'the sacred cord of reason'. The cord is ambivalent as being both the agent of binding and limitation and also the possibility of infinite extension and freedom; it can lead man onwards or tie him to his destiny. The Iranian sacred cord is passed three times round the waist, symbolizing good thought, good word, good action. The knotted cord on a Hindu devotee or saint depicts the many acts of devotion performed. The cord round the waist of a Christian monk binds him to his vocation and symbolizes his commitment to celibacy. See also KNOTS.

Corn Ears or sheaves of corn or wheat are attributes of all corn deities, especially in the

Greek Mysteries, and symbolize the fertility of the earth, awakening life, life springing from death; germination and growth through solar power; abundance. The golden ears of corn are the offspring of the marriage of the luminous sun with the virgin earth. The corn goddess is identified with the constellation Virgo. Corn and wine together, like bread and wine, represent the balanced product of man's agricultural labours and provision for life. Corn measures depict fruitfulness, abundance. As funerary, corn signifies abundance in the next world. Forced growths of corn, wheat, or barley were used in many funeral cults and mourning rites, notably Egyptian (see BARLEY), Mediterranean, Persian and Chinese rites and in Eastern Christian Holy Week ceremonies. The growing grain denoted both the revived hero's resurrection and the spring crops. *Amerindian*: the ear of corn (maize) with all its seeds represents the people and all things in the universe. *Christian*: Ears of wheat are the bread of the Eucharist, the body of Christ; bounty; the righteous; the godly. Corn and the vine together also represent the Eucharist. *Egyptian*: The ear of corn is an attribute of Isis and a corn measure is an emblem of Serapis. *Graeco-Roman*: Fertility; abundance; life springing from death; creation; emblem of Demeter/Ceres, Gaia and Virgo. Corn was offered to Artemis. The ear of corn was the central symbol of the Eleusinian Mysteries: 'There was exhibited as the great, the admirable, the most perfect object of mystic contemplation, an ear of corn that had been reaped in silence' (*Philosophoumena*). In the cult of Cybele, Attis is 'the reaped yellow ear of corn'. The Roman planting of corn on graves secured the power of the dead for the living. *Mexican*: The maize plant with a humming-bird indicates the Sun Hero; awakening vegetation. *Sumero-Semitic*: Corn was sacred to Cybele and bread was eaten sacramentally at her feast; it was also an attribute of Tammuz/Dumuzi. Dagon, the pre-eminent deity of Philistia, was a corn and earth god at Ascalon and Gaza.

Cornelian See JEWELS.

Cornucopia The Horn of Plenty. Abundance; endless bounty; fertility; fruitfulness; the gathered fruits of the earth; the Horn of Amaltheia, 'giver of wealth'. As a horn it is phallic; as hollow and receptive it is feminine. The cornucopia is an attribute of deities of vegetation, vintage and fate and of the Mother Goddesses such as Demeter/Ceres, Tyche, Fortuna and Althea; it is also carried by Priapus as fecundity.

Cow The Great Mother; all moon goddesses in their nourishing aspect; the productive power of the earth; plenty; procreation; the maternal instinct. The horns are the crescent moon and, as representing both the moon and earth goddesses, the cow is celestial and chthonic. *Celtic*: The chthonic cow is depicted as red with

Eleusis, the site and sanctuary of the Great Mysteries, abounds in symbols of fertility and generation, like this bas relief of **corn**, the Mysteries' supreme and principal symbol.

This late 26th-dynasty statue of the Pharaoh Psammetichus I depicts him under the protection of Hathor, the Great Mother of the Egyptians, symbolized as a **cow**, with the sun disk of royal divinity between her horns.

white ears. *Chinese*: The yin, earth principle, with the horse as the yang and the heavens. *Egyptian*: Pre-eminently Hathor, the Great Mother of Egypt. The double-headed cow represents Upper and Lower Egypt. The legs of the Celestial Cow, Nut, Lady of Heaven, are the four quarters of the earth and she has the stars of the firmament on her underbody. Hathor, Isis and Nut can all be depicted as cows, or with horns. *Greek*: A form of Hera and Io. *Hindu*: The sacred animal. Fertility; plenty; the earth; Nandini, the wish-fulfilling cow, gives milk and an elixir; Aditi the all-embracing; the cow Prithivi. As the earth the cow appears with the bull of heaven. The four legs of the Sacred Cow are the four castes. A barren black cow is sacred to Nirriti, goddess of ill-luck and disease. *Scandinavian*: The primordial cow, the Nourisher, sprang from the ice; she licked the ice to produce the first man.

Cowrie Fertility; giver of life; the Great Mother and the feminine principle; childbirth; the feminine power of the waters; the vulva. The 'cowrie pattern' in art is a funerary and death pattern, depicting both life and death. The cowrie protects against the evil eye.

Coyote *Amerindian*: A transformer; hero-saviour, a demiurge; leads out of danger; it is also lunar and a flood-bringer; the spirit of night; the TRICKSTER (q.v.) of the Indians of the western mountains. *Aztec*: A form of Quetzalcoatl, the double coyote is his chthonic aspect.

Crab As Cancer it is the oblique, retrograde movement of the sun after the summer solstice. The oblique movement also symbolizes dishonest people; unreliability; crookedness; money-changers. *Buddhist*: The sleep of death; the period between incarnations; regeneration between successive births. *Inca*: The terrible aspect of the Great Mother; the waning moon; the devourer of the temporal world. *Sumerian*: Crabs, lobsters and scorpions are associated with Nina, the Lady of the Waters.

Cradle The cosmic barque; the ship of life rocking on the primordial ocean; new life; a fresh beginning. The cradle is made of WOOD (q.v.) which gives shelter at birth, in life and at death.

Crane A messenger of the gods; communion with the gods; the ability to enter into higher states of consciousness. *Celtic*: A form of Pwyll, king of the underworld; a herald of death or war; parsimony; meanness; evil women. *Chinese*: 'The Patriarch of the Feathered Tribe'; messenger of the gods; an intermediary between heaven and earth; carries souls to the Western Paradise; immortality; longevity; protective motherhood; vigilance; prosperity; high official position; happiness. The crane is usually associated with the sun and the pine tree. Pure

white cranes, sacred birds, inhabit the Isles of the Blest. *Christian*: Vigilance; loyalty; goodness; good order in monastic life. *Graeco-Roman*: Sacred to Apollo as herald of Spring and light. *Japanese*: 'Honourable Lord Crane' has the same significance as in China.

Crescent The crescent moon is, par excellence, the symbol of the Great Mother, the lunar Queen of Heaven, and is the attribute of all moon goddesses; it is the passive, feminine principle and is both the Mother and Celestial Virgin. The changing moon depicts change in the phenomenal world. The crescent is represented by cows' or bulls' horns, but it also takes the form of the lunar barque and the receptive cup; it is the ship navigating the night sky, 'the ship of light on the sea of night'. Crescents backing each other, or placed above and below, are the waxing and waning moon. The solar disk with the lunar crescent, or with the disk placed between cow's horns, together depict unity, the two-in-one, or joint sun and moon deities and the sacred marriage of the divine pairs. A crescent with rays is funerary, an apotheosis of the dead. *Celtic*: The crescent moon and two crescents back to back symbolize immortality. *Christian*: The Virgin Mary, Queen of Heaven. *Egyptian*: Isis, Queen of Heaven, and Hathor as the cow with the solar disk between her horns. *Hindu*: The crescent moon the newborn; quick and eager growth; the cup of the elixir of immortality. In Siva's hair it represents the bull Nandi. *Islamic*: The crescent with the star depicts divinity; sovereignty. *Maori*: Light out of darkness. *Sumerian*: Attribute of the moon god Sin. The emblem of Byzantium, Islam and the Turks.

Cricket In the West a symbol of the domestic hearth. In China it denotes Summer; courage.

Crocodile The devourer; the necessity of passing through death to life. With open mouth it depicts going against the current, hence liberation from the limitations of the world. The crocodile is sometimes a guardian of the door. As living on land and in water it denotes the dual nature of man. Pliny says that the crocodile and lizard typify silence: both were thought to be tongueless. The crocodile is also equated with the fertility of the waters. Being swallowed by a crocodile is the descent into hell. It is an emblem of Set in his typhonic aspect as brutality and evil. Sebek is crocodile-headed and symbolizes vicious passions; deceit; treachery; dissimulation and hypocrisy: having swallowed the moon he weeps, hence 'crocodile tears'. Sacred to Apep, Serapis, Sebek, and portrayed at the feet of Ptah.

Cromlech Sacred to the Great Mother with the menhir as the complementary phallic principle; takes on the circular symbolism of the sacred CENTRE (q.v.); also shares the solar symbolism of the circle and cyclic time.

Crook/Crozier The shepherd's crook denotes
authority; guidance; jurisdiction; mercy; faith
and is an attribute of all Good Shepherds.
Christian: Christ as the Good Shepherd; the staff
of the Apostles; an attribute of a bishop as
shepherd of his flock; emblem of SS Gregory,
Sylvester, Zeno. *Egyptian*: Attribute of Osiris as
judge of the dead and often represented with the
flail as supreme power. Egyptian kings were
shepherds of their people and carried a crook as
sceptre. *Greek*: Attribute of Proteus, shepherd of
the ocean flocks, of Orpheus as Good Shepherd,
also of Apollo, Thalia, Pan, Argus and
Polyphemus. *Sumero-Semitic*: One of the royal
insignia of Assyria and Babylon.

Crooked Line In Chinese symbolism the
crooked line is used to signify the insincere;
artificial standards; showy and flashy elegance
as opposed to the straight line of rectitude of the
perfect man.

Cross A universal symbol from the most remote
times; it is the cosmic symbol par excellence. It
is a world centre and therefore a point of
communication between heaven and earth and
a cosmic axis, thus sharing the symbolism of the
cosmic tree, mountain, pillar, ladder, etc. The
cross represents the Tree of Life and the Tree of
Nourishment; it is also a symbol of universal,
archetypal man, capable of infinite and
harmonious expansion on both the horizontal
and vertical planes; the vertical line is the
celestial, spiritual and intellectual, positive,
active and male, while the horizontal is the
earthly, rational, passive, and negative and
female, the whole cross forming the primordial
androgyne. It is dualism in nature and the
union of opposites and represents spiritual
union and the integration of man's soul in the
horizontal-vertical aspects necessary to full life;
it is the Supreme Identity. The cross is the figure
of man at full stretch; also the descent of spirit
into matter. As capable of infinite expansion in
every direction it denotes eternal life. It is also
formed by the four rivers of Paradise flowing
from the root of the Tree of Life. It comprises
the cardinal axes; the quaternary under its
dynamic aspects; the quincunx, the four
elements of the world united at the fifth point,
the Centre. Cosmologically the upwards and
downwards are the Zenith and Nadir, the
North–South axis is the solstitial axis and the
East–West is the equinoctial axis.
  Crux ansata: the Egyptian 'ankh'; combining
the male and female symbols, is the union of the
sexes; the union of heaven and earth; life;
immortality; eternal life; 'life to come' and
'time that is to come'; hidden wisdom; the key
to the mysteries of life and knowledge. It is
suggested also as a Tree of Life; or the oval may
have been eternity and the cross extension in
length and breadth, that is from infinity to
space. It might also have represented the sun
rising over the horizon. *Cross in circle*: Solar
mobility; the wheel of change; the wheel of

The white **cranes** on this 16th-century Chinese blue
porcelain vase symbolize, like all of their race,
longevity and prosperous happiness; their whiteness
here makes them, besides, sacred birds, dwellers in
the Isles of the Blest.

In this Theban painting from the tomb of
Sennedjem, Osiris as judge of the dead holds the
crook of guidance and control; his flail symbolizes his
supreme power to judge the souls of men, separating
their good deeds from their bad.

fortune. The Christian Church frequently forms a cross inside the circle of the churchyard. See also CIRCLE. *Cross in square*: The Chinese symbol of the earth; stability. *Cross with wheel at centre*: The Hindu *chakra*; power; majesty; solar. *Cross pattée*: The open wings of a bird; emblem of Knights Hospitaller. *Cross saltire*: Perfection; the number 10; St Andrew's cross. *Maltese cross*: The four great gods of Assyria: Ra, Anu, Belus, Hea. Emblem of the Knights of Malta. *Rose cross*: Harmony; the heart; the centre. *Tau cross*: The Tree of Life; regeneration; hidden wisdom; divine power and rule; life to come. It is also the hammer of thunder gods, 'the Avenger', 'the Grinder', the battle axe of Thor. *Double cross*: Solar symbol of Zeus as sky god; also appears on Buddhist stupas and accompanies Chaldean sky gods and Aryan divinities. *Cross with hand*: An ancient talisman against the evil eye. *Cross with crescent*: The crescent is the lunar barque, the feminine receptive element, the cross is the axis of the mast and a phallic symbol, together the two depict the union of male and female, heaven and earth. Sacramental bread is usually marked with a cross.

African: (Bushmen and Hottentot) The divinity; protection in childbirth. *Alchemic*: The natural order of the elements; the central point of the *quinta essentia*. *Amerindian*: The human form; rain; stars; wood-fire; maidenhood; the four cardinal directions and the four winds. The north arm of the cross is the north wind, the most powerful, cold, the all-conquering giant, the head and intelligence; the east is the east wind, the heart, the source of life and love; the west the gentle wind from the spirit land, the last breath and going out into the unknown; the south wind is the seat of fire and passion, melting and burning. The centre of the cross is earth and man, moved by conflicting forces of gods and winds. The lodge cross, inscribed in the circle, is sacred space, a cosmic Centre. The four dimensions of space in the celestial circle symbolize the totality comprising the Great Spirit; the cross also represents the Cosmic Tree, extending horizontally over the earth and touching heaven through the vertical central axis. *Buddhist*: The axis of the Wheel of the Law and of the Round of Existence. *Celtic*: Phallic; life; fecundity. *Chinese*: The cross in the square is the earth symbol with the circle as the heavens. *Christian*: Salvation through Christ's sacrifice; redemption; atonement; suffering; faith. The Y cross on the chasuble depicts Christ's arms extended on the cross and the 'lifting up of hands' (Ps. 141, 2). The cross also signifies acceptance of death or suffering and sacrifice. St Andrew's cross depicts martyrdom, suffering and humiliation. Ecclesiastical crosses with two crossbars denote archbishops and patriarchs and with three crossbars the Pope. The pectoral cross is jurisdiction. In mediaeval symbolism the cross of Christ was said to have been made from the wood of the Tree of Knowledge, the cause of the Fall, which thus became the instrument of redemption. The tree is represented as bearing

good and bad fruit (also symbolized by the good and bad thieves) on opposite sides, with Christ, as the trunk of the unifying Tree of Life, as the central cross of the three on Calvary. The two arms of the cross also represent mercy and judgment and, in Christian art, often have the sun and moon on either side to portray these two qualities as well as the two natures of Christ which are also symbolized by the vertical and heavenly and horizontal and earthly axes of the cross. The floriated cross, or 'cross botoné' has been suggested as both the budding of Aaron's rod and the resurrection of Christ as life resurgent. *Egyptian*: The *crux ansata*, or ANKH (q.v.), is life; union; immortality; health. It is held by Maat, goddess of truth; it also represents the union of Isis and Osiris. The tau cross is the hammer, the Avenger, the Grinder. *Gnostic*: The balance of perfection. *Greek*: Depicted on the brow of the Ephesian Artemis. *Hebrew (Qabalism)*: The six-rayed cross signifies the six days of creation and the six phases of time and world duration. *Hindu*: The *rajas*, the expansion of being, the vertical represents the *sattvas* or higher, celestial states of being, while the horizontal is the *tamas* or lower earthly states. The cross is also associated with the sacred Ganges and with the crossed fire sticks of Agni. *Islamic*: Perfect communion of all states of being, both in 'amplitude' and 'exaltation'; horizontal and vertical expansion; the Supreme Identity. *Manichean*: The Cross of Light symbolizes the Suffering Jesus, the light that penetrates all nature. *Maori*: The moon goddess; the common good. *Maya*: The tau cross is the Tree of Life and Tree of Nourishment. *Mexican*: The Tree of Life. God is sometimes represented on the cross and his sacred victims as crucified. The cross also depicts the four winds, hence fertility. It is a symbol of Tlaloc and Quetzalcoatl. *Platonic*: The Creator, 'splitting the whole world along its entire length into two parts and joining them together across one another'. *Roman*: Doom for the malefactor. *Scandinavian and Teutonic*: The tau cross is Thor's hammer and represents thunder, lightning, storm, rain and fertility; also the power of the storm gods. *Sumero-Semitic*: In Babylon the cross with the crescent appears in connection with moon deities; in Assyria the cross represents the four directions in which the sun shines, and the sun-cross was worn as a pendant by the aristocracy. In Phoenicia the cross denotes life and health. In Chaldea the six-rayed cross depicts the six days of creation and the six phases of time and of world duration.

Crossroads Choice, but also the union of opposites; the meeting place of time and space; a magic but also dangerous place where witches and demons meet. Burials of suicides, vampires and felons at crossroads ensured their confusion of ways and prevented their return to haunt the living. Sacred to Hecate, dogs were sacrificed to her at crossroads. Associated with Ganesha and Janus.

Crow *Alchemic*: The *nigredo*, the first stage of matter in the Great Work. *Amerindian*: In some tribes the crow takes on the functions of a demiurge. *Chinese*: When black it is evil; malice; bad luck and business; if portrayed as red or gold it is the sun, also filial piety. There is, however, some question whether it should not be the cock, rather than the crow, which is connected with the sun since stylized creatures can be confused. The three-legged crow, or cock, lives in the sun. The black crow paired with the white heron symbolizes the yin-yang. *Christian*: Solitude. As plucking out eyes it is the Devil blinding sinners. *Egyptian*: A pair of crows denote conjugal felicity. *Greek*: Sacred to Apollo and Athene. *Hebrew*: Carrion; a corpse. *Hindu*: An attribute of Varuna. *Japanese*: Ill-omen; misfortune, but also, in Shintoism, holy crows, as messengers of deities, are associated with temples. The crow is sometimes depicted in front of the sun.

Crown Sovereignty; victory; honour; dignity; reward; the highest attainment; dedication; completeness; the circle of time, of continuity and endless duration. The radiate crown represents the energy and power contained in the head, which was regarded as the seat of the life-soul; it is variously an attribute of sun gods and depicts their sun disk; of supernatural people; saints, etc.; the points of the crown symbolize the rays of the sun. A crown of evergreen indicates life; immortality; victory. A crown at the feet denotes renunciation of royalty. The turreted crown signifies the turreted walls of the holy place of the deity and is often worn by Great Mothers. *Buddhist*: The crown of Buddha symbolizes his realization of the five *gyanas*. The five-leaved *chodpan* depicts the five celestial Buddhas. *Chinese*: Imperial power; supremacy. If the crown covers the ears it signifies 'hear no slander', or covering the eyes with a short screen of threaded jewels hanging from the crown is 'see nothing unworthy'. *Christian*: The righteous; blessing and favour; victory over death; attainment; the reward of martyrs. The golden crown depicts victory over vice. The crown, often of stars, is worn by the Virgin Mary as Queen of Heaven; the triple crown, representing the Trinity, is worn by the Pope as triple royalty on non-liturgical important functions; it is also an emblem of St Elizabeth of Hungary. The crown of thorns placed on Christ's head, as a parody of the Roman Emperor's crown of roses, portrays the passion and martyrdom and is also an attribute of SS Catherine of Siena, Louis of France, Mary Magdalene, Veronica. The crown of roses is an emblem of SS Casimir, Cecilia, Flavia. Three crowns are an emblem of St Charlemagne and, with the cross, of St Helena. *Egyptian*: The Pharoah was crowned with the double crown of the white crown of the South and the red crown of the North, symbolizing the higher world and the higher mind and the lower world and the lower mind. *Greek*: The laurel crown, sacred to Apollo, was awarded to the victor at the

A 7th-century **cross** from the Rhineland depicts a crucifixion scene above a cross saltire, or St Andrew's cross, representing suffering and martyrdom.

A Tsimshian shaman's **crown**, of mountain goat horns, symbolizes the wearer's power to move surely and safely among the high places of the gods.

Surely the most ornate **crown** in history, the imperial crown of the Holy Roman Empire was probably made for the coronation of Otto I in 961. The CROSS and ARCH, the JEWELS and PEARLS are a unique collection of symbols of sacred and secular power.

Pythian games; the parsley crown, sacred to Zeus, at the Nemean games; the pine crown, sacred to Poseidon, at the Isthmian games; the crown of wild olives, sacred to Zeus, at the Olympian games (see also WREATH). Tyche wears the turreted crown, Flora a crown of flowers and Ceres of ears of corn. *Hindu*: The crown at the top of the central pillar of a temple represents divine glory, also indicates the passage to heaven; it is the architectural symbol of the celestial world and forms the point of exit from this world and entry into the divine. *Roman*: Victory. The radiate crown denotes a sun god or divinity. The Emperor wore a crown of roses. Fortuna has a turreted crown. *Sumero-Semitic*: The crown of feathers depicts authority, power, celestial power; it is an attribute of Marduk and Shamash. The turreted crown is worn by all Mother Goddesses of the Middle East.

Crozier See CROOK.

Crucible *Alchemic*: Woman; the matrix; the feminine receptive principle, used in conjunction with the fire-active-male forge. It is the melting pot, used in the 'dry' method in which the *materia* is exposed to direct fire. It is the womb to which all must return to die before regeneration and rebirth; the place of severe testing, suffering and initiatory trials before rebirth into a higher state. The oven or athanor; in it the *materia* is dissolved, purified and transformed. The vessel contains the primordial forces of sulphur and quicksilver (combined with the salt of new birth), the male and female, volatile and solid, joined in marriage in the *solve et coagula*, the dissolution and final union.

Crutch Support, but also, by implication, lameness, hence moral shortcoming. Old age; a beggar. *Christian*: Emblem of SS Anthony the Hermit and Romauld. *Graeco-Roman*: Attribute of Hephaestos/Vulcan and Saturn as the lame smith. *Islamic*: Forms the letters of the name of Nasiree, the Preserver, the Powerful.

Crystal Purity; spiritual perfection and knowledge; the self-luminous. Crystal or glass boats, towers, slippers, etc. signify a transfer from one plane to another or change of state or to the inner plane. The crystal has magic powers and is an aboriginal symbol of the Great Spirit. It is also the passive aspect of the will, with the sword as the active aspect. *Buddhist*: The state of transparency; the sphere of spiritual knowledge; the pure mind; perfect insight. It reflects the five colours symbolizing the five aggregates of body and mind. *Christian*: A glass or crystal ball denotes the world of the light of God. *Graeco-Roman*: Sacred to Selene as moon goddess. *Shamanism*: Celestial power and light.

Cube With the sphere as the primordial state, a cyclic beginning and movement, the cube represents the final state of a cycle in immobility; symbolically it is squaring the circle. The cube is also Truth as being always the same however viewed; it is perfection; completion; stability; static perfection; immaculate law. It is also the folded cross. In traditional architecture the cube, as stability, is used as the foundation stone, the lower part of the building, with the circle of the dome as the higher. *Alchemic*: The cube represents salt, the product of the crystallization of sulphur and quicksilver. *Chinese*: The earth deity, with the sphere as the heavenly. *Hebrew*: The Holy of Holies. *Islamic*: The Ka'aba is a cube; stability; static perfection. *Maya*: The earth; the Tree of Life grows from the centre of a cube.

Cuckoo Symbolizes Spring in southern Europe and Summer in northern regions. *Greek*: Wedlock; one of the transformations of Zeus to win Hera. *Japanese*: Unrequited love. *Phoenician*: The kingly bird, mounted on royal sceptres.

Cup The open, receptive, passive, feminine form. The draught of life; immortality; plenty. The Sacred Cup symbolism appears in many initiatory traditions. An overturned cup depicts emptiness, hence vanity. See also GRAIL. *Buddhist*: See BOWL. *Celtic*: The heart; life; with the mallet the cup is an attribute of Sucellus. *Christian*: Christ's agony in Gethsemane. A cup with a serpent issuing from it is an emblem of St John; a broken cup is an emblem of SS Benedict and Donato. *Graeco-Roman*: An attribute of Heracles/Hercules. *Hindu*: The four sacrificial cups of the Vedas represent the four rivers of Paradise forming the cross of the terrestrial world; the four elements, phases of cyclic development, ages, seasons, castes, etc. A cup placed on top of a support symbolizes the being who offers himself up to heaven and who receives from heaven its grace and abundance. *Islamic*: The cup of Jamshi, into which the Sufis look, denotes a mirror of the world.

Cupola The dome of the sky; the celestial vault; the celestial world. On the top of a Hindu or Buddhist stupa, chörten or temple it is the 'little place' and takes the place of the CROWN (q.v.) or the umbrella of spiritual protection or of royalty.

Cyclamen *Christian*: An attribute of the Virgin Mary; its red spot is the bleeding of Mary's heart; it is also the 'bleeding nun'.

Cymbals The two hemispheres of the earth; the motion of the elements. Used in orgies with the drum and tambourine in ecstatic dancing, especially in the rites of Dionysos/Bacchus and the cult of Cybele and Attis; in the latter the initiate ate from the tambourine and drank from the cymbal. Attribute of Cybele.

Cypress Phallic; also largely a death and mortuary emblem. It was supposed to have the power of preserving the body from corruption, hence its use in cemeteries. Surmounted by either the sun or the moon it represents the androgyne. *Chinese*: Grace; happiness, but also death. *Christian*: Endurance, hence the Christian; perseverance in virtue; the just man; also mourning and death. *Graeco-Roman*: As an emblem of Zeus, Apollo, Venus and Hermes the cypress denotes life; as an attribute of gods of the underworld and of fate it is funereal and signifies death and is sacred to Hades/Pluto. *Phoenician*: Sacred to Astarte and Melcarth; it is the Tree of Life.

Dagger Masculine, phallic, like the SWORD, SPEAR (qq.v.), etc. Attribute of Mars, Mithra and Melpomene, also of SS Thomas and Lucia.

Daisy In the West it represents innocence and purity; emblem of the nymph Belides. Solar, as the 'day's eye'.

Dalmatic *Christian*: Ministerial office, the deacon's vestment; salvation; justice; worn on festal occasions. Shaped like a cross, it represents Christ's passion and is also an emblem of SS Lawrence, Stephen, Vincent and Leonard. It is the sakkos of the Eastern Church and is also used by the British sovereign at coronation.

Dance/Dancing Cosmic creative energy; the transformation of space into time; the rhythm of the universe; imitation of the divine 'play' of creation; the reinforcement of strength, emotion and activity. Round dances follow the sun's course in the heavens and can also enclose a sacred space. Sword dances and morris dances are sympathetic magic to help the sun on its rounds, specially in Spring. Dancing round an object encloses it in a magic circle, both protecting and strengthening the object. Chain dances symbolize the linking of male and female, heaven and earth. Troy, or labyrinth, dances were probably apotropaic as well as giving strength to the object at the centre, or, when there was a maiden at the centre as was often the case, the attainment of the object and the centre both represented a goal, either of initiation or regaining Paradise. Thread or rope dances depict the thread of Ariadne, or secret knowledge giving the way both in and out of the maze; the rope or thread is also suggested as the umbilical cord. In Hinduism the Dance of Siva is the eternal movement of the universe, the rhythm of the universe, the 'play' of creation with Siva as Creator, Preserver and Destroyer of the world. He dances on the vanquished demon of chaos and matter and on ignorance overcome; the dance symbolizes release following the destruction of illusion; but when dancing on the figure of a reclining child Siva's dance is so light that he does not hurt the child beneath his feet, and when he dances with a woman the dance is gentle, graceful and

A 19th-century American Plains Indian bison hide commemorates the Sun **Dance**, recreating and confirming the course of the sun through the heavens and giving the dancers a participating share in that course.

For the Dervishes, the **dance** is the customary means of achieving union with God, whose presence and grace come down to the dancer through his uplifted arm, pass through his body and spirit, and are united with the Earth after leaving through his downward-held arm.

natural, like the true play of the sexes; but when he dances alone it takes on the symbolism of the solitary, unnatural ascetic and becomes violent and destructive. Although the dance is closely connected with Siva, Lord of the Dance, many other Hindu deities are associated with dance and music. Vishnu dances and Krishna dances on the head of the serpent Kaliya. In post-Vedic texts dancing is associated with ageing and death. Death is a dance in the *Upanishads*, for the dance is destroyed in the moment of its creation, but, like death, it is also liberative. In Dionysian/Bacchic frenzy dancing is symbolic of emotional chaos. In the monotheistic religions the round or ring dance imitates the dance of angels round the throne of God. In Christianity the Apocryphal Acts of St John has a round dance in which the 12 Apostles circle round Jesus as the centre, who 'would have it called a mystery'. In Islam the dervishes portray the whirling of a planet on its own axis and around the sun; also the cycles of existence and their circling by the Spirit.

Darkness Primordial chaos; the powers of chaos; the source of existential dualism; the foetal state of the world. Darkness is not essentially evil since it is the ground of the light which emerges from it, and in this sense it is unmanifest light; the pre-cosmogonic, pre-natal darkness precedes both birth and initiation and darkness is associated with states of transition as in death and initiation; germination and creation take place in darkness and everything returns to darkness in death and dissolution. Darkness and light are the dual aspect of the Great Mother as creator and destroyer; birth, life and love, also death and disintegration. This is also symbolized by the Black Virgins, by the yin and yang, the shakta and shakti. *Chinese*: The yin, feminine, passive principle. *Christian*: The Devil, the Prince of Darkness; spiritual darkness; captivity. *Hindu*: The dark aspect of Kali as Time the destroyer; the malefic character of Durga. *Iranian*: The power of Angra Mainyu, or Ahriman, Lord of Lies and darkness. *Islamic*: Indiscretion.

Date Fertility; fecundity. In Mandaean symbolism the date is masculine fertility with the grape as feminine.

Dawn Illumination; hope. In Buddhism it is also the clear light of the Void; in Christianity it is the resurrection and advent of Christ bringing light to the world.

Days Frequently used in the Orient and with Semitic peoples to symbolize long periods of time, e.g. the days and nights of Brahma and the Sumerian and Hebrew days of the creation. Day and night are also brought about by the opening and closing of the eyes of Siva.

Death The unseen aspect of life; omniscience, since the dead are all-seeing. Death to the earthly life precedes spiritual rebirth; in initiation the darkness of death is experienced before the birth of the new man, resurrection and reintegration. Death is also the change from one mode of being to another, the reunion of the body with the earth and the soul with the spirit. The King of Death is often depicted as a skeleton, with sword, scythe, sickle and hourglass; other death symbols are the veil, serpent, lion, scorpion, ashes, the drummer. Death is symbolized as a dancer, sometimes a beautiful girl, in Hinduism. Siva is a God of Dance and Death.

Deer Frequently depicted with the Tree of Life. *Amerindian*: Swiftness; fleetness of foot. *Buddhist*: Deer on either side of the circle of the Wheel of the Law represent Buddha's preaching in the deer park at Sarnath which set the wheel in motion; the deer depicts meditation, meekness and gentleness, but it is also one of the 'three senseless creatures' of Chinese Buddhism as signifying love-sickness, with the tiger as anger and the monkey as greed. *Celtic*: Deer are the supernatural animals of the fairy world and are fairy cattle and divine messengers. Deer skin and antlers are ritual vestments. Flidass, Goddess of Venery, has a chariot drawn by deer. *Chinese*: Longevity; high rank; official success; wealth (deer being a homophone of *lu*, emolument). *Egyptian*: Sacred to Isis at Phocis. *Greek*: Sacred to Artemis, Athene, Aphrodite and Diana as moon goddesses, and to Apollo at Delphi. *Japanese*: An attribute of gods of longevity, but it is also solitariness and melancholy when associated with the maple. See also STAG.

Delta The feminine generative power; the door of life.

Deluge See FLOOD.

Descent Going down into the underworld, or searching for underground treasure, is equated with the quest for mystic wisdom, rebirth and immortality. It is also the understanding of, and redeeming of, the dark side of man's own nature and overcoming death; the *regressus ad uterum*; descent into the primordial darkness before rebirth and regeneration; descent into Hell before resurrection and ascent into Heaven; it is the journey taken in all initiatory rites and by all dying gods.

Desert Desolation; abandonment; but also a place of contemplation, quiet and divine revelation.

Dew The light of dawn; spiritual refreshment; benediction; blessing. Sweet dew is peace and prosperity. Dew can also represent change, illusion and evanescence. Related also to the moon, nightfall and sleep. *Celtic*: The most sacred form of water among the Druids. *Chinese*: Immortality. The Tree of Sweet Dew grows on the sacred mountain Kwan-lung, the *axis mundi*, and takes on the symbolism of the Tree of Life. *Hebrew*: In Qabalism it is resurrection. The Dew of Light emanates from the Tree of Life by which the dead are revived. *Mexican*: The dew of the peyotl, the sacred cactus, found at the intersection of the two perpendicular diameters traced in a circle, is the dew of immortality. *Neo-Platonic*: Dew is the natural envelope of souls; generation. *Roman*: The seminal fluid of Jupiter.

Diadem Royal power; sovereignty; the circle of continuity; endless duration.

Diamond See JEWELS.

Diamond Mace, Throne, Seat On the Footprint of Buddha the diamond mace is thunder striking at the passions of mankind in the world; it is also resolution. See VAJRA. The Diamond Throne or Seat is the place of enlightenment.

Dice/Die Throwing dice is Fate, the irrevocable, fickleness. Breaking dice in two is a contract or renewal of friendship. In Hinduism the die takes on the symbolism of the CUBE (q.v.) and is the four-square of the sacred four, the cycles of the yugas, etc. In Christianity it is a symbol of Christ's passion.

Directions of Space See NORTH, SOUTH, EAST and WEST. Chinese and Toltec astronomy both divide the world into five directions, with the Centre as the fifth. The cardinal points play an important part in burial ceremonies and customs. There are four Sumero-Semitic gods identified with the four cardinal points.

Disk The sun; renewal of life; perfection; divinity; power. The winged disk is variously suggested as power from heaven; the solar god; fire from heaven; a combination of the solar disk and the wings of the solar hawk or eagle; the movement of the heavenly sphere round the pole; divinity; transfiguration; immortality; the brooding and generative power of nature; the dual powers of the life-giving and protective and death-dealing aspects of nature; or that it is apotropaic. The disk with a hole in the centre denotes the circle of the cosmos with the centre as the Void, the transcendent and unique Essence. Twirling the disk is the revolution of the universe on its axis. The sun disk with the crescent moon, or with horns, symbolizes unity; the two-in-one; the sacred marriage of the divine pair; joint solar and lunar deities. *Buddhist*: The circle is the round of creation, the centre the Void; it is an attribute of Vairocana. *Chinese*: The sun is the 'sacred disk'; heaven; divinity; spiritual and celestial perfection. Disks with the encircling, contending dragons depict the Void. *Egyptian*: The sun god Ra; power; renown. The disk of the rising sun is renewal of life; life after death; resurrection. The winged

This **deer** mask, 29 cm high, carved from a single block of cedar and inlaid with shell, was probably worn by a shaman in a ritual dance to promote good hunting.

This page of a 16th-century fortune-telling book indicates how, with three **dice**, an individual's fate and future can be discovered; the configurations of the spots are interpreted with reference to numerology, astrology and alchemy.

disk is the 'Great God, Lord of the Upper Regions'. *Hebrew*: 'The Sun of Righteousness with healing on its wings' (Mal. 4, 2). *Hindu*: The flaming disk is an attribute of Krishna; the disk of Brahma. The twirling, rayed disk is the weapon of Vishnu and the revolving of the universe on its axis, also the revolution of the chakras. *Iranian*: The winged disk as light and the power of light is a symbol of Ahura Mazda or Ormuzd. *Sumero-Semitic*: The winged disk is the empyrean, symbol, or direct representation, of the sun gods, the Assyrian Asshur and the Babylonian Shamash. *Zodiacal*: The disk on the horns of the ram is Aries.

Dismemberment The death and rebirth symbolism of initiation; the necessity of the death of the self before reintegration and rebirth; the two complementary phases of disintegration and reintegration. It also represents unity giving way to fragmentation, multiplicity and disintegration in creation, the many arising out of the One. Dismemberment is closely connected with sacrifice. Gods, such as Osiris, Zagreus, Dionysos, dismembered and scattered and reintegrated, represent the multiplicity of the manifest world in creation and the final restoration of primordial unity. Mystic dismemberment can be a feature of the initiation of a Shaman. Dismemberment also occurs in the Yoruba breaking in pieces and reintegration of Orisha.

Distaff Time; creation; the attribute of all goddesses of spinning, weaving and fate. Athene is patroness of spinning and weaving; Clotho is the Spinner. A symbol of the work of women. See also SPIDER and WEAVING.

Dog Fidelity; watchfulness; nobility (dogs and falcons being emblems of the nobility); Plutarch says that dogs symbolize 'the conservative, watchful, philosophical principle of life'. 'The dog, raising his rough neck, his face alternately black and golden, denoted the messenger going hence and thence between the Higher and Infernal powers' (Apuleius). A keeper of boundaries between this world and the next; guardian of the passage; guardian of the underworld; attendants on the dead; a psychopomp. When a lunar animal, with the hare and lizard, the dog is an intermediary between moon deities; also solar in the Far East as a yang animal in the daytime, but yin at night. In Egypt and Sumeria it is solar. It is associated with all messenger gods and gods of destruction and is an attribute of Anubis and Hermes/Mercury. The dog and otter are special among the 'clean' animals of Zoroastrianism; to kill them is a sin. Hecate has her dogs of war; the northern Garmr, 'the devourer', is often depicted as a dog and Brimo, as destroyer, is accompanied by a dog. The dog sometimes accompanies the Good Shepherd and usually is the companion of healers, such as Aesculapius,

and of all huntresses and Mother Goddesses, the Mother Goddess often being called 'the Bitch' and portrayed as a whelping bitch. A black dog is sorcery, diabolical powers, the damned, death. Cats and dogs, as witches' familiars, can represent witches as rain-makers, hence 'raining cats and dogs'.

Dogs as winds can chase away the boar of Winter or drought. The cynocephalus destroys or imprisons the enemies of light. The dog is often a culture hero or mythical ancestor. Also, having been a companion in life it continues as such after death and intercedes and interprets between the dead and the gods of the underworld. It has also the qualities of a fire-bringer and master of fire, having either invented fire by friction or, in some cultures, watched the masculine secret of fire-making and then reported it to the women. When associated with fire it takes on a sexual symbolism, fire and sexual power being related. *African*: It is often a culture hero and inventor and bringer of fire. *Alchemic*: The dog, with the wolf, is the dual nature of Mercurius, the philosophical mercury, the *nous*. *Amerindian*: Interchangeable with the coyote; a thunder animal, a rain-bringer, also a fire-inventor and, as the coyote, a culture hero and mythical ancestor; an intercessor and messenger. A white dog was sacrificed at the New Year, by the Iroquois, to take prayers to the next world. *Aztec*: Xoltl, God of Death and the Setting Sun, has a dog's head and was patron of dogs. The dog was a psychopomp and was often sacrificed at the tomb to accompany the dead on the journey to the next world. The last sign of the Mexican Zodiac, representing the period of no-time or chaos, was the dog as the end of the year and death, but also resurrection and rebirth. *Buddhist*: The Lion Dog, a guardian, is a defender of the Law; motionless obedience and the subjection of the passions through the Law. It is also an attribute of Yama, God of the Dead. *Celtic*: Associated with the healing waters and accompanies hunter gods, war gods and heroes, and the god of healing, Nodens. Sucellos is also accompanied by a dog. *Chinese*: Fidelity; unswerving devotion. The coming of a dog signifies future prosperity. The red Celestial Dog, T'ien Kou, is yang and helps Erh-lang drive off evil spirits; but as a guardian of the night hours the dog becomes yin and symbolizes destruction, catastrophe, and is connected with meteors and eclipses when the dog goes mad and bites the sun or moon. The Lion Dog of Buddha is frequently depicted in Chinese art. *Christian*: Fidelity; watchfulness; conjugal fidelity. As a guardian of the flock the dog represents the Good Shepherd, a bishop or a priest. Black and white dogs denote the order of the Dominicans. The dog is an emblem of SS Bernard, Roch (who was fed by his dog), Sira, Tobias, Wendelin. *Egyptian*: A guide to the hawk-headed solar god to keep the sun on its right path. Sacred to Anubis, the dog or jackal-headed god, and to Hermes as messenger god;

attribute of the Great Mother, Amenti. *Graeco-Roman*: In Greek, the pejorative term 'cynic', 'dog-like', implies impudence, flattery. According to Homer the dog is shameless, but it is also a psychopomp and an attribute of Hermes/Mercury as both a messenger and presiding mind and who, as a good shepherd, is accompanied by his dog Sirius, the 'all-seeing vigilance', who also accompanies the hunter Orion. Associated with Aesculapius, the dog heals by rebirth into a new life; its fidelity survives death. The dogs of Hades represent the gloom of dawn and dusk which contain hostile powers and are dangerous and demonic times. The monster dog Cerberus guards the entrance to the underworld. Hecate has the dogs of war and dogs were sacrificed to her at crossroads; they were also sacrificed to Eileithyia. Sacred to Heracles/Hercules and Diana/Artemis. *Hebrew*: Impurity. See also *Semitic* below. *Hindu*: The hunting dog is an attribute or companion of Indra; a dog with four eyes depicts Yama, God of the Dead, and has the same symbolism as Hades, see *Greek* above. *Islamic*: Impurity; permissible only as a guard-dog. *Japanese*: Protection; a guardian. *Mayan*: A dog carrying a torch represents lightning. *Mithraic*: As a psychopomp the dog is associated with the bull sacrifice and is then depicted with the snake and scorpion. *Oceanic*: An inventor and bringer of fire. *Parsee*: The sag-dig, a white dog with yellow eyes, or white with four eyes, is unexplained; it is possibly a psychopomp since a dog is introduced to a death-bed and accompanies a funeral procession. The death of a woman in childbirth requires two dogs for the two souls. *Scandinavian*: Odin/Woden has two dogs as well as two ravens as counsellors. The monster dog Garmr guards the underworld. *Shamanistic*: The messenger of the forest spirits. *Sumero-Semitic*: In Semitic symbolism the dog is associated with the scorpion and serpent and all reptiles as baleful, evil and demonic, but in Phoenician iconography the dog accompanies the sun and is an emblem of Gala, the Great Physician, as an aspect of the Mother Goddess and the Accadian Belit-ili whose throne is supported by dogs, or a dog sits by it. An attribute of Astarte.

Doll/Dolly The doll is often an image of the soul of some particular person who can, through the doll, be harmed by sympathetic magic or witchcraft. The Corn Dolly or Maiden represents the seed, the child of the future growth and harvests and is also an image of the Corn Goddess, Mother or Maiden. See CORN. It is made from the last sheaf at harvest-time and is carried ceremoniously back to the farm. The dolly was often lowered to the ground with wailing, then raised high with shouts of joy, to signify the death and rebirth of the corn deity. Rice dollies are made in the Far East and decorate wayside shrines. A dolly hung up in the farm keeps away witches, fairies and evil influences until the next harvest.

On this basalt bas-relief from 9th-century BC Nimrud, a scene of homage and reverence takes place under the protection of the sun-**disk**, here winged, and its consort the moon, a conjunction of pure light and its dark reflection.

The corn **dolly**, made from the last blades of the harvest and dressed as an image of the Great Mother, was kept until the next harvest and then destroyed, a symbol of the birth, growth, death and rebirth of the corn deity.

Dolmen The feminine gate-womb entrance to the underworld, associated with the MENHIR as the phallic pillar, symbolizing the beyond and rebirth.

Dolphin A saviour and psychopomp; a guide to souls in the underworld; saver of the shipwrecked; the King of Fishes; sea-power; safety; swiftness. Two dolphins facing in opposite directions are the duality of nature. The dolphin with an anchor signifies speed and slowness, the two together representing the medium between extremes and 'hasten slowly'. *Celtic*: Associated with well-worship and the power of the waters. *Christian*: Christ as saviour of souls and as bearer of souls over the waters of death. A dolphin with a ship or anchor depicts the Church guided by Christ; in Christian art this sometimes replaces the ship or ark of salvation and rebirth. A dolphin pierced by a trident, or on an anchor, is Christ on the cross. As taking the place of the whale, the dolphin denotes resurrection. See also FISH. *Egyptian*: An attribute of Isis. *Greek*: A psychopomp guiding souls to the Isles of the Blessed; it has both solar and lunar associations: as connected with Apollo Delphinos it is light and the sun, but it is also the feminine principle and the womb on account of the assonance between *delphis* (dolphin) and *delphys* (womb). It has an amatory symbolism when associated with Aphrodite, 'the woman of the sea', and with Eros; it is also an attribute of Poseidon as sea power, and of Dionysos. Thetis rides naked on a dolphin. *Minoan*: Sea power. Also associated with Apollo Delphinos. *Mithraic*: Associated with Mithras as light. *Roman*: The soul's journey across the sea of death to the Blessed Isles. *Sumero-Semitic*: Used as an alternative to the fish in representations of Ea-Oannes; an attribute of Ishtar and sacred to Atargatis as connected with water.

Donkey Patience; stupidity; obstinacy. *Chinese*: Stupidity. 'The year of the donkey and the month of the horse' is Never. See also ASS.

Door Hope; opportunity; opening; passage from one state or world to another; entrance to new life: initiation; the sheltering aspect of the Great Mother. The open door is both opportunity and liberation. *Christian*: Christ – 'I am the door.' The three doors of a cathedral or church signify faith, hope and charity. *Hindu*: Divinities are carved on door jambs, indicating the deity through which man enters the Supreme Presence. *Mithraic*: The entrance to the seven zones of Paradise or the cave of initiation. *Roman*: Janus is the god of the doorway and holds the keys of the power of opening and closing. *Zodiacal*: The summer solstice, in Cancer, is the 'door of men' and symbolizes the dying power and descent of the sun, the *Janua inferni*. The winter solstice, in Capricorn, the 'door of the gods', is the ascent and rising power of the sun, the *Janua coeli*. These doors are also associated with the entrances and exits of initiation caves and with souls entering and leaving the world. In Hinduism they are the *deva-yana* (*Janua coeli*) and the *pitri-yana* (*Janua inferni*).

Dorje The Tibetan Buddhist rod or sceptre, the 'noble stone', of the highest power, justice and authority; the active, masculine, virile power associated with the bell as the feminine, passive power; together they are Method and Wisdom; compassionate action; supreme bliss, also the seven positive and permanent virtues. The diamond sceptre, the 'adamantine', the thunderbolt, is the divine force of the doctrine, transcendental truth and enlightenment; it is the subduer of evil passions and desires. It is the indestructible, but can also destroy the seemingly indestructible. Of the Dhyani Buddhas, Amoghasiddhi carries the double thunderbolt and Akshobhya a single thunderbolt, symbolizing mastery over life and dominion over phenomenal existence. The crossed dorjes signify equilibrium, harmony and power. See also VAJRA.

Dove The life spirit; the soul; the passing from one state or world to another; the spirit of light; chastity (but in some traditions lasciviousness); innocence; gentleness; peace. Doves are sacred to all Great Mothers and Queens of Heaven and depict femininity and maternity; often two doves accompany the Mother Goddess. The dove with an olive branch is a symbol of peace, also of renewal of life; it is an emblem of Athene. Doves drinking from a bowl depict the Spirit drinking the waters of life. Sacred doves are associated with funerary cults. *Chinese*: Longevity; faithfulness; orderliness; filial piety; Spring; lasciviousness; also associated with the Earth Mother. *Christian*: The Holy Spirit; purity; inspired thought; peace; baptism; the Annunciation; the waters of creation. Seven doves denote the seven gifts of the spirit; a flock of doves is the faithful; a dove with an olive branch is peace, forgiveness and deliverance; as the dove of Noah's Ark brought back the olive branch of peace between God and man, and as it found no resting place outside the Ark, so the Christian finds no safety outside the Church. The dove with the palm branch is victory over death. A white dove is the saved soul, the purified soul as opposed to the black raven of sin. Doves in a vine are the faithful seeking refuge in Christ. Two doves together are conjugal affection and love. A dove on Joseph's staff depicts the husband of a pure virgin. The dove is the emblem of the Knights of the Grail and of SS Benedict, Gregory, Scolastica. *Egyptian*: Innocence. The dove sits in the branches of the Tree of Life and appears with the fruit of the tree and vases of the waters of life. *Graeco-Roman*: Love; renewal of life; an attribute of Zeus who was fed by doves. The dove with an olive branch is an emblem of Athene as renewal of life. The dove is sacred to Adonis and to Bacchus as the First Begotten of Love also to Venus as voluptuousness. A dove with a star is an emblem of Venus Mylitta. *Hebrew*: White doves, as purity, were offerings at the Temple for purification. A symbol of Israel. In the Old Testament the dove represents simplicity; harmlessness; innocence; meekness; guilelessness; incubation. Embodies the soul of the dead. *Hindu*: Yama, god of the dead, has owls and doves or pigeons as messengers. *Islamic*: The three Holy Virgins are represented by stones, or pillars, surmounted by doves. *Japanese*: Longevity; deference; sacred to Hachiman, god of war, but a dove, bearing a sword, announces the end of a war. *Manichean*: In Christian Manichean iconography the third person of the Trinity is sometimes depicted as a white dove. *Minoan*: Associated in Minoan art with the Great Mother; doves and snakes, symbolizing the air and earth, were her attributes. *Parsee*: The Supreme Being. *Sumero-Semitic*: Divine power; sacred to Astarte and an attribute of Ishtar as the Great Mother. A dove was sent forth from the Babylonian Ark on the seventh day of the deluge.

Dragon A complex and universal symbol. The dragon, the 'winged serpent', combines the serpent and bird as matter and spirit. Originally it was wholly beneficent as the manifestation of the life-giving waters (the serpent) and the breath of life (the bird), and was identified with sky gods and their earthly delegates: emperors and kings. Later it became ambivalent as both the fertilizing rains, following thunder, and the destructive forces of lightning and flood. Generally the dragon, in the Orient, is a beneficent, celestial power while, in the Occident, it becomes chthonic, destructive and evil. It can be solar or lunar, male or female, good or evil. In the Far East it symbolizes supernatural power; wisdom; strength; hidden knowledge; the power of the life-giving waters; it is the emblem of the Emperor as Son of Heaven and, following him, the wise and noble man. The monotheistic religions depict the dragon as evil, except in isolated instances, when it can be the Logos, the vivifying spirit, or omnipotent divinity, the Pleroma. The DRAGON and SERPENT (q.v.) are usually interchangeable in symbolism as representing the unmanifest; the undifferentiated; chaos; the latent; untamed nature; also the life-giving element of water. Its hurling of the thunderbolt or striking by lightning, is the change from the unmanifest to the manifest – creation, form, matter. Here also the dragon can be two-sided, either as a rain god or an enemy of the rain god, preventing rain from falling. It is associated with the sea, the great deeps, also with mountain tops and clouds and with the solar eastern regions.

Dragons, as monsters, are autochthonous 'masters of the ground', against which heroes, conquerors and creators must fight for mastery or occupation of the land; they are also guardians of treasures and of the portals of esoteric knowledge. The struggle with the

To the Greeks, the **dolphin** was a psychopomp, guiding souls to the Islands of the Blest.

In Poussin's *Annunciation*, the **dove** hovering over the Virgin's head simultaneously symbolizes the fecundating Spirit, the bird sacred to the Great Mother and Queen of Heaven, and Mary's submissive innocence.

The **dragon** casting up Jason at the feet of Athena. Here, as so often, the dragon is the guardian of treasure, and against it the hero must contend.

dragon symbolizes the difficulties to be overcome in gaining the treasures of inner knowledge. Killing the dragon is the conflict between light and darkness, the slaying of the destructive forces of evil, or man overcoming his own dark nature and attaining self-mastery. Rescuing the maiden from the dragon is the releasing of pure forces after killing evil powers. The dragon is often the opponent of the dying god. *Alchemic*: The winged dragon depicts the 'volatile'; without wings it is the 'fixed'. In Chinese alchemy the dragon is mercury, the blood and the semen. *Celtic*: Sovereignty; a chief. The Red Dragon is the emblem of Wales. *Chinese (Taoist, Buddhist)*: The dragon and serpent are not separated in Chinese symbolism. The dragon represents the highest spiritual power; the supernatural; infinity; the spirit of change; the divine power of change and transformation; the rhythms of Nature; the law of becoming; supernatural wisdom; strength. It is 'the Celestial Stag'; the sun; light and life; the Heavens; sovereignty; the masculine yang power. The dragon of the clouds is also thunder and the fertilizing rain, the waters of the deep and Spring. The Azure Dragon, *lung*, the highest, lives in the sky and is the vital spirit; celestial power; infinite supernatural power and, on earth, the delegated imperial power, the Emperor. The *lung*, or Imperial Dragon, has five claws and its head is to the South and its tail to the North. It also represents the East and fertilizing rain. The common dragon, *mang*, has four claws and is temporal power. The three-clawed dragon was an early Chinese form, later to become the Japanese dragon. *Li*, the hornless dragon, lives in the sea and controls the deeps; he also symbolizes the scholar. *Chiao* lives in the mountains or on land and represents the statesman. The 'nine resemblances' of the dragon are, according to Wang Fu: 'His horns resemble those of a stag, his head that of a camel, his eyes those of a demon, his neck that of a snake, his belly that of a clam, his scales those of a carp, his claws those of an eagle, his soles those of a tiger, his ears those of a cow.' The two 'contending dragons', facing each other, are the yin-yang forces of dualism, all opposites and complements, celestial and terrestrial powers; they usually have either the sun or the 'night-shining pearl', the moon, between them; backing each other they symbolize the yin-yang and eternity; chasing each other's tails they depict the two-way creative action of the yin-yang powers. The dragon is often portrayed with the 'dragon ball' or 'flaming pearl' and this has been variously suggested as rolling thunder or the moon as rain-bringer with the dragon swallowing the pearl as the wane of the moon and belching it forth as the waxing moon, but in Taoism and Buddhism it is the 'pearl which grants all desires', the pearl of perfection, that is to say, wisdom, enlightenment and the spiritual essence of the universe. It can also represent the Bodhisattva of instantaneous enlightenment. The dragon with the phoenix is the union of

Heaven and Earth, Emperor and Empress, the divine potentiality containing all opposites, also the interaction of the macrocosm and microcosm, the two aspects of the androgyne, the rhythms of involution and evolution, birth and death. These are also symbolized by the double spiral. The dragon can depict lustfulness if portrayed with the tiger as anger and hostility. *Christian*: The dragon is equated with the serpent, 'that old serpent', the power of evil, the Devil, the Tempter, the enemy of God; it also represents death and darkness, paganism and heresy. In the Old Testament the 'place of dragons' was associated with the 'shadow of death' (Ps. 44, 19) and the waters of the deep, a 'habitation of dragons', was a place of desolation and destruction. Subduers of dragons represent victory over the powers of evil and heresy. A dragon with a knotted tail depicts evil defeated since it was thought that, like the scorpion, its power was in the tail. The Archangel Michael defeating the dragon is the victory of the sun god over darkness, adapted to Christianity as the defeat of Satan. Dragons are attributes of SS Cado, Clement of Metz, George, Keyne, Margaret, Martha, Samson, Sylvester and the Apostle Philip. *Egyptian*: An emblem of Osiris as god of the dead. Apophis, dragon of darkness and chaos, is overcome each morning by the Sun-god Ra. *Graeco-Roman*: An attribute of Heracles/Hercules as a slayer of monsters. Dragons sometimes draw the chariot of Ceres. *Hebrew*: Desolation; a dweller in the wilderness. *Hindu*: Manifest power; the uttered word. Attribute of Soma and Varuna. Indra was a slayer of the dragon. *Iranian*: An attribute of Haoma. *Japanese*: The three-clawed dragon represents the Mikado, Imperial and spiritual power. *Sumero-Semitic*: 'The Adversary', the power of evil.

Dragonfly Can share BUTTERFLY symbolism as immortality and regeneration. *Amerindian*: The whirlwind; swiftness; activity. *Chinese*: Summer; instability; weakness. *Japanese*: A national emblem of 'The Dragonfly Island', but also irresponsibility; unreliability.

Drinking Drinking a divine fluid such as wine, soma, nectar, water, milk, etc. is symbolic of absorbing divine life and power. Drinking from the same cup is, ritually, union, marriage and the end of single life.

Drowning Can symbolize the loss of the self or ego in the ocean of non-differentiated unity.

Drum Sound; the primordial sound; speech; divine truth; revelation; tradition; the rhythm of the universe. Attribute of all thunder gods. The drum, cymbals and tambourine are all used in ecstatic dancing. *African*: The heart; magic power. *Buddhist*: The voice of the Law; joyous tidings; 'the drum of the immortal in the darkness of the world'. The beating of the drum of the Dharma wakens the ignorant and slothful. *Chinese*: The voice of heaven. An emblem of the Taoist genii, or immortal, Chang Kuo-lao. *Greek*: Sexual orgy; used in ecstatic dancing. *Hindu*: Attribute of Siva and Kali as destroyers; also of Durga. Sarasvati, goddess of music and arts, has the drum as an emblem. Siva's drum gives the primordial sound of creation. *Japanese*: The drum calls to prayer; it is associated with the cock. *Phrygian*: An attribute of the Magna Mater indistinguishable from Cybele and her counterparts. Drum, cymbals and tambourine were used in ecstatic dances in her rites. *Shamanistic*: Magic power summoning spirits; the drum is symbolically made from the Cosmic Tree.

Dryness The solar, fire, positive, masculine principle.

Duck As floating on the surface it is superficiality; it is also chatter and deceit. *Amerindian*: The mediator between sky and water. *Chinese* and *Japanese*: Conjugal happiness and fidelity; felicity; beauty. The duck and drake together depict the union of lovers; mutual consideration; fidelity. The duck is yin to the cock's yang. *Egyptian*: Associated with Isis. *Hebrew*: Immortality.

Dwarf The unconscious and amoral forces of nature, such as gnomes, elves, etc. *Egyptian*: Bes is depicted as a dwarf. *Graeco-Roman*: Hephaestos/Vulcan is sometimes portrayed as a dwarf. *Hindu*: The dwarf under the foot of Siva is human ignorance. Vishnu sometimes assumes the form of a dwarf. *Japanese*: The river god is a malignant dwarf. *Scandinavian*: Four dwarfs stand at the corners of the earth and support the sky.

Dying Gods In fertility religions dying gods symbolize cyclic death and rebirth, vegetative death and renewal, life eternally dying and eternally reborn. Dying gods combine both the masculine and feminine principles of the vegetation gods and the Great Mother, whose symbol is the Tree. They are often dismembered and scattered as symbolic of the end of primordial unity and the beginning of fragmentation in manifestation and time and also represent the conferring of life on the multiplicity of creation.

Characteristics of dying-god symbolism are: announced by a star at birth, or connected with a light; born of a virgin in a cave; sometimes visited by wise men; as a child the god teaches his instructors; predicts his own death and second coming; dies on a tree; descends into the earth for three days (the dark of the moon) and is resurrected. He is usually depicted as a beautiful young man or as androgynous; he never attains maturity; is always identified with the Father. The shrines of dying gods are places of ritual re-enactment of the passion and sacrifice and of lamentation for the God, King and Sacrifice. Proclus says that in Orphic

To this Siberian shaman, his **drum**, made from a sacred tree and the skin of a consecrated animal, is his means of translating his sacred power into rhythm and sound which will summon his supporting spirits.

The Egyptian **dwarf** god Bes, here depicted in reinforcing duplication, is the apotropaic guardian of roads and highways: his own ultimate unknowability and sinister nature were invoked by travellers against unseen and threatening dangers on a journey.

theology he comes back to establish his kingdom. Euripides says that he is served by women who lament him. He patiently submits to his fate, having incarnated to instruct and save mankind; the divine prisoner maintains a dignified silence before his judges who have eyes but cannot see or know what they do. All dying-god religions are initiatory and the candidate for initiation must also die to the world. Dying gods are: Osiris, Dionysos, Tammuz/Dumuzi, Attis, the Dictean Zeus, Men, Orpheus, Mithra, Baal, Baldur, Adonis, Woden/Odin, etc. Baldur does not return to the earth each Spring but awaits the end of the old order and the beginning of the new. The Christian Jesus dies only once and ascends to remain in heaven until the second coming. The search for the dead god by his sister or consort is common in Canaanite, Mesopotamian and Egyptian rituals of Tammuz, Marduk and Osiris. The kid can be used as a substitute for the dying god in Canaanite and Babylonian death and resurrection rites.

Eagle Solar; the symbol of all sky gods; the meridian sun; the spiritual principle; ascension; inspiration; release from bondage; victory; pride; contemplation; apotheosis; royalty; authority; strength; height; the element of air. Thought to be able to fly up to the sun and gaze unwaveringly upon it and to identify with it, the eagle represents the spiritual principle in man which is able to soar heavenwards. Double-headed eagles are attributes of twin gods and can represent omniscience or double power. The contest between the eagle and the bull, or eagle and lion, in which the eagle is always victorious, is the triumph of the spirit or intellect over the physical.

The conflict between the eagle and serpent, or an eagle with a snake in its talons, depicts spiritual victory, the eagle being symbolic of the celestial powers of good and the serpent representing evil and chthonic powers; the eagle is also unmanifest light with the serpent as unmanifest darkness; together they are a totality, cosmic unity and the union of spirit and matter. The eagle surmounting a pillar is an emblem of sun gods as *sol invictus* victorious over darkness. *Alchemic*: The soaring eagle is the liberated spiritual part of the *prima materia*. The double eagle depicts the male-female mercury. The crowned eagle and lion are wind and earth, quicksilver and sulphur, the volatile and fixed principles. *Amerindian*: The eagle-feather head-dress represents the Thunder Bird, Universal Spirit; the eagle is revelation and a mediator between sky and earth; it is also the day. In some cases the white eagle symbolizes man and the brown eagle woman. *Australian aboriginal*: The eagle or hawk is equated with the deity. *Aztec*: Celestial power; the luminous sky; the rising sun, devourer of the serpent of darkness.

Buddhist: A vehicle of Buddha; attribute of Amoghasiddhi. *Celtic*: Associated with the healing waters. *Chinese*: The sun; the yang principle; authority; warriors; courage; tenacity; keen vision; fearlessness. The eagle and raven are connected with war gods. *Christian*: The Spirit; ascension; aspiration; spiritual endeavour; the Last Judgement, when it throws the damned out of the nest; renewal of youth (Ps. 103, 5). Looking at the sun without blinking, it is Christ gazing on the glory of God; carrying its young to the sun, it is Christ bearing souls to God; plunging to take fish out of the sea, it is Christ rescuing souls from the sea of sin. The eagle was thought to renew its plumage by flying up to the sun and plunging into the sea, hence it symbolized resurrection and the new life in baptism; the soul renewed by grace. It also represented the inspiration of the Gospels, hence its use as a lectern. Grasping the serpent in its talons it is victory over sin; tearing its prey it is the Devil. Emblem of the Apostle John and SS Medard, Prisca, Servatius. One of the four beasts of the Apocalypse. In the Tetramorph it represents St John the Evangelist. *Egyptian*: Solar; the sons of Horus. *Greek*: Solar; spiritual power; royalty; victory and favour. An attribute of Zeus and as his lightning-bearer sometimes has a thunderbolt in its talons. Originally an emblem of Pan who yielded it to Zeus; emblem of Ganymede as funerary; Ganymede depicted as watering an eagle is the overcoming of death. An eagle with a snake in its talons is, according to Homer, a symbol of victory. *Hebrew*: Renewal; the East. *Hindu*: The solar Garuda Bird on which Vishnu rides; also an emblem of Indra. It is the Aryan stormcloud bird. *Mithraic*: Both the eagle and hawk are attributes of the solar Mithra. *Roman*: The solar storm bird, lightning-bearer of Jupiter. Represents the Emperor; dignity; victory; favour; quickness of perception. Holds Jupiter's thunderbolt in its talons. The symbol and agent of apotheosis after death. *Scandinavian*: Wisdom; appears in the boughs of the Yggdrasil as light in conflict with the serpent of darkness. An emblem of Odin/Woden. *Sumero-Semitic*: The noontide sun; attribute of Ninurta or Ningvisu, the beneficent sun and war god of Canaan and Babylon; emblem of the Phrygian Sabazios and sacred to the Assyrian Asshur as storm god, lightning and fertility. The double-headed eagle symbolizes Nergal, the fierce heat of the Summer and noon sun. It is also essentially Hittite and is solar power and omniscience; it often holds either a lunar hare or the serpent in its talons. Marduk is often depicted as an eagle.

Ear Associated with the spiral, the whorled shell and the sun; this accounts for the otherwise strange notion of birth from the ear, since the shell is a birth symbol connected with the vulva. Karma, son of the sun god Surya, was born from his mother's ear. The shell has also been regarded as a talisman to assist in easy birth. The ear hears the 'word' of creation and so is associated with the breath of life. In Egyptian symbolism the right ear receives the 'air of life' and the left ear the 'air of death'. In Christian art the Holy Ghost is sometimes represented in the form of a dove entering the ear of the Virgin Mary. Ears of gods, kings and any rain-bearing reptiles or animals are connected with the spiral. Elongated lobes on Hindu, Jain, Buddhist or Chinese figures indicate royalty or spiritual authority or greatness; they are one of the Chinese 'auspicious signs'. Pointed ears are associated with Pan, satyrs and devils. Asses' ears appear on a jester's cap and are an attribute of Midas; they depict folly.

Earth The Great Mother; Mother Earth; the universal genetrix; the Nourisher; the Nurse. The Earth Mother is the universal archetype of fecundity, inexhaustible creativity and sustenance. The Earth and Heaven are matter and spirit. *Amerindian*: The Earth is the Mother; the Earth Lodge is an omphalos, a cosmic centre. The circular floor depicts the earth, the dome-shaped roof the heavens and the four posts are the stars and the four directions. *Celtic*: The corruptible body, with salt as the immortal spirit. Earth was placed on the breast of the dead. *Chinese*: The feminine, yin, principle, symbolized by the square, the colour yellow and the tiger.

East The rising sun; dawn; Spring; hope; childhood; dawning life; youth. It is the direction towards which worship is oriented, especially for all solar gods. In China it is symbolized by the green dragon, in Egypt a man, in Mexico a crocodile, in Tibet a man-dragon. Ceremonies concerned with death and resurrection stress the East as sunrise and life and the West as sunset and death.

Easter Egg, Rabbit A pre-Christian symbol of rebirth and renewal of life at the beginning of the vernal equinox. A hare, or rabbit, is the emblem of Ostara or Eastre, Teutonic goddess of Spring and dawn and the probable origin of the term Easter.

Eating Imparts the quality of that which is consumed to the consumer, e.g., fish are prolific, hence fish-eating confers fecundity; also fish was the food of all feasts of the Great Mother and eaten on her day, Friday. Cannibalism, in eating the flesh of a warrior or hero, imparts prowess and heroism. Eating the flesh of a god imparts sanctity and spiritual power.

Echidna In Australian aboriginal symbolism it plays the part of the lunar hare or rabbit and represents initiation, death and resurrection.

Eden See PARADISE.

Eels Phallic; slipperiness. *Chinese*: Carnal love.

On this mid-6th century BC Greek cup, Zeus, Father and head of all the gods, is attended by his **eagle**, the symbol of his supremacy, his solar nature as ruler of the skies where the gods dwell, and his divine kingship.

This 5th-century Constantinopolitan mosaic communicates all the power, tension and struggle in the battle between the **eagle** and the serpent, symbols of the eternal conflict between opposites and respectively of man's higher and lower natures, of the solar and chthonic, of intellect and instinct.

Egg The Cosmic Egg, also symbolized by the sphere, is the life principle; the undifferentiated totality; potentiality; the germ of all creation; the primordial matriarchal world of chaos; the Great Round containing the universe; the hidden origin and mystery of being; cosmic time and space; the beginning; the womb; all seminal existence; the primordial parents; the perfect state of unified opposites; organic matter in its inert state; resurrection; hope. In Hindu, Egyptian, Chinese and Greek symbolism the Cosmic Egg, as the origin of the universe, suddenly burst asunder. Hitherto a whole, it had yet contained everything existing and potential in the limited space of the shell. The egg as the origin of the world is found in Egypt, Phoenicia, India, China, Japan, Greece, Central America, Fiji and Finland. The golden egg is the sun. The serpent encircling the egg is OUROBOROS (q.v.). An ostrich egg, or large porcelain egg, suspended in temples, Coptic churches and mosques, depicts creation, life and resurrection and, as such, is sometimes found on tombs. In Christianity it can signify the virgin birth. *Alchemic*: Out of the egg grows the white flower (silver), the red flower (gold), and the blue flower, (the flower of the wise). The egg is also the sealed hermetic vase in which the Great Work is consummated. The philosophers' egg is symbolic of creation. *Buddhist*: The eggshell is the 'shell of ignorance' and breaking through it is second birth and the attainment of enlightenment, transcending time and space. *Chinese*: Totality; the yolk is the sky and the albumen the earth. At creation the Cosmic Egg split open and the halves formed the earth and sky. *Christian*: Resurrection; re-creation; hope. *Druidic*: The Cosmic Egg is the 'egg of the serpent', symbolized by the sea-urchin fossil. *Egyptian*: The Cosmic Egg from which the sun, Ra, was hatched was laid by the Nile Goose: 'It groweth, I grow; it liveth, I live' (*Book of the Dead*). Kneph, the Serpent, also produced the Cosmic Egg from his mouth, symbolizing the Logos. *Greek*: In Orphism the egg is the mystery of life; creation; resurrection; it is surrounded by Ouroboros. The Dioscuri, born of the egg by Zeus and Leda, wear the two halves of the egg as domed caps. The egg is sometimes depicted as containing the four elements. *Hindu*: The Cosmic Egg was laid by the divine bird on the primordial waters. Brahma sprang from the golden egg of creation and the two halves formed heaven and earth: 'This vast egg, compounded of the elements, and resting on the waters, was the excellent natural abode of Vishnu in the form of Brahma, and there Vishnu ... assumed a perceptible form. ... In that egg were the continents and seas and mountains, the planets and divisions of the universe, the gods, demons and mankind' (*Vishnu Purana*). The Cosmic Egg corresponds to the egg of Brahma and is divided into three regions, the realm of the senses, the heavens and the formless world. The egg also signifies the yoni. The Cosmic Tree is sometimes depicted as growing from the Cosmic Egg floating on the waters of chaos. *Iranian*: Creation; the life principle. In Zoroastrianism the sky was created in the form of an egg of shining metal. *Oceanic*: In some islands the first man was said to be hatched from a bird's egg. *Sumero-Semitic*: The Cosmic Egg produced creation.

Elder In Europe it signifies witchcraft; magic; ghostly powers. It is worn on Walpurgis night.

Elements The passive forces of nature. In the West there are four elements: water is symbolized by undulating lines, the downward-pointing triangle and the colours blue or green, and has the quality of humidity, the fluid and cohesive; fire is depicted by flame, rays, pyramids or the upward-pointing triangle and the colours red or orange, and has the quality of heat, the consuming, the moving; earth is represented by a square or cube and the colours brown, black or yellow, and has the quality of coldness, the solid, that which can bear a load; air's symbols are the circle of the heavens, or an arc, and the colours blue, or gold of the sun; it has the quality of dryness, the light and mobile. In Chinese symbolism the four sacred or 'spiritually endowed creatures' combine the elements. The blue or green Dragon, portrayed ritually by the round blue jade tablet, is the air; there is also a Dragon of the Waters, of the Earth and of the Mountains. The Phoenix, with the red jade tablet, combines air and fire. The Tortoise, with the black semi-circular or yellow tubular jade, is earth and water. The White Tiger, with the white jade figure of a tiger, combines fire and water. Fire and air are yang, active and masculine; water and earth are yin, passive and feminine. In Graeco-Roman symbolism the elements are usually female figures or deities: water is symbolized by the flowing overturned vase, Neptune, Tritons, Nereids, Dolphins or Hippocampi; fire is a woman with the head on fire, or a phoenix, or Vulcan; the earth is represented by a goddess of fertility, the cornucopia, the chthonic snake or scorpion, or the turreted crown of Cybele; air is Juno and the Peacock, or Juno in mid-air with anvils suspended from her feet, or the chameleon, which was thought to live on air. There are five elements in Taoism, which each conquer the other in turn: wood conquers earth; earth, water; water, fire; fire, metal; metal, wood. In Hindu and Buddhist symbolism there are five elements: the earth is a square or cube; water a globe or circle; fire a triangle or pyramid; air a crescent; and the crescent surmounted by a gem or flame is the fifth element, ether.

Elephant Strength; fidelity; long memory; patience; wisdom; conjugal felicity. The white elephant is solar. *Buddhist*: Sacred to Buddha, a white elephant having appeared to Queen Maya to announce the birth of a royal world-ruler. The white elephant is also the Jewel of the

Law, the *vahan* of the Bodhisattva; compassion; love; kindness. An elephant is ridden by Akshobhya. The elephant's hide symbolizes ignorance. *Chinese*: Strength; sagacity; prudence; energy; sovereignty. *Christian*: A symbol of Christ as an enemy of the serpent, trampling the serpent underfoot; chastity; benignity. *Graeco-Roman*: An attribute of Mercury as intelligence. Pliny says the elephant is a religious animal, worshipping the sun and stars and purifying itself at the new moon, bathing in the river and invoking the heavens. In Roman art, longevity, immortality, victory over death. *Hindu*: The vehicle of the god Ganesha; the strength of sacred wisdom; prudence; kingly rank; invincible might; longevity; intelligence. Indra, guardian of the East, rides on the elephant Airavata. The world is supported by elephants.

Elk/Moose *Amerindian*: Supernatural power; the whirlwind.

Ellipse The Cosmic Egg; the yoni; the two sides signify descent and ascent, involution and evolution.

Elm *Christian*: Dignity; its great growth and spreading branches are the strength and power of the scriptures for the faithful.

Embryo Symbolized by the point, or by the point in the centre of the circle; it is the centre from which creation began and is identified with the waters, the egg and the lotus.

Emperor/Empress The Emperor is the incarnation of the sun god and is his delegate on earth. In China the Emperor, 'The Son of Heaven', symbolized the spiritual power of Heaven, the Empress the earthly; supreme perfection and wisdom. His emblem was the five-clawed Dragon and that of the Empress was the Phoenix. The Emperor of Japan, the Mikado, claims descent from the sun goddess Amaterasu.

Enchantress The feminine principle in its binding and destroying aspect; the spell-binding power of life; the illusion of Maya; self-delusion.

Enclosing All enclosing forms are symbols of the Great Mother in her aspect of protection, sheltering and nourishment and of the womb. Symbolized by the cave, city, temple, church, house, tent, gate, door, fence, tomb, wall, chest, cauldron, chalice, cup, etc., and by the sea and all waters, especially the well. The enclosure in connection with the womb also represents fertility.

Ephod *Hebrew*: According to Josephus, the universe compounded of the four elements. The breastplate in the middle of the Ephod is the Cosmic Centre.

To the ancient Egyptians, the god Ptah was the Father Creator, the Great Artificer, shown here at his potter's wheel fashioning the world **egg**, which contained his own spirit and was matched by the sun and moon eggs which he also created.

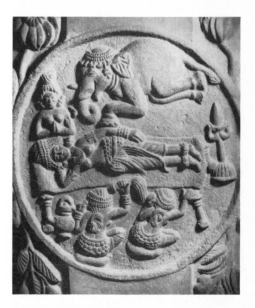

Before his birth the Buddha's mother, Queen Maya, dreamed of an **elephant** (the scene is reproduced on this 2nd-century BC Indian bas-relief), the symbol of the future Prince Gautama's patience, wisdom, long memory and supremacy among the world's great teachers.

Ermine As white in winter it is purity, chastity, innocence, also associated with justice, and on robes it denotes royalty or nobility in Church or State. Aristocratic Christian virgin saints are sometimes depicted wearing ermine, notably St Ursula.

Evaporation Transformation; the passage from the lower to the higher waters; connected with the symbolism of the sun, rain, fire and water as opposite and complementary forces. As producing steam it represents purification by fire and water, as in the North American Indian Sweat Lodge.

Evergreens Immortality; perpetuity; vitality; youth and vigour; the eternal; generative power. Wreaths of evergreen denote undying fame, consecration to immortality.

Evil The powers of darkness; demons; the Devil; Satan; Beelzebub; Angra Mainu or Ahriman. Symbols of evil are: the serpent or dragon (except in the East); the viper; scorpion; scorpion-man; the hurricane; all devouring beasts and some horned beasts; the ant; the single eye of the Cyclops.

Ewer Purity; the washing of the hands in innocence. Emblem of Dionysos as wine god.

Excrement Associated with gold and riches; contains the power of the person. In Alchemy it is the *nigredo*.

Eye Omniscience; the all-seeing divinity; the faculty of intuitive vision. The eye is a symbol of all sun gods and of their life-giving power of fertilization by the sun; their power is incarnated in the god-king. Plato calls it the most solar of instruments. It is also the mystic eye; light; enlightenment; knowledge; the mind; vigilance; protection; stability; fixity of purpose, but also the limitation of the visible. The 1,000, or 10,000, eyes of the sky gods are the stars, the eyes of the night, representing omniscience; never-sleeping watchfulness; infallibility. The 'eye' as applied to sacred architecture is the opening heavenwards in the centre of the dome of a temple, cathedral, lodge, or any other traditionally constructed 'world centre'; it represents the solar door giving access to celestial regions. The 'eye of the heart' is spiritual perception; illumination; intellectual intuition. The eye can also depict the androgyne as being formed of the oval female symbol and the circle of the male.

The single eye is either symbolic of evil as with the Cyclops or monsters of destructive power, or as the single eye of enlightenment, the eye of God and of eternity, the self-contained. A triangle with an eye in the centre is the 'All-seeing Eye', omnipresence and omniscience. In the Occident the right eye is the sun, the eye of the day, and the future, with the left eye as the moon, the eye of the night, and the past. In the

Orient the position is reversed. The peacock feather can take on the symbolism of the eye. *Amerindian*: 'The eye of the heart sees everything.' It is the eye of the Great Spirit, omniscience. *Buddhist*: Light; wisdom. The third eye of Buddha, the 'flaming pearl', is spiritual consciousness, transcendent wisdom. *Celtic*: The evil eye, symbolic of ill-will and envy, is the antithesis of the kind heart of generosity and compassion. *Chinese and Japanese*: The left eye is the sun, the right eye the moon. *Christian*: The all-seeing God; omniscience; power; light, 'The light of the body is the eye' (Matt. 6, 22). The seven eyes of the Apocalypse are the seven spirits of God. The eye of God in a triangle depicts the Godhead; in a triangle surrounded by a radiant circle, the infinite sanctity of the Godhead. A pair of eyes is the emblem of SS Lucy and Ottilia. *Egyptian*: Highly complex. 'The Eye of Horus', the Utchat, the 'All-seeing', is suggested as the Pole Star and illumination; the eye of the mind. The eye and eyebrow of Horus depict strength and power. Two winged eyes are the two divisions of heaven, the North and South; the sun and moon; celestial space. The right eye is the sun and Ra and Osiris, the left eye the moon and Isis. The eye of Ra is also the Uraeus. The eye of Horus could be associated with the moon and its phases, and could also symbolize offerings made to the gods in the temples. *Greek*: The eye symbolizes Apollo as 'viewer of the heavens', the sun, which is also the eye of Zeus/Jupiter. *Hindu*: The third eye of Siva, the pearl in the middle of his forehead, represents spiritual consciousness, transcendent wisdom. The eye of Varuna is the sun. *Iranian*: Yima, the Good Shepherd, possesses the solar eye and holds the secret of immortality. *Islamic*: The 'eye of the heart' is the spiritual centre, the seat of the Absolute Intellect; illumination. *Japanese*: The right eye of Izanagi gave birth to the moon god. *Oceanic*: The sun is the 'great eye-ball'. *Platonic*: 'There is an eye of the soul ... by it alone is Truth seen.' *Sumero-Semitic*: The eye depicts Ea, or Enki, 'Lord of the Sacred Eye', and is wisdom; omniscience; vigilance. The Phoenician Cronos has four eyes, two open, two closed, as perpetual watchfulness.

Fabulous Beasts The combination of different characteristics suggests other possibilities of creation and potentialities, also freedom from the conventional principles of the phenomenal world. Composite monsters are also symbolic of the primordial chaos or the fearsome and terrifying powers of nature. Sometimes two fabulous beasts or winged beasts are depicted on either side of the Tree of Life and frequently at doors as guardians, or as guardians of treasures, either of underground wealth or of esoteric knowledge. Frightful monsters represent the evil or chaotic forces in the world or in man's own nature, or they can be symbols of pestilence or destructive forces. They are usually fought by a god or hero such as Marduk, the Creator, overcoming Tiamat as primordial chaos; Theseus and the Minotaur, or knights slaying dragons; these represent the triumph of order over chaos and good over evil or light over darkness. The gaping jaws of a monster signify the gates of hell or the entrance to the underworld.

Amemait: Lion, crocodile and hippopotamus, is the Devourer; retribution. *Amphisbaena*: Similar to the Basilisk, but with a head at each end and so able to see both ways. *Anata*: The giant serpent on which Vishnu lay in pre-cosmic sleep.

Basilisk/Cockatrice: A bird and reptile combination, with the head and claws of a bird and body of a serpent; when the tail ends in another head it is the Amphisbaena. In Christianity it is the Devil or the Antichrist, one of the four aspects of the Devil. *Behemoth*: Usually supposed to be the hippopotamus, represents the power of the land as opposed to Leviathan, the power of the sea, and Ziz, the power of the air. *Benhu/Bennu*: The bird sometimes equated with the phoenix; it incarnates the soul of Osiris. *Bucentaur*: Half-man, half-bull; the dual nature of man.

Capricornus: Half-goat, half-fish; the Winter Solstice. It is also a form of the Babylonian Ea-Oannes, 'Lord of the Abyss'. *Celestial Dog*: T'ien Kou; destruction; catastrophe; eclipses; meteors. *Centaur*: (q.v.) Half-man, half-horse; holding an arrow and drawn bow, the Sagittarius of the Zodiac. *Cerberus*: A huge three-headed dog, representing the underworld Trinity; guardian of the threshold of the underworld. *Charybdis*: A roaring monster or whirlpool which swallowed the sea and threw it up again; with Scylla as the other monster of the Sicilian sea, together they are symbolic of the difficult PASSAGE (q.v.). *Chimera*: Head, mane and legs of a lion, body of a goat and tail of a dragon; storm and winds; dangers on land and sea; the non-existent. *Cockatrice*: See *Basilisk*.

Dragon: (q.v.) Various forms; largely evil powers in the West and beneficent in the East.

Epimacus: see *Opinicus*.

Furia: Woman with wings and serpent; depicts vengeance.

Gargoyles: Monstrous heads, either human, animal or fabulous; suggested as evil spirits flying from the church, or objectivized powers of evil, or the frightening away of evil powers. *Garuda*: The Bird of Life, sometimes equated with the Phoenix; the sun; the sky; victory; a vehicle of Vishnu, creator and destroyer of all. It emerges fully grown from the egg and nests in the wish-fulfilling Tree of Life; it is at war with the Nagas. *Gorgon*: The three Gorgons have women's heads with hair of snakes; the Great Mother in her terrible aspect as destroyer; terror. *Grylli*: As *Chimera*. *Gryphon*: (q.v.) Head of an eagle and body of a lion; the sun; the

'Lady with an **Ermine**' by Leonardo. The ermine stands for chastity and purity – but here the symbolism may have been double-edged, for the lady is thought to be the mistress of Lodovico il Moro, of the Sforza family, and the ermine was their emblem.

This circle of plaster-stiffened linen, called a hypocephalus, was placed beneath a mummy's head by the ancient Egyptians to symbolize the **eye** of a god – Ra, Horus or another – accompanying the dead person's spirit on the dark journey to the underworld.

wealth of the sun; strength; vigilance; vengeance. Without wings it is the male Gryphon.

Harpy: Head and breasts of a woman and claws of a vulture; associated with sudden death; whirlwinds and storms; the feminine principle in its destructive aspect. *Hippogryph*: Half-horse, half-gryphon; probably solar, as were the winged horses of Apollo's chariot. *Hippolectryon*: Half-horse, half-cock; solar. *Hydra*: Dragon or serpent with seven heads; blind, animal life-force.

Kala-makara: Lion and makara or crocodile; solar and the power of the waters. *Ky-lin*: (q.v.) The yin-yang, it is sometimes equated with the unicorn; it is the union of the male and female; perfection; purity of nature; the essence of the five elements.

Lamia: A cruel queen turned into a beast; equated with sirens and having a fish symbolism. *Leogryph*: Lion and serpent or gryphon; illusion; the terrible aspect of the Great Mother as Maya. *Leviathan*: A huge fish, 'that crooked serpent'; the primordial monster of the ocean and chaos; the serpent and power of the deep, with Behemoth as the power of the land and Ziz as the air. *Lindworm*: A wyvern or dragon sans wings; war and pestilence.

Makara: Fish and crocodile or elephant; a sea monster ridden by Varuna as god of the deeps. *Marine Monsters*: Usually symbolize the unfathomable depth, primordial chaos, or divine power in manifestation. *Mermaid*: half-woman, half-fish; a divinity of the waters. *Minotaur*: (q.v.) A man with a bull's head; the savage passions of nature; the miasma.

Naga: Many-headed snake; guardian of treasures and esoteric knowledge; serpent kings and queens; the life forces of the waters, the swamp-like passionate nature. See SERPENT, *Hindu*.

Opinicus/Epimacus: A type of gryphon having the body and legs of a lion, head, neck and wings of an eagle and tail of a camel, sometimes depicted without wings; shares the symbolism of the gryphon. *Pegasus*: Winged horse; the combination of the lower and higher nature striving for the higher; solar. *Phoenix*: (q.v.) A fabulous bird rising from flames; death and resurrection; rebirth by fire.

Roc: A huge bird, a storm bird, with the wind as the rush of its wings and lightning as its flight. According to Arabic tradition it never lands on earth except on the mountain Qaf, the *axis mundi*; it is solar and the sky.

Salamander: (q.v.) Usually depicted as a small, wingless dragon or lizard; sometimes dog-like, leaping out of flames; it is the element of fire. *Sermurv/Simurgh*: A combination of peacock, gryphon, lion and dog; it is the sky, the intermediary between two worlds. *Scylla*: With Charybdis, a monster of the Sicilian sea. Originally a beautiful nymph, she was changed into a monster with six heads with triple rows of teeth, the necks of the heads inordinately long; together, Scylla and Charybdis are symbolic of the difficult passage and powers of the waters. *Siren*: A bird with a woman's head, a seducer of seafaring men; also a funerary. The attributes of sirens are lyres and flutes and they represent the seductive powers of the senses and of the realm of illusion. *Sphinx*: (q.v.) Has the head of a man, or woman, body of a bull, feet of a lion and wings of an eagle; it combines the four elements and symbolizes the mysterious, the enigmatic and solar power.

Tengu: A man with a bird's head and wings and with claws on his feet; depicts war, conflict, hypocrisy, mischief. *Tiamat*: The monster of the deep; primeval chaos; the waters; darkness. *Triton*: A merman, half-man half-fish; holds or blows a horn or conch shell and controls the powers of the waters.

Unicorn: (q.v.) A one-horned animal with the body of a horse or stag; it symbolizes the feminine, lunar principle; chastity; purity. *Wyvern*: A serpent or dragon with wings, but with only two legs like an eagle's; betokens war and pestilence. *Ziz*: A large bird, the power of the air, with Behemoth on land and Leviathan in the sea. *Zu*: A storm bird, stealer of the Sumerian Tablets of Fate which conferred omnipotence.

Face The outward personality. Multiple faces on Hindu gods show the different aspects, elemental powers, exploits or functions of a deity, or can combine various gods. The four or five faces on statues of Siva or Brahma also represent the elements.

Falcon Shares much of the solar symbolism of the EAGLE (q.v.), with which it can change places. It is aspiration; victory; ascension through all planes. It also typifies freedom, hence hope for all those in bondage, either moral or spiritual. *Celtic*: Like the eagle, it was one of the primordial manifestations. It is opposed to the lascivious hare and thus depicts victory over lust. *Chinese*: In China it was ambivalent as solar power, but also the destructive force of war. *Egyptian*: In Egypt the falcon was the King of Birds; the heavenly principle; the bird of hunting. It was a representation of Horus, the all-seeing, who appears either as a falcon or falcon-headed. Ra of the Rising Sun, as identified with Horus with the Horizon, can also be falcon-headed. *Inca*: A solar symbol; a guardian spirit. *Scandinavian*: Odin could travel to earth as a falcon. Attribute of Frigg and an aspect of Loki as associated with fire.

Fall The Fall of Man is involvement in the material and individual world; man forgetting his divine origin and nature; the loss of Paradise; the congenital duality in man and in manifestation.

Fan The spirit, as moving air; power; dignity. The shape of the fan typifies life, starting at the point of the rivet and expanding as experience of life widens out. The folding fan depicts lunar changes and feminine changeability. The waving of the fan wards off evil forces. *African*: Frequently a symbol of royal dignity. *Chinese*: Authority; royal dignity; the power of the air which can infuse new life into the dead; delicacy of feeling; the dignity of the mandarin. An 'Autumn fan' is a deserted wife. *Hindu*: An attribute of Agni, the Vedic fire god, and of Vishnu. *Japanese*: Authority; power. The white-feather fan is the power of the winds. *Taoist*: Associated with birds and flight as a means of liberation from the formal world and release into the realm of the Immortals. Emblem of Chung-li Chuan, one of the Taoist genii.

Fasces *Roman*: Magisterial power and judicial authority; punishment; the rods denote scourging and the axe beheading; together they symbolize strength in unity. As unity it can be an attribute of Eros/Cupid.

Fasting An Aryan-Celtic method of drawing attention to a grievance.

Fat Regarded as a seat of life and as possessing the powers of the body from which it is taken. A choice part.

Father The sun; the Spirit; the masculine principle; conventional forces of law and order as opposed to the feminine and intuitive instinctual powers. The sky god is the All-Father. In myth and legend the figure of the father symbolizes physical, mental and spiritual superiority. Father Time, identified with Cronos/Saturn, holds a scythe or sickle as god of agriculture and as the Reaper, Time. An hourglass is also his attribute.

Fawn Emblem of the Bacchant and Orphic devotee who wore a fawn skin and fawn-skin sandals; accompanies Diana.

Feather Truth, which must rise; lightness; dryness; the heavens; height; speed; space; flight to other realms; the soul; the element of wind and air as opposed to the humid principle. To wear feathers or feathered headdress is to take on the power, or *mana*, of the bird and puts the wearer in touch with the knowledge of the birds ('a little bird told me'), and with their transcendent and instinctual knowledge and magic power. Two feathers together represent light and air; the two poles; also resurrection. Three feathers are associated with the FLEUR-DE-LIS (q.v.) and are an emblem of the Prince of Wales. The white feather symbolizes clouds, sea-foam and cowardice since a white feather or feathers in the tail of a fighting cock was taken as a sign of faulty breeding and therefore disinclination to fight. A feather-crown represents the rays of the sun. *Amerindian*: Eagle feathers depict the Thunder Bird, the Great Spirit, universal spirit, also rays of light. See

On this ancient Greek bronze plaque, the female *gryphon*, here with her young, combines the fierceness and majesty of the lion and the eagle, of whose bodies she is composed and whose solar natures combined she symbolizes.

A Buddha from Angkor Thom, in Cambodia, sits in recollected calm on the coiled body of a *naga*, symbolizing the knowledge hidden in instinct which he has conquered and transformed into his guardian and support.

FEATHERED SUN. *Celtic*: Feathered cloaks worn by priests represent the journey to the other world; fairies also wear feather-trimmed dresses. *Christian*: Contemplation; faith. *Egyptian*: Sovereignty; truth; flight; weightlessness; dryness; height; emblem of the goddess Maat as Truth. Deities with feathers as attributes are also the solar Amen Ra and Anheru, Osiris, Horus, Shu, Hathor, Amsu, Mentu, Nefertium. In Amenti Osiris weighs the soul against feathers of truth. *Scandinavian*: Freyja owned a magic robe of feathers which enabled its wearer to fly through the air. *Shamanistic*: The feathered robes of shamans give power of flight to other realms and to undertake knowledge-gaining journeys. *Taoist*: Attribute of the priest, the 'feathered sage' or 'feathered visitor'; communication with the next world. *Toltec*: Feathered sticks represent prayer, contemplation.

Feathered Sun A Plains Indian symbol with stylized feathers pointing both inwards and outwards; inward toward the centre and outward to the circumference; it combines the symbols of the sun and the eagle and depicts the universe; the Centre; solar power; radiation of power; majesty.

Feet/Foot Freedom of movement; willing service; humility; the lowly. Kissing or washing the feet signifies complete abasement and reverence. Footmarks are the road man has covered (see also FOOTPRINTS). Absence of feet, as in the case of fire gods, indicates the instability of flame. Other limbs taking the place of feet, such as the fish-body of Ea-Oannes, indicates the element controlled, or the dual nature of the deity. In Chinese symbolism the sole of the foot denotes the measurement of time or a section of time. Deities treading people underfoot depict the treading down of worldly passions and existence, the realm of *maya*, the illusory nature of existence. Stamping the foot indicates frustrated rage.

Fennel Sacred to Sabazios, fennel wreaths were worn in his rites.

Fermentation The process of fermentation allows the spirit to surpass ordinary limitations, to release intuitive powers and to produce dreams. It is also associated with decomposing and excrement. In Alchemy it is connected with the work of transformation and transmutation and hence regeneration; the passage from death to life. Metals ferment in the earth and the process is symbolic of cyclic ideas and the eternal return.

Fern Solitude; sincerity; humility.

Field The Earth Mother, the great provider and nourisher. *Hindu*: 'The woman is the field, the male the seed.' *Islam*: 'Women are the field.'

Fig, Fig Tree or Pipal Fecundity; life; peace; prosperity. The fig tree is sometimes the Tree of Knowledge and combines symbols of both the masculine and feminine principles, the fig leaf being the male, the linga, and the fig the female, the yoni. The fig leaf depicts lust and sex: 'The fig leaf is interpreted as denoting drinking and motion and is supposed to resemble the male sexual organ' (Plutarch). A basket of figs is fertility and represents woman as goddess or mother. Associated with the vine as a place of peace and quiet and with the breast as 'the tree of many breasts'. *Buddhist*: The sacred Bo-Tree under which Buddha attained enlightenment. *Christian*: Has been used in place of the apple in the Garden of Eden. *Graeco-Roman*: Sacred to Dionysos/Bacchus, Priapus, Jupiter and Silvanus; phallic. *Hebrew*: Peace; prosperity; plenty; a symbol of Israel, with the vine. *Islamic*: The Tree of Heaven, sacred since Mohammed swore by it. *Oceanic*: Often a Tree of Life and the object of cultural rituals.

Finger Pointing the finger is magic power, or an insult; a finger to the mouth indicates silence or thought or a warning. Fingers raised in benediction convey spiritual power. Two fingers raised depict teaching or judging. The first and fourth raised (the Cornuto) are apotropaic, protection against the evil eye, but are insulting if pointed at a person. *Christian*: Raising three fingers in blessing represents the Trinity. *Egyptian*: Two fingers raised in benediction are help and strength and portray the two fingers of Horus extended to help Osiris mount the ladder from this world to the next; the first finger is divine justice and the second is the Spirit, the Mediator. The infant Horus has a finger in his mouth. *Greek*: A finger on the mouth is silence or meditation and is a symbolic attitude of Polyhymnia and Nemesis.

Fir Tree Boldness; integrity. In Chinese symbolism it depicts the Elect and patience. It is sacred to Pan and to Woden. See also PINE.

Fire/Flame Transformation; purification; the lifegiving and generative power of the sun; renewal of life; impregnation; power; strength; energy; the unseen energy in existence; sexual power; defence; protection; visibility; destruction; fusion; passion; immolation; change or passage from one state to another; the medium for conveying messages or offerings heavenward. Fire manifested as flame symbolizes spiritual power and forces, transcendence and illumination, and is a manifestation of divinity or of the soul, the pneuma, the breath of life; it is also inspiration and enlightenment. A flame resting on the head, or surrounding it, like the NIMBUS, represents divine power, potency of soul or genius, the head being regarded as the seat of the life-soul. A flame leaves the body at death. Fire and flame can both typify the heart. Both are ambivalent as being either divine or demonic, creative or destructive; they are the means of devouring all created things to return them to original unity. Both represent truth and knowledge as consumers of lies, ignorance, illusion and death and as scorchers of the impure. Baptism by fire restores primordial purity by burning away the dross and is associated with passing through fire to regain Paradise which, since it was lost, has been surrounded by fire or protected by guardians, with swords of flame, who symbolize understanding barring the way to the ignorant or unenlightened. Fire is polarized into the two complementary aspects of light and heat, often depicted one by straight, the other by wavy, lines or rays. Light and heat can also represent the intellect and the emotions, also the flash of the rain-bringing and fecundating lightning and the warmth of the domestic hearth; the awe-inspiring and the comforting.

Kindling a fire is equated with birth and resurrection and in primitive cultures with sexual creation. Torch-bearing at weddings and fertility rites denotes the generative power of fire. Fire and water together are the two great principles, the active and passive, of the universe; they are the Sky Father and Earth Mother and all the opposites in the elemental world; fire and water are in conflict, but as heat and moisture they are necessary for all life. Fire is represented in the vegetable world by the seed of mustard. Fire and wind represent the mountain and volcanic gods. The fire of the domestic hearth is the centre of the home and is the feminine-earth aspect of fire. Symbols of fire are the upward-pointing triangle, swastika, lion's mane, hair, sharp weapons, fir tree, azalea. *Alchemic*: Fire is the central element as unifier and stabilizer. 'The operation begins with fire and ends with fire' (ibn Bishrun). *Amerindian*: In the Medicine Lodge fire is the sacred, central dwelling place of the Great Spirit; it is also an intermediary between God and man. *Aztec*: Ritual death; redemption; penitence. *Buddhist*: Wisdom, which burns all ignorance. A fiery pillar is an aniconic symbol of Buddha. Fire is consuming and water purifying. *Chinese*: Flame signifies the presence of divinity. Fire is danger; anger; ferocity; speed; but as a spiritual power it is solar, yang, combined with the yin of water; it is symbolized by the trigram ☲ which has yang lines without and a yin line within. *Christian*: Religious fervour; martyrdom. 'Tongues of fire' are the advent of the Holy Spirit; the voice of God; divine revelation; the emblem of St Anthony of Padua. *Egyptian*: Associated with Thoth as inspiration. *Graeco-Roman*: The attribute of all thunder and volcanic smith-gods such as Hephaestos and Vulcan who symbolize the power of terrestrial fire; also an emblem of Vesta, the hearth goddess. Associated with Hermes/Mercury as inspiration. Hestia/Vesta, Goddess of the hearth, was the 'Lady of Fire' (Euripides). *Hebrew*: Divine revelation; the voice of God. 'The Lord thy God is a consuming fire' (Deut. 4, 24). *Hindu*: Transcendental light and know-

The **feather** and wood-grain pattern in the glaze of this 13th-century Chinese bowl combines in a single symbol the opposites of lightness and loftiness, as expressed by the feather, and the earthly vitality and growth of the tree, whose grain is the chart and map of life itself.

The Kings of the earth – their crowns surround a globe – worship through their surrogate the supreme transforming **fire** in an illustration from a 17th-century alchemical text.

ledge; the vital energy of wisdom; fire is also identified with the forces of destruction, release and recreation wielded by Siva. The column of flame and mounting smoke of the Vedic fire god, Agni, represents the world axis. As fire, Agni is both the rain-bringing fecundity of lightning and the domestic hearth. Flames are portrayed by Agni's golden teeth, sharp tongue and dishevelled hair; he rides the solar ram, holds an axe, fan and bellows and is born from wood. Three fires are lit on the Vedic fire altars at the South, East and West, representing the sun and sky, ether and winds, and the earth. The black and horrific aspect of fire is symbolized by Kali/Durga (who is also all-consuming Time), usually depicted as a fearful black or red figure with long canine teeth and tongues of fire and holding the attributes of her husband Siva: the trident, sword, drum and bowl of blood. Kindling the fire is a re-enactment of the act of creation, of integration and reunion by means of sacrifice. The ring of flame round Siva depicts the cosmic cycle of creation and destruction. Fire, as the vital flame, is also Krishna: 'I am the fire residing in the bodies of all things which have life' (*Bhagavad Gita*). *Iranian*: The Parsee temple has the fire as the Sacred Centre, the place of divinity and the divine light in the soul of man. It is also solar power, symbolized by Atar, the divine fire in the sky and in wood. It is also associated with law and order. In Zoro-astrianism 'the seeds of men and bulls have their origin in fire, not in water'. *Islamic*: Fire and flame are light and heat, divinity and hell. *Pythagorean*: Associated with the tetrahedron, fire being the first element and the tetrahedron the first figure in geometry. *Sumero-Semitic*: Marduk was a fire god, 'the flame which causes foes to be burned.'

Firefly In Buddhism it portrays shallow knowledge incapable of lightening the darkness.

Fish Phallic; fecundity; procreation; life renewed and sustained; the power of the waters as origin and preservation of life; the watery element; associated with all aspects of the Mother Goddess as genetrix and with all lunar deities. Fish, with bread and wine, was the sacramental meal of the mystery religions and fish meals and sacrifice were solemnized in the ritual worship of all gods of the underworld and lunar goddesses of the waters and of love and fecundity, such as Atargatis, whose son, Ichthys, was the Sacred Fish; also Ishtar, Nina, Isis and Venus; their day was Friday on which day fish was eaten in their honour but also with the object of partaking of the fecundity of the fish.

Fishes were also symbolic of devotees and disciples swimming in the waters of life. Fishes depicted with birds are chthonic and funerary and represent hope of resurrection. Fish deities and sea gods riding on fishes or dolphins typify independence of motion in the waters; the all-possible. Fish swimming downwards portray

the movement of involution of spirit in matter and swimming upwards the evolution of spirit-matter returning to the First Principle. Two fishes are temporal and spiritual power. Three fishes with one head portray the unity of the Trinity; this symbolism is found in Egyptian, Celtic, Indian, Mesopotamian, Burmese, Persian and French iconography and occurs almost universally from ancient to modern times. Three intertwined fishes are also a Trinity symbol. *Alchemic*: The arcane substance. *Buddhist*: Symbolic, on the footprint of Buddha, of freedom from restraint; emancipation from desires and attachments. Buddha is a Fisher of Men. *Celtic*: Salmon and trout were associated with sacred wells as symbols of the fore-knowledge of the gods. Nodon was a fisher god. *Chinese*: Abundance (fish and abundance are homophones); wealth; regeneration; harmony; the Emperor's subjects. A single fish depicts a solitary or a lonely person, an orphan, widow or bachelor. A pair of fishes portrays the joys of union; marriage; fertility. An emblem of Kwan-yin and of the T'ang Dynasty. *Christian*: Baptism; immortality; resurrection (the sign of Jonah). The sacramental fish with wine and a basket of bread represents the eucharist and the Last Supper in Christian art. The Early Fathers called the faithful *pisciculi*, and the Apostles were fishers of men. Christ was depicted by the rebus ICHTHUS (*I*esous *Ch*ristos *Th*eou *Hu*ios *S*oter, Jesus Christ, Son of God, Saviour). The fish represented Christ in the Latin church, but not in the Greek Orthodox. The fish is an emblem of SS Anthony of Padua, Chrysogonus, Congall, Corentin, Benno, Peter the Fisherman, Mauritius, Ulrich, Zeno. The three fishes with one head denote the three-in-one of the Trinity and the three intertwined fishes are baptism under the Trinity. *Egyptian*: The phallus of Osiris. Two fishes are the creative principle; prosperity of the Nile; fertility; emblem of Isis and Hathor. The barbel is the unclean; hatred; emblem of Typhon as the irrational and passionate element in nature. *Greek*: Attribute of Aphrodite as love and fecundity, also of Poseidon as the power of the waters. The fish was an offering for the dead in the worship of Adonis. Orpheus was the Fisher of Men. *Hebrew*: The *coena pura* of the meal of the Sabbath; food of the blessed in Paradise; symbol of the heavenly banquet of the future life of bliss. Fishes are the faithful of Israel in their true element, the waters of the Torah. The old Jewish Passover was in the month of Adar, the Fish. *Hindu*: A vehicle of Vishnu as Saviour in his first incarnation when he saved mankind from the flood and founded a new race at the start of the present cycle; also a symbol of Varuna, a golden fish, as the power of the waters and redeemer of Manu from the flood. The fish depicts wealth and fertility and is an attri-bute of divinities of love. Two fishes touching nose-to-tail depict the yoni. *Japanese* Love (a homophone of carp); an attribute of Kwannon. *Mandaean*: Eaten sacramentally at feasts for the dead. *Roman*: Funerary; new life in the next world; an emblem of Venus as love and fertility and of Neptune as the power of the waters. *Scandinavian*: Attribute of Frigga as love and fertility. *Sumero-Semitic*: The fish skin was used as a theriomorphic dress by the priests of Ea-Oannes, Lord of the Deeps, who is also depicted as a fish-goat or fish-ram; the fish headdress of the priests of Ea later became the mitre of Christian bishops. The fish is an emblem of Ea and of Tammuz as phallic and masculine, but it represents the feminine, love and fertility as associated with Ishtar. Adapa, the Wise, son of Ea, is portrayed as a Fisher. In Assyria the fish appears with the axe, possibly as lunar and solar power, the powers of the waters and the sky gods. It appears with the axe also in Crete. In Phoenicia, Phrygia and Syria fish was the eucharistic food of the priests of Atargatis, who had sacred fish pools; it was an emblem of divinities of love and signified good fortune. *Zodiacal*: The arcane substance is symbolized by the opposite fishes; the fish-goat is Capricorn.

Five See NUMBERS.

Flail Sovereignty; rule; dominion; supreme power. The flail is often depicted with the crook. In Egyptian art it is an attribute of Osiris as judge of the dead.

Flame See FIRE.

Fleece Represents the fat, regarded as the life-force of the sheep and, by implication, all life-sustaining produce, such as cattle, corn, etc., also progeny and longevity.

Fleur-de-lis The stylized lotus or lily, the flower of light and life; the flame of light and life; the Queen of Heaven and the triple majesty of God; of Trinity; royalty. It is also associated with the androgyne as the male trinity combined with the female circle and connected with the trident, caduceus and thyrsus; as resembling a spearhead it is phallic and represents masculine and military power. Emblem of the kings of France and SS Louis of France and Toulouse.

Flight/Flying Transcendence; the release of the spirit from the limitations of matter; the release of the spirit of the dead; passage from one ontological plane to another; passing from the conditioned to the unconditioned; access to a superhuman state. The ability of sages to fly or 'travel on the wind' symbolizes spiritual release and omnipresence.

Flint Fire, bringing forth fire; hardness of heart, hence indifference; the spark of love; procreation. Flint arrowheads are fairy weapons; apotropaic.

Floating Floating on waters is the *regressus ad uterum*; orgasm; passivity. On air it is lightness

The Mayan god Huehuetlotl, god of **fire**, holds on his head a brazier in which the symbol of himself and his divinity would be kindled and fed.

These **flying** male and female Indian deities, carved in the 6th century AD on the ceiling of a cave in Badami, express the Eastern belief that through physical love both partners may, paradoxically, rise above their earthly passion.

and a power of fairies and witches. Witches float on water and cannot drown.

Flock The faithful; communities of believers; members of churches.

Flogging Ambivalent as both expiation and punishment and as encouragement and stimulation. Ritual flogging restores male vitality. Flogging was also used to cast out devils in bewitched persons. See also WHIP.

Flood The lunar power of the waters; the end of a cycle and the beginning of a new; causes death but also regeneration.

Flowers The feminine, passive principle; the form of the receptacle, the 'cup' of the flower, thus taking on the CUP symbolism. In the bud the flower is potentiality; in opening and expanding from the centre outwards it depicts development in manifestation; this is particularly stressed in the symbolism of the lotus in the East and the rose and lily in the West. The expansion in the phenomenal world and the form of the open flower also connect it with the symbolism of the wheel with its rays emanating from the centre. Flower gardens are also associated with Paradise, the Fields of the Blessed, the 'better land', the abode of souls. Five-petalled flowers, the rose, lily, etc., symbolize the Gardens of the Blessed, also the microcosm of man fixed in the five extremities of the five senses. The six-petalled flower, especially the lotus, is the macrocosm. Flowers often grow from the blood of a god when it is split on the ground, e.g. the anemone or red roses from the blood of Adonis, the violet from the blood of Attis, the hyacinth from that of Hyacinthus and roses from the blood of Christ. Divinities also emerge from flowers, in particular from the lotus as representing the light of the sun and the primaeval waters, the matrix, e.g. Brahma, Buddha, Horus.

Flowers also portray the fragile quality of childhood or the evanescence of life. A child rising from a flower depicts either the birth of a god or the birth of day, dawn, new life. A blue flower is the unattainable; the red flower depicts dawn, the rising sun, passion; it is an attribute of the Mother Goddess; white flowers typify purity and innocence, white and red together denote death. Scented flowers or plants, which are apotropaic and help the departed, are used in rites of the dead, notably Parsee, Jewish and Mandaean. The Christian practice of sending flowers for the funeral and grave is probably an extension of this custom. *Alchemic*: The white flower is silver, the red flower gold and the blue flower is the flower of the wise which grows from the Cosmic Egg. *Buddhist*: The transitoriness of the body; flowers are offered in worship. The LOTUS (q.v.) is highly symbolic in Buddhism. *Celtic*: The soul; the sun; spiritual flowering. *Chinese*: The feminine element; in the yin-yang symbolism

flowers are the yin with the horse and lion, as speed and strength, as the yang; this combination is also used in marriage symbolism and decoration. *Christian*: The rose springs from the blood of Christ and the rose and lily are emblems of the Virgin Mary. Three flowers are the emblem of St Hugh of Lincoln. *Greek*: Anemones are sacred to Adonis, having sprung from his blood. Zephyr and Flora beget the flowers of Spring and gardens. *Mexican*: Xochiquetzal was the goddess of flowers and her twin brother Xochipilli was the prince of flowers. *Roman*: Funerary; continuing life in the next world; roses were scattered on Roman graves at the festival of the Rosalia. *Taoist*: The GOLDEN FLOWER (q.v.) is the crystallization of light; the Tao; attainment of immortality; spiritual rebirth. A basket of flowers, denoting longevity and happy old age, is the emblem of Lan Ts'ai-ho, one of the eight Taoist genii or immortals.

Flute Sometimes equated with anguish and the extremes of emotion. *Chinese*: Emblem of Han Hsiang-tzu, one of the eight Taoist genii or immortals and symbolizing harmony. *Graeco-Roman*: Emblem of Euterpe and an attribute of the Sirens as seduction and the emotions. *Hindu*: The flute of Krishna is 'the voice of eternity crying to the dwellers in time'. *Phrygian*: An attribute of Cybele.

Fly Usually associated with evil gods and corruption. Can represent supernatural power, mostly evil; demons are often portrayed as flies. *Christian*: Evil; pestilence; sin. Depicted in Christian art with the goldfinch as the Saviour and the fly as disease. *Phoenician*: Beelzebub, Lord of the Flies, is the agent and power of destruction and putrefaction.

Flying See FLIGHT.

Fly Whisk Authority; command. *Buddhist*: Sparing life in obedience to the command not to kill. *Chinese*: Leadership; authority. *Hindu*: The whisk with the golden handle denotes spiritual and temporal power.

Font *Christian*: Placed at the West door of the church, that is at the entrance to the building, it signifies admission to the Church by baptism. As square in shape it depicts the Holy City; as a pentagon, the five wounds of Christ; as an octagon it represents the NUMBER 8 (q.v.), which is regeneration.

Fool The extreme opposite of the highest temporal power, the King. The fool, clown or jester is the lowest at the court and frequently took the place of the king, in ritual sacrifice, as the scapegoat. The King symbolizes the forces of law and order, the fool those of chaos, hence the licence of the fool or jester who could say or do what he pleased. The fool also represents unregenerate man who does not know whence he came or where he is going but goes on blindly towards the abyss.

Footprints Divine presence or visitation; the form impressed on the universe by the presence or passage of a deity or saintly person or by the Forerunner as a guide to the follower or devotee. Footprints going in opposite directions denote coming and going, past and present, or past and future. *Buddhist*: The Footprints of Buddha have imprinted upon them the Seven Appearances: the swastika, fish, diamond mace, conch shell, flower vase, Wheel of the Law, the crown of Brahma; they symbolize the vestige of divinity, that which man may follow after. *Islamic*: 'If you do not know the way, seek it where his footprints are' (Rumi).

Forelock The crown of the head, the point of complete control. To grasp the forelock is to gain control of the person or animal, or to grasp opportunity.

Forest The realm of the psyche and the feminine principle. A place of testing and initiation, of unknown perils and darkness. Entering the Dark Forest or the Enchanted Forest is a threshold symbol; the soul entering the perils of the unknown; the realm of death; the secrets of nature, or the spiritual world which man must penetrate to find the meaning. It can also represent lack of spiritual insight and light, mankind lost in the darkness without divine direction. Retreat into the forest is symbolic death before initiatory rebirth. *Australian aboriginal*: The Beyond; the realm of shades; the place of initiation. *Druidic*: The sun and the forest are married as male and female, light and darkness. *Hindu*: The 'forest dweller' is one who has left the active world for a life of contemplation, who has 'died' to this world. *Shamanistic*: The dwelling place of the spirits.

Forge *Alchemic*: The sacred fire of the furnace; the power of transmutation of the flame; the generative, masculine, active, inflicting force in conjunction with the passive, receptive, enduring female crucible; the matrix from which metals are born.

Forty See NUMBERS.

Fountain The mother-source; the waters of life as with the 'fountain of life' or the fountain of immortality; eternal life. In the symbolism of Paradise the waters of life issue from the base of the Tree of Life as a fountain which gives rise to the four rivers of Paradise. Fountains in centres of squares, courtyards, cloisters, walled gardens, etc. represent the Cosmic Centre, like the central fountain in Paradise, and are also a source of the living waters and of youth and immortality. Fountains, or jets of water issuing from a mouth, depict the power of speech, of the word, as well as instruction and refreshment. 'Fountains of light' are symbolic of light and

The four arms of Krishna on this 17th-century Dravidian sculpture indicate his divine nature as an avatar of Vishnu, and his human **fluting** is the symbolic expression of the divinity which expressed itself through his body.

The **fountain** in the Van Eycks' *Adoration of the Lamb* is the source of eternal life in that Paradise Garden where the mild, but triumphant, lamb symbolizes the reconciliation of redemption through its own gushing blood.

water proceeding from the same central source. The sealed fountain is virginity. *Christian*: Redemption and purification by the living waters; the flow of the Logos; the fountain of life confers immortality and is also the Holy Spirit. The sealed fountain represents the Virgin Mary. *Hebrew*: The fountain of the living waters is God. *Islamic*: The heaven-sent waters of reality, the drinking of which is gnosis. The sudden access of knowledge or the opening of the 'eye of the heart'. The fountain of grace. The waters of life are the knowledge of God.

Four See NUMBERS.

Fox Slyness; cunning; hypocrisy; craftiness; guile. *Amerindian*: Cunning; craftiness; trickery. *Chinese*: Longevity; craftiness; powers of transformation; ghosts of dead souls. *Christian*: The Devil, the deceiver; cunning; guile; fraud. Feigning death to trap its prey it is the treachery and stratagems of Satan. Spoiling the vines signifies the actions of heretics and enemies of the Church. *Japanese*: Longevity; magic power for good or evil; a messenger; an attribute and messenger of the rice god Inari. Fox-fire is the *ignes fatui*. A black fox is good luck, a white fox, calamity; three foxes, disaster. *Scandinavian*: The 'light of the fox' is the aurora borealis.

Frog Lunar and a rain-bringer; fertility; fecundity; eroticism. As rising from the waters it is renewal of life and resurrection; it is also life and resurrection as possessing the moist skin of life as opposed to the dryness of death. The Great Frog, supporting the universe, represents the dark and undifferentiated *prima materia*; the watery element and the primordial slime, the basis of created matter. *Celtic*: The Lord of the Earth; the power of the healing waters. *Chinese*: The lunar, yin principle. A frog in a well depicts a person of limited vision and understanding. *Christian*: Ambivalent as resurrection but also the repulsive aspect of sin; evil; heretics; grasping at worldly pleasure; envy; avarice. *Egyptian*: The green frog of the Nile is new life and prolific generation; abundance; fertility; the reproductive powers of nature; longevity; strength out of weakness; an attribute of Hekt as the embryonic powers in the waters, protector of mothers and the newborn; also an emblem of Isis. *Graeco-Roman*: Emblem of Aphrodite/Venus; fertility; licentiousness; harmony between lovers. *Hindu*: The Great Frog, supporting the universe, symbolizes the dark, undifferentiated *materia*. See also TOAD.

Fruit Immortality; the essence, the culmination and result of one state and the seed of the next. First fruits represent the best of that which is sacrificed. In Christianity Christ is the First Fruit of the Virgin. The fruit of the Tree of Passion is world-attachment. The fruit of the Tree of Knowledge is the Fall, self-consciousness as separate from God. The fruit of the Tree of Life is immortality. Fruit and flowers

often figure as offerings in rites of the dead; they are also carried by Priapus as fertility. See also various fruits herein.

Fungus *Chinese*: Longevity; immortality; persistence; appears also with cranes and bats as symbols of longevity and happiness. It is a Taoist food of the genii or immortals.

Furnace See FORGE.

Gall Bitterness; rancour.

Garden Paradise; the Fields of the Blessed; the 'better country'; the abode of souls. The Gardener is the Creator and in the centre of the garden grows the life-giving Tree, fruit, or flower, the reward of him who finds the centre. The garden is also the symbol of the soul and the qualities cultivated in it and of tamed and ordered nature. Enclosed gardens are the feminine, protective principle; they also represent virginity. *Christian*: The enclosed garden is a symbol of the Virgin Mary. *Hermetic*: The Good Gardener of Life, who brings to fruit the blossom of the new life, is the Logos. *Inca*: The 'garden of the sun' is an *imago mundi*. *Islamic*: The four gardens of Paradise are those of the Soul, Heart, Spirit, Essence, symbolizing the mystic journey of the soul. *Roman*: Enclosed funerary gardens were regarded as the counterpart of Elysium, with earthly funerary banquets held in the gardens representing Elysian banquets; these gardens were frequently planted with vines, both to provide libations and as a symbol of life and immortality; roses were also planted as signifying eternal Spring. *Taoist*: Miniature gardens are an earthly copy of Paradise.

Gardenia *Chinese*: Feminine grace; subtlety; artistic merit.

Garland Dedication; holiness; setting apart; honour; distinction for a hero or guest; a happy fate; good luck. Garlands also involve the symbolism of binding and linking together; they were used in initiation as a setting-apart and in sacrifice on sacrificial animals or captives of war as sacrifices. In funerary rites they represent the after-life, fruitfulness and happiness, sharing the symbolism of flowers.

Garlic Magic protection; lightning (the smell being regarded as similar).

Garnet See JEWELS.

Gate Shares the symbolism of the THRESHOLD (q.v.) as entrance; communication; entry into a new life; communication between one world and another, between the living and the dead.

It is also the protective, sheltering aspect of the Great Mother. In Christianity the Virgin Mary is the Gate of Heaven. Gates and portals are usually guarded by symbolic animals such as lions, dragons, bulls, dogs or fabulous beasts. At the gates of the House of Osiris a goddess keeps each gate, whose name has to be known. The Gates of the East and West are the doors of the World Temple through which the sun passes morning and night. The 'strait gate' is the central point of communication between the lower and the higher; the passage, in 'spiritual poverty' for initiates or at death, leading to new life. Like the eye of the needle, it symbolizes the spacelessness of the soul in passing through. The gate is associated with wisdom (Proverbs 8, 3); kings sat in judgment at gates, probably as sacred places of divine power. See also DOOR and PASSAGE.

Gazelle The gazelle can change places, symbolically, with the antelope, deer or goat. *Christian*: As fleeing from an animal of prey it is the soul fleeing from earthly passions. *Egyptian*: With the oryx and the goat the gazelle is an attribute of Set in his typhonic aspect. Horus trampling on the gazelle is victory over typhonic powers. *Graeco-Roman*: An attribute of Diana. *Hindu*: With the antelope it is a vehicle of Chandra, the moon god, and a symbol of Siva who rides in a chariot drawn by antelopes. The gazelle or antelope represents Capricorn in the Hindu Zodiac. *Islamic*: Spiritual states: 'My heart, a pasture for gazelles' (ibn Arabi). *Sumero-Semitic*: Attribute of Astarte and of Mullil, god of storms; it occasionally appears with Ea as an antelope.

Gemini See TWINS and ZODIAC.

Giant The brute forces of nature; primordial power and forces; the elemental; darkness; night; winter. The giant can be beneficent or malefic, a defender or an enemy. In Scandinavian mythology frost and hell giants are chthonic powers; fire giants depict the power of fire.

Gilding Gilding or, alternatively, painting red associates an object with solar power and represents the radiance of divine power or the power of flame and fire.

Girdle Ambivalent as either binding to fate or death; or it can depict the circle of life, or sovereignty, wisdom and strength; it can also signify virginity, marital fidelity, or fertility. The girdle of the sword is strength and power; to put on the girdle, or to gird oneself, is to prepare for, or be bound to, some action or to go forth on a mission or journey. The ocean is the girdle of the earth. The girdle of purity of a goddess, saint or virgin is a protective talisman and inhibits the power of a monster, e.g. St George and the Princess, Sir Gawain and the Green Knight, Tripitaka and Monkey. *Christian*: a girdle of cords

On this 18th-century Chinese saucer, the **fungus** expresses the wish that whoever eats from the dish may, like the Immortals whose food it is, enjoy longevity and eventually immortality.

In the **Garden** of Paradise painted by the 15th-century 'Frankfurt Master', nothing is lacking, neither food nor drink, companionship, bird song, living water, nor the company of angels.

represents the cords with which Christ was bound and scourged and binds the wearer to his service; girding the loins is undertaking his work. Monastic girdles are both the cords of Christ and continence in monastic life, also humility; the three knots in the girdle denote poverty, chastity, obedience. The girdle is one of the six eucharistic vestments, depicting sacerdotal chastity and spiritual watchfulness. *Greek*: An attribute of Hippolyta, Queen of the Amazons, as strength and sovereignty. Aphrodite's magic girdle, the Cestus, induced love in all beholders; it is a symbol of fertility. *Hebrew*: The girdle of vestments represents the surrounding ocean. *Hindu*: The varicoloured girdle depicts the cycles of time and its circular shape is the wheel of cosmic order and a symbol of the twice-born, the sacred thread assumed at initiation. *Scandinavian and Teutonic*: The girdle of strength is an attribute of Thor.

Glass See CRYSTAL.

Globe The world as the circle and sphere; eternity; the self-contained; universal sway; dominion over the earth; power; imperial dignity. The globe shares the symbolism of the SPHERE (q.v.) as wholeness. Usually held in the left hand, it represents far-reaching dominion, either of a deity or sovereign. A globe surmounting a pillar depicts the sky, a boundary or terminus. *Alchemic*: A crowned globe is the philosophers' stone and is sometimes called the Great King. *Christian*: A globe surmounted by a cross signifies the rule of Christ over the world, also dominion by faith in Christ. In art the feet of the Father sometimes rest on a globe. Emblem of St Charlemagne. *Graeco-Roman*: Fortune, fate, associated with Tyche/Fortuna who stands on a globe. The globe and compass are emblems of Urania. The blue globe is an attribute of Zeus/Jupiter as sky god, also of Apollo and Cybele.

Glove Evidence of good faith; a gage of honour; purity of heart ('clean hands and a pure heart'); white gloves worn by priests represent purity of heart and freedom from bribery. Taking off gloves signifies respect, sincerity, since the gloved can also be the concealed. To throw down the glove is to engage the honour in a challenge. Iron gloves are an attribute of Thor and smith gods. Gloves accentuate hand gestures and symbolism.

Glow-worm *Chinese*: Perseverance; industry; beauty.

Goad Action; control; movement. *Chinese*: Power; spiritual authority. *Hindu*: Action; the elephant goad is an attribute of Ganesha.

Goat Masculinity; abundant vitality; creative energy. The goat can change places, symbolically, with the gazelle or antelope. Living on high places it also represents superiority. The female goat denotes the feminine generative power; fertility; abundance. *Chinese*: A homophone of yang, it becomes the masculine principle; the good; peace. *Christian*: The Devil; the damned; sinners; lust; lubricity. The scapegoat is Christ burdened with the sins of the world. *Graeco-Roman*: Virility; creative energy; lust. Sacred to Zeus Dictynnos, who was suckled by the goat Amalthea, whose skin became the aegis, the protector and preserver, and whose horn was the cornucopia, abundance and plenty. The wild goat is sacred to Artemis and is an attribute or form of Dionysos. Satyrs are half goats with goats' horns. Pan has the legs, horns and beard of a goat. Sacrificed to Faunus. *Hebrew*: Lewdness. *Hindu*: Fire; creative heat; an attribute, with the ram, of the Vedic fire god Agni, who rides a he-goat. *Scandinavian and Teutonic*: The chariot of Thor, god of thunder and fertility, is drawn by goats, sacred to him. *Sumero-Semitic*: Often appears with Marduk and with hunting goddesses; an emblem of the Babylonian Ningirsu. The goat, or goat-fish, represents Ea-Oannes, Lord of the Watery Deep.

Gold The sun; illumination; the self-luminous; the quality of sacredness; incorruptibility; wisdom; durability; the equilibrium of all metallic properties; nobility; honour; superiority; wealth. Showers of gold symbolize the sun's rays. *Alchemic*: The living gold, product of the interplay between sulphur and quicksilver, the masculine and feminine principles, is the Great Work; attaining the centre; the goal; the sun; the heart; perfection; wholeness; congealed light; the equilibrium of all metallic properties. 'The philosopher's gold resembles common gold neither in colour nor in substance' (*The Golden Tract*). *Aztec*: 'The excrescence of God.' *Buddhist*: Light; illumination. *Chinese*: Harmony; the sun; the yang, with silver as the lunar yin. In Chinese alchemy gold is the cinnabar; the essence of the heavens. *Christian*: Ambivalent as both the pure light, spiritual treasure given by Christ, triumph in adversity, incorruptibility (immersed in filth it retains its purity), but also idolatry (the Golden Calf) and worldly wealth. *Egyptian*: Gold is the flesh of the gods. *Hindu*: Light; immortality; a form of the gods; a life-giver. See also COLOURS.

Golden Bough See BOUGH.

Golden Fleece Doubly solar as the colour gold and being from a solar animal, the golden ram, on which Zeus mounted to the sky. The lamb is also innocence and gold the supreme treasure, hence the quest for the golden fleece is also the search for spiritual illumination, the supreme identity, regaining immortality and the attempt to gain the seemingly unattainable. To attain this it is necessary to overcome the dark side of nature, symbolized by the dragon and Medea, requiring heroic or mystical conquest. The fleece is found on a tree, symbolizing the Tree of Life and is guarded by the dragon as guardian of treasures.

Golden Flower *Taoist*: The light; the Tao; the crystallization of light and the experience of light; the transcendent power; spiritual rebirth. The unfolding of the flower is the development of the spiritual potential in man. Also, in Taoist alchemy, it is the production of gold, the cinnabar, the Elixir of Immortality, the union of the yang sulphur and the yin quicksilver in the unity of the primordial or paradisal state.

Golden Oriole *Amerindian*: Harmony; equilibrium; it is the opposite of the woodpecker.

Goldfinch In Christian art the goldfinch is portrayed as connected with the passion of Christ and with Christ as Saviour, the bird being associated with thorns and thistles. It also denotes fruitfulness and gallantry.

Golgotha 'The place of the skull' is the traditional burying place of Adam's skull and Christ sacrificed there on a cross made from the wood of the Tree of Life symbolizes the redemption of man who fell by the Tree of Knowledge.

Goose Solar (said to follow the sun on migrations); breath; the wind; the 'breath bird'; watchfulness; love; the good housewife. The Michaelmas and Christmas goose represent the waning, then rising, power of the sun. The goose and swan are often interchangeable in symbolism. *Celtic*: War; an attribute of war gods. *Chinese*: The wild goose is a bird of heaven; yang; masculinity; light; inspiration; swiftness; a messenger bird; the bearer of good tidings; conjugal happiness; seasonal change; Autumn. Although solar, the goose is associated with the Autumn moon in Chinese art. *Christian*: Vigilance; providence; emblem of St Martin of Tours. *Egyptian*: The Nile Goose, 'the Great Chatterer', is the creator of the world and laid the Cosmic Egg from which the sun, Amon-Ra, was hatched. The goose is also an attribute of Seb, or Geb, the earth god, and symbolizes love; it is also an emblem of Isis, Osiris and Horus. *Greek*: Love; watchfulness; a good housewife; attribute of Hera, Queen of Heaven. It also symbolizes the solar Apollo; Hermes, the messenger; Mars as war; Eros as love and Peitho as goddess of eloquence and winning speech. *Hindu*: The wild goose, or gander, is a vehicle of Brahma, the creative principle, self-existent being. It also denotes freedom from bondage; spirituality; devotion; learning; eloquence. The Hamsa is depicted as either a goose or a swan. *Japanese*: Autumn; swiftness; a messenger bird; also associated with the Autumn moon in art. *Roman*: Watchfulness; sacred geese were kept in Rome and associated with Mars as war, Juno as Queen of Heaven and Priapus as fertility. *Sumerian*: Sacred to Bau, goddess of the farmyard.

Four stylized **goats**, symbols of Ea-Oannes, Lord of the Waters, are shown on a piece of painted Sumerian pottery, running round a pool.

Jason's **golden fleece**, as painted on this 5th-century BC Greek crater, hung from the tree of life and was guarded by an encircling dragon or serpent; the hero's quest for immortality and knowledge may not avoid an encounter with evil and peril.

Gorgon The Great Mother in her terrible and destructive aspect.

Gourd *Chinese*: Longevity; mystery; necromancy; an emblem of Li T'ieh-kuai, one of the eight Taoist genii or immortals. Smoke rising from a gourd is the setting free of the spirit from the body. *Christian*: Resurrection; pilgrimage; attribute of the Archangel Raphael and of St James the Great.

Graces The Three Graces depict Beauty, Love, Pleasure; Giving, Receiving, Requiting. They are handmaids of Venus and are naked because they 'must be free of deceit' (Servius), or if they are dressed they are in transparent, ungirdled garments 'because benefits want to be seen' (Seneca). In Neo-Platonism they are the threefold aspect of love. In mediaeval art they are Charity, Beauty, Love. Their attributes are the rose, myrtle, apple and sometimes dice.

Grail Variously described as a miraculous provider of food and abundance; a wish-fulfilling dish or vessel whereby 'every knight had such meats and drinks as he best loved'; a stone, the *lapis exilis*, with magical powers which conferred new life on the Phoenix and gave perpetual youth to those who served the Grail, also suggested as the Philosophers' Stone; something which had the power of appearing and moving about without visible means of support and which was made of gold or precious stone and emitted a great radiance; or it is called a chalice and, as such, is taken, in Christian legend, to be the cup of the Last Supper and the cup in which Joseph of Arimathea caught the blood of Christ on the cross. The Grail is generally taken to symbolize the Waters of Life; the Holy of Holies; the Cosmic Centre; the heart; the source of life and immortality; the cup of the magician; the source of abundance; fertility. It occupies the same place in western tradition as the vase in the East, or the sacrificial cup which contained the Vedic Soma, the Mazdean Haoma or the Greek Ambrosia and carries a eucharistic significance, and is the symbolical source of physical and spiritual life.

The Grail, cup or vase can be depicted as the downward-pointing triangle, the receptive, watery, feminine element, and as such is associated with the symbolism of the lance, the active, fiery, masculine element depicted as the upward-pointing triangle. The two together are connected with, and united in, the blood or sacred draught in the cup; the life-blood. The cup-vase and downward triangle is also a symbol of the heart, with which the Grail and Vase are associated as the Centre, both cosmic and in man. In both Egyptian and Celtic symbolism there is an association between the Cup or Vase of Life and the Heart as life-centre. In Christianity the Grail is also the Sacred Heart of Christ. The loss of the Grail represents the loss of the Golden Age, Paradise, man's primordial spirituality, purity and innocence. In Christian legend the Grail was given to Adam but was left in Paradise at the Fall. It is at the centre of Paradise and must be refound, hence the Redeemer (of whom Seth, who achieved re-entry and received the Grail, is the prototype) recovers the chalice and restores Paradise to mankind. The Quest for the Grail is the return to Paradise, the spiritual centre of man and the universe, and follows the symbolic pattern of initiation through trials, tests and encounters with death in the search for the hidden meaning and mystery of life. The quest is usually undertaken by a solar hero, often the son of a widowed mother and brought up in seclusion and in ignorance of his true nature. Grail symbols are the cup or vase, a radiant chalice, a chalice with a heart, the lance, sword, dish, downward-pointing triangle, magical stone. The Quest is sometimes symbolized by the Book, in which case the search is for the Lost Word.

Grain Potentiality; the seed of life; the *multum in parvo*; fertility. *Chinese*: Justice, mercy and virtue due to all beings; the Empire; the earth. *Christian*: The human nature of Christ.

Grapes Wisdom – *in vino veritas*. A bunch of grapes is an attribute of agricultural and fertility deities and represents the wine of life, hence immortality; particularly associated with Dionysos/Bacchus. It also symbolizes sacrifice through the connection between wine and blood; as such it is used in Christian iconography with Christ the sacrificial Lamb of God depicted between bunches of grapes. Sometimes they are used to cover Eve's genitals as opposed to the male fig-leaf. Grapes take on the symbolism of wine in intoxication, hospitality, orgy, youthfulness.

Grass Usefulness; submission. As turf it is the native land. A handful of grass signifies victory, conquest of a land, surrender. *Roman*: A crown of grass was awarded to a military hero or saviour.

Grasshopper *Chinese*: Abundance; numerous sons; virtues; good luck. *European*: Irresponsibility; improvidence; Summer enjoyment. *Greek*: The golden grasshopper depicts nobility, a native aristocrat. *Hebrew*: A scourge.

Grave See TOMB.

Gryphon A fabulous beast with the head and talons of an eagle and body of a lion, without wings, in heraldry. It symbolizes the sun, the sky, the light of dawn turning to gold, also the combined powers of the eagle and lion. As a guardian of treasures it denotes vigilance and vengeance. In the East the gryphon shares the symbolism of the dragon as wisdom and enlightenment. In Greece it was sacred to Apollo as solar, Athene as wisdom and Nemesis as vengeance. In Christianity it depicts evil as the Devil flying away with souls, also those who persecute Christians. Later, with Dante, it became the two natures of Christ and the role of the Pope as spiritual and temporal power.

Guitar *Buddhist*: Excellence in the arts and sciences; harmony of existence in the *deva* world.

Hair The life-force; strength; energy; the life-substance from the head; the power of thought; virility. The hair of the head represents the higher powers and inspiration, while the body hair is the lower power of mind and body. Hair flowing loose depicts freedom, the nubile state; bound, it is the married state and subjection. Shaving off the hair, or cutting it in a tonsure, denotes the ascetic or the dedicated person renouncing the physical powers. Hair standing on end signifies magic power, divine possession, or fear. Dishevelled or torn hair is grief or mourning, but in Hinduism the dishevelled or matted hair of Siva portrays the ascetic, while the black hair of Kali is Time. The systematically curled hair of Buddha represents control of the life-force, serenity, tranquillity. In Christianity long loose hair indicates penitence, or the virgin saints, and long hair in a man is the strength of Samson. Serpent hair, as with the Erinyes and Medusa, represents the baleful aspect of the feminine power. Egyptian royal children are depicted with a heavy tress of hair on the right side of the head. Face-covering hair can play the part of a VEIL (q.v.) and share its symbolism. To steal the hair, or cut off a lock, is to overpower and rob the masculine principle of its solar power in the hair-rays; a castration symbol, e.g. Samson and Delilah.

Hallowe'en The return of Winter, chaos, the breakdown between the living and the dead worlds. Samhuinn, the festival of the dead; the beginning of the Celtic year.

Halo See NIMBUS.

Halter Shares the symbolism of BONDS (q.v.) but has the additional power of control over the head, regarded as the seat of the life-force of the intellect.

Hammer The formative, masculine force; an attribute of all thunder gods. The hammer and anvil together are the formative forces of nature, creation in both the masculine, active, and feminine, passive, aspects. As striking and crushing the hammer represents justice and avenging. The hammer and tongs and the double hammer, or Tau cross, are depicted with all thunder gods, but especially with Hephaestos, Vulcan and Thor. *Chinese*: Divine shaping of the universe; sovereign power driving away darkness and evil. *Christian*:

The **gorgon** on this 6th-century BC Athenian plate epitomizes the dark side of the Great Mother: devouring, fearsome, threatening, staring.

The longevity symbolized by this **gourd**-shaped Ming vase is echoed in the character *shou* (long life) which decorates it.

The **grapes** and wheat in Botticelli's *Madonna of the Eucharist* are the starting point in the Christian miracle of transubstantiation.

A symbol of the passion of Christ. *Egyptian*: The Tau cross is the emblem of Ptah; it is the 'Avenger' and 'Grinder'. *Graeco-Roman*: Thunder, vengeance; attribute of Hephaestos/Vulcan and also of the sky god Zeus/Jupiter. *Hindu*: Thunder; a stone hammer is an emblem of Parashu-Rama. *Japanese*: Wealth; good fortune. *Scandinavian and Teutonic*: The thunder hammer of Thor, the 'Destroyer', when hurled never missed its mark and returned to Thor; it could also revive the dead. It corresponded to Indra's *vajra* and Jupiter's thunderbolt.

Hand One of the most symbolically expressive members of the body. According to Aristotle the hand is 'the tool of tools'. Quintilian says 'the hands may almost be said to speak. Do we not use them to demand, promise, summon, dismiss, threaten, supplicate, express aversion or fear, question or deny? Do we not use them to indicate joy, sorrow, hesitation, confession, penitence, measure, quantity, number and time? Have they not the power to excite and prohibit, to express approval, wonder, shame?' Hands signify power; strength; providence; blessing. The Hand of God is divine power; transmission of spirit; protection; justice. The Great Hand depicts supreme power, the Deity. The hand pushes away evil and trouble. Symbolic attitudes of hands are: *On the breast* – submission, the attitude of a servant or slave. *Clasping* – union; mystic marriage; friendship; allegiance. *Folded* – repose; immobility. *Covering the eyes* – shame; horror. *Crossed at wrists* – binding or being bound. *Laying-on* – transference of power and grace or healing. *On the neck* – sacrifice. *Open* – bounty, liberality, justice. *Clenched* – threat, aggression. *Outstretched* – blessing, protection, welcome. *Placed in another's* – pledge of service, the right hand pledges the life principle. *Placed together* – defencelessness; submission of the vassal before the sovereign; inferiority; inoffensiveness; greeting; allegiance. *Placed on each other palm upwards* – meditation; receptiveness. *Raised* – adoration; worship; prayer; salutation; amazement; horror; also the receiving of the influx of power; *with palm outwards* – blessing, divine grace and favour; *both hands raised* – supplication, weakness; an implication of ignorance; dependence; surrender; also invocation and prayer. *Raised to head* – thought, care. Shaking the hand forms the cross or ankh of covenant, a pledge; washing hands denotes innocence, purification, repudiation of guilt; wringing hands is excessive grief or lamentation.

The right hand is the 'hand of power', it is held up in blessing and pledges the life principle. Josephus writes: 'None of them will deceive you when they have given the right hands nor will anyone doubt their fidelity.' The left hand is the passive aspect of power, receptivity; it is often associated with theft and cheating.

A hand with three fingers, or a mutilated hand, depicts the phases of the moon; with fingers extended and ending in the sun's rays it is

the life-giving power from heaven or the sky. A hand emerging from a cloud denotes divine power and benefits, also majesty. The Talismanic Hand portrayed with the eye and other power symbols typifies clairvoyance and the pyschic power it confers. *Buddhist*: The hand of Buddha is protection; with the palm upwards it represents unlimited giving; in Buddhist iconography the right hand of Buddha touches the earth, depicting his lordship over it, calling the earth to witness; it is the active pole. His left hand, holding the alms bowl, or turning upwards, is receptivity and surrender; the passive pole. In Buddhism and Hinduism *mudra* is the manual expression of divine powers and is a complete language of symbolic positions and movements of hands, too numerous to itemize, but, in general representations, the right hand raised is dauntlessness, or, with the palm upwards, giving; hands together, palm upwards or on the lap, indicate meditation and receptiveness; hands together in front of the heart are the unity of Wisdom and Method. The hand with an eye in the palm denotes the helping hand of compassion and wisdom which is not blind but discriminating. *Celtic*: Lugh's 'long hand' symbolizes the rays of the sun. *Chinese*: Clasped hands are friendliness, allegiance; concealing the hands denotes respect and deference. The right hand is yang and strength and is the opposite of the left hand of honour, except in time of war when the right hand becomes the military hand of honour as the sword hand. The left hand is yin, the weak, the side of honour since strength leads to violence and destruction. *Christian*: The power and might of God. In Christian art the hand appearing from the cloud is the presence and power of God the Father; it sometimes looses the Dove of the Holy Spirit. Hand raised, palm outwards, is blessing, divine grace and favour; with three fingers raised it signifies the Trinity; with the whole hand raised the thumb symbolizes the Father, the first finger the Holy Spirit, the second, Christ and the third and fourth the two natures of Christ. Laying-on of hands at Confirmation is the transmission of the Spirit, power and grace. A hand holding a bag of money represents Judas Iscariot. *Egyptian*: The 'hand of the Egyptians' X̄ depicts the union of fire and water, male and female. *Greek*: The votive Hand of Sabazios has the thumb and first finger extended, with the third and fourth fingers crooked (the Cornuto), and has on it the cone, snake, cross, crescent, caduceus, lizard, insects. It is suggested as the helping hand of the god, or protection, healing and blessing, or that the three fingers are the triad or male trinity, or that it is merely talismanic and apotropaic. *Hebrew*: The Hand of God is 'the right hand of the majesty on high'. *Hindu*: With the hands of Siva, the uplifted hand is peace and protection, the lowered hand, pointing to the foot, depicts deliverance, the drum beat is the creative act and the flame in the hand denotes the destruction of the world by fire. *Islamic*: The open hand signifies benediction, adoration and hospitality. The Hand of Fatima represents the Hand of God, divine power, providence and generosity. The thumb is the Prophet and the fingers are his four companions, the first the Lady Fatima, second Ali, her husband, third and fourth Hasan and Husain, their sons. The fourth finger is also spiritual and moral excellencies and the five together are the five fundamental dogmas and the five pillars of religion. *Mandaean*: In ceremonies the joining of the hands symbolizes truth and faithfulness. *Manichean*: Shaking the right hand signifies the saving power of the deity. *Sumero-Semitic*: The hand is an attribute of the Great Mother as bounteous giver and protector. The votive hand, as that of Sabazios, is frequently found in Syria. *Toltec*: The 'long hand' of Huemac depicts the sun's rays.

Hare A lunar animal, attribute of all moon deities; as closely connected with the moon it represents rebirth, rejuvenation, resurrection, also intuition, 'light in darkness'. It is often associated with sacrificial fire and 'life through death'. It is universally a fertility symbol and typifies feminine periodicity; it is a love gage; timidity; the inverted; crafty wisdom; fleetness. The hare in the moon is almost universal and, as lunar, with the dog and lizard it acts as an intermediary between lunar deities and man. In the West the white hare symbolizes snow; the March hare madness. A hare's head or foot is a specific against witchcraft, but the hare is often the servant or companion of witches. *African*: Associated with the moon by the Hottentots. *Amerindian*: The Great Hare, Manabozho, father and guardian, is a creator and transformer, changing man's animal nature. He is the Hero Saviour, a demiurge, Hero of the Dawn, the personification of Light; the Great Manitou who lives in the moon with his grandmother and is 'provider of all waters, master of winds and brother of the snow'. A later development of Trickster into Hero signifies integrated man. As Trickster it is also nimble mind outwitting dull brute force. He slew the snake, or fish, devouring the people. *Buddhist*: The hare in the moon was translated there by Buddha and symbolizes total sacrifice of the self since, when Buddha was hungry, the hare offered itself as a sacrifice and jumped into the fire. *Celtic*: An attribute of lunar and hunter deities, often held in the hand of hunter gods. *Chinese*: The moon; a yin animal; the feminine yin power; the imperial female consort; longevity. The hare is the fourth of the symbolic animals of the Twelve Terrestrial Branches. The hare in the moon, with pestle and mortar, mixes the elixir of immortality. The hare is the guardian of wild animals. The white hare is divinity; the red, good fortune, peace, prosperity and virtuous rulers; the black, good fortune and a successful reign. Figures of hares or white rabbits were made for the moon festival. *Christian*: Fecundity; lust. A white hare

A **hand** carved on the doorway of the Alhambra is a perennial symbol of the five basic precepts of Islam: profession of faith, prayer, pilgrimage, fasting and charity.

The **hare** in the moon on this Tung dynasty bronze mirror-back is pounding the elixir of immortality in the pestle and mortar of appearances and humdrum daily life.

at the feet of the Virgin Mary depicts triumph over lust. The defencelessness of the hare represents those who put their trust in Christ. *Egyptian*: The dawn; the beginning; the opening; uprising; periodicity; an emblem of Thoth; also associated with the moon. *European*: The Easter hare, rabbit or bunny symbolizes dawn and a new life; it is an attribute of the hare-headed moon goddess, probably Oestra (Teutonic) or Eostre (Anglo-Saxon) who gives her name to Easter; hence rebirth and resurrection as the rebirth of the moon. The Easter hare lays the Easter egg. *Graeco-Roman*: Fertility; lubricity; a messenger animal; attribute of Hermes/Mercury, also of Aphrodite and Eros. Cupids are often portrayed with hares. *Hebrew*: The unclean. *Hindu*: Appears with the crescent moon in Hindu and Buddhist art. *Scandinavian*: Freyja has attendant hares. *Teutonic*: Holda, Harke, or Harfa, the moon goddess, is followed by hares as a train of torch-bearers. The Easter hare is connected with Oestra.

Harp Shares the symbolism of the LADDER (q.v.) as leading to the next world. The harpist is Death. An emblem of King David in the Old Testament, and of Wales, and an attribute of Dagda, the Celtic fire god, who calls up the seasons and whose playing originally brought about the change of the seasons.

Harpy See FABULOUS BEASTS.

Hart Solitude; purity. In Christian symbolism it signifies religious aspiration and fervour, the catechumen thirsting after knowledge as 'the hart panteth after the water-brook'. The hart trampling on the serpent is Christ overcoming the power of evil.

Hat Authority; power. Since the hat covers the head it contains thought, hence to change hats is to change attitudes or opinions. The covered head, as with the cap, denotes nobility and freedom in contradistinction to the bare-headed slave. Different hats depict social or hierarchical orders, e.g. the cardinal's hat, the mitre, biretta, clerical hat, top hat, 'mortar board', dunce's cap. Raising the hat is the courtesy of suggesting social inferiority to the person saluted; removing the hat on entering a building shows homage.

Hawk A solar bird with much the same symbolism as the EAGLE (q.v.); it is an attribute of all sun gods and represents the heavens; power; royalty; nobility. Like the eagle, it was regarded as being able to fly up to the sun and gaze on it without flinching. Gods with a hawk, or hawk-headed, are sun gods. *Aztec*: A messenger of the gods. *Egyptian*: The royal bird; the Spirit; the soul; inspiration; the Bird of Khensu; Ra, the sun. Other gods with hawks, or hawk-headed, are Ptah, Horus, Mentu, Rehu, Sokar, Kebhsenuf. The hawk-headed crocodile

is Sebek-Ra; the sphinx is sometimes hawk-headed. The hawk is also an emblem of Amenti, Great Mother and goddess of the West and the underworld. *Graeco-Roman*: The 'swift messenger of Apollo'; attribute of Circe. *Hindu*: Gayatri, the hawk, brought soma from heaven. The hawk is also a vehicle of Indra. *Iranian*: An attribute of Ahura Mazda, or Ormuzd, as light. *Mithraic*: An attribute of Mithra as sun god.

Hawthorn *European*: A fairy flower; apotropaic. Wearing a may-flower garland symbolizes virginity, chastity, or miraculous virgin conception. Hawthorn was the Graeco-Roman bridal flower, sacred to Hymen, Chloris, Hecate, Flora and the Roman Maia; it protected against sorcery. Spirits and fairies meet at hawthorn trees.

Hazel Like all nuts, a symbol of hidden wisdom and associated with the Mother Goddess. Hazel nuts also represent peace and lovers. The hazel wand has magic powers, it is a rain-maker and used in dowsing to find water. Hazel was the sacred tree of the Celtic groves and represented wisdom, inspiration, divination, magic and chthonic powers. As the Tree of Life it grew in Avalon beside the sacred pool or well containing the SALMON (q.v.) and only the salmon might eat the nuts. It was also associated with the milk-yielding goddess and the fire god as its twigs were used in fire-making. In Greece it was the rod of Hermes, messenger of the gods, hence it symbolized communication and reconciliation. It also signified poetic inspiration. In Scandinavian and Teutonic religions it was sacred to Thor. In the Old Testament Jacob used the magic hazel-twigs to produce the mottled sheep and cattle.

Head Regarded, with the heart, as the chief member of the body, the seat of life-force and the soul and its power; it denotes wisdom; mind; control; rule. The head is the seat of both intelligence and folly and is the first object of both honour and dishonour: the crown of glory and wreath of victory are placed on the head, but so are the ashes of mourning and penitence, the fool's cap and 'coals of fire'. In consecration and dedication the head is crowned or shaven. Images of heads on tombs or as memorials represent the life-force or genius of the person contained in the head, hence the use of 'busts'. The heads of flowers contain the seeds of future life. Heads with wings signify the life-force, the soul and supernatural wisdom. Heads of horses, oxen or boars, sacrificed or hunted, contained the vital force and fertility and were hung up or carried in ritual processions, or served as food on ritual occasions. Head-hunters acquire the vital force and fertility of the victim. Bowing the head lowers the seat of the life-force before another in honour or submission. To nod the head is to pledge the life-force.

The veiled head (see also VEIL) is either inscrutability, secrecy and hidden knowledge,

or the heads of sacrifices were often veiled and
garlanded, hence the veil and garland of the
bride, or nun, who sacrifices, and dies to, her old
life. The veil also protects the inner life in the
head, as covering the head with hats, caps etc.
and the head-covering of married women.

Two-headed gods and figures, such as Janus,
symbolize the beginning and the end; past and
future; yesterday and today; solar and lunar
power, also Lunus-Luna; the descending and
ascending power of the sun; the choice of the
cross-roads; destiny; the beginning of any
enterprise or journey, departure and return; the
powers of opening and closing of doors, hence
keys are an attribute of Janus and of guardians
of doors. The two heads also represent judgment
and discernment; cause and effect; seeing
inwards and outwards. With male and female
heads joined, or the king and queen, the
androgyne is portrayed, unifying the opposites;
this figure also symbolizes spiritual and
temporal power. There is also the two-headed
figure of Prudence, looking both ways. The two
heads of Janus also signify the *Janua inferni*, the
Summer solstice in Cancer, the 'door of men'
and the descent and waning power of the sun,
and the *Janua coeli*, the Winter solstice in
Capricorn, the 'door of the gods' and the ascent
and increasing power of the sun. The two heads
of the Dioscuri, looking upward and downward,
depict the alternate appearance of the sun in the
upper and lower hemispheres; also day and
night. Triple-headed gods symbolize the three
realms; past present and future; the three phases
of the moon; the rising, noon and setting sun.
Serapis, Hecate and sometimes Cernunnos are
so represented. Astral divinities with plural
heads are the All-seeing, or can depict the
number of cycles or seasons. Animal or monster
heads holding a ring in the jaws are guardians of
the way. Heads as fountains depict the power of
speech, also refreshment. *Celtic*: Solar; divinity;
other-world wisdom and power. A head
surmounting a pillar is phallic; a head with
phallus denotes fertility and is also funerary and
apotropaic: there is a traditional Celtic association between the head and phallus. The god
Cernunnos is sometimes portrayed as triple-
headed. *Christian*: Christ, the Head of the
Church. Beheaded saints, with a head as
emblem, are Alban, Clair, Denis, Peter,
Valerie. *Greek*: The 'head' of corn which,
according to Plato, is 'the image of the world',
was identified with Ceres as fertility and was the
central symbol of the Eleusinian mysteries.
Hebrew (Qabalism): The *Arik Anpin*, the Vast
Countenance, is the Supreme Deity. *Hindu*: The
four heads of Brahma are the sources of the four
Vedas. *Scandinavian*: The head of the boar,
emblem of Freyja, contained the vital force,
hence at Yuletide it symbolized abundance and
good fortune for the coming year. *Slav*: The
early Slav triple-headed god looked at the sky,
earth and sea; heaven, earth and hell; past,
present and future. *Sumero-Semitic*: The Semitic
El and Sumerian Marduk are depicted with two

The Egyptian god Horus with arms outstretched in
libation, perhaps to his mother Isis, to whom he was
born as the sun, symbolized by his **hawk** head.

Hermes with two **heads**, guardian of roads and
ways, looks in both directions, scrutinizing past and
future, destiny and choice, departure and return – all
double aspects of a single phenomenon.

heads, looking left and right and having the same significance as Janus.

Heart The centre of being, both physical and spiritual; the divine presence at the centre. The heart represents the 'central' wisdom of feeling as opposed to the head-wisdom of reason; both are intelligence, but the heart is also compassion; understanding; the 'secret place'; love; charity; it contains the life-blood. The heart is symbolized by the sun as a centre of life and the rayed sun and radiant or flaming heart share the same symbolism as centres of the macrocosm and microcosm, as the heavens and man and as transcendent intelligence. The heart is also portrayed by the downward-pointing triangle. *Aztec*: The centre of man, religion and love; the unifying life-principle. The heart sacrifice represented the liberating of the life-blood, the seed of life, to germinate and flower. The pierced heart is penitence. *Buddhist*: The essential nature of Buddha. The Diamond Heart is purity and indestructibility and the man whom nothing can 'cut' or disturb. In Chinese Buddhism the heart is one of the Eight Precious Organs of Buddha. *Celtic*: The kind heart symbolizes generosity and compassion; it is the antithesis of the evil eye. *Christian*: Love; understanding; courage; joy and sorrow. The flaming heart depicts religious fervour, zeal and devotion. A heart in the hand portrays love and piety; a heart pierced by an arrow is the contrite heart, repentance; an emblem of St Augustine. A heart crowned with thorns is an emblem of St Ignatius Loyola; a heart with a cross is an emblem of SS Bernadine of Siena, Catherine of Siena, Teresa. *Hebrew*: The heart is the Temple of God. *Hindu*: The Divine Centre, dwelling-place of Brahma: 'It is Brahma; it is all'; the Atman. The heart is symbolized by the lotus. The 'eye of the heart' is the third eye of Siva, transcendent wisdom, the omniscient spirit. See also 'Diamond Heart' in *Buddhist* above. *Islamic*: The Centre of Being; the 'eye of the heart' is the spiritual centre; the absolute intellect; illumination. *Taoist*: The seat of the understanding. The Sage has seven orifices in his heart, all open.

Hearth An omphalos; the interior spiritual centre; the transference of the spirit by fire. The centre of the home; feminine domination; fire in its feminine-earth aspect, but the fire can also take on the masculine aspect with the earth as the feminine; warmth; provision of food. The Vedic round hearth is the earth, the realm of man, while the fire to the East is the realm of the gods. Among South American Indians the hearth-stone is named the 'bear', signifying subterranean powers and the point of communication with them. In Celtic countries the cult of the dead centred on the hearth.

Heaven Heaven and earth represent spirit and matter and, usually, the Father and Mother principles, with notable exceptions in Egyptian,

Teutonic and Oceanic symbolism, when the position is reversed. In sacred architecture the heavens are depicted by the dome, stupa, chörten, or the open central hole of a tepee, tent or sacred lodge. Universally portrayed as blue in colour, but occasionally as black, and as round or domed in shape. In the Far East the heavens are symbolized by the Dragon and the earth by the White Tiger, also by mist and mountain, horse and bull.

Hedgehog *Christian*: The Evil One; evil-doing; robbing vines of grapes as the Devil robs men of souls. It is also a Sumerian emblem of Ishtar, and more generally a symbol of the Great Mother.

Heel The vulnerable part of an otherwise invulnerable person, e.g. Krishna, Achilles, but it is also the part which kills the serpent and grinds under evil.

Heliotrope *European*: The herb of the sun; eternal devotion; love. Sacred to Apollo and Clytie.

Helmet Protection; preservation; the attribute of a warrior or hero. In heraldic symbolism the helmet denotes hidden thought. It is an attribute of Ares/Mars as war and of Athene/Minerva as thought; it is also an emblem of Hades/Pluto as the helmet of darkness. The golden helmet is an emblem of Odin/Woden.

Hemlock Death; deceit; ill-luck.

Hen Procreation; providence; maternal care. A black hen is a diabolical agent, or an aspect of the Devil. A crowing hen is feminine dominion or a bold woman. In Christianity, the hen with chickens depicts Christ with his flock.

Hermaphrodite See ANDROGYNE.

Hero/Heroine The prototype of the Saviour; the miraculous. The hero is usually of humble birth, or of noble birth unknown to him, and is reared in simple circumstances in ignorance of his state; he undergoes early trials of strength, frequently alone or with some animal companion; he struggles with evil and temptation, is betrayed and killed or sacrificed. Alternatively he may start alone but collects crowds, or a select band of disciples, who finally leave him to suffer and die alone, symbolizing the journey of the soul and emergence into manifestation and multiplicity and the final return to primordial unity. In the case of the hero and an immortal bride, he often has to seek her in the underworld or some mysterious place. The heroine may be haughty, disdainful or in an ugly disguise, symbolizing the egoistic side of man's nature which must be subdued; but the symbolism remains that of separation and reunion; fall and redemption – the two sides of man's nature which must be reconciled and integrated.

Heron A solar bird which shares much of the symbolism of the stork and crane; it is also vigilance and quietness. It is also a bird of the waters. *Buddhist and Taoist*: Takes on the symbolism of the CRANE (q.v.). *Chinese and Japanese*: The white heron is associated with the black crow as yin-yang, solar and lunar, light and darkness, the one serious and silent, 'the Thinker', and the other mischievous and chattering. The crane represents tact and delicacy since it rises from the water without stirring the mud; it is associated with the willow tree in art. *Egyptian*: The first transformer of the soul after death. The Bennu is thought to have been a species of heron, or possibly the phoenix, as it is also symbolic of the rising sun, regeneration, the return of Osiris, as the bird of the flooding of the Nile and renewal of life, since it leaves the river and flies over the fields when the Nile rises.

Hexagram As the two interlocking TRIANGLES (q.v.) the hexagram symbolizes 'as above so below', etc. *Chinese*: The Eight Trigrams, or PA KUA (q.v.), are symbolically linked, each representing yin-yang powers and forces in nature. These are expanded into the sixty-four hexagrams, signifying the endless interaction between those forces.

Hippogryph See FABULOUS BEASTS.

Hippopotamus Sometimes equated with the Behemoth of the Old Testament. In Egyptian symbolism it represents the Great Mother, Amenti, the 'bringer-forth of the waters'; Taueret, the hippopotamus goddess, signifies bounty and protection. The red hippopotamus is Set in his typhonic aspect, and the thigh of the hippopotamus is the 'phallic leg of Set' as power and virility; it also depicts the North Pole.

Hive The earth governed by the feminine power in nature; the earth-soul; protective motherhood; industry; thrift. The hive is also an attribute of the figure of Hope. In Christianity St Bernard equates it with the ordered, cloistered community. See also BEEHIVE.

Hog See SWINE.

Hole The Void; emptiness. The hole takes on the symbolism of both depth and height: as the hole in the earth it is the feminine fertility principle and shares the symbolism of all hollow things; as the hole in the roof of a temple, tepee, sacred lodge, etc., it is the opening upwards to the celestial world and is the door or gateway to the spiritual. Passing through it man leaves the earthly and assumes the heavenly guise. The heavens are depicted as a round hole, the earth as a square hole.

Holly Good will; joy; an attribute of sun gods. In Rome the holly was sacred to Saturn and

Seal of the Catholic Confederacy, which was proclaimed in Ireland in 1642. The flaming **heart** is the dominant symbol, for religious zeal; it is accompanied by CROWN, CROSS, DOVE and HARP.

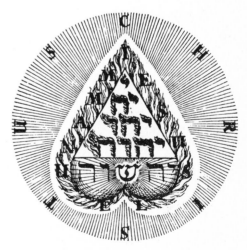

Inverted **heart**, a Qabalist figure by Jakob Boehme (1575–1624) in which JHVH, the name of God, in Hebrew letters, is converted into JHSHVH, Jehoshua (Jesus).

used in the Saturnalia as a symbol of health and happiness. In Christianity it is sometimes depicted as the tree of the cross (as are also the oak and aspen), its spiked leaves signifying the crown of thorns and the passion and its red berries being the blood of Christ. It is an emblem of SS Jerome and John the Baptist. It is apotropaic.

Honey Immortality; initiation; rebirth. Honey was supposed to impart virility, fertility and vigour and to have an aphrodisiac quality. It was used as an offering to supreme deities and fertility spirits. The imagined parthenogenic origin of bees made honey an uncontaminated sacred food. In astrology honey was associated with the moon and thus with increase and growth. *Chinese*: Honey, with oil, is false friendship. *Christian*: The earthly ministry of Christ; the sweetness of the divine word. *Greek*: Poetic genius; eloquence; wisdom; the food of the gods. Bees filled the mouths of Homer, Sappho, Pindar and Plato with honey. It was also used in chthonic rites. *Hindu*: The food of the Hamsa, feeding on the lotus of knowledge. *Jain*: A forbidden food on account of its aphrodisiac quality and as being offered to fertility spirits. *Minoan*: Played an important part in ritual as a food for both the living and the dead. *Mithraic*: Offered to Mithra, probably indicating the bees as the stars of heaven. It was also poured on the hands and tongue of the initiated. *Sumerian*: A food for the gods.

Hood Invisibility and, by analogy, death; withdrawal. As a covering for the head it is also thought, spirit. Cronos/Saturn sometimes has a hood, with his sickle, as the setting, or waning Autumn, sun. An attribute of the Celtic god of the underworld, the Peaked Red One.

Hook Ambivalent as both drawing towards, hence attraction, and captivity and punishment. *Christian*: That which draws out of the floods of the world, Christ, or the Logos. *Egyptian*: In the hands of Osiris the hook depicts attraction. *Graeco-Roman*: An attribute of Dionysos and Priapus. *Hindu*: The iron hook signifies doom.

Hope Symbolized in the West by the anchor, or a woman with a globe, cornucopia, pear or beehive; sometimes she has a galleon in full sail surmounting her head. In Christian art she is represented as a winged woman with hands raised to heaven and with an anchor or St James the Great at her feet. Other emblems of hope are the cross of the resurrection and a crown presented by an angel. In Egypt Isis also signifies hope.

Horns Supernatural power; divinity; the power of the soul or life-principle arising from the head, thus horns on helmets or headdress confer double power; the power and dignity of divinity; manifestation of the spirit; royalty; strength; victory; protection; virility; abun-

dance in cattle and agriculture. Horns are both solar and lunar as attributes of the sun gods and as the lunar crescent and the waxing and waning moon; lunar animals without horns depict the last phase of the waning moon. Horns are attributes of all Mother Goddesses, Queens of Heaven; the cow-horn crescent often appears with the solar disk, particularly in Egyptian art.

Horned gods represent warriors, fecundity in both humans and animals, and are lords of animals; their attributes are horns of bulls or cows as signifying honour, dignity and power, and horns of rams or goats as generative power and fertility; they also wear antlers and have with them the serpent, or the ram-headed serpent. Horns with a long ribbon falling from them denote a storm god. As sharp and piercing horns are masculine and phallic, but as hollow they are feminine and receptive. The power of horns can be beneficent or malefic according to the context. Later, in mediaeval England, horns became a symbol of disgrace, contempt, turpitude and the cuckold, Christianity having adapted the Horned God to the Devil and an evil power. *Amerindian*: The head is armed with horns 'that he may appear terrible'. *Celtic*: Fecundity; the Horned God is the Lord of Animals. Cernunnos, 'the Horned One', a stag-god, is accompanied by a ram-headed or stag-headed serpent. *Christian*: The two horns are the Old Testament and New Testament by which the adversary can be overcome. The seven horns of the Apocalypse are the Seven Spirits of God; omniscience and power. Horns were later adopted as a symbol of the Devil. *Egyptian*: The cow horns are the symbol of Hathor as the Great Mother; as the lunar crescent they appear with Isis and Nut, Lady of Heaven. The horns of the bull are solar, while the solar and lunar symbols appear together as the cow horns supporting the solar disk. The horns of Ammon are curled like a ram's horns. Set/Sutek has horns with a long ribbon falling from them, denoting the storm god. *Graeco-Roman*: Dionysos is often depicted with horns. Pan is a horned nature god and his satyrs are horned depicting virility and fertility. Pluto, as god of wealth, has the horn of plenty and the cornucopia is the horn of plenty or the 'horn of Amaltheia', giver of wealth and abundance. *Hebrew*: Power; the 'raising of horns' is victory and the 'breaking of horns' is defeat. Moses is sometimes depicted with horns of power. *Hindu*: The four horns of the Rig Veda are the four cardinal points. *Islamic*: Strength; 'exalting the horn' is victory; success. *Minoan*: Horns are found in conjunction with the tree, altar and double axe as symbols of power and divinity. The 'horns of consecration' are suggested as the lunar crescent, also as an aniconic representation of an indwelling divinity. *Scandinavian*: Power, virility; warriors. *Sumero-Semitic*: Divinity; the supreme principle; power, both solar and lunar. The horned headdress is worn by Asshur, Anu and Bel; Adad, as storm god, has horns with a long ribbon falling from a crown.

Horse Ambivalent as it is solar power when the
white, golden or fiery horses appear with sun
gods, drawing their chariots, but lunar as the
humid element, the sea and chaos and the steeds
of the oceanic gods; thus the horse is both a life
and a death symbol, solar and lunar. It also
symbolizes the intellect; wisdom; mind; reason;
nobility; light; dynamic power; fleetness; the
swiftness of thought; the swift passage of life; it is
also instinctual animal nature; magic powers of
divination; the wind; the waves of the sea. The
horse appears also with fertility gods and the
Vanir. It can be ridden by the Devil and then
becomes phallic, or by the Wild Huntsman or
the Erl-King, when it becomes death. The
winged horse is the sun or the Cosmic Horse, as
is also the white horse, and represents pure
intellect; the unblemished; innocence; life and
light, and is ridden by heroes.

At a later date the horse replaced the bull as a
sacrificial animal; both represented the sky and
fertility gods, masculine virility and fertility as
well as the chthonic and humid powers. The
white horse of the ocean is also related to both
the fiery and humid principles. The lion slaying
the horse or bull depicts the sun drying up
moisture and mists. The black horse is funerary
and heralds death and symbolizes chaos; it
appears at the twelve days of chaos between the
old and new year. The sacrifice of the October
horse signified the death of death. *Buddhist*: The
indestructible; the hidden nature of things. The
winged, or cosmic, horse 'Cloud' is a form of
Avalokitesvara or Kwan-yin. Buddha left his
home on a white horse. In Chinese Buddhism
the winged horse bore the Book of the Law on its
back. *Celtic*: The attribute, or form, of horse
deities such as Epona, the Great Horse, the
goddess-mare, Medb of Tara and Macha of
Ulster, protectors of horses, as chthonic
divinities and powers of the dead. The horse can
also be solar as virility and fecundity; also a
psychopomp and messenger of the gods. *Chinese*:
The heavens; fire; yang; the South; speed;
perseverance; good omen. The horse is the
seventh of the symbolic animals of the Twelve
Terrestrial Branches. Its hoof (not shoe) is good
luck. When the cosmic horse is solar it is
opposed to the cow of the earth; but if it appears
with the dragon, which symbolizes heaven, the
horse then represents the earth. The winged
horse, bearing the Book of the Law on its back,
depicts good fortune and wealth. In marriage
symbolism the horse signifies speed and
accompanies the lion of strength for the
bridegroom, while flowers represent the bride.
The horse also typifies fertility and power of the
ruler. *Christian*: The sun; courage; generosity.
Later, at the Renaissance, it became lust. In the
catacombs it depicted the swift passage of life.
The four horses of the Apocalypse are war,
death, famine and pestilence. The horse is the
emblem of SS George, Martin, Maurice,
Victor, and wild horses of St Hippolytus.
Egyptian: The horse is notably absent from
Egyptian symbolism. *Greek*: White horses draw

On this Cheyenne Indian ritual rattle the **horns**
enhance the spectral look of the face and the
frightening noise made when it was shaken.

The **horse** on this Roman sarcophagus is lunar,
mortal, as it endures its death-struggle in the power
of the supreme solar animal, the lion, symbol of
vigorous life and endurance.

the solar chariot of Phoebus and are associated also, as the humid principle, with Poseidon as god of the sea and earthquakes and springs who can appear as a horse. The Dioscuri ride white horses. Pegasus depicts the passage from one plane to another; he carries the thunderbolt of Zeus. Centaurs appear frequently in the rites of Dionysos. See also CENTAUR. *Hindu*: The horse is the bodily vehicle and the rider the spirit. Manu's mare is deified earth. Kalki, a white horse, is to be the last incarnation or vehicle of Vishnu when he appears for the tenth time, bringing peace and salvation to the world. Varuna, the cosmic horse, is born of the waters. The Gandhavas, men-horses, represent a combination of natural fecundity and abstract thought, intelligence and music. The horse is the guardian of the South. *Iranian*: The chariot of Ardvisura Anahita is drawn by the four white horses of wind, rain, cloud and sleet and the chariot of the Magi is drawn by four chargers, the four elements and their gods. *Islamic*: Happiness; wealth. *Japanese*: A white horse is the vehicle or form of Bato Kwannon (the Buddhist Avalokitesvara of India and the Kwan-yin of China), goddess of mercy and a Great Mother; she can appear either as a white horse, or horse-headed, or having a horse figure in her crown. The black horse is the rain god's attribute. *Mithraic*: White horses draw the chariot of Mithra as a Sun God. *Roman*: White horses draw the chariots of Apollo and Mithra. Epona, adopted from the Celts, became the Roman horse goddess and the protector of horses; she was also a funerary deity. The Dioscuri ride white horses. The horse is an attribute of Diana, the huntress. *Scandinavian and Teutonic*: Sacred to Odin/Woden who had an eight-legged mare, Sleipnir. The horse appears with the Vanir as gods of the fields, forests, sun and rain. Clouds are the steeds of the Valkyrie. *Shamanistic*: A psychopomp; passage from this world to the next. The horse is also associated with sacrifice and is the sacrificial animal of Shamanism in Siberia and the Altai; its skin and head take on ritual importance, the skin, like the fleece, representing the fat and the head containing the life-principle. *Sumero-Semitic*: The chariot of the sun god Marduk was drawn by four horses. The horse's head was the emblem of Carthage. The winged horse appears on Assyrian bas-reliefs and Carthaginian coins. *Taoist*: The horse is an attribute of Ch'ang Kuo, one of the eight Taoist genii or immortals. See also STALLION.

Horseshoe When turned upwards and crescent-shaped it represents the moon and moon goddesses and takes on the symbolism of the horns of power and protection. It can also depict the yoni; it is apotropaic and good luck. Inverted, it is emptied of power and luck.

Hourglass Time; transitoriness; the swift passage of life; the running out of time; death. The two sections also portray the cyclic

recurrence of life and death; the heavens and the earth; the sand running down is the attraction of the lower nature, the world. The hourglass is an attribute of the Reaper, Death, Father Time, who, as a skeleton, holds it with the scythe. In Christian art the figure of Temperance sometimes holds an hourglass. It is also a symbol of INVERSION (q.v.).

House A world centre; the sheltering aspect of the Great Mother; an enclosing symbol; protection. The cult house, hut, lodge or tepee of tribal religions is the Cosmic Centre, 'our world'; the universe; it is the *regressus ad uterum* of initiation, descent into the darkness before rebirth and regeneration.

Hunt/Huntsman Death; active participation; desire; the pursuit of worldly ends. The Wild Huntsman with his pack of hounds is Death in pursuit of his victim.

Hyacinth *European*: Prudence; peace of mind; heavenly aspiration. The blood of Hyacinthus, from which the hyacinth sprang when he was killed accidentally by Apollo, symbolizes vegetation scorched by the heat of the Summer sun; but the flower springing from the blood represents resurrection in Spring. Also an emblem of Cronos.

Hydra See FABULOUS BEASTS.

Hyena Nameless vice; impurity; instability; inconstancy; a two-faced person. In Christianity it is an image of the Devil feeding on the damned.

Hyssop Purging; purification; an apotropaic. In Christianity it signifies penitence; humility; its purgative properties depict innocence regained, hence baptism.

Ibex In Egypt sacred to Set and Reshep and shares the symbolism of the GAZELLE (q.v.).

Ibis *Egyptian*: The soul; aspiration; perseverance; the morning; sacred to Thoth. The crested ibis is the sun; the 'Blessed Spirit'; as a destroyer of reptiles in their malefic aspect the ibis is solar, but as belonging to the watery element it is lunar and is sometimes depicted with the crescent moon on its head.

Ice Rigidity; frigidity; brittleness; impermanence. Ice represents the gross waters of the earth as opposed to the 'fresh' and living waters of the fountain of Paradise. It also denotes hardness of heart; the coldness and absence of love. Melting ice is the softening of the hardness of heart.

Icon An icon symbolizes a microcosm; its colours must be unmixed, and the gold background is the light and grace of God and God as the background of all. Its materials represent the manifest world, comprising the animal, vegetable and mineral kingdoms and symbolizing the inter-relatedness of all creation. The icon is sacramental in that it is 'the outward and visible sign of an inward and spiritual grace' or meaning, a channel of divine grace. The icon screen, the iconostasis, in the Eastern Church, divides heaven and earth vertically by the arch (heaven) and the sides and ground (earth) and horizontally by separating the chancel from the nave. It is a boundary between the sacred and profane, the divine and human.

I.H.S. Symbol of Dionysos, its meaning is unknown but has been suggested as *in hoc signo, in hac salus* or the ritual cry 'Iacchos'. Adopted by Christians as an abbreviation of 'Jesus' and later taken as *Iesous Hominum Salvator*. Inscribed on a heart it is an emblem of SS Bernardino of Siena, Ignatius Loyola, Teresa.

Immersion Baptism by immersion symbolizes the return to the primordial waters of life and pristine innocence; transformation; renewal; rebirth. Immersion in water is an act of rebirth, as a rite it purifies, revitalizes and protects.

This 14th-century Islamic ceramic is shaped like a **horseshoe**, so that the building into whose wall it was set would always prosper and enjoy good luck.

Immobility Like the central point of the circle, immobility symbolizes the Eternal Now, the *nunc stans*: the unconditioned state; the non-dual present; the 'unmoved mover'; the liberated Self. In iconography rigidity and immobility express inflexibility, superhuman impassivity and impartiality.

Imp Disorder; tormenting. In Christian art imps help the Devil in hell.

Incense Homage to the deity; purification; suggests the 'subtle body' as rising and a spiritual substance; the 'perfume that deifies'; a medium for passing the 'double' in communication between man and gods; a medium for wafting the soul to heaven; prayer rising to heaven; the perfume of virtue and fragrance of a pure life. Incense is also apotropaic, puts demons to flight and exorcises evil spirits. As the resin exuded from trees and which was regarded as the soul-substance, it is 'the tears of the Great Mother'. Pine and cedar from which the resin is obtained are of great vitality and were thought to preserve from corruption, and these qualities are shared by their soul-substance. Incense was also regarded as symbolizing, and a substitute for, burnt offering.

A 4th-century Egyptian sculpture of an **ibis** combines the bird as symbol of the soul's perseverance with the ostrich feather, symbol of truth and justice.

Incest Among gods and in legend and myth, incest is a symbol of original identity; reinstating the original unity by marriage of the separate parts. In alchemy it denotes regeneration, return to the matrix, the *prima materia*. In the Work it is sometimes symbolized as incest in which the mother unites with the son; the necessary *regressus ad uterum* before rebirth.

Infant See CHILD.

Initiation The archetypal pattern of death and rebirth; transition from one state to another, from one ontological plane to another; death before rebirth and victory over death; return to the darkness before the rebirth of light; death of the old man and rebirth of the new; acceptance, or rebirth, either spiritual or physical, into adult society. Initiation usually requires a 'descent into hell' to overcome the dark side of nature before resurrection and illumination and the ascent into heaven, thus initiation ceremonies are usually held in caves, or some underworld place, or a labyrinth from which the reborn man emerges into light. Dying gods sacrifice themselves for rebirth and resurrection.

Ink *Islamic*: The reflection of all existential potentialities; also 'the ink of the learned is like the blood of the martyrs' (Mohammed).

Intersection Conjunction; the union of opposites; communication, the point of intersection being a 'centre' from which change can take place.

Intestines 'Bowels of compassion', the intestines were thought to be the seat of the emotions. Associated with the serpent and labyrinth. Used in divination. *Chinese*: Compassion; affection; the mystic knot.

Intoxication Revelation; the overwhelming power of divine possession; the release of truth, *in vino veritas*.

Inundation See FLOOD.

Inversion The interplay of opposites; one quality giving rise to its opposite, death giving rise to life, good to evil, etc. Symbols of inversion are the hourglass; the inverted tree, the double triangle or 'Solomon's Seal', the double spiral, the letter X, the man hanged upside-down. It also signifies that 'every true analogy must be applied inversely', 'as above so below'.

Invisibility Death; magic powers. Symbolized by the cloak, mantle, veil and hood.

Iris The power of light; hope; often depicted as the FLEUR-DE-LIS and shares its symbolism and that of the LILY (q.v.). *Chinese*: Grace; affection; beauty in solitude. *Christian*: As the lily it is the flower of the Virgin Mary, Queen of Heaven, and the Immaculate Conception. As the 'sword lily' it depicts the sorrow of the Virgin. *Egyptian*: Power. *Greek*: The symbol of Iris, the feminine messenger of the gods and a psychopomp.

Iron Hardness; durability; strength; firmness; inflexibility; fetters. *Chinese*: Evil power. *Egyptian*: Evil; an attribute of Set and 'the bones of Typhon'. *Graeco-Roman*: Symbolized by the shield and spear of Ares/Mars. *Hindu*: The *kali-*

yuga, the age of iron and darkness, is the fourth and final age of the cycles of manifestation, the present age. *Islamic*: The power of evil. *Mexican*: The masculine principle. *Minoan*: The masculine principle and associated with shells as the feminine principle in funerary rites. *Teutonic*: Slavery.

Island Ambivalent as a place of isolation and loneliness but also a place of safety and refuge from the sea of chaos. Enchanted islands depict Paradise, the abode of the Blessed, like the Isles of the Blest and the Celtic Green Island.

Ivory The ivory tower symbolizes the inaccessible, also the feminine principle. In Christianity it represents the Virgin Mary; purity; incorruptibility and moral strength.

Ivy Like all evergreens, the ivy is immortality and eternal life; it is also revelry; clinging dependence; attachment; constant affection; friendship. *Christian*: Everlasting life; death and immortality; fidelity. *Egyptian*: 'The plant of Osiris', immortality. *Greek*: Sacred to Dionysos who is crowned with ivy and whose cup is an 'ivy cup'; his thyrsus is encircled with ivy and one of his emblems is a post sprouting ivy leaves. *Semitic*: Sacred to the Phrygian Attis; immortality. The ivy-leaf is phallic, depicting the male trinity.

Jacinth See JEWELS.

Jackal The jackal, able to see by day and night, is the symbol of the Egyptian Anubis, 'the Pathfinder', the 'Opener of the Way', a psychopomp guiding souls from this world to the next; also associated with the cemetery. Anubis is depicted as a black jackal or as jackal-headed. *Buddhist*: A person rooted in evil, incapable of understanding the Dharma. *Hindu*: Jackals and ravens as scavengers follow Kali as the destroyer.

Jade *Chinese*: 'All that is supremely excellent'; the yang; the Heaven-Father principle. It is the Jewel of Heaven, the product of the interaction of mountain and water, the unified powers of yin and yang. 'The perfect man competes in virtue with jade.' 'Polished and brilliant, it represents purity; smooth and lustrous, it appears as benevolence; its compactness and strength represent the sureness of the intellect; angular, but not sharp or cutting, it represents justice; hanging in beads it is like humility; the clear, prolonged note it gives when struck represents music. Its flaws do not mar its beauty, nor does its beauty conceal its flaws, calling to mind loyalty; its transparency represents sincerity. Iridescent as a rainbow, it is like the heavens; exquisite and mysterious, formed of

mountain and water, it is like the earth. Cut
without ornamentation, it represents chastity.
Valued by all it represents truth and beauty'
(*The Book of Rites*). The various colours of jade
are *wan*, the Ten Thousand Things, symbolizing infinity. The jade disk with a square hole at
the centre, the *pi*, depicts the circle of the
heavens and the square of earth and is the 'Sun
Door' or 'Gate of Heaven'. The four points of
the compass with the six jade ritual objects
which do homage to heaven and earth are the
round blue tablet – Heaven; the yellow tube –
Earth; the green tablet – the East; the red tablet
– the South; a white tablet in the form of a tiger
– the West; a black semi-circular piece of jade –
the North. White jade with yellow streaks is an
image of the forces and virtues of Heaven and
Earth combined. Jade always symbolizes good
fortune.

Jaguar *Aztec*: The powers of darkness in
conflict with the solar eagle. *Mexican*: The
messenger of the forest spirits. *Shamanistic*: The
jaguar is sometimes a familiar spirit of, or a form
taken by, the shaman.

Japa See MANTRA.

Jar A feminine, receptive symbol, like the VASE
(q.v.). *Buddhist*: One of the auspicious signs on
the Footprint of Buddha, denoting triumph
over birth and death, also spiritual triumph.
Egyptian: Hopi, watering from two jars,
represents the Upper and Lower Nile. See also
CANOPIC JARS. *Greek*: *Pithos* represents the grave,
burial and the underworld; grain was stored in
jars underground during the season of the death
of vegetation.

Jasmine *Chinese*: Femininity; sweetness;
grace; attraction. *Christian*: Grace; elegance; the
Virgin Mary.

Jasper See JEWELS.

Jaw The jaws of a monster depict either the
gates of hell and entry into the underworld, or
they share the symbolism of the clashing rocks,
the wall with no door, the eye of the needle, etc.
as the contraries, polarity and duality, which
must be transcended in order to attain to
ultimate reality and spiritual enlightenment;
they must be passed in the 'timeless moment'.
See also PASSAGE.

Jay Mischief; ill luck.

Jester See FOOL.

Jewels The heart; the sun and moon; light and
heat. As guarded by serpents, dragons or
monsters, jewels symbolize hidden treasures of
knowledge or truth, but also profane love and
transient riches. The cutting and shaping of
precious stones signifies the soul shaped from the
rough, irregular, dark stone into the gem,

Dionysos trailing fronds of **ivy**, his particular symbol,
adorns a cup by the Hermaios Painter, *c.* 525–500 BC.

The **jackal**-headed Egyptian god Anubis taking a
mummified body into his care as he prepares to
escort the dead soul to the Underworld.

regular in shape and reflecting divine light. In Buddhism the jewel typifies wisdom, and the Triple Jewel is the Buddha, the Dharma and the Sangha; with the Jains the three jewels are right belief, right knowledge and right conduct. In Japan the jewel, as compassion or wisdom, is one of the Three Treasures together with the sword and mirror as courage and truth. Counting jewels symbolizes aimless work; possessing the gem is equated with realization.

Agate: (black) symbolizes courage, boldness, vigour, prosperity; (red) spiritual love of good, health, wealth, longevity, peace. *Amber*: Congealed light; magnetism. *Amethyst*: Humility, peace of mind, piety, sobriety, resignation; the gem of healing. *Aquamarine*: Youth, hope, health.

Beryl: Hope, happiness, eternal youth, married love. *Bloodstone*: Understanding, peace, the granter of all wishes.

Carbuncle: Determination, assurance, success, energy; also war and bloodshed. *Carnelian*: Friendship, courage, self-confidence, health. *Cat's eye*: Longevity, the waning moon; apotropaic. *Chalcedony*: Bodily vigour; apotropaic. *Chrysolite*: Wisdom, discretion, prudence; apotropaic. *Chrysoprase*: Gaiety, joy. *Corundum*: Stability of mind. *Crystal*: (q.v.) Purity, simplicity, magic.

Diamond: Light, life, the sun, durability, incorruptibility, invincible constancy, sincerity, innocence.

Emerald: Immortality, hope, Spring, youth, faithfulness, the waxing moon.

Garnet: Devotion, loyalty, energy, grace.

Hyacinth: Fidelity, second-sight. *Jacinth*: Modesty. *Jade*: (q.v.) 'All that is supremely excellent', the yang power of the heavens. *Jasper*: Joy, happiness. *Jet*: Grief, mourning, safe travel.

Lapis Lazuli: Divine favour, success, ability. *Lodestone*: Integrity, honesty, virility.

Moonstone/Selenite: The moon, tenderness, lovers.

Olivine: Simplicity, modesty, happiness. *Onyx*: Perspicacity, sincerity, spiritual strength, conjugal happiness. *Opal*: Fidelity, religious fervour, prayers, assurance.

Pearl: (q.v.) The feminine principle, the moon, the waters, chastity, purity. *Peridot*: Friendship, the thunderbolt.

Ruby: Royalty, dignity, zeal, power, love, passion, beauty, longevity, invulnerability.

Sapphire: Truth, heavenly virtues, celestial contemplation, chastity, apotropaic. *Sardonyx*: Honour, renown, brightness, vivacity, self-control.

Topaz: Divine goodness, faithfulness, friendship, love, sagacity, the sun. *Tourmaline*: Inspiration, friendship. *Turquoise*: Courage, fulfilment, success; apotropaic.

Zircon: Wisdom, honour, riches.

Journey Heroic journeys symbolize crossing the sea of life, overcoming its difficulties and attaining perfection; they are also transformation symbols; the search for the lost Paradise; initiation; facing trials and dangers in the quest for perfection and realization; testing and training the character; passing 'from darkness to light, from death to immortality'; finding the spiritual Centre. Such journeys are those of Heracles, the Argonauts, Ulysses, Theseus, the Knights of the Round Table, etc. The symbolism of the journey is also bound up with that of the crossroads and the choice of the left-hand or right-hand path.

Jubilee The return to the beginning, the primordial state. After the 7×7 years, the fiftieth becomes hallowed and a fresh start.

Ju-i In Chinese Buddhism the *Ju-i* is the diamond mace symbolizing Buddha and the Doctrine; supremacy; conquering power. See also DORJE and VAJRA.

Juice See SAP.

Jumping Ambivalent as denoting joy, while in China and ancient Egypt signifying grief.

Juniper *Graeco-Roman*: Protection; confidence; initiative; sacred to Hermes/Mercury.

Justice Depicted as a woman, blindfolded and holding a sword and scales. In Christian art she has the Emperor Trajan at her feet. The Virgin Mary is called the Mirror of Justice. Justice is also symbolized by the Roman FASCES.

Ka'aba *Islamic*: An omphalos; the point of communication between God and man; the Essence of God; the heart of existence. The seven circuits made by the pilgrim represent the seven attributes of God. As a CUBE (q.v.) the Ka'aba also shares that symbolism.

Kettle In magic the kettle symbolizes transforming power.

Key An axial symbol which includes all powers of opening and closing, binding and loosing. The key also denotes liberation; knowledge; the mysteries; initiation. It is closely connected with the symbolism of Janus, a binder-and-looser, the 'inventor of locks' and god of initiation; he holds the Keys of Power to open and close and the key to the door giving access to the realm of gods and men, the doors of the solstices of Winter and Summer, the *Janua coeli* in Capricorn being the door of the gods, the ascending and increasing power of the sun, and the *Janua inferni* in Cancer the door of men and the descending and waning power of the sun. Silver and gold keys represent, respectively, temporal and spiritual power, the Lesser and the Greater Mysteries and the earthly and heavenly Paradise. *Alchemic*: The power of opening and closing, dissolution and coagulation. *Celtic*: The stable key is an attribute of Epona, guardian of horses. *Christian*: Emblem of St Peter as guardian of the gate of Heaven, also an attribute of the Pope. St Martha has a bunch of keys. *Graeco-Roman*: Attribute of Hecate as guardian of hell; also of Persephone and Cybele. See JANUS. *Hebrew*: The keys of God are the raising of the dead; birth, fertilizing rain. *Japanese*: The three keys of the granary are love, wealth and happiness. *Mithraic*: Mithras holds the Keys of Power to open and close.

Kid Sacrificed to Silvanus and Faunus as Spring gods, and used as a substitute for the dying god in Canaanite and Babylonian death and resurrection rituals.

Kidneys *Chinese*: The element of water; the sacred fish; the emotions.

King The masculine principle; sovereignty; temporal power; supreme achievement in the temporal world; the supreme ruler, equated with the Creator God and the Sun, whose delegate he is on earth. In many traditions it was held that the vitality of the king reflected, or was responsible for, the vitality of his people and the fertility of the land, hence the sacrifice of the king, or, later, his scapegoat, when his vitality waned. The king and queen together represent perfect union, the two halves of the perfect whole, completeness, the androgyne; they are also symbolized by, and symbolize, the sun and moon, heaven and earth, gold and silver, day and night and, in Alchemy, sulphur and quicksilver. Attributes of the king are the sun, crown, sceptre, orb, sword (with the exception of the Chinese Emperors), arrows, the throne.

Kingfisher *Chinese*: Halcyon days; calm; beauty; dignity; speed; fine feminine raiment; retiring nature.

Kiss A token of good will; peace; sealing a pact; good faith; fellowship; reconciliation; affection. In the Middle and Near East and in Catholic Christianity it also provides contact with some holy object such as the Ka'aba, icons, a crucifix or holy book, statue or vestment. Kissing the hand or foot implies humility or soliciting protection. The kiss of Judas is betrayal.

Knee/Kneeling The generative force; vitality; strength. To place on the knee symbolized recognition of paternity; adoption; maternal care. Kneeling depicts homage to a superior, supplication, submission and inferiority.

Knife Sacrifice; vengeance; death. Cutting with a knife signifies severance; division; freeing. *Buddhist*: Cutting with a knife represents deliverance as cutting the bonds of ignorance and pride. *Christian*: Martyrdom;

When a Muslim pilgrim makes seven circuits round the **Ka'aba**, here shown in a 16th-century manuscript illustration, he paces out the seven attributes of God round the geographic point where God and man most closely and intimately meet.

The **keys** of St Peter, which he holds in this statue in St Peter's Basilica, symbolize the axial power on which all loosing and binding, opening and closing, justice and mercy depend.

an emblem of SS Bartholomew, Crispin, Crispianus, Peter the Martyr and of Abraham.

Knight As mounted on a horse, the knight is the spirit guiding the body; his quest represents the journey of the soul through the world, with its temptations, obstacles, trials, testing and proving of character and development towards perfection. He also typifies the initiate. The Green Knight is either the neophyte or initiate, or, if in giant form, the powers of Nature and sometimes Death. The Red Knight is the conqueror, baptized in blood. The White Knight depicts innocence, purity, the elect, the illuminated. The Black Knight represents the powers of evil, sin, expiation and sacrifice. See also CHESS.

Knot An ambivalent symbolism since all powers of binding also imply those of loosing, of restraining but also uniting; the harder it is pulled the firmer it becomes and the greater the union. Knots also represent continuity; connection; a covenant; a link; Fate; that which binds man to his destiny; determinism; the inescapable. Knots can also be the instruments of the enchantress, magician or witch, in which case the tying of knots is the power and weaving of spells; other knots can be apotropaic. Loosening knots is freedom; salvation; the solving of problems. Cutting a knot denotes the taking of the short, steep path to salvation and realization. *Buddhist*: The MYSTIC KNOT (q.v.) is one of the Eight Auspicious Signs and represents continuity of life; infinity and eternity. *Chinese*: Longevity; binding the good and an obstacle to evil. *Christian*: The three knots in the monastic girdle are the three vows of poverty, chastity and obedience. *Hindu*: The Mystic Knot of Vishnu depicts continuity; immortality; infinity. *Iranian*: The sacred cord, *kosti*, is knotted twice in front and twice behind. See CORD. *Witchcraft*: Obstruction; 'hitches'; ill-wishing.

Kundalini Symbolized by the serpent which lies coiled at the base of the spine in the chakra known as the muladhara and which lies dormant until awakened by yogic and spiritual practices when it begins to ascend through the chakras, bringing increasing powers into play, until it reaches the highest point in total awareness and realization. It is latent energy; unawakened being; the sleeping serpent power; the primordial shakti in man. To awaken and uncoil it is to break the ontological plane and attain the sacred Centre; enlightenment. The symbolism of kundalini is associated with that of the serpent or dragon and the spine, the world axis.

Ky-lin The Chinese fabulous beast, sometimes called the unicorn; it is the union of the yin-yang forces with the Ky as the masculine and the Lin as the feminine. The whole animal symbolizes benevolence, good will and fertility; it heralds the birth of a great sage or wise emperor. To 'ride a ky-lin' is to rise to fame, and in Chinese art sages and immortals are represented as mounted on a ky-lin to denote their exceptional qualities. An exceptionally clever child is a 'son of a ky-lin'. It is an animal of great gentleness and does not strike with its horn, which is soft and signifies benevolence; having only one horn denotes the unity of the world under one great ruler. The ky-lin is an incarnation of the five elements and the five virtues and has five symbolic colours. If not portrayed as a unicorn it is a composite creature with the head of a dragon with a single horn, the mane of a lion, the body of a stag and the tail of an ox.

Labarum or **Chi-Rho**. The full significance of this symbol is in doubt. It is an abbreviation of CHRESTON, 'a good thing' or good omen, and was used in Greece to mark an important passage. The vertical line is suggested as a Cosmic Tree and axial symbol. The labarum was also an emblem of the Chaldean sky god and in Christianity it was adopted as the Chi-Rho, the first two letters of 'Christ'; it was the emblem of Constantine, said to have been revealed to him in a dream; it was placed on his standard and on the shields of his soldiers, thus putting them under the protection of Christ. It is frequently depicted with the Alpha and Omega symbols on lamps, vessels and tombs.

Labours The twelve labours of Hercules represent the passage of the sun through the twelve signs of the Zodiac. They are also taken as the toils and struggles of man in attaining self-realization and as divine powers working to help mankind.

Labyrinth A highly complex symbol; it can be a design, a building, an open path, a path enclosed by banks or hedges, a dance, or Troy Towns and Troy dances, games or walls. It is often situated underground, in darkness. Labyrinths are mainly of two kinds: (1) the unicursal, in which a single route leads straight to the centre and out again, with no choice, puzzle or confusion, taking the traveller over the maximum ground without treading the same path twice (starting towards the centre it then turns backwards towards the perimeter and, doubling back on itself each time, works gradually to the centre and out again); (2) the multicursal, which is designed with the intention of confusing and puzzling and contains blind paths, requiring knowledge of the key or solution to the problem. The symbolism of the labyrinth is variously suggested as the return to the Centre; Paradise regained; attaining realization after ordeals, trials and testing; initiation, death and rebirth and the rites of passage from the profane to the sacred; the mysteries of life and death; the journey of life through the difficulties and illusions of the world to the centre as enlightenment or heaven; a proving of the soul; the path of travel and escape to the next world (this world being easy to enter, but once entered into difficult to leave); a knot to be untied; danger; difficulty; fate.

The labyrinth is also suggested as the courses of the sun, its declining and increasing, or the Spring release of the sun after its long captivity by the demons of Winter; or as the body of the Earth Mother, the centre being the virginity of the divinity and to reach the centre is to make the mystic return to the matrix, the *regressus ad uterum*; or the beginning of the night sea voyage in which the male descends into the underworld, the domain of the Great Mother in her devouring aspect. The labyrinth is often presided over by a woman and walked by a man and guarded or governed by the Lord of the Labyrinth, the Judge of the Dead, at the centre, as with Minos. It is also said to symbolize the world; totality; inscrutability; movement; any complex problem; its continuous line is eternity, endless duration, immortality, the thread being the 'rope to Heaven' on which all things depend and are threaded. The labyrinth, at one and the same time, permits and prohibits, a symbol of both exclusion in making the way difficult and of retention in making the exit difficult; only those qualified and equipped with the necessary knowledge can find the centre, those venturing without knowledge are lost. Here the labyrinth shares the symbolism of the enchanted forest.

As the way to the hidden centre the labyrinth is connected with the search for the Lost Word and the quest for the Holy Grail, or, in Eastern symbolism, the escape from *samsara* and the laws of *karma*. It is also related to the symbolism of the cave with the idea of an underworld, mysterious journey, or the journey to the next world and with initiation rites, often held in a cavern or crypt, or with funerary rites, all of which are associated with death and rebirth. It also shares the symbolism of the knot in binding and loosing, restricting but uniting. The labyrinth is also thought to have been concerned with the symbolism of the coiled snake, or with patterns of entrail divination and the bowels of the earth. It can also be represented by a net, or a spider at the centre of its web. The labyrinth in a square depicts the four cardinal points and the cosmos and may be connected with the swastika.

Labyrinth designs on houses are apotropaic and a form of magic to confuse, and prevent entry of, hostile powers and evil spirits. Graves, burial caves and mounds of labyrinthine form protected the dead but also prevented them from returning. The labyrinth dance or Troy dances and games typify the difficult path, journeying from birth to death and rebirth, the centre being the place of both death and rebirth, of going inwards and outwards, sinking and rising, journeying to the depth and rising to the heights. This is also connected with the Crane Dance with the crane as psychopomp; it is also a mimetic solar ritual path or dance.

The **labarum**, here decorating an early Roman Christian tombstone, is said to have appeared to Constantine in a dream. Although traditionally interpreted as formed of the first two letters of Christ's name in Greek, it was earlier an emblem of the ancient Chaldaean sky-god.

Theseus' **labyrinth**, here in a Florentine 15th-century drawing, implies a paradoxical answer to an apparently hopeless question, both of which arise out of the labyrinth's symbolism: once you have made the difficult and complicated journey, what is at the centre? – You are.

Going into a labyrinth symbolizes death, coming out is rebirth. *Celtic*: It is suggested that 'Troy', 'Troja' or 'Troia' may be derived from the Celtic 'tro', to turn, i.e. rapid revolution, to dance through a maze. *Christian*: In early Christianity the symbol was inverted and made to represent the path of ignorance, with hell at the centre and the Minotaur as the Devil, until Christ, as Theseus, shows the way. It was also a trap for devils. The labyrinth was unknown in catacomb art. Later it was used in churches and cathedrals and the symbolism is variously suggested as the perplexities and problems which beset the Christian's path through the world; the confusing and entangling nature of sin in leaving the straight path; the pilgrimage of the soul from earth to heaven; the devious course of the wrongdoer who yields to temptation; finding the way through the entanglements of sin; the way from Pilate's house to Calvary, sometimes called 'Chemin de Jerusalem'. It is suggested also that church labyrinths were designed as pilgrimages for penitents who were unable to undertake journeys to distant shrines or the Holy Land. *Egyptian*: There is a possible parallel with the Amenti, the sinuous path taken by the dead on their journey from death to resurrection, guided by Isis, with Horus overcoming the difficulties and Osiris as Judge of the Dead. *Greek*: Theseus, the hero-saviour, travels the path, guided by Ariadne's golden thread of divine instinct, and slays the savage nature of the Minotaur. The labyrinth is not mentioned by Homer. *Minoan*: The bull at the centre is suggested as the male, solar, generative force situated at the centre of the labyrinth which, as the spiral, is the female, lunar aspect; or as heat acting on humidity, the sun sucking up the mists and miasma. *Oceanic*: The pattern of the journey of the soul in the realms of the dead. *Roman*: Secrecy; inscrutability. 'As none may know the secret of the labyrinth, so none may know the monarch's councils.' *Sumero-Semitic*: 'An artificial imitation of the lower world' (from a tablet of a priest's initiation).

Ladder The passage from one plane to another of from one mode of being to another; the break through to a new ontological level; communication between heaven and earth with a two-way traffic of the ascent of man and the descent of the divinity, hence the ladder is a world axis symbol which, in turn, connects it with the Cosmic Tree and the pillar. It also represents access to reality, the Absolute, the Transcendent, going from 'the unreal to the real, from darkness to light, from death to immortality'. The transition is also a way to the next world through death. The ladder is a means of access, but it is also removable. Originally a ladder existed between heaven and earth in Paradise and there was uninterrupted communication between God and man, but this was lost at the Fall.

The rungs of the ladder typify the ascending power of man's consciousness passing through all degrees of existence; they also represent the degrees of initiation, always seven or twelve in number; in initiation one ascends by knowledge and realization of each successive stage and descends by the virtues, that is to say, the fruits of knowledge and realization. The two sides of the ladder are the left and right PILLARS (q.v.) or the two trees of Paradise, unified by the rungs. As in all initiation, attainment is fraught with danger and the climbing of the ladder is accompanied by the dual emotions of joy and fear. The ladder is also associated with bridge symbolism in the rites of passage and, like the bridge, can have razor-edges. (This symbolism is seen in a decadent form in the sword-rungs of the ladders of jugglers in the East.) *Amerindian*: The rainbow is the ladder of access to the other world. *Buddhist*: The ladder of Sakya-muni is often depicted with the footprint of Buddha on the bottom and top rungs. *Christian*: An emblem of Christ's passion, also of Jacob and St Benedict. *Egyptian*: A symbol of Horus surmounting the material world and connecting it with heaven. 'I set up a ladder to Heaven among the gods' (Book of the Dead). Hathor also holds a ladder for the good to climb to heaven. *Hebrew*: The means of communication, through angels, between God and man. *Islamic*: The ladder seen by Mohammed leads the faithful to God. *Japanese*: The ladder is an attribute of the thunder god and represents traffic between heaven and earth. *Mithraic*: The initiate ascends the stages of the seven-runged planetary ladder, which is the passage of the soul through the seven heavens. *Shamanistic*: The shaman ascends the ladder, or seven-notched pole, to communicate with spirits and the spirit world.

Lake The feminine, humid principle; often the dwelling place of monsters or magical feminine powers, such as 'The Lady of the Lake'. In Chinese symbolism the Lake is the *Tui* (see PA KUA), the collected waters, receptive wisdom, absorption, the humid and passive. In Egypt it represented the Lower Waters.

Lamb Gentleness; young innocence; meekness; purity; the unblemished. Sorcerers are powerless against its innocence. Lambs symbolize neophytes and mystic rebirth. The lamb with the lion depicts the paradisal state. *Chinese*: Filial piety. *Christian*: The crucifixion, Christ sacrificed for the sins of the world, the Lamb of God, the 'sacrifice without blemish'. The lamb represents Christ as both suffering and triumphant, the passion and the resurrection. It is used extensively in the symbolism of Christian art: Christ carrying a lamb is the Good Shepherd caring for his flock, or having rescued the lost lamb that went astray, the sinner, or leading his flock; the lamb with the cross depicts the crucifixion; the lamb with the pennant or flag is the resurrection; the Apocalyptic lamb, with the book and seven

seals, is Christ as Judge at the Second Coming;
the lamb of the Apocalypse with seven horns
and seven eyes denotes the seven gifts of the
Spirit; the lamb with a hill and four streams
signifies the Church as the hill and the streams
are the four rivers of Paradise and the four
Gospels; where a lamb is flanked by a row of
sheep, the lamb is Christ and the sheep the
disciples; John the Baptist with a lamb depicts
the forerunner pointing to the coming of Christ.
Cyril of Alexandria says that the lamb and dove
together portray the body and soul of Christ, his
human and divine natures. The lamb is an
emblem of SS Agnes, Catherine, Clement,
Genevieve, Joanna, John the Baptist, Regina.
Hebrew: The coming Messiah, the Lamb
without Blemish.

Lameness With Hephaestos/Vulcan and the
smith gods, lameness indicates the imperfection
of the demiurge who forges the imperfect world.
Lameness and a limp also represent the zig-zag
movement of the lightning of storm gods. It is a
castration symbol.

Lamia See FABULOUS BEASTS.

Lamp Life; the light of divinity; immortality;
wisdom; the intellect; guidance; the stars; also
individual life in its transitoriness; good works,
shedding light in the darkness; remembrance.
The Seven Lamps of Christianity are the seven
gifts of the Spirit. The lamp is an emblem of SS
Agatha, Bridgit, Gudula, Genevieve, Hugh,
Hiltrudis, Lucy, Nilus. Lamps on altars indicate
the light of the presence of divinity; they can
also be used as a substitute for the sun in sun or
fire worship. In Hinduism the oil of the lamp is
the ocean and devotion, the wick is the earth
and mind, and the flame is love.

Lance An aspect of the masculine power;
phallic; solar; war. The lance, sword and
arrows can all represent solar rays. The lance is
an attribute of the lower forms of knighthood
with the sword, as discernment, as the higher.
The symbolism of the lance as masculine and
the cup, or chalice, as feminine, is bound up
with that of the mountain and cave; the
mountain and the vertical shadowless lance are
both symbols of the *axis mundi*. The lance and
cup are also associated with the GRAIL(q.v.).
Christian: The lance and cup are connected with
the Holy Grail as the cup which caught the
blood of Christ on the cross when wounded by
the lance. It is an emblem of the passion and of
SS George of Cappadocia, Thomas and Jude.
Graeco-Roman: Solar; war; an attribute of Ares/
Mars and Athene. The lance of Achilles, like the
solar rays and lightning, could heal the wounds
it inflicted. *Hindu*: Strength; power; victory
over evil; an attribute of Indra. Divine wisdom
which pierces ignorance. *Japanese*: Attribute of
Izanagi who wields the celestial lance of
creation with which he stirs the waters to
produce the land.

Jacob, in this frontispiece to an 18th-century
alchemical text, is being summoned by the angels to
rouse himself from the sleep of the senses and
transcend earthly phenomena by scaling the waiting
ladder to heaven.

The **lamb** on a 6th-century Christian tomb in
Ravenna is accompanied by several other symbols of
Christ, of redemption and of sacrifice: the cross as
LABARUM, the dove, the wreath of victory.

Lantern See LAMP.

Lapis Lazuli Divine favour; success. *Chinese*: One of the seven precious stones; success; ability. *Graeco-Roman*: Love; an emblem of Aphrodite/Venus. *Sumerian*: Lapis lazuli was used extensively in temples and depicted the firmament and its sacred power.

Laurel Triumph; victory. As evergreen it is eternity; immortality; as consecrated to vestal virgins it is chastity. In Graeco-Roman symbolism it is victory, truce and peace and is sacred to Apollo, Dionysos, Juno, Diana and Silvanus and represents the nymph Daphne who was changed into a laurel. In Christianity it is the crown of martyrdom.

Lead In Alchemy lead is the heavy 'sick' condition of metal or of human existence or the soul; it is the base metal, density, the opaque bodily consciousness, unregenerate man, subject of the work of transforming and transmuting. The metal of Saturn.

Leaf Fertility; growth; renewal. Green leaves depict hope; revival; renewal. Dead leaves are sadness; Autumn; decay. Crowns of leaves symbolize divinity or triumph and victory. In Chinese symbolism the leaves of the Cosmic Tree represent all beings in the universe – the Ten Thousand Things.

Leek Victory; protection against wounds. Its smell, like that of garlic, was regarded as similar to the smell of striking lightning and, as such, an emblem of the Celtic god Aeddon. The leek is an emblem of St David and of Wales.

Left The left side is usually the sinister, dark, illegitimate, lunar, inward-looking aspect and represents the past. In Christianity at the Judgment the sheep are on the right hand and the goats on the left and in crucifixion scenes the good thief is depicted as on the right hand of Christ and the bad thief to the left, or the Virgin Mary on the right with St John on the left, or the Church on the right and the Synagogue on the left. In China, on the contrary, the left was the side of honour as the weak, yin, side, since the right side, being yang and strength, tends to violence and so to self-destruction. In time of war, a time of violence and destruction, the position was reversed.

Leg One-legged gods are suggested variously as axis symbols, or as lunar, or phallic. In Qabalism the leg represents firmness and glory. In Egypt it denotes lifting.

Lemon Sourness; sharpness. In Christianity it also depicts faithfulness in love. In Hebrew symbolism it represents the harvest, was carried in the left hand at the Feast of Tabernacles and appears to have some connection with the fir-cone of the Semitic rites of Dionysos.

Leo See ZODIAC.

Leopard Cruelty; ferocity; aggression; intrepidity. The leopard's spots resembling eyes, the animal is called the Great Watcher. *Chinese*: Bravery; warlike ferocity. *Christian*: The Devil; sin; the duplicity of Satan; the Antichrist; concupiscence. *Egyptian*: An emblem of Osiris. *Greek*: An attribute of Dionysos as creator and destroyer. *Hebrew*: Swiftness. *Heraldry*: Bravery; impetuosity; activity.

Leper The unclean; the outcast; the spiritually and morally fallen.

Lettuce An Egyptian fertility symbol. Sacred to the Phoenician Adoni as representing ephemeral existence.

Level Equality; justice. In sacred architecture it represents transcendent knowledge, the archetype controlling all works. In Chinese symbolism it is the magistrate or a just man, a 'man of the level'.

Leviathan See FABULOUS BEASTS.

Libations The life-giving power of water, necessary for the production and maintenance of life.

Libra See ZODIAC.

Light Manifestation of divinity; cosmic creation; the Logos; the universal principle in manifestation; the primordial intellect; life; truth; illumination; gnosis; direct knowledge; the incorporeal; *nous*; the source of goodness. Radiance symbolizes new life from the divinity; it is the first thing created; the power of dispelling evil and the forces of darkness; glory; splendour; joy. Illumination conveys, or is the result of, supernatural powers. Light is associated with rain in the symbolism of the descent of heavenly and beneficent influences. The experience of light is the encounter with ultimate reality. Light is connected with the beginning and the end; it existed in the Golden Age, darkness descended at the Fall and the regaining of Paradise restores the primordial light; to reach the light is to attain the Centre.

Light and darkness are dual aspects of the Great Mother, life and love, death and burial, creation and destruction. The light of the sun represents direct knowledge as opposed to the indirect or analytical lunar knowledge. The Feast of Lights, at the beginning of February, when torches and candles were carried in procession, was for protection against plague, famine and earthquakes; later adopted by Christianity as Candlemas. Light is symbolized by rays, either straight or undulating, by the sun's disk, or the nimbus; the straight line is usually light, with the undulating as heat; light and heat are symbolically complementary and polarize the element of fire. *Buddhist*: Light is truth; liberation; direct knowledge; identification with the Buddha; transcendence of the world and of conditioned being. The Clear Light is ultimate reality; pure being; the colourless and formless Void. Impure lights denote a formal after-life and rebirth into the phenomenal world. Lights in worship are the lights of the Three Worlds. *Celtic*: Bridgit had a light festival at the beginning of February when candles were lighted round corn. *Chinese*: The yang heavenly power. In Chinese Manichean texts Vahman is the Light of Wisdom and the Kind Light. *Christian*: Christ, 'the Light of the World', 'the Father of Lights with whom there is no variableness, neither shadow of turning' (James 1, 17). The Virgin Mary is the 'Light-bearer' in her son and the Feast of Lights was adopted and adapted as the Purification or Candlemas. *Graeco-Roman*: Zeus/Jupiter, 'brightness', 'god of the bright sky'. Lights were carried in Eleusinian rites of the search of Demeter for Kore and the return of Spring. *Hebrew (Qabalism)*: the Ain Soph, the 'Limitless light'. *Hindu*: The Self; Atman; cosmic creation; 'the progenitive power'; spirituality; wisdom; sanctity; the manifestation of Krishna, Lord of Light. *Iranian*: Pure being; pure Spirit. In Zoroastrianism the power of truth is light as Ormuzd or Ahura Mazda, Lord of Light, opposed to the darkness of Ahriman or Angra Mainyu, Lord of Lies. Sacred to the Magi. *Islamic*: The effulgent light of Allah who illumines the world; pure being; the heavens; air; the manifestation of Divine Knowledge, Majesty and Beauty; the Intellect; the Word; the Divine Name Nur. The weaver of forms is the vehicle of light. 'Allah is the Light of the Heavens and of the earth' (*Qoran*). *Parsee*: Sacred as the flame of light. *Taoist*: The Tao; the Light of Heaven; the manifestation of non-being; unity.

Lightning Spiritual illumination; enlightenment; revelation; the descent of power; sudden realization of truth cutting across time and space, the Eternal Now; the destruction of ignorance; fecundation; nutrition; the masculine power. Lightning, like the sun's rays, is regarded as both fertilizing and destructive, also like the lance of Achilles which could both wound and heal. It is associated with all storm and thunder gods and is symbolized by the zig-zag, trident, axe (the 'sky axe'), hammer, thunderbolt, vajra, dorje, ju-i, arrow and bird of prey. Death by lightning is to be translated immediately to heaven. To be struck by lightning, in Shamanistic belief, confers immediate initiation. In Hinduism 'in the thunder flash is Truth'; Agni dwelt in the waters of heaven in the form of lightning. For the North American Indian it is the Great Spirit, revelation. Lightning is a Manichean symbol for the Virgin of Light.

Lily Purity; peace; resurrection; royalty. Sacred to all Virgin Goddesses, the Mother and

A 1st-century Roman gold coin commemorates and honours the military and naval victories of Brutus by encircling his head within a wreath of **laurel**, the evergreen plant symbolic of triumph.

In Jan van Eyck's *Annunciation*, the Angel Gabriel holds a **lily** plant, reinforcing the paradoxical situation of Mary's chastity and her pregnancy, and of her role as the Virgin Mother Goddess.

Maid, the One and the Many. The lily also represents the fertility of the Earth Goddess and later of the sky gods. The lily, in the West, shares the symbolism of the LOTUS (q.v.) in the East. A branch of lilies depicts virginity, also regeneration and immortality. *Alchemic*: The white lily is the feminine principle. *Christian*: Purity; innocence; the Virgin Mary; its straight stalk is her godly mind, its pendant leaves her humility, its fragrance is divinity, its whiteness is purity; it is also a symbol of the Annunciation and of virgin saints, as chastity; it is the flower of Easter. Dante calls it the 'lily of faith'. The lily among thorns depicts the Immaculate Conception as purity in the midst of sins of the world. The lily is an emblem of SS Anthony of Padua, Francis of Assisi, Casimir, Catherine of Siena, Clare, Dominic, Euphemia, Francis Xavier, Joseph. In art a lily on one side and a sword on the other depict innocence and guilt. *Egyptian*: Fruitfulness, but the lotus is more frequently used in Egyptian symbolism. *Graeco-Roman*: Purity; it sprang from the milk of Hera and is an emblem of Hera/Juno and of Diana as chastity. *Hebrew*: Trust in God; emblem of the Tribe of Judah. *Islamic*: Its symbolism can be taken by the hyacinth. *Minoan*: Chief attribute of the goddess Britomartis. *Sumero-Semitic*: Fruitfulness; fecundity.

Lily of the Valley Sweetness; virginity; humility. In Christianity an emblem of the Virgin Mary and a symbol of the Advent of Christ as the advent of new life in Spring.

Lime/Linden *European*: Feminine grace; beauty; happiness; a Greek emblem of Baucis, with Philemon as the oak, as conjugal love. The linden is a Germanic emblem in towns and villages.

Line Division; measurement; boundary. The straight line represents infinite time from a point in which it is possible to proceed backwards and forwards indefinitely; simple indefiniteness. The line is associated with the cord as being an agent of both limiting and binding and as a possibility of endless extension and freedom, that which both leads and limits man to his destiny; the path man takes through life. When horizontal, the line is the temporal world, the passive aspect; vertical, it is the spiritual world, the active aspect, the cosmic axis. Undulating lines convey the idea of motion, either of water or of the heat of the sun's rays or of celestial bodies. The straight line also denotes rectitude and an undeviating line of conduct.

Linen *Christian*: The linen cloth on the altar represents the winding sheet which covered the body of Christ in the tomb. Fine linen signifies purity and righteousness, the vesture of the bride of Christ, the Church Triumphant. *Hebrew*: The linen of the vestments symbolizes the earth aspect.

Linga *Hindu*: The phallus; creativity; the masculine generative principle with the yoni as the feminine. It is pre-eminently the symbol of Siva as creator. The symbol is not one of a merely physical force but of cosmic creation and renewal of life; it is also a symbol of spiritual virility in the ascetic or yogi; it is the self-existing; an omphalos; symbolized by the pillar, column, cone, etc. It rises symbolically from, and is rooted in, the waters. In Buddhism it preceded figures as an aniconic representation of the Buddha. It is frequently associated with the tree.

Lion Ambivalent as both solar and lunar, good and evil. As solar it represents the heat of the sun, the splendour and power of the noonday sun; the fiery principle; majesty; strength; courage; fortitude; justice; law; military might; the King of the Beasts; but it is also cruelty; ferocity; and the sub-human modes of life; it is a symbol of war and an attribute of war gods. As lunar it is the lioness accompanying the Great Mother, or drawing her chariot, and typifying the maternal instinct; it is often depicted with virgin warrior goddesses; goddesses of Crete, Mycenae, Phrygia, Thrace, Syria, Lycia and Sparta all have the lioness as an emblem; it also appears with the winged Artemis, Cybele, Fortuna and the Gorgons, and in India and Tibet as an attribute of Tara, as an earth and maternal symbol.

The lion and the unicorn represent the contending solar-lunar, male-female forces. The lion killing the boar depicts the power of the sun killing the boar of Winter. The lion and dragon devouring each other signifies union without loss of identity. The lion and lamb together symbolize Paradise regained and primordial unity, the Golden Age; also the end of the temporal world and freedom from conflict. The solar hero slaying the lion is the sun god modifying the scorching heat of the noonday sun. Macrobius says that lions are emblematic of the Earth, 'Mother of the Gods'. Pairs of lions are 'the master of double strength', the guardians of doors, gates and treasure, or the Tree of Life. They often support a solar symbol and represent vigilance and courage. The winged lion, or griffin, can depict the union of two natures or the androgyne. The green lion is the young corn god before maturing into the golden corn. Lions' heads as waterspouts or fountains depict the diurnal sun, the gift of water exhaled over the earth. The lion throne represents the subjugation of the cosmic forces. *Alchemic*: The red lion, sulphur, is the masculine principle, with the unicorn, quicksilver, as the feminine. The green lion is the beginning of the alchemical work, the all-transmuting elixir. Two lions depict the dual nature of Mercurius, the philosophical mercury, the *nous*. *Buddhist*: The defender of the law, the wisdom of Buddha; spiritual zeal; advancement and cognizance; bravery; an enlightened one depicting sovereignty. Buddha is sometimes seated on a lion throne. The lioness is an attribute of Tara. Ratnasambhava rides a lion. A lion cub represents a newly initiated Bodhisattva; a lion with a cub under its paw is also Buddha ruling the world and compassion. The lion's roar is Buddha's fearless teaching of the Dharma. *Chinese*: Valour; energy; strength. The lion-with-ball depicts either the sun or the Cosmic Egg; dualism in nature. The lion as strength, with the horse as speed, represents the man in marriage, while flowers represent the woman. *Christian*: Ambivalent as both Christ's power and might, his kingly nature as the Lion of Judah, or the power of Christ to deliver the Christian from the lion's mouth which is the Devil as 'a roaring lion'. The lion was supposed to sleep with its eyes open, hence it depicted vigilance, spiritual watchfulness and fortitude; as a sentinel it supported the pillars of the Church. It was also believed that the cubs were born dead and life was breathed into them by the sire, hence the lion as a symbol of resurrection. As a solitary animal it signified the hermit and solitude. The lion was taken as the emblem of St Mark since his gospel emphasized the royalty and majesty of Christ. It is also an emblem of SS Adrian, Euphemia, Jerome, Mary of Egypt, Paul the Hermit, Prisca, Thecla. In catacomb paintings the story of Daniel in the lions' den is symbolic of God's redemption of his people. *Egyptian*: Protection; a guardian; it is solar when depicted with the sun disk and lunar with the crescent moon. A lion with a head at each end of the body represents the sun gods of sunrise and sunset. Two lions back-to-back, with the solar disk, are past and present, or yesterday and tomorrow. The lioness is an attribute of Sekmet and the mother goddesses and symbolizes maternity, but as Sekmet it can also be vengeance. With the solar disk the lion represents Ra, the sun god, and with the crescent Osiris, Judge of the Dead. Tefnut is lion-headed. *Greek*: Accompanies Phoebus, Artemis, Cybele, Tyche and the Gorgons and occasionally Dionysos. Lions draw the chariots of Cybele and Juno. The lion skin is an attribute of Heracles who, wrestling with a lion, as funerary, is the solar hero overcoming death. *Hebrew*: The mighty; cruelty. The winged lion represents the South, the Lion of Judah. *Hindu*: The fourth avatar of Vishnu; sometimes half-man, half-lion, the lion of Agni; the lion and lioness together depict the shakta-shakti, the lion is the Supreme Lord, rhythm, and the lioness the power of the uttered word. The lion is the guardian of the North and is an attribute of the goddess Devi and of Durga as destroyer of demons. *Iranian*: Royalty; solar power; light. *Islamic*: Protection against evil. *Japanese*: The lion is the King of Beasts and appears with the peony as Queen of Flowers. The lion ball signifies emptiness. *Mithraic*: Solar; the fourth grade of initiation. The lion-headed Cronos is Aion, time and destiny devouring all things; the sun as fire. The lion and bull together are symbols of death; the lion

A 17th-century Mughul artist has painted a ruler of India and a Shah of Persia embracing in peace and standing on the traditional symbols of peace in the world, the **lion** and the lamb lying together in concord.

The **lion** in his symbolic role as guardian of the door: from Ferrara Cathedral, *c*. 1140.

and stag together represent the moment of death. *Roman*: Solar fire; royalty; an attribute of Apollo, Hercules and Fortuna. The ravening power of death; also man's victory over death. *Sumero-Semitic*: Solar fire; sovereignty; strength; courage; attribute of the Sumerian sun god Marduk. Inanna/Ishtar, as the Great Mother, is accompanied by two lions. A lion with a bough in its paws, or a lion with two heads, represents Ninib, solar and war god. The Chaldean Nergal, a god of war and death, is depicted as a lion, symbolizing the hostile aspect of the sun, the devouring heat of the solstice, or as two lions' heads, back to back, as god of the sun and the underworld. A lion accompanies Atargatis as Great Mother. *Taoist*: The hollow 'brocade ball' or 'lion ball' is the Void; emptiness; withdrawal of the mind.

Lizard A lunar creature; the humid principle; believed to be tongueless and subsist on dew, the lizard was a symbol of silence. In Egyptian and Greek symbolism it represented divine wisdom and good fortune and was an attribute of Serapis and Hermes; in Zoroastrianism it was a symbol of Ahriman and evil. In Christianity it is also evil and the Devil. The lizard is an attribute of Sabazios and usually appears on the Hand of Sabazios. In Roman mythology it was supposed to sleep through the winter and so symbolized death and resurrection. The lizard Tarrotarro is an aboriginal Australian culture hero.

Loaf/Loaves Shares the CORN symbolism (q.v.) as fertility, nourishment and life. In Hebrew symbolism the twelve loaves on the table of the Temple represent the twelve months of the year, according to Josephus. It is also suggested that they represent the Twelve Tribes and the Zodiac.

Lobster *Japanese*: Longevity; congratulation; a happy event, especially associated with New Year festivities or feasts.

Lodge *Amerindian*: In the Sweat Lodge of purification and rebirth the whole lodge is the body of the Great Spirit; the circular shape is the world in totality; the steam is the visible image of the Great Spirit performing a purifying and spiritual transformation. Coming out of the dark lodge is leaving behind all impurities and errors. The Sun Dance Lodge is also a sacred Centre; the central pole is the world axis, joining heaven and earth and making communication possible between them and leading to the sun, the symbol of the Great Spirit. The opening at the top of a lodge or tepee also gives access to the heavens and spiritual power.

Loom Fate; time; the weaving of destiny. Attribute of Penelope and Arachne. See also WEAVING.

Loop See BONDS.

Lost Object The search for the lost object is the quest for life, immortality, spiritual treasure, enlightenment, the 'pearl of great price'. It also symbolizes the quest for the Lost Word or the Holy Grail or Paradise.

Lotus An almost universal symbol as the eastern lotus or the western lily or rose. It is solar and lunar, birth and death, appearing with Egyptian and Hindu sun gods and with Semitic moon gods and with the Great Mother as lunar goddess. It is 'the flower that was in the Beginning, the glorious lily of the Great Waters'; 'that wherein existence comes to be and passes away'; it is the cosmos rising from the waters of pre-cosmic chaos as the sun rose from the lotus at the beginning of the world. It is the Flower of Light, the result of the interaction of the great creative forces of the fire of the sun and the lunar power of the waters. As the product of the sun and the waters it symbolizes spirit and matter as fire and water, the source of all existence. It is 'the universal ground of existence, inflorescent in the waters of its indefinite possibilities'; the solar matrix; opening with the sun and closing at sunset, it represents solar renaissance, hence all renaissance, creation, fecundity, renewal and immortality. It is also perfection of beauty.

Associated with the wheel as the solar matrix, the expanded flower forms the rosette and sun-wheel of the perpetual cycles of existence; it also forms the cup of the receptive feminine principle. According to Iamblicus it is a symbol of perfection since its leaves, flowers and fruit form the figure of the circle. The lotus depicts spiritual unfolding as it starts with its roots in the slime and, growing upwards through the opaque waters, it flowers in the sun and the light of heaven. Its root signifies indissolubility, the stem the umbilical cord attaching man to his origins; the flower is in the form of the sun's rays; the seed pod is the fecundity of creation. The flower rests on the waters of repose; in bud it is all potentiality, in bloom it is expansion, enlightenment, the heart, the cosmic wheel of manifestation, its seed pods are creation, the 'mover on the waters' (the seed pod openings are smaller than the seeds generating within the pod which bursts and lets the seeds out to put down tap roots wherever carried by the waters).

The lotus is also a symbol of a superhuman or divine birth issuing unsullied from the muddy waters. Gods springing from the lotus signify the world arising from the watery element, with the lotus depicting the sun emerging from the primaeval waters of chaos. As solar-lunar the lotus is also the androgyne, the self-existent and immaculate purity. A flame rising from a lotus is both divine revelation and the union of the dualistic forces of fire and water, sun and moon, male and female. Either the flower or the leaf of the lotus can be a source of support for any plane of existence. In Assyrian, Phoenician and Hittite culture and in Graeco-Roman art the lotus has a funerary and mortuary significance

and depicts death and rebirth, resurrection and
future life, and the reproductive powers of
nature.

Portrayed with the bull the lotus is solar and
is associated with sun gods, with the cow it
becomes lunar and an attribute of moon
goddesses. It frequently appears with the lion,
ram, deer, goose, swan and swastika. With the
cobra it depicts the lifegiving, death-dealing
powers of the Great Mother and the duality of
manifestation, the tension of opposites in the
process of transformation into ultimate unity.
The Thousand-Petalled Lotus is the sun, the
dome of the firmament and, in man, it
represents the skull. The Lotus Throne
symbolizes perfect receptive harmony in the
universe, the summit of spiritual perfection.
Two lotuses represent the Upper and Lower
Waters. *Buddhist*: The primordial waters; the
potentialities of the manifest world and of man
in it; spiritual flowering and unfolding;
wisdom; Nirvana. The stem is the world axis
which supports the flower of the lotus throne,
the spiritual summit. Sacred to Buddha who is
manifest as a flame issuing from a lotus, the
'Jewel in the Lotus' of which Buddha is the
heart; he is also enthroned on a fully-opened
lotus and it is one of the Eight Treasures or
Auspicious Signs of Chinese Buddhism. The
'lotus of the heart' is solar fire, also Time, the
unseen and all-devouring, the unfolding of all
existence; peace; harmony; union. The full
bloom, as the wheel-shape, depicts the Round of
Existence and is also a symbol of Amitabha,
Kwan-yin and the Maitreya Buddha.
Bodhisattvas stand on the flower which has not
yet opened. The book of illuminating wisdom,
resting on the lotus of spiritual flowering, is an
attribute of the white Tara, the Mother of all
Buddhas. See also *Hindu* below. *Chinese*: Purity;
perfection; spiritual grace; peace; feminine
genius; Summer; fecundity. The lotus also
represents the past, present and future since the
same plant bears buds, flowers and seeds at the
same time. It depicts the gentleman who grows
out of dirty water but is uncontaminated by it.
Egyptian: 'The fire of intelligence'; creation;
fecundity; rebirth; immortality; royal power;
emblem of the Upper Nile with the papyrus as
the Lower Nile; depicted together, they
represent the union of the two. Sacred to Horus,
'He of the lotus', 'a pure lotus, issue of the field of
the sun' (*Book of the Dead*). The four sons of
Horus stand on a lotus before Osiris. As
associated with Amon Ra at Thebes the lotus is
solar, but is lunar when held by Hathor, and as
an attribute of Isis is fecundity but also purity
and virginity, the Maiden-Mother. The lotus
appears with the bull, lion, ram, gryphon,
sphinx and serpent in Egyptian iconography.
Graeco-Roman: An emblem of Aphrodite/
Venus. *Hindu*: The universe in the passive
aspect of manifestation; the highest form or
aspect of earth; the procreative power of the
eternal substance; the mover on the face of the
waters; the self-generative; the self-born,

In both this ancient Egyptian inscription and the
18th-century Indian painting, the **lotus** is used as
primal and ultimate container and receptacle of life
and whatever there is of the divine in human life.

immortal and spiritual nature of man; the unfolding of all possibilities; eternal regeneration; superhuman origin; purity; beauty; longevity; health; fame; fortune, especially for children. It is also the solar matrix, the throne of Brahma, born from the lotus. Agni also rises from a lotus. As solar it is an emblem of the sun gods Surya and Vishnu; as lunar it is an aniconic symbol of Sri Lakshmi or Padma, 'the goddess moisture', consort and 'the beloved of Vishnu'. As resting on the waters and opening to the sun's rays, the lotus symbolizes the interaction between Purusha and Prakriti. The lotus on the threshold of a temple signifies the dwelling place of divinity and the state of purity and dispassion required of the devotee. The lotus on the triple stalk depicts the triple aspect of time. The lotus is also a world symbol since the centre of the flower is sometimes represented as Mount Meru, the world axis. The CHAKRAS (q.v.) are portrayed as lotuses which, in this context, are also connected with the wheel symbolism as, when awakened, these centres open and revolve. *Iranian*: Solar; light. *Mayan*: The earth; the manifest universe. *Sumero-Semitic*: Solar with the sun gods and lunar with the great mothers. Creative, generative power; but also funerary, hence life-and-death; resurrection; immortality. *Taoist*: The GOLDEN FLOWER (q.v.); the cosmic wheel of manifestation; spiritual unfolding; the heart; emblem of Ho Hsien-ku, one of the Eight Taoist genii or immortals.

Lowness/The Low Inferiority; submissiveness; humility; typified by kneeling and prostration. Evil is equated with descent as opposed to height and ascent as the good.

Lozenge The feminine creative principle; the vulva; a life symbol of fertility goddesses; with a central point it is the *pudenda mulieris*.

Lungs *Chinese*: The seat of righteousness, source of inner thoughts. One of the Eight Precious Things of Buddha, symbolized by the sacred canopy.

Lute *Chinese*: Harmony between rulers and ministers; friendship; connubial bliss. One of the four symbols of the scholar, with literature, painting and chess. *Christian*: The symbolism of Orpheus and his lute was used by early Christians to depict the followers attracted by Christ and the Gospels. The wild beasts subdued were human passions subdued by Christ who was also portrayed as the Good Shepherd. *Greek*: Orpheus, as the Good Shepherd, was a mediator, and his lute symbolized harmony and the reconciliation of natural forces; charming wild beasts signified self-knowledge and mastery resolving conflict.

Luxury Symbolized by the goat, pig and monkey; also Aristotle on all fours and Virgil suspended in a basket.

Lynx Keenness of sight, 'lynx-eyed'. The lynx was believed to be able to see through walls. In Christianity it indicates the vigilance of Christ. In Heraldry it is watchfulness and keen vision.

Lyre The underlying numerical harmony of the universe. The heptachord represents the harmony of the planetary spheres and its seven strings correspond to the planets. The tetrachord symbolizes Fire, the subtle, acute, movable; Air, the subtle, blunt, movable; Water, the dense, blunt, movable; Earth, the dense, blunt, immovable (Proclus). The lyre is an attribute of Erato, Apollo, Orpheus, Harmonia, Aeolus.

Mace Absolute authority; power; office. For diamond mace see DORJE, VAJRA, JU-I. The mace with seven heads is a Sumerian battle symbol.

Magnolia *Chinese*: Self-esteem; ostentation; Spring; feminine charm and beauty.

Magpie *Chinese*: The 'Bird of Joy'; good fortune. A chattering magpie signifies good news, the arrival of guests. Under the Manchu dynasty it also represented imperial rule. *Christian*: The Devil; dissipation; vanity.

Maize In America it takes the symbolism of CORN (q.v.); in European and Mediterranean civilizations it represents the Mother Goddess, the life-sustaining power of the earth; plenty; nourishment; peace. A cob of maize is a symbol of life among the Pawnee and other tribes.

Makara See FABULOUS BEASTS.

Mallet Authority; directing will; masculine force. Shares some of the symbolism of the hammer as a thunder god attribute. *Celtic*: An attribute of Sucellus. *Chinese*: The mallet and chisel are attributes of Lei-kung, god of thunder. *Japanese*: It is 'the creative hammer', the combined masculine and feminine powers; good luck.

Mallow *Chinese*: Quietness; peace; rusticity; humility.

Man Cosmic man is the microcosm, a reflection of the macrocosm and the elements, with the body representing the earth; the heat of the body, fire; the blood, water; the breath, the air. The masculine principle is symbolized by the sun and the heavens in most traditions, with Teutonic and Oceanic exceptions, and by all that is phallic, piercing, penetrating, upright and associated with heat, e.g. the sun, sword, spear, lance, arrow, dart, spade, plough, ship's prow, pillar, pole, cone, obelisk, fire, flame, torch, also the linga, the shakta and yang forces, etc. In Amerindian symbolism the male principle is represented by the white eagle feather. In Taoism man is the central and mediating power of the Great Triad of Heaven-Man-Earth. In Islam he signifies universal existence, 'the link between God and Nature'. The Sufis define man as 'the symbol of universal existence'.

Manacle See BONDS.

Mandala A symbolical diagram, either imagined or depicted, and typically a circle enclosing a square with a central symbol which can be a figure. It is a pattern of existence and a system on which meditational visualization is based. It is also an *imago mundi*; the enclosure of sacred space and penetration to the sacred centre; totality; the microcosm; cosmic intelligence; integration. Qualitatively the mandala represents spirit, quantitatively it is existence. The alternating squares depict the dualistic but complementary principles of the universe, and the whole is the re-enactment of the cosmic drama and a pilgrimage of the soul; it is symbolic of the universal spirit and is the ritual, diagrammatic form of Purusha. It is also a centre of power, a circumscribed area safe from hostile influences. The centre is a Sun or Sky Door, a means of access to the heavens.

The Hindu Temple is built as a mandala, symbolizing the universe at its different levels and having gates, or doors, to the four cardinal points. The quinary grouping of images depicts the four points revolving round the centre – 'the ego revolving round itself in Time and Space'. These five points represent the five elements of the human personality, the five Buddhas, the five 'families', which correspond to the five faces of Siva: the West, white, Sadyojata; North, yellow, Vamedeva; South, black, Aghora; East, red, Tatpurusha; Centre, green, the face of Isana (creative power); also the five gnoses, of which the five Tathagatas are symbols: Vairocana (Brilliant) – knowledge reflecting the archetypes as in a mirror; the Centre; the Wheel; white. Akshobhya (Imperturbable) – primordial consciousness; the One; the Vajra; the East; blue. Ratnasambhava (Jewel-born) – knowledge of the fundamental identity of things; the Jewel; the South; yellow. Amitabha (Boundless Light) – knowledge of the One Being as this or that; the Lotus; the West; red. Amoghasiddhi (Infallible Success) – knowledge as power and action; the Sword; the North; green. The demons (Vighna) in the mandala symbolize the menacing aspect of the psychic and passional forces which hamper man's progress towards the light. The mandala is based on the 8×8 squares, the order of the celestial world established on earth, or on 9×9 squares, leading to and enclosing the universe.

Mandorla The *vesica piscis*, or *ichthus*, the almond-shaped aureole, the 'mystical almond' which depicts divinity; holiness; the sacred;

The **lyre** of Orpheus, whose death is the subject of this Greek vase painting, was the symbol of his power to enforce the rhythm of discipline on the instinctual life as embodied in animals.

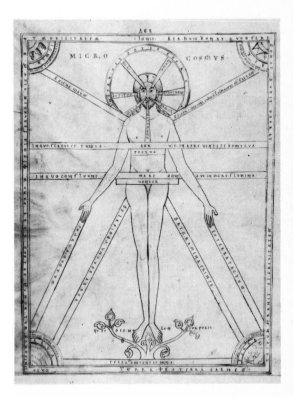

Christ as the microcosmic **man**, holding within himself the perfect reflection of all the qualities, powers, elements and other characteristics of the universe.

virginity; the vulva. It also denotes an opening or gateway and the two sides represent the opposite poles and all duality. The mandorla is also used to portray a flame, signifying the Spirit or a manifestation of the spiritual or soul principle.

Mandrake A symbol of the Great Mother, giver of life; the plant of enchantment; emblem of Circe. In Hebrew symbolism it represents conception and fertility; in witchcraft it is the power of magic.

Maniple *Christian*: The fetters or rope with which Christ was bound; repentance; vigilance; good works.

Manna Food from Heaven; food for the soul; the bread of Heaven; the grace of God. Said to be exuded from the tamarisk, the Tree of Life, sacred to Anu. Ma-nu is also connected with the date palm.

Mantis The praying mantis appears among the Bushmen as a Trickster.

Mantle Shelter and protection for mankind, but also concealment, mystery, power and a particular role. Wearing a ritual mantle symbolizes transformation. The mantle of the Great Mother, Queen of Heaven, is usually sky-blue in colour.

Mantra/Japa The sonorous form of the Divinity, corresponding to a name or aspect. The cosmic, creative vibrations; the uttered word; primordial sound; the word of power; a name or syllable of power with *japa* as the repetition of a particular invocation of the Name and its continual remembrance.

Maple Leaf Emblem of Canada. *Chinese and Japanese*: Autumn; the emblem of lovers.

Mare See HORSE and STALLION.

Marigold Fidelity. In Chinese symbolism it is longevity, 'the flower of 10,000 years'. In Hinduism it is the flower of Krishna.

Marriage The reconciliation, interaction and union of opposites; relationship between the divinity and the world; the *hieros gamos*, the sacred marriage between god and goddess, priest and priestess, king and queen, representing the mystic union of heaven and earth, sun and moon, the solar bull and lunar cow, on which the vital forces of the sky and earth and the fertility of the cattle and crops depend. It also symbolizes spiritual union, attaining perfection and completion by the union of opposites in both life and death, each partner 'giving up' to the other, but with the death forming a new life. In Alchemy it is the *conjunctio*, the union of sulphur and quicksilver,

sun and moon, gold and silver, king and queen, etc. In Christianity it represents the union of the soul with the Divine Lover, Christ, the bridegroom.

Marrow The marrow of the bone represents the life-force; vitality; strength.

Mask Protection; concealment; transformation; non-being. The mask can be either unifying or identifying, either 'masked' and lost in the mass, or wearing a mask of some identifying character. The Mask of God is the illusion of the phenomenal world, *maya*. Masks in sacred plays portray the supernatural forces of the deities represented; in ordinary plays they symbolize the inner characteristics which may normally be hidden by the outward personality.
    Animal or bird masks denote the re-establishment of communion with animals and birds and regaining the paradisal state; they also represent animal instinctual wisdom from which man can learn, also man's animal nature with which he must come to terms. The mask also depicts the rigidity of death and can be apotropaic. In Greece the mask symbolized either the death-dealing power of the Gorgon, or the tragic or comic nature of the character in plays. The comic mask is an attribute of Thalia and the tragic mask of Melpomene. The Australian aboriginal 'bush soul' masks identify the wearer with the power of the animal, bird or plant represented. Among African tribes masks can symbolize and confer a power of their own.

Maypole The *axis mundi* round which the universe revolves. The tree, stripped of its foliage which symbolizes change, becomes the changeless axis or centre. The pole is the phallic, masculine symbol and the discus at the top of the pole is the feminine; the two together depict fertility. The seven ribbons are the colours of the rainbow. The maypole also symbolizes the number 10, with the pole as the central '1' and the 'o' as the discus and the circle danced round the maypole.
    Originally it was the sacred pine of Attis which was taken in procession, or on a chariot, to the temple of Cybele and set up for veneration; it was followed by men, women and children and dances were performed round it. Later this ceremony appeared in the Roman Hilaria, the Spring Festival, and then in the May Day celebrations of the May Queen and the Green Man. The ribbons of the maypole are also suggested as the bands of wool bound round the Attis pine. The entire ceremony is symbolic of renewed life, sexual union, resurrection and Spring.

Maze See LABYRINTH.

Meander Clouds; thunder; the movement of water; a possible development of the SPIRAL (q.v.). See also LABYRINTH.

Menat The Egyptian whip of authority; strength; also, as driving away care, it can be happiness and pleasure.

Menhir Phallic, the masculine creative force, associated with the DOLMEN as the feminine womb-gate; it is also an *axis mundi* and a sacred place of sacrifice.

Menorah See CANDLE.

Mermaid See FABULOUS BEASTS.

Metals Associated with gold as the Sun; silver, the Moon; lead, Saturn; tin, Jupiter; iron, Mars; quicksilver, Mercury; copper or brass, Venus. Base metals are the sensuous world of unregenerate man and gold symbolizes the attainment of illumination and spirituality. In Alchemy the base metal is lead which is worked upon to attain to the superior metal of gold as enlightenment. Metals are embryonic in the womb of the earth.

Might Symbolized by the lion, dragon, hammer and anvil, thunderbolt, broken column.

Milk Milk from the Mother Goddess is the food of divinity for the gods, divine nourishment. As food for the newborn it is used in initiation ceremonies as a symbol of rebirth. It is also a family blood-tie and symbol of motherhood. When used ritually it is a life-fluid. Bedouins regard the sale of milk as impious. Milk and honey are both life-foods and often used in initiation and funeral rites as the food of Paradise; they connect the cow and bee with the tree of the Mother Goddess. Milk and water are combined as the milk of the spirit and the water of matter; they are also taken as representing weakness. Milk, water and honey is the libation to the Muses. *Buddhist*: The nourishment of the Buddha Dharma. *Christian*: the Logos; the heavenly milk from the mystic bride, the Church; milk is also the simple teaching given to the neophyte before initiation and the wine of the sacrament. Milk and honey, food for the newborn, was given to the newly baptized. In Christian iconography the milk pail, *muletra*, portrays the spiritual nourishment of Christ and the Church. *Greek*: Orphic: the initiate entered the womb of the Earth Mother, was reborn and partook of the milk of her breasts. *Hindu*: There is a milk-yielding tree in Paradise. *Zoroastrian*: Sacred as a product of the cow.

Mill/Millstone The transformer; fate. The cosmic mill which grinds out creation has the lower stationary stone as the earth and the upper revolving stone as the heavens and the turner, the sky god is the Great Turner. The two stones also signify will and intellect. Millstones also denote punishment; a heavy burden; crushing; hardness; martyrdom. They are related to the fertility of the corn and the

The wearer of this Aleutian death **mask** provided an encounter with death to his fellow ritual participants, thus transforming their primal fear into an acquaintance with dying as an instant in a process of change rather than ending.

Menhir from southern France: phallic, and a sacred place of sacrifice.

symbolism of the wheel. In Buddhism the millstone represents the Round of Existence, *samsara*. In Norse mythology it is the revolving universe. In Christianity it is an emblem of SS Aurea, Christina, Callixtus, Florian, Quirinus, Vincent, Victor, also of a deacon.

Minotaur Variously suggested as the savage passions of nature; the solar bull; the humid principle; the miasma slain by the sun as Theseus, a solar hero; with the labyrinth as the tortuous way of life and the thread as the divine instinct in man. Emblem of Crete.

Mirror Truth; self-realization; wisdom; mind; the soul, the 'mirror of the universe'; the reflection of the supernatural and divine intelligence; the clear shining surface of divine truth; supreme intelligence reflected in the sun, moon and stars. The reflection in the mirror is the manifest and temporal world, also man's knowledge of himself. The mirror is both solar and lunar as the sun disk, sky and light, and as the reflected light of the moon. It is also regarded as having magical properties and is the gateway to the realm of inversion. Hanging face down in a temple or tomb it establishes an 'axis of light', the way of ascent for the soul. *Buddhist*: The soul in a state of purity; reflected truth; the enlightened mind; form; the body reflected; sincerity; purity. As reflected light it depicts *samsara*. It is one of the Eight Precious Things of Chinese Buddhism. *Chinese*: Sincerity; a square mirror is the earth and a round the heavens. The central boss of the metal mirror is the axis and the balance between the Two Powers; it is also attaining the centre and the Sun Door or Gate of Heaven. *Christian*: A spotless mirror depicts the Virgin Mary; she is also called the 'Mirror of Justice'. *Hindu*: A reminder that all images and forms are mere reflections, creations of the karmic state, the contrivances of thought. *Islamic*: 'God is the mirror in which thou seest thyself as thou art his mirror' (ibn Arabi). 'The universe is the mirror of God ... man is the mirror of the universe' (ibn al-Nasafi). *Japanese*: The *kagami*, the 'mirror of accusation', reflects truth and reveals faults; the mirror is also the divine sun. The sacred mirror is entered by a deity, on ritual occasions, to manifest itself. The mirror, as truth, is one of the Three Treasures, with the sword and jewel. Symbol of the sun-goddess Amaterasu. *Mexican*: An attribute of Tezcatlipoca, the 'shining' or 'smoking' mirror, both solar and lunar as the sun god of the Summer and a lunar god of the evening. *Taoist*: Self-realization. On looking into one's nature evil is killed by seeing the horror of its reflection: 'When evil recognizes itself it destroys itself.' The mirror also symbolizes the mind of the Sage, the calm of the Sage: 'The mind of the Sage, being in repose, becomes the mirror of the universe' (Chuang Tzu). *Semitic*: The mirror symbolizes the feminine divinity with a bunch of grapes as the masculine, in Hittite art.

Mist The condition of error and confusion. Mystery religions employ the symbolism of mist in initiation; the soul must pass out of the darkness and confusion of the mist to the clear light of illumination.

Mistletoe The life-essence; divine substance; the all-healing; immortality. As neither tree nor shrub it symbolizes that which is neither one nor the other, which, by extension, is the realm of freedom from limitation, so that anyone under the mistletoe is free from restrictions, but also free from protection, and re-enters the world of chaos. Mistletoe is the Golden Bough of the Druids and Aeneas, and represents the sacred feminine principle with the oak as the male. It symbolizes new life and rebirth at the winter solstice. It was believed to be the result of lightning striking the branch of the oak tree and was thus imbued with special spiritual qualities (see LIGHTNING). The milk of the berries is food for both body and spirit. Associated with the Norse Baldur. Some authorities relate the gathering of mistletoe by the Druids, with a golden sickle, to the myth of Cronos castrating Ouranos.

Mitre Authority. It was the fish-head cap of the priests of Ea-Oannes. Worn also by the Jewish high priest, in Mithraism and by Christian bishops.

Mole As an underground dweller it is chthonic and represents the powers of darkness; it is also the misanthrope.

Monkey Impudence; inquisitiveness; mischief; the baser instincts. The Three Mystic Monkeys, with eyes, ears, or mouth covered, depict 'See no evil, hear no evil, speak no evil'. *Buddhist*: One of the Three Senseless Creatures, always greedy and grasping. *Chinese*: Ugliness; trickery; the power of transformation; apotropaic. The ninth animal of the Twelve Terrestrial Branches. *Christian*: Vanity; luxury; the Devil. *Hindu*: Attribute of the monkey god Hanuman, possessed of divine power, son of Vayu, a wind god. Hanuman is also sometimes monkey-headed. See also APE. *Mayan*: The God of the North Star has a monkey's head.

Monolith Unity; solidarity; strength. The monolith also shares the symbolism of the MENHIR (q.v.).

Moon Is usually represented as the feminine power, the Mother Goddess, Queen of Heaven, with the sun as the masculine; exceptions to this are some African and North American Indian tribes, Teutonic, Oceanic, Maori and Japanese symbolism where the moon is the male fertilizing principle. Whether male or female the moon is universally symbolic of the rhythm of cyclic time; universal becoming. The birth, death and resurrection phases of the moon symbolize immortality and eternity, perpetual renewal; enlightenment. The moon also represents the dark side of Nature, her unseen aspect; the spiritual aspect of light in darkness; inner knowledge; the irrational, intuitional and subjective; human reason as reflected light from the divine sun. It is the eye of the night as the sun is the eye of the day. As periodic re-creation it is Time and measurement, time being first measured by lunar phases, and, as such, the bringer of change, suffering and decay, man's condition on earth; as variable in its phases it symbolizes the realm of becoming. It controls tides, rains, waters, floods and the seasons, hence the span of life. All moon goddesses are controllers of destiny and weavers of fate, and are sometimes depicted as the spider in the centre of its web; the spindle and distaff are also their attributes.

The sun and moon depicted together represent the *hieros gamos*, the sacred marriage of heaven and earth, king and queen, gold and silver, etc. The three days of the dark of the moon are the period of descent of the dying god into the underworld, from which, like the moon, he rises again. The full moon signifies wholeness, completion, strength and spiritual power. The half moon is funereal; the waning moon the sinister, demonic aspect, the crescent and waxing moon is light, growth, regeneration.

The moon is symbolized pre-eminently by the crescent or the horns of the cow; it is also the 'ship of light on the sea of the night'. All nocturnal animals, such as the cat and fox, are lunar, as are animals which appear and disappear, for example, the bear which hibernates and reappears with a newborn cub in Spring; the snail, hare and rabbit, amphibians and everything associated with the waters, swamps and floods. The frog and toad live in the moon, as do, almost universally, the hare and rabbit. Often the toad, or hare, is three-legged, portraying the three lunar phases and past, present and future. There is also a man in the moon who carries a load of logs as a punishment; Christianity equates him with Cain or Judas Iscariot. A decrepit old man can symbolize the waning moon. Lunar deities are frequently triune, especially as Fates (see NUMBER: Three). Trees and various plants are connected with the moon, such as the Hindu soma, the American maize and the South American pachimba palm. Semitic moon gods are associated with trees and bushes. *African*: Ashang: Time and death; some African tribes associate the moon with a tree; in some tribes the moon is the masculine deity. *Alchemic*: Luna, silver, is the affections purified; sol and luna are soul and body, gold and silver, king and queen. *Amerindian*: 'The old woman who never dies'; also the 'water maiden' with a pitcher of water. Associated with the palm and maize in South America and with a tree in the North. The full moon resembles the light of the Great Spirit, but in some tribes the moon is an evil and malevolent power. *Astrology*: The animal soul;

On the back of this Chinese Han period **mirror**, the central boss, the Axis of the Universe, balances the tension between the surrounding circle – the Heavens, the true world – and the outer square – the Earth, realm of appearances and reflections.

An ancient Palmyran relief depicts the **Moon** as a male god, whose armour, sword and, especially, crescent suggests the horns of power associated with male fertility gods in their aggressive, impregnating aspect.

the seat of sensation; sexual life and impulse. With the sun as the heart and its desires and the element of character, the moon represents the general style of behaviour. *Buddhist*: Peace, serenity; beauty. The full and new moons are times of strength of spiritual power. The crescent moon is an emblem of Avalokitesvara, Kwan-yin and Kwannon. Also a symbol of unity, the Self. 'One moon appears reflected in all waters/Wherein all moons from the One Moon derive' (Yang Chia's *Song of Enlightenment*). The moon and waters together represent the unobstructive nature of the Dharma. *Chinese*: The essence of the yin, feminine, principle in nature; the passive and transient, but also immortality. The hare in the moon, with pestle and mortar, mixes the elixir of immortality. *Christian*: The moon with the sun depicted in crucifixion scenes represents the dual nature of Christ. The moon is the abode of the Archangel Gabriel, with Michael in the sun. *Egyptian*: 'The maker of eternity and the creator of everlastingness'. The crescent moon is pre-eminently an attribute of Isis as Queen of Heaven. Thoth is a lunar deity. *Eskimo*: 'The sender of snow'. *Greek*: Associated with the tree. Moira, the moon goddess, was above the gods, and the Moirai, the three Fates, are the power of destiny of the moon. In Orphic symbolism the moon represented the liver, with the heart as the sun of the universe. *Hindu*: The crescent moon is the newborn babe, quick and eager in growth. It is also the cup of the elixir of immortality and is associated with the plant soma, which yields the sacred draught. *Iranian*: Venerated as Mah, with Hvare-Khshaeta as the sun. The moon is masculine in both Zend and Pahlevi. *Islamic*: 'The number of years and the measure of time' (Qoran). The Islamic year is lunar. The cloven moon depicts duality in manifestation ultimately returning to unity. The crescent moon, divinity and sovereignty, is a symbol of Islam. The Tree of Life, sometimes represented on Moslem tombs, is usually surmounted by a crescent or full moon. *Japanese*: The moon is masculine, the god Tsukiyomi, born of the right eye of Izanagi. The hare with the pestle and mortar lives in the moon. *Manichean*: The moon is Jesus the Splendour, with the sun as Mithra. *Maori*: 'The husband of all women'; the Father god. *Mithraic*: Luna, in a one-horse chariot, with the Cautopates, is usually depicted on the left in iconography, with Sol, his quadriga and Cautes on the right. *Oceanic*: The moon is masculine and also symbolizes eternal youth. *Scandinavian*: Freyja's lunar chariot is drawn by lunar cats. *Sumero-Semitic*: Sin, the moon deity, is the masculine god of wisdom and the measurer of time. The night of the full moon was a time of prayer, rejoicing and sacrifice. His moon can be portrayed as lying on its back. *Shamanistic*: Magic power. *Taoist*: Truth, 'the eye that shines in darkness'. The moon is yin, but the sun and moon together are all radiance; supernatural being. *Teutonic*: The moon is the masculine divine power.

Mortar See PESTLE.

Mosquito *Chinese*: Rebellion and wickedness.

Moth A form of Psyche.

Mother/Great Mother/Mother Goddess 'Nature, the universal Mother, mistress of all the elements, primordial child of time, sovereign of all things spiritual, queen of the dead, queen also of the immortals, the single manifestation of all gods and goddesses that are, whose nod governs the shining heights of Heaven, the wholesome sea breezes, the lamentable silences of the world below. She is worshipped in many aspects, known by countless names and propitiated with all manner of different rites' (Apuleius). 'She is called nurse and myrionymos, from having, in a word, innumerable forms and semblances' (Plutarch). Brahma prays to the Great Goddess: 'Thou art the pristine spirit, the nature of which is bliss; thou art the ultimate nature and clear light of heaven which illuminates and breaks the self-hypnotism of the terrible round of rebirth and thou art the one that muffles the universe, for all time, in thine own very darkness.'

She is the archetypal feminine; the origin of all life; the *primum mobile* and the ultimate *plenum*, the containing principle; she symbolizes all phases of cosmic life, uniting all the elements, both celestial and chthonic. She is the Queen of Heaven, Mother of God, 'opener of the way'; the keeper of the keys of fertility and the gates of birth, death and rebirth. As the Moon Goddess she is perpetual renewal, the bringer of the seasons, the controller of the life-giving waters and the growth from the fertilized earth and the resurrection of its life, the Tellus Mater. As the moon she is the measurer of time, dividing the year into months of a twenty-eight-day cycle, and as time she is the weaver of fate, hence all great Mothers are weavers and spinners, weaving the web and pattern of life with the thread of destiny, symbolic of her powers of ensnaring and binding, but also of loosing and freeing. She has the dual nature of creator and destroyer and is both nourisher, protector, provider of warmth and shelter, and the terrible forces of dissolution, devouring and death-dealing; she is the creator and nourisher of all life and its grave.

Mythologically she is the Virgin Mother, the Mother of God, and bears a male and is begotten by her son-lover, or by the spirit or the will; she is both the Bride and Mother of God and the Mater Dolorosa, mourning the death of her son or lover. Spiritually she is archetypal wholeness; the self-sustaining and self-sufficient; the Virgin who gives birth to the Son of Light; she is the mother of all wisdom, self-mastery and redemption through illumination and transformation, 'she who leads out beyond darkness and bondage' and, as wisdom, encompasses the transformation of man from the most elementary to the highest level. She is the ultimate mystery: 'I am all that has been, and is, and shall be, and my veil no mortal has yet lifted.'

In Alchemy the Great Mother is dynamic as fire and heat, transforming, purifying, consuming and destroying; she is also the bearer of the embryo ores in the earth-womb. In Gnosticism she is an Aeon of the pleroma. In Buddhism and Taoism she is the passive, static principle, wisdom, realization and beatitude, with the lotus and open book of wisdom as her attribute. In her beneficent, nourishing, creative aspect she is the Magna Mater as Isis, Hathor, Cybele, Ishtar, Lakshmi, Parvati, Tara, Kwan-yin, Demeter, Sophia, Mary, 'clothed with the sun and having the moon at her feet'. As ensnaring and death-dealing she is Astarte, Kali, Durga, Lilith, Hecate, Circe, and is the black virgin, or has serpent-hair or is of frightful appearance. Her symbols are legion: the crescent moon, crown of stars, turreted crown, blue robe, horns of the cow, the spiral, concentric circles, the lozenge, all waters, fountains, wells, etc., all that is sheltering, protecting and enclosing – the cave, wall, earth mound, gate, temple, church, house, city, etc. – all vessels of nourishment, and breasts as nourishment, all containers of abundance, and all that is hollow and receptive – the cup, cauldron, basket, chalice, horn of plenty, vase, yoni, etc. – all that comes from the waters – shells, fishes, pearls, the dolphin, etc. Among birds her attributes are the dove, swan, goose, swallow, partridge, etc., and among plants and flowers, the lotus, lily, rose, bryony, peony, incense tree, cedar, together with trees and their fruits also stones connected with trees and pillars as depicting tree-trunks. In her beneficent aspect, all food-producing animals, the cow, sow, goat, deer, etc.; in her dark aspect she is associated with the king-sacrifice: the king, identified with irrigation and fertility, was sacrificed to the Earth Mother when his fertility waned; later a scapegoat was substituted. This killing identified her, in turn, with the man-killing cobra and lunar serpents and with the lioness. The unicorn is her symbol as virginity and purity.

The Great Mother is associated with the Great Bear in the heavens, with the number seven and the day of the week, Friday, when the fish sacrifice was made and eaten in her honour. In her guise of Artemis, Britomartis and other goddesses she is also Lady of the Beasts, associated with hunting and wild life and accompanied by various animals.

Mound The Earth Mother; dwellings of the dead; entrance to the otherworld. The mound can take on the symbolism of the mountain as an omphalos, or as an abode of the gods at its summit.

Mountain The Cosmic Mountain is a world

Isis, the **Great Mother** of the Egyptians, wears the sun-and-moon horns of her supremacy, and holds her son Osiris in a pose prefiguring the later Christian Madonna.

Tlazolteotl, **Great Mother** of the Aztecs, has none of the celestial aloofness of Isis and Mary, but crouches and grimaces in the travail of birth and creation.

centre, an omphalos, 'through which the polar axis runs and round which glide the dragons of the cosmic powers' (Flamel). The highest point of the earth is regarded as central, the summit of Paradise, the meeting place in the clouds of heaven and earth, reaching up 'on high'. As axial and central it provides passage from one plane to another and communion with the gods; it is also the support and abode of the gods. It is the embodiment of cosmic forces and life; the rocks are bones, the streams blood, the vegetation the hair and the clouds the breath.

The mountain symbolizes constancy; eternity; firmness; stillness. Mountain tops are associated with sun, rain and thunder gods and, in early traditions of the feminine godhead, the mountain was the earth and female, with the sky, clouds, thunder and lightning as the fecundating male. On the spiritual level mountain tops represent the state of full consciousness. Pilgrimages up sacred mountains symbolize aspiration, renunciation of worldly desires, attaining to the highest states and ascent from the partial and limited to the whole and unlimited. The sacred mountain is also the 'navel of the waters' since the fountain of all waters springs from it. Passing between closing or clashing mountains represents passing to new spiritual planes, the passing being possible only in the spirit and in the 'timeless moment'.

Mountains with two summits are either the seat of solar or astral divinities, or, as in Sumeria and China, the seat of the sun and moon, as is also the case with the twin Hebrew mountains of Horeb, Mount of the Sun, and Sinai, Mount of the Moon. Temples built in the form of mountains, such as the Sumerian ziggurats, Borobadur and Inca temples, symbolize the Cosmic Centre and the ascending planes of being and the ascent of the soul. In Christian art the four rivers issue from the sacred mountain and the throne of God.

Mouse Chthonic; the powers of darkness; incessant movement; senseless agitation; turbulence. *Christian*: The Devil, the devourer; the mouse is depicted as gnawing at the root of the Tree of Life. *Greek*: An attribute of Zeus/ Sabazios and Apollo (it is suggested that they represent food for his snakes). *Hebrew*: Hypocrisy; duplicity.

Mouth The rending, devouring aspect of the Great Mother. It is also symbolic of the entrance to the underworld or the belly of the whale. In Aztec iconography a gigantic, open mouth is the hungry and all-consuming earth. Opening the mouth is judgment, powers of speech, uttering words of power. The Golden Mouth is the precious doctrine of the Buddha. The mouth of a river takes on the symbolism of the door or gate as access to another realm and the ocean of unity.

Mud The receptive earth impregnated by the fertilizing waters; the source and potential of fertility and growth. It also represents primitive and unregenerate man. See also HAND.

Mudras In Hinduism and Buddhism mudras are a whole language of symbolic movements, gestures and attitudes.

Mulberry The three colours of its three stages of ripening, white, red and black, are used to symbolize the three stages of initiation, also the three stages of man's life: white, the innocent child; red, the active; black, old age and death. *Chinese*: The mulberry is a Tree of Life and has magic powers against the forces of darkness. It also represents industry and filial piety. *Greek*: Misfortune in love as the mingled blood of Pyramus and Thisbe.

Multiplicity Intensification of a quality, such as a multiplicity of heads or hands in iconography. It also represents dispersion in manifestation, the circumference of the circle in the Round of Existence as opposed to the unity of the central point.

Muses The nine aspects of the feminine power of the Goddess.

Music Sacred music is symbolic of nature in her transitory and ever-changing aspect; it is the relative, but contains an underlying reality, the Absolute. The music of the spheres signifies the harmony of the spheres and of life. Musical instruments denote felicity; some pipe instruments are phallic and many of the stringed instruments represent the female form.

Myrrh Suffering and sorrow.

Myrtle Joy; peace; tranquillity; happiness; constancy; victory; the feminine principle; the *vesica piscis*. It is the 'flower of the gods', a magic herb. The myrtle wreath is that of the initiate. *Chinese*: Fame; success. *Christian*: The gentiles converted to Christianity. *Egyptian*: Love; joy. Sacred to Hathor. *Graeco-Roman*: Love and marriage; conjugal felicity; childbirth. Sacred to Poseidon/Neptune as the power of the waters, also to Adonis, Aphrodite/Venus, Artemis, Europa. *Hebrew*: The flower of the Tabernacle; marriage. *Mandaean*: Used in all rites as part of a priest's ritual headdress, on the heads of those baptized, on a newborn babe, on bride and bridegroom and the dying. A myrtle ring is used in religious ceremonies. Myrtle is a vital essence and transmits the breath of life, and is symbolic of life germinating and rebirth and life renewed.

Mystic Knot The continuity of everlasting life; infinity; never-ending wisdom and awareness. It is one of the Eight Treasures or Auspicious Signs of Buddha's Footprint. In China it symbolizes longevity, also the bowels of compassion.

Nagas See SERPENT (Hindu), also FABULOUS BEASTS.

Nail A symbol of the Cosmic Axis. It also shares the symbolism of binding (see BONDS) and is fate and necessity. In Christianity nails are a symbol of Christ's passion; attribute of SS Helena and Bernard of Clairvaux.

Nakedness See NUDITY.

Narcissus The self-sufficient; self-love; vanity; mistaking shadow for substance. *Chinese*: Introspection; self-esteem, but also good fortune for the coming year. *Christian*: The narcissus can take the place of the lily in pictures of the Annunciation and signifies divine love; sacrifice. *Greek*: Self-love; coldness; death in youth. The sweet and intoxicating scent of the flower, causing madness, symbolizes the results of self-love and vanity. Sacred to Narcissus, Demeter, Nemesis, Selene and Hades. *Japanese*: Silent purity; joy.

Navel See OMPHALOS.

Necklace The necklace, chain or collar indicates office and dignity, but also binds to that office. The necklace and chain also represent diversity in unity, the beads or links being the multiplicity of manifestation and the thread and connection the non-manifest; the beads are also men, animals and all living things depending on, and being kept together by, the divine power.

Net/Network Ensnaring; entanglement; the attribute and property of all gods who bind (see BONDS) and the ensnaring, negative aspect of the feminine power, the Great Mother, who is often a goddess of nets. Network is symbolic of a complex relationship beyond a mere time-space sequence, unlimited relationship; a structure formed of the visible and the invisible; it is also unity. *Chinese*: The 'net of heaven' is the stars of the firmament. *Christian*: Ambivalent as the unbreakable net of the Church, and the ensnaring net of the devil. An attribute of the disciples as fishers of men. *Egyptian*: 'The net of the underworld.' *Graeco-Roman*: An attribute of Hephaestos/Vulcan as smith gods and gods who bind. In the Orphic fish cult, like the Semitic, the net is the Word of divinity, 'the great net encircling heaven and earth'. *Scandinavian*: Attribute of the goddess Ran, 'the Ravisher'. *Sumero-Semitic*: In the fish cult 'the great net encircles heaven and earth'; it is an emblem of gods who bind. Bel is invoked as 'the catching net' and Marduk overcomes Tiamat with a net; Ishtar is a goddess of the net. *Taoist*: Heaven's Net is unity.

New Jerusalem The final transformation of the world; Paradise regained, but in a final and

An 18th-century Chinese carved this piece of turquoise matrix into an icon of the cosmic **mountain**, where human, animal and vegetable life exist in perfection and mutual harmony, all joined and nourished by a never-failing waterfall and stream.

The devouring **mouth** of Hell, entrance to the whale's belly of oblivion, receives the souls of the damned in this miniature in the 12th-century Winchester Psalter, while an angel turns the key in the lock of eternity.

fixed state, not in the growing garden symbolism of the edenic condition. The Holy City is based on the symbolism of the square; it has twelve gates, corresponding to the Twelve Tribes and the signs of the Zodiac. It is guarded by twelve angels. The Tree of Life is in the centre, bearing twelve fruits, one for each month of the year.

New Year Cosmic regeneration; the increasing power of the sun; the promise of new growth; the yearning for renewal; starting afresh.

Niche In sacred buildings the niche is symbolic of the 'cave of the world', containing the Holy, the presence of the divinity. A niche with a lamp represents the light of the deity shining in the world.

Night Like darkness, night signifies the pre-cosmogenic, pre-natal darkness preceding rebirth or initiation and illumination, but it is also chaos; death; madness; disintegration; reversion to the foetal state of the world. Night is also, according to Hesiod, the 'Mother of the Gods', the enveloping, maternal aspect of the feminine power, usually symbolized by a female figure with a star-spangled veil, holding a child, one black (death) and one white (sleep), on either arm; or by the crescent moon, or poppies, or the owl, or black wings. As all-devouring time, day and night can be depicted as a white and a black rat. Going by night symbolizes esotericism.

Nimbus Halo or Aureole. Originally indicative of solar power and the sun's disk, hence an attribute of sun gods. Also symbolizes divine radiance and power composed of the fire and gold of solar or divine energy; radiance issuing from sacredness; the spiritual power and force of light; holiness; glory; 'the circle of glory'; genius; virtue; the emanation of the life-force contained in the head; the vital energy of wisdom; the transcendental light of knowledge. The aureole sometimes surrounds the entire figure.

A round nimbus or halo denotes a dead person; a square or hexagonal aureole depicts a living saint or holy person, or it can symbolize the totality of the godhead, with three sides as the Trinity and the fourth as totality; the tri-radiate portrays a holy trinity. The double nimbus, halo, or rays, represents the dual aspect of the divinity. The cruciform halo is specifically Christian. Hexagonal haloes depict fundamental virtues. The nimbus is sometimes used to denote spiritual power as distinct from the temporal power represented by the crown. Occasionally the nimbus is employed as an attribute of the phoenix as symbolic of solar power and immortality. Colours are blue, yellow or rainbow. *Buddhist*: The red halo of Buddha is solar, dynamic activity. *Christian*: The halo was not used in Christianity until the fourth century. It signifies the holy; sainthood.

The triangular and the diamond-shaped nimbus denote God the Father; the halo with the cross indicates Christ. In Byzantine art Satan was sometimes depicted with a halo as the radiation of power. *Greek*: The blue nimbus is an attribute of Zeus as sky god; Phoebus has an aureole as sun god. *Hindu*: Siva's halo, with the fringe of flames, symbolizes the cosmos. *Mithraic*: The halo depicts the light of the sun and Mithra as sun god. *Roman*: A blue nimbus is an attribute of Jupiter as sky god, and of Apollo. The ordinary halo implied majesty or a demi-god or a deified Emperor.

Noose See BONDS.

North Coldness; darkness; obscurity; the land of the dead; night; Winter; old age, except in Hindu and Egyptian symbolism when it is lightness and the day, and a masculine power. *Chinese*: Cold; Winter; water; yin; fear; the Black Tortoise as primordial chaos. *Christian*: Darkness; night; coldness; the region of Lucifer and powers of evil; barbarians. The gospel read from the North end of the altar represents the Church's work to convert the heathen. *Egyptian*: The light; masculine power; depicted as the baboon-headed Hopi. *Hebrew*: Depicted as the winged ox. *Hindu*: The light; day; masculine power. *Iranian*: Evil, the powers of darkness and Ahriman.

Nourishment All symbols of nourishment are associated with the Mother Goddess, e.g. the vessel, jar, cup, chalice, cauldron, bowl, horn of plenty, etc., as are food-producing animals, the cow, sow, goat etc., also all waters, rivers, fountains, wells and trees and fruits. On the spiritual level these represent knowledge, feeding the soul and conferring life and immortality.

Nudity The natural, innocent, paradisal state; birth; creation; resurrection in rebirth; also stripping the self of worldly wealth and ambition; renunciation; unveiled reality and truth. A nude woman symbolizes the Tellus Mater, Dame Nature. A hero or divinity depicted as nude signifies freedom from all earthly taint. In art a nude woman is ambivalent as either truth, innocence, virtue, or as lust and lack of virtue, shamelessness. Ritual nudity is re-entry into the paradisal state and into timelessness where there is no 'wear and tear' of Time; it is also to be naked before God, to be naked and unashamed in primordial innocence; the soul stripped of the 'garment of shame', the body and selfhood, and standing 'clothed in its own power'. Baptismal nudity is putting off the old sinful nature and being reborn into a new spiritual nature.

In Hindu, Jain, Buddhist and Tantric symbolism nudity is to be 'clothed in space', the primordial state, formlessness and simplicity, and a naked woman represents Prakriti as primordial nature and cosmic power. The naked Kali depicts the state of freedom from illusion; plenitude and integrity. For the Romans nudity was shame and poverty. In Christian art it was ambivalent as it could represent the martyr, lack of possessions in poverty or in holy renunciation of worldly goods, penitence, or, on the other hand, pagan or satanic shamelessness.

Numbers In many traditions, notably the Babylonian, Hindu and Pythagorean, number is a fundamental principle from which the whole objective world proceeds; it is the origin of all things and the underlying harmony of the universe. It is also the basic principle of the universe in proportion in the plastic arts and in rhythm in music and poetry. In Hermetic philosophy the world of numbers is equated with the world of reason. Numbers are not merely quantitative, but also symbolic qualities. (It is impossible to include the whole vast complexity of Pythagorean and mediaeval Christian symbolism of numbers as employed by theology, cosmogony and science.) *Chinese*: Odd numbers are yang, celestial, immutable, auspicious; even numbers yin, terrestrial, mutable, inauspicious. *Christian*: There was little Christian number symbolism until St Augustine and the Alexandrian scholars; for St Augustine number is the archetype of the Absolute. *Greek*: 'Everything is disposed according to numbers' (Pythagoras). For Plato, numbers are the harmony of the universe; for Aristotle number was 'the origin and, as it were, the substance of all things and, as it were, their affections and states'. Odd numbers are masculine and even numbers feminine. 'Sacrifice to the celestial gods with an odd number and to the terrestrial with an even' (Plutarch). Pythagorean numbers are both quantitative and qualitative. *Hindu*: Numbers are the primary substance of the universe.
   ZERO Non-existence; nothingness; the unmanifest; the unlimited; the eternal; the absence of all quality or quantity. In Taoism it symbolizes the Void; non-being; in Buddhism it is the Void and no-thingness; in Qabalism it is the Boundless; Limitless Light; the Ain; for Pythagoras, zero is the perfect form, the Monad, the originator and container of all; in Islam it is the Divine Essence. Zero also represents the Cosmic Egg, the primordial Androgyne, the Plenum. As an empty circle it depicts both the nothingness of death and the totality of life contained within the circle and shares the symbolism of the CIRCLE (q.v.). As an ellipse the two sides represent ascent and descent, evolution and involution. Before the One there is only the Void, or non-being; thought; the ultimate mystery, the incomprehensible Absolute.
   ONE Primordial unity; the beginning; the Creator; the First Mover; the sum of all possibilities; essence; the Centre; the indivisible; the germinal; isolation; an upsurging and uprising, the principle which gives rise to duality and thence to multiplicity and back to

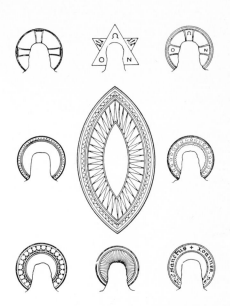

The **nimbus**, or halo, surrounding the head of a holy person symbolizes the divine light shining from the sanctified personality; the MANDORLA, or *vesica piscis*, here at the centre, encloses the entire body of a person of special dignity and holiness.

The tortoise on a 3rd-century Chinese sarcophagus symbolizes the **North**, land of darkness and of the dead.

final unity. *Chinese*: Yang, masculine; celestial; auspicious. The Monad. *Christian*: God the Father; the Godhead. *Hebrew*: Adonai, the Lord, the Most High, the 'I am'; hidden intelligence. *Islamic*: God as unity; the Absolute; the self-sufficient. *Pythagorean*: Spirit; God, from whom all things rise; the essence; the Monad. *Taoist*: 'Tao begets One, One begets Two, Two begets Three and Three begets all things.'

TWO Duality; alternation; diversity; conflict; dependence; otherness; the static condition; the rooted, hence balance, stability; reflection; the opposite poles; the dual nature of man; desire, since all that is manifest in duality is in pairs of opposites. As one represents a point, so two signifies length. The Binary is the first number to recede from Unity, hence it also symbolizes sin which deviates from the first good and so denotes the transitory and corruptible. Double animals of the same symbolism even if of different species, e.g. two lions or a lion and bull, both solar, represent twofold strength. *Alchemic*: The opposites, sun and moon, king and queen, sulphur and quicksilver, at first antagonistic but finally resolved and united in the androgyne. *Buddhist*: The duality of *samsara*; male and female; theory and practice; wisdom and method; also the blind and the lame united to see the way and walk in it. *Chinese*: Yin, feminine; terrestrial; inauspicious. *Christian*: Christ with two natures as God and man. *Hebrew*: The life-force. In Qabalism wisdom and self-consciousness. *Hindu*: Duality; the shakta-shakti. *Islamic*: The Spirit. *Platonic*: Plato says that two is a digit without meaning since it implies relationship, which introduces the third factor. *Pythagorean*: The Duad, the divided terrestrial being. *Taoist*: The K'ua, the Two Determinants, the yin-yang. Two is a weak yin number, since it has no centre.

THREE Multiplicity; creative power; growth; forward movement overcoming duality; expression; synthesis. 'Three is the first number to which the word "all" has been appropriated' and 'The Triad is the number of the whole, inasmuch as it contains a beginning, a middle and an end' (Aristotle). The 'power of three' is universal and is the tripartite nature of the world as heaven, earth and waters; it is man as body, soul and spirit; birth, life and death; beginning, middle, end; past, present, future; the three phases of the moon, etc. Three is the 'heavenly' number, representing the soul, as four is the body; together the two equal seven and form the sacred hebdomad; while 3 × 4 is twelve, representing the signs of the Zodiac and the months of the year, etc. The ternary can be divided into duality and unity, of which it is the sum; it is the 'strong' number of Taoist symbolism since it has a central point of equilibrium. Three introduces the all-embracing Godhead – Father, Mother, Son, which is also reflected in the human family. Three also carries the authority of accumulated effect, once or twice being possible coincidence,

but three times carries certainty and power, e.g. Thrice Greatest Hermes; Thrice Noble Lord; Thrice Happy Isles, etc. Folklore has three wishes, three tries, three princes or princesses, witches, weird sisters, fairies (often two good, one bad). Three, being equivalent to the many, can symbolize a large number, a crowd, 'three cheers', and also signifies fulfilment. There are innumerable trinities of gods and powers, and triune lunar deities and threefold goddesses are prominent in Semitic, Greek, Celtic and Teutonic religions; they are often different aspects, or potencies, of one deity. The chief symbol of three is the TRIANGLE (q.v.) and three interwoven circles or triangles can represent the indissoluble unity of the three persons of a trinity. Other symbols are the trident; fleur-de-lis; trefoil; trisula; triple thunderbolt; trigrams, etc. Lunar animals are often three-legged, as the three phases of the moon, but sometimes, as in France, there are three rabbits or people in the moon. *African*: Ashanti. The moon goddess is three persons, two black and one white. *Alchemic*: The ternary; sulphur, quicksilver, salt, represents spirit, soul and body. *Arabic*: Pre-Islamic. Manat is a threefold goddess represented as the three Holy Virgins, Al-Itab, Al-Uzza, Al-Manat, depicted as aniconic stelae, stones or pillars, or as pillars surmounted by doves. *Buddhist*: The Tri-ratna, the Three Precious Jewels, the Buddha, Dharma, Sangha. *Celtic*: Bridgit is threefold; there are the Three Blessed Ladies and innumerable Triads, often a threefold aspect of the same divinity. Three is a particularly significant number in Celtic tradition. *Chinese*: Sanctity; the auspicious number; the first odd, yang number. The moon toad, or bird, is three-legged. See also *Taoism*, below. *Christian*: The Trinity, the soul, the union of body and soul in man and in the Church. There are three gifts of the Magi to Christ as God-King-Sacrifice; three figures of transformation, temptations, denials by Peter, crosses on Calvary, days of the death of Christ, appearances after death, Marys, and the qualities, or theological virtues, of Faith, Hope and Love. *Egyptian*: Thoth is the Thrice Great, 'Trismegistus'. *Graeco-Roman*: Fate, the Moirai, who are three-in-one as Moira; Hecate is threefold; the Erinyes are three-in-one as Erinys, as are the Gorgons as Medusa. There are three charities, graces, sirens, Horae, Hesperides, Graiai. Cerberus is triple-headed and Scylla has a three-bitch tail; the Chimera has a three-part body. Three, four, and their sum, seven are sacred to Aphrodite/Venus as queen of the three worlds and four elements. Orphic symbolism has the triad of Being, Life, Intelligence. *Hebrew*: Limitless Light; sanctifying intelligence. In Qabalism three represents understanding and the trinity of male, female and uniting intelligence. *Hermetic*: The Supreme Power, 'Trismegistus', the Thrice Great. *Hindu*: The Trimurti, the triple power of creation, destruction, preservation, of unfolding, maintaining and concluding. There are various trinities of gods; the moon chariot has three wheels. *Japanese*: The Three Treasures are the Mirror, Sword and Jewel – Truth, Courage, Compassion. *Maori*: The Great Spirit, the Divine Creator, is a trinity of sun, moon and earth, the god of nature, of past, present and future; mind, character and physique, symbolized by three raised fingers. *Mexico*: The Trinity is represented by three crosses, one large and two smaller. *Pythagorean*: Completion. *Scandinavian and Teutonic*: Fate, as the Three Norns, Mani, Nyi, Nithi, who also denote the full, new and waning moon. In Teutonic mythology the moon is Fate, and Holda, the lunar goddess, is triune with her two daughters. The hare in the moon has three legs. Thor is sometimes depicted with three heads and the triskele, or triquetra, is a symbol of Odin/Woden. Three is the number of good fortune. 'Aller guten Dinge sind drei.' *Sumero-Semitic*: There are numerous trinities. In Carthage, the Great Goddess, as lunar, is represented by three aniconic pillars. *Slav*: The moon god is triple-headed. *Taoist*: The Great Triad is Heaven-Man-Earth. Three is the first 'strong' number as when divided it has a centre remaining, the central point of equilibrium. It is yang, auspicious, and is also symbolic of multiplicity: 'The One gave rise to the Two, the two gave rise to three; three gave rise to all numbers.'

FOUR From four the first solid figure is produced; it is the spatial scheme or order of manifestation, the static as opposed to the circular and dynamic. It is wholeness; totality; completion; solidarity; the Earth; order; the rational; measurement; relativity; justice. There are four cardinal points, seasons, winds, sides of the square, arms of the cross, rivers of Paradise and of the infernal regions, seas, sacred mountains, watches of the night and day, quarters of the moon, tetramorphs, and in the West there are the four elements (there are five elements in the East). The Divine Quaternity is in contrast to the Trinity. Four is an emblematic number in the Old Testament. The four rivers of Paradise forming the cross, the four quarters of the earth, etc. are almost universal in symbolism. The quaternary can be depicted as the quatrefoil as well as the square and the cross. *Amerindian*: The number most frequently used, with the four cardinal directions and winds, depicted with the cross and swastika. Ceremonial and ritual acts are repeated in fours. *Buddhist*: The Damba Tree of Life has four limbs and from its roots gush forth four sacred streams of Paradise, representing the four boundless wishes of compassion, affection, love, impartiality, the four directions of the heart. In Chinese Buddhism the four celestial guardians of the cardinal points are Mo-li Ch'ing, the East, with the jade ring and spear; Virupaksha, the West, the Far-gazer, with the four-stringed guitar; Virudhaka, the South, with the umbrella of chaos and darkness and earth-quakes; Vaisravenna, the North, with the whips, leopard-skin bag, snake and pearl.

The **three** gods – Brahma, Siva, Vishnu – of the Hindu trinity are joined in the single but threefold power of creation, preservation and destruction on this relief from the Adhipuricvara temple.

The **four** canopic jars, whose covers bear the heads of the sons of Horus – Amset, Hapi, Duamutef and Senuf, the guardians of the four directions – were the receptacles for a dead Egyptian's internal organs.

Chinese: Four is the number of the Earth, symbolized by the square. There are four streams of immortality. Four is an even, yin, number. *Christian*: The number of the body, with three as the soul. There are the four rivers of Paradise, Gospels, Evangelists, chief archangels, chief devils, Fathers of the Church, Great Prophets, cardinal virtues (prudence, fortitude, justice, temperance), winds from which the One Spirit is to come, horsemen of the Apocalypse, tetramorphs. *Egyptian*: The sacred number of time, measurement of the sun. Four pillars support the vault of heaven; the four canopic jars placed round the dead at the four corners, are guarded by the four sons of Horus who are associated with the cardinal points. *Gnostic*: Barbelo, the Four-ness of God. *Greek*: The sacred number of Hermes. *Hebrew*: Measuring; beneficence; intelligence. In Qabalism it is memory; the four worlds of the Qabala; the four directions of space and the four levels of the hierarchical organism of the Torah. *Hermetic*: The divine quaternity; God. *Hindu*: Totality; plenitude; perfection. Brahma, the Creator, is four-faced. The temple is based on the four sides of the square, symbolizing order and finality. There are four tattvas, the four bodies of man and kingdoms of nature (animal, vegetable, mineral, mind) and four yugas. Four is the winning throw at dice. There are four castes and pairs of opposites. *Islamic*: The four terms of the quaternary are the Principle, the Creator; Universal Spirit; Universal Soul; the primordial matter. These correspond to the four worlds of Qabalism. There are also four angelic beings and four houses of death. *Mayan*: Four giants support the celestial roof. *Pythagorean*: Perfection; harmonious proportion; justice; the earth; four is the number of the Pythagorean oath. Four and ten are divinities; the Tetraktys $1+2+3+4 = 10$. *Scandinavian*: There are four rivers of milk flowing in Asgard. *Sumero-Semitic*: Four astral gods are identified with the four cardinal points. *Teutonic*: Four dwarfs support the world. *Taoist*: The four celestial guardians are Li, with the pagoda; Ma, with the sword; Cho, with two swords; Wen, with a spiked club. There are four Spiritually Endowed, or Sacred, Creatures: the Dragon, Phoenix, Ky-lin or Unicorn, and Tortoise, who also represent the cardinal points.

FIVE The human microcosm; the number of man, forming a pentagon, with outstretched arms and legs. The pentagon, being endless, shares the symbolism of the perfection and power of the circle and five is a circular number as it produces itself in its last digit when raised to its powers. Like the circle, the pentacle symbolizes the whole, the quincunx being the number of the centre and the meeting-point of heaven and earth and the four cardinal points plus the centre. It is also the Godhead as the Central Creator of the four great forces. Five is the marriage number of the *hieros gamos* as the combination of the feminine, even, number two and the masculine, odd, three. It also symbolizes

meditation; religion; agency; versatility and, except in the East, the five senses. Five-petalled flowers and five-pointed leaves, e.g. rose, lily, vine, represent the microcosm. The five-pointed star, like the pentagram, depicts integral individuality and it also represents spiritual aspiration and education when it points upwards: pointing downwards it is a witchcraft and black magic symbol. The five digits formed the first counting mechanism. *Alchemic*: The five-petalled flower and five-pointed star symbolize the quintessence. *Buddhist*: The heart has four directions which, with its centre, make five and represent universality; this is also symbolized by the Sacred Mountain surrounded by four islands. There are five Dhyani Buddhas: Vairocana, the Brilliant, whose attributes are the wheel, the centre and whiteness; Akshobhya, the Imperturbable, with the vajra, the East and blue; Ratnasambhava, the Jewel-born, jewel, South, yellow; Amitabha, Boundless Light, the lotus, West, red; Amoghasiddhi, Infallible Success, sword, North, green. *Chinese*: There are five elements; atmospheres; conditions; planets; sacred mountains; grains; colours; tastes; poisons; powerful charms; cardinal virtues; blessings; eternal ideals; relations of mankind. *Christian*: Five depicts man after the Fall; there are five senses; points of the cross; wounds of Christ; fishes feeding the five thousand; books of Moses. *Egyptian*: There are the five crocodiles of the Nile. *Graeco-Roman*: The nuptial number, love and union; the number of Venus, Venus years being completed in groups of five. Apollo as god of light has five qualities: omnipotence; omniscience; omnipresence; eternity; unity. *Hebrew*: Strength and severity; radical intelligence. In Qabalism five signifies fear. *Hindu*: The quinary groups of the world; the five elements of the subtle and coarse states; the primary colours; senses; the five faces of Siva and the twice-five incarnations of Vishnu. *Islamic*: The five pillars of religion; the five Divine Presences; fundamental dogmas; actions; prayer five times daily. *Parsee*: A significant number in Parsee and Mandaean rites, possibly connected with the five sacred intercalary days of light. *Pythagorean*: The *hieros gamos*, the marriage of heaven and earth; light; Apollo as god of light and his five qualities.

SIX Equilibrium; harmony; the perfect number within the decad: $1+2+3 = 6$. 'The most productive of all numbers' (Philo). It also symbolizes union of polarity, the hermaphrodite being represented by the two interlaced triangles, the upward-pointing as male, fire and the heavens, and the downward-pointing as female, the waters and the earth. Six also signifies love; health; beauty; chance; luck; it is the winning throw at dice in the West. There are six rays of the solar wheel and the interlaced triangles, the six-pointed star or Seal of Solomon, also represents perfect balance. *Chinese*: The universe takes the number six, with the four cardinal points and the Above and

Below making the six directions; there are six
senses (mind being the sixth); the day and night
each have six periods. *Christian*: Perfection;
completion; the six days of creation. *Hebrew*:
The six days of creation; meditation; intelligence. In Qabalism it is creation, beauty.
Pythagorean: Chance; luck. *Sumerian*: The six
days of creation.

SEVEN The number of the universe, the
macrocosm. Completeness; a totality. With the
three of the heavens and the soul and the four of
the earth and the body, it is the first number
which contains both the spiritual and temporal.
It is perfection; security; safety; rest; plenty;
reintegration; synthesis, also virginity and the
number of the Great Mother. There are seven
cosmic stages, heavens, hells, major planets and
metals of the planets, circles of the universe, rays
of the sun, ages of man, pillars of wisdom, lunar
divisions of the rainbow, days of the week, notes
of the scale, wonders of the world etc. The
seventh ray of the sun is the path by which man
passes from this world to the next. Seven days is
a period of fasting and penitence. The seventh
power of any number is, according to Philo,
both a square and a cube and thus of great
importance. The seven-headed dragon appears
in India, Persia, the Far East, especially
Cambodia, and in Celtic and Mediterranean
myths. *Alchemic*: There are seven metals
involved in the Work. *Astrology*: The seven stars
of the Great Bear are 'indestructible', i.e. seen
all the year round. There are seven Pleiades,
major planets, rays of the sun. *Buddhist*: The
number of ascent and of ascending to the
highest and attaining the centre. The seven
steps of Buddha symbolize the ascent of the
seven cosmic stages transcending time and
space. The seven-storied *prasada* at Borobadur is
a sacred mountain and *axis mundi*, culminating
in the transcendent North, reaching the realm
of Buddha. *Chinese*: There are seven fairies and
animal spirits. *Christian*: God is represented by
the seventh ray in the centre of the six rays of
creation. There are seven sacraments; gifts of
the spirit; the seven of the 3+4 theological and
cardinal virtues; deadly sins; tiers or mountains
in Purgatory; liberal arts; crystal spheres
containing the planets; major prophets; angels
of the Presence; devils cast out by Christ; period
of fasting and penitence; joys and sorrows of
Mary; champions of Christendom; councils of
the early Church; the seventh day after the six
of creation was one of rest. In the Old
Testament there are the seven altars of Baalam;
oxen and rams for sacrifice; trumpets; circuits of
Jericho; times Naaman bathed in the Jordan;
number of Samson's bonds; the child raised
from the dead by Elisha sneezed seven times;
the Ark rested on the seventh month and the
dove was sent out after seven days. *Egyptian*:
There are seven Hathors as Fates and the
priestesses of Hathor have seven jars; the seven
daughters of Ra made seven knots in their seven
tunics; the seven hawks of Ra are the seven wise
ones; seven cows with the bull depict fertility;

The 12th-century mystic and visionary Hildegarde of
Bingen saw the **six** days of creation, here illustrated
in a manuscript of her writings, with their
individuality united within the circle of their
integrity as parts of a single process.

In this 11th-century Kashmiri bronze group, the
seven planets, each carrying its own symbol, stand
arm in arm, depicting the number's significance of
completeness, totality and synthesis.

there are seven houses of the underworld with three times seven gates. The number is sacred to Osiris. *Graeco-Roman*: Sacred to Apollo, whose lyre has seven strings, and to Athene/Minerva and Ares/Mars; Pan has seven pipes; there are the seven Wise Men of Greece. *Hebrew*: Occult intelligence. There are seven great holy days in the Jewish year; the Menorah has seven branches; the Temple took seven years to build; there are seven pillars of wisdom. *Hindu*: There are the Seven Jewels of the Brahmanas and seven gods before the flood, with seven wise men saved from it. *Islamic*: The first perfect number. There are seven heavens, climates, earths and seas, colours, prophets, active powers, states or stations of the heart; the Ka'aba is circumambulated seven times, representing the seven attributes of God. *Magic*: There are seven knots in a cord for 'spellbinding', and incantations are sevenfold. *Mithraic*: The cave of Mithras has seven doors and altars, and a ladder of seven rungs depicting the seven grades of initiation into the mysteries. *Pythagorean*: The cosmic number with the three of heaven and four of the world; the God of the world; perfection. *Sumero-Semitic*: There are seven lunar divisions and days of the week. 'Thou shalt shine with horns to determine six days and on the seventh with half a crown', the seventh thus becomes opposition to the sun and symbolizes darkness and balefulness, and therefore it is dangerous to undertake anything on the seventh day, which becomes a day of rest. There are seven zones of the earth; heavens, symbolized by the planes of the ziggurat; branches of the Tree of Life, each having seven leaves; gates of hell; demons of Tiamat and winds to destroy her; colours; seals; Fates.

EIGHT Spiritually, eight is the goal of the initiate, having passed through the seven stages or heavens, and it is, thus, the number of Paradise regained; regeneration; resurrection; felicity; perfect rhythm; the eighth day created the new man of grace. After the seven days of fasting and penance the eighth day becomes plenty and renewal. As $7 + 1$ it is the number of the octave and a beginning again. It is also solidarity as the first cube and it denotes perfection by virtue of its six surfaces. There are eight winds and intermediate directions of space. Eight also represents the pairs of opposites. The octagon is the beginning of the transformation of the square into the circle and vice versa. *Buddhist*: Completion; all possibilities. There are eight symbols of good augury. *Chinese*: The whole; all possibilities in manifestation; good luck. The PA KUA (q.v.) is the design depicting the eight trigrams and pairs of opposites, usually placed in a circle, the circumference of which symbolizes time and space. There are eight delights of human existence. *Christian*: Regeneration; rebirth. The font is usually octagonal as symbolizing the place of regeneration. There are eight beatitudes. *Egyptian*: The number of Thoth. *Hebrew*: Perfect intelligence; splendour; the digit value

of IHVH, the 'Number of the Lord'. The Temple was sanctified in eight days. *Hermetic*: The magic number of Hermes. In Hermetic theology there is one chief God, Thoth/Hermes, inventor of numbers and geometry, and eight minor gods. *Hindu*: 8×8 is the order of the celestial world established on earth. Temples are built on the pattern of the MANDALA (q.v.), the 8×8 symbolism. There are eight regions of the world; suns; divisions of the day; chakras. *Islamic*: The throne which encompasses the world is supported by eight angels, corresponding to both the eight divisions of space and the groups of letters in the Arabic alphabet. *Japanese*: Eight is the 'many'; there are eight gods in the heavens. *Platonic*: Plato has eight spheres of different colours surrounding the luminous pillar of the heavens. *Pythagorean*: Solidarity; stability. *Sumero-Semitic*: The magic number of Nebo. *Taoist*: All possibilities in manifestation with the Pa Kua representing the forces in the phenomenal world. There are eight Taoist genii or immortals.

NINE Composed of the all-powerful 3×3, it is the Triple Triad; completion; fulfilment; attainment; beginning and end; the whole; a celestial and angelic number; the Earthly Paradise. It is an 'incorruptible' number. Nine is also the number of the circumference, hence its division into 90 degrees and into 360 for the entire circumference. It is symbolized by the figure of the two triangles △ which, in turn, is a symbol of the male and female, fire and water, mountain and cave principles. *Buddhist*: The supreme spiritual power; a celestial number. *Celtic*: A highly significant number in the Celtic tradition; a central number with the eight directions and the centre making nine. The Triple Goddesses are thrice three; there are nine Celtic maidens and nine white stones symbolize the nine virgins attendant on Bridgit; nine is connected with the Beltane Fire rites which are attended by eighty-one men, nine at a time. *Chinese*: Celestial power, the 3×3 being the most auspicious of all numbers. It also signifies the eight directions with the centre as the ninth point, as in the Hall of Light. There are nine great social laws and classes of officials. In land division for *feng-shui* there are eight exterior squares for the cultivation of the land by holders and the central, and ninth, square is a 'god's acre', dedicated to Shang-ti, the supreme ruler; it is also called the 'Emperor's Field', denoting his position as delegate of the heavenly power. *Christian*: Nine appears little in Christian symbolism. There are the triple triads of choirs of angels and nine spheres and rings round hell. *Egyptian*: The Ennead. *Graeco-Roman*: There are nine gods and, later, nine muses. *Hebrew*: Pure intelligence; truth, since it reproduces itself when multiplied. In Qabalism it symbolizes foundation. *Hindu*: The number of Agni, fire; the square of the nine forms the mandala of eighty-one squares and leads to, and encloses, the universe. *Mayan*: There are nine underworlds, each ruled by a God. *Pythagorean*: The limit of numbers, all others existing and revolving within it. *Scandinavian*: Odin/Woden hung for nine days and nights on the Yggdrasil to win the secrets of wisdom for mankind. Skeldi, the northern Persephone, goddess of snow, lives in her mountain for three months and by Niord's sea for nine months. Nine is the sacred number in Scandinavian-Teutonic symbolism.

TEN The number of the cosmos; the paradigm of creation. The decad contains all numbers and therefore all things and possibilities; it is the radix or turning-point of all counting. It is the all-inclusive; law; order; dominion. The tetraktys $1+2+3+4 = 10 \therefore$ symbolizes divinity; also one represents a point; two, length; three, a plane surface (as the triangle); four, solidity or space. Ten is the perfect number, the return to unity. Based on the two hands, it is completeness and the foundation of all counting. Its higher ranges of completeness, 100 and 1000, are the basis of all Hindu cosmology, and in China the Ten Thousand Things, i.e. the uncountable, symbolize the whole of manifestation. Ten is also the number of completion of journeys and the return to origins: Odysseus wandered for nine years and returned on the tenth; Troy was besieged for nine years and fell on the tenth. It is also the sum of the number nine of the circumference with the one of the centre, hence perfection. It is also symbolized by the maypole, the one of the axis with the circle danced round it. *Chinese*: Represented by a cross formed centrally by the character *chi*, symbolizing the self facing both ways as both yin and yang; the perfect figure. The Ten Celestial Stems (*Kan*) are possibly connected with the names of the ten-day week on the prevailing cyclic calculations (see *Sixty*). *Christian*: There are ten Commandments of the Decalogue; parables of ten lamps, virgins and talents. Tithes were to be given to God. *Gnostic*: The ten Aeons become the Sephiroth, emanating from the Pleroma. *Hebrew*: In Qabalism it is the numerical value of Yod, the Eternal Word, the first letter of the divine name; resplendent intelligence; divine support; the Decalogue; the Kingdom; the ten names of God; the number of the Sephiroth, the spheres or emanations from the Ein Soph, usually symbolized by the Tree of Life, the first being the Monad, the First Cause of the other nine which are composed of three trinities, each an image of the original Trinity of male-female and uniting intelligence; the tenth, Adoni, represents the mystic return to unity. In Solomon's Temple there were ten lavers, tables and candlesticks; the cherubim were ten cubits high and ten Levites minister before the Ark. *Hindu*: the higher ranges of ten, i.e. 100 and 1000, are the basis of all Hindu cosmology. *Islamic*: Tithing holds an important place. *Pythagorean*: The Monad, the recommencement of a series and infinite expansion; perfection. *Roman*: The number is represented by X, the perfect figure; completion. *Sumero-Semitic*: The

Each of the **eight** sides of this 19th-century Chinese brass incense-burner is governed by one of the eight basic trigrams, all ruled over and integrated by the yin-yang, central and uniting symbol of perfect rhythm and the combination of opposites.

Nine squares by nine, arranged in nine sub-squares, each of nine, feature in this 18th-century Indian diagram. It was used for computing astronomical periods, and also as an aid to meditation.

tenth day of the Spring Festival was celebrated by a procession comprising the whole of the gods.

ELEVEN Sin; transgression; peril. Ten being the perfect number and the law, eleven represents the exceeding of both.

TWELVE The Duodecad is a complete cycle; cosmic order. As 3×4 it is both the spiritual and temporal order, the esoteric and exoteric. There are the twelve Signs of the Zodiac and months of the year, of which there are six male and six female; twelve hours of the day and night; fruits of the Cosmic Tree, etc.; there are also the twelve days of return to chaos at the Winter Solstice, when the dead return, celebrated in the Saturnalia in Rome and the twelve days of Yuletide and Christmas; these celebrations are also found in Vedic, Chinese, Pagan and European symbolism. The days are said to forecast the meteorological pattern of the twelve months of the coming year. *Buddhist*: There are twelve members of the council of the Dalai Lama. *Celtic*: There were twelve paladins or peers of Charlemagne and knights of the Round Table. *Chinese*: For the Twelve Terrestrial Branches see ZODIAC. *Christian*: There are twelve Fruits of the Spirit; stars as the Tribes of Israel and the Apostles; gates and foundation stones of the Holy City; days of Christmas. *Egyptian*: There are twelve gates of hell, in which Ra spends the hours of the night. *Graeco-Roman*: Herodotus says there are twelve gods and goddesses of Olympus; Hesiod mentions twelve Titans. Twelve is also the number of the tables of the law and of the days and nights of the Saturnalia. *Hebrew*: There are twelve fruits of the Tree of Life; gates of the Heavenly City; loaves of the Table of the Temple, which represented the months of the year; precious stones of Aaron's breastplate; Tribes of Israel; sons of Jacob. *Hermetic*: There are twelve months of the year and torments. *Islamic*: The twelve descendants of Ali, the Imams, or 'directors', rule the twelve hours of the day. *Mithraic*: Mithra had twelve disciples. *Roman*: Twelve *flamines minores* followed the Pontifex Maximus at sacred rites. *Sumero-Semitic*: There are twelve days of duel between Chaos and Cosmos.

THIRTEEN In Christianity there are thirteen Tenebrae, or Lenten-hearse, candles, which are extinguished one by one, symbolizing the darkness on earth at Christ's death. Thirteen is regarded as unlucky as being the number of Judas Iscariot with Jesus and the twelve disciples; it is also the number of a witches' coven. There are thirteen Mayan heavens, each ruled by a god. Thirteen is an important number in the Aztec calendar, divided into thirteen-day periods; it was also the number used in divination.

TWENTY As the sum of the fingers and toes, twenty carries the significance of the whole man and of reckoning by the score.

FORTY Probation; trial; initiation; death. As an elevation of four it is wholeness and totality. The importance of the 'forty days' probably arises from the Babylonian forty days' disappearance of the Pleiades, a period of rains, storms, floods and dangers. The return of the Pleiades was a time of rejoicing, and a bundle of forty reeds was burned for the forty days of evil power. The Roman 'quarantine' kept ships isolated for forty days. Temples in Persia, Baalbec, Tartary, and those of the Druids and the Temple of Ezekiel, had forty pillars. *Christian*: There are forty days of Lent, from Christ's forty days in the wilderness; days of the resurrection, from Easter to Ascension; time of privilege or sanctuary; St Swithin's weather. In the Old Testament there are forty days of Moses on Sinai; Elijah in hiding; the Deluge; probation for Nineveh under Jonah; forty years of the Jews wandering in the wilderness; under the yoke of the Philistines; reign of David; reign of Solomon; Eli judging Israel. Ezekiel bore the iniquity of Israel for forty days. *Egyptian*: The forty days of the death and absence of Osiris is a period of fasting. *Islamic*: The number of change and death, but also of reconciliation and return to the principle. Mohammed received his 'call' at forty years; the Qoran should be read every forty days. *Mithraic*: Forty is the number of days of initiation rites and of festivals and sacrifice.

FIFTY After the completion of the 7×7 cycle of years the fiftieth becomes a Great Year, a Jubilee, a return to the beginning and the primordial state and so a fresh start. There are fifty lunations, i.e. four years, between the Olympic Games.

SIXTY The number of time in minutes and seconds. It is a 'round number' as three score. It frequently occurs in sagas. In Egypt sixty represented longevity. It is the Chinese cyclic number, a 'cycle of sixty', in the West called a 'cycle of Cathay'. By the revolving interaction of the Ten Celestial Stems (*kan*) and Twelve Terrestrial Branches (*chih*), a cycle becomes complete in all its combinations in the sixtieth year; it is then repeated. Six cycles approximately comprise a tropical year.

SEVENTY In Hebrew symbolism the seventy branches of the candelabra are the Decans, the twelve Zodiacal divisions of the seven planets in tens. Seventy is the allotted span of human life.

666 Ambivalent as both the 'Number of the Beast' and the number of Hakathriel, the Angel of the Diadem. In Christianity it is the Mark of the Beast, the Antichrist. In Qabalism it is the number of Sorath, the solar demon opposed to the Archangel Michael. It is the solar number, the sum of the square of the sun, a basic figure in sacred geometry.

888 In the Hebrew alphabet this is the sacred number of Jesus, as opposed to the 666 of the beast.

Nymphs Emanations of the feminine productive powers of the universe; later guardian spirits, especially of groves, fountains, springs and mountains.

In his *Last Supper*, Leonardo catches the **thirteen** figures' instant of sinister confusion and agitation at the announcement of Judas's betrayal and treachery.

Oak Strength; protection; durability; courage; truth; man; the human body. The oak is often associated with thunder gods and thunder; sky and fertility gods have the oak as an emblem, hence it can also represent lightning and fire. *Amerindian*: Sacred to the Earth Mother. *Celtic*: Sacred to Dagda, the Creator; a holy tree. *Chinese*: Masculine strength, also the weakness of strength which resists and breaks in the storm, in contrast to the strength in weakness of the willow which bends before the storm and survives. *Christian*: A symbol of Christ as strength in adversity; steadfastness in faith and virtue. The oak, holly and aspen are variously said to be the tree of the cross. *Druidic*: The sacred tree, the masculine principle with the mistletoe as the feminine. *Graeco-Roman*: Sacred to Zeus/Jupiter; the marriage of the oak god Jupiter to the oak goddess Juno was celebrated each year in an oak grove and worshippers wore crowns of oak leaves. The crown of oak leaves was also awarded for saving life and for victory in the Pythian games. The oak is an emblem of Cybele and of Silvanus, and in Greece of Philemon as conjugal devotion and happiness. The dryads were oak nymphs. *Hebrew*: The Tree of the Covenant, the Divine Presence. *Scandinavian and Teutonic*: Thor's Tree of Life; also sacred to Donar. Oak groves were places of worship in Germanic rites.

Oar Power; skill; knowledge. The oar is the rod, or spear, which stirs the primordial ocean, also the pole which guides the Ship of the Dead across the waters to the other shore. In this context the oar, wand, or pole is related to the symbolism of the Golden Bough. In Egypt the oar depicted sovereignty, rule and action. An attribute of river gods.

Obelisk Phallic; male generative power; fertility; regeneration; stabilizing force. It is also an *axis mundi* and Tree of Life, a ritual world centre, a 'finger of the sun'. In Egypt it denotes Ra; the ray of the sun; solar generative power.

Oblation See SACRIFICE.

Obsidian *Aztec*: The source of life; bringer of both life and death.

Ocean The primordial waters; chaos; formlessness; material existence; endless motion; it is the source of all life, containing all potentials; the sum of all possibilities in manifestation; the unfathomable; the *anima mundi*, the Great Mother. The ocean also symbolizes the sea of life which has to be crossed. *Hindu*: The cosmic ocean is the recumbent Vishnu who sleeps on the coiled serpent on the waters; the ocean is also symbolized by the enclosing stones of the Vedic altar: 'That household altar is this world and the enclosing stones are the waters'

Re-erected in Rome in 1667 to the design of Bernini, this **obelisk** was first erected in Egypt in the 6th century BC – the skyward-pointing sign of Ra, the sun god.

(*Satapatha Brahmana*). *Islamic*: Infinite divine wisdom. The two seas, one sweet and fresh, the other salt and bitter, are Heaven and Earth, the Higher and the Lower Waters, which were originally one; the salt sea is exoteric knowledge, the fresh, esoteric. *Sumero-Semitic*: The Accadians associated the primordial waters with wisdom. All life arose from the sweet waters, Apsu, and the salt water, Tiamat, who symbolized the power of the waters, the feminine principle and blind forces of chaos. *Taoist*: The ocean is equated with the Tao, the primordial and inexhaustible, 'informing at creation without being exhausted' (Chuang Tzu).

Ocelot In Amerindian symbolism the ocelot assumes the powers and attributes of the lioness goddesses of Egypt and Babylon and the tigress of East Asia.

Octagon Eight is the number of regeneration; renewal; rebirth; transition. After the seven steps of initiation the eighth is Paradise regained and the eighth day created the new man of grace. In sacred architecture an octagonal structure may support a dome, thus forming a transition from the square to the circle; in some temples the circle of the roof is supported by eight pillars standing on a square base, thus squaring the circle. The four cardinal and four intermediate points, which form the octagon, are called, in various traditions, the 'eight winds'; they are also the eight doors giving passage from one state to another; in Hinduism they also represent the eight divisions of the day. In Christianity the font, as symbolizing regeneration and rebirth, is frequently octagonal in shape.

Octopus Related to the dragon, spider and spiral symbolism; it is suggested as a thunder symbol, or as depicting lunar phases; it is associated with the zodiacal sign of Cancer, the depth of the waters and the Summer Solstice, the malefic *Janua inferni*. In Celtic and Scandinavian art the arms of the octopus are straight, but in Minoan and Mycenean representations the arms are coiled and take on the symbolism of the SPIRAL (q.v.). The octopus is often accompanied by the swastika.

Oil Consecration; dedication; spiritual illumination; mercy; fertility. Anointing with oil is infusing new divine life; consecration; bestowing the grace of God or conferring wisdom.

Old Man Mortality. As naked, or partly clothed, he is Time and is frequently depicted as bald or having a single lock of hair on the forehead: 'that bald sexton, Time'. With a scythe and hourglass, and sometimes with crutches, he portrays the Reaper, Death. In Qabalism he represents esoteric and occult wisdom; in the Zodiac he is Saturn.

Olive Immortality; fruitfulness; bridal, to impart fertility; peace; plenty (the oil being valuable). The olive branch, especially with the dove, is a symbol of peace, par excellence, and of the Golden Age. The olive branch was also the prize at the Moon Virgin's race as was the apple bough at the race of the Sun-bridegroom. The olive tree is the dwelling place and an emblem of the moon. The crown of olives worn by the victor at the Heraea identified the victorious virgin with Hera and the moon, while the crown of wild olives for the victor at the Olympic Games represented Zeus; the two together symbolized the sacred marriage of Zeus and Hera, sun and moon. The olive leaf denotes renewal of life. *Chinese*: Quiet; persistence; grace; delicacy. *Christian*: The fruit of the Church; the faith of the just; peace. The dove with the olive twig depicts the souls of the faithful departed in peace. The olive branch is sometimes carried by the Archangel Gabriel in annunciation scenes. *Graeco-Roman*: Achievement; peace. The olive tree of the Acropolis held the life and fate of the people. Emblem of Zeus/Jupiter, Athene/Minerva, Apollo and Cybele; the olive wreath was worn by the victor at the races in honour of Hera and Athene. *Hebrew*: Strength; beauty; safety in travel.

OM (AUM) The sacred sound; the imperishable Word; the Absolute; Brahman; the primordial AUM, the totality of all sounds and that which penetrates and sustains the whole cosmos; the Self; the light of the supernal sun. It is also a Trinity as it has the three factors A.U.M., the threefold Brahman. 'All this universe is but the result of sound' (*Vakya Padiya*).

Omega Ω The end; finality. With ALPHA (q.v.) it is the Totality, the beginning and end of all things. It is often depicted with Ouroboros as totality.

Omphalos The Cosmic Centre; the centre from which the universe is nourished; the navel of the world; a place of refuge. It is both cathartic and apotropaic. It is the place of communication between the three worlds and every sacred place is an omphalos. It is also the point of expansion or a principal space not yet expanded. It is the navel and world centre as the sun is the centre of the universe. The omphalos is a symbol of the earth and all birth, represented often as a mountain or island rising from the waters of chaos; as a meeting place of heaven and earth it is also a dwelling place of the gods, such as Mt Meru, Heliopolis, Olympus, Sinai, Himinbjorg, Genizim. In Hinduism there is 'Mighty Agni' stationed at the navel of the earth (*Rig Veda* 11, 33).

One See NUMBERS.

Onion Unity, the many in the one; the cosmos;

the First Cause; immortality; revelation as peeling off the layers to reach the centre. Apotropaic, especially potent against baleful lunar powers.

Opal See JEWELS.

Orange Orange blossom is a symbol of fertility and fruitfulness; it was worn by Saracen brides as signifying fecundity. See also COLOURS. *Chinese*: Immortality; good fortune. *Christian*: Orange blossom is purity, chastity, virginity, which is its significance as a bridal wreath. If depicted in Paradise it is the fruit of the Fall, and can be portrayed instead of the apple in the hand of the Christ Child. *Greek*: The blossom is an emblem of Diana. Oranges were thought to be the Golden Apples of the Hesperides. *Japanese*: The blossom denotes pure love.

Orb See GLOBE.

An ancient Mycenaean gold disk embossed with the **octopus**, whose coiled tentacles duplicate and enforce the spiral symbolism inherent in the animal itself.

Orchid Magnificence; favours; luxury. In Chinese symbolism it is the Perfect Man; harmony; refinement; love; beauty; feminine charm; the scholar in seclusion.

Orgy Re-entry into chaos, the primordial state before creation; cosmic night; dissolution; the lower potentialities of beings. Agricultural, Spring and May Day orgies represent the union of the Sun God with Mother Earth, encouraging the forces of nature; imitative fertility; sowing the seed; regeneration. The return of chaos also took place at the Winter Solstice, the New Year, in the twelve days following the rebirth of the dying god, the vegetation god, in the Roman Saturnalia. In Babylon there were twelve days of duel between chaos and cosmos and in Christianity the twelve days of Christmas under the direction of the Lord of Misrule. The same symbolism applies to carnivals and fêtes.

Ostrich The ostrich feather depicts truth and justice (the feathers being perfectly equal). On the heads of divinities, as 'masters of truth', it is shown in scenes of the judgment of the dead in Egypt. It is an emblem of Maat, goddess of truth, justice and law; of Ament, as goddess of the West and the dead, and of Shu, as air and space. In Semitic mythology the ostrich is a demon and can represent a dragon. In Zoroastrianism the ostrich is the divine storm bird. The ostrich egg, suspended in temples, Coptic churches, mosques, and sometimes over tombs, depicts creation; life; resurrection; vigilance. In Africa, among the Dogons, the ostrich is both light and water, its undulations and erratic movements representing the waters.

A 21st-dynasty Egyptian figure of Osiris is crowned by twin **ostrich** feathers, in opposition here as the qualities of truth and justice which the god, as judge of the dead, must exercise in perfect balance.

Otter One of the 'clean' animals of Zoroastrianism which, with the dog, it is a great sin to kill. It is a Christian emblem of St Cuthbert.

Ouroboros Depicted as a serpent or dragon

The tail-biting **ouroboros**, the eternal circle of disintegration and re-integration, is a world-wide symbol. This one comes from Dahomey, W. Africa.

biting its own tail. 'My end is my beginning.' It symbolizes the undifferentiated; the Totality; primordial unity; self-sufficiency. It begets, weds, impregnates, and slays itself. It is the cycle of disintegration and reintegration, power that eternally consumes and renews itself; the eternal cycle; cyclic time; spatial infinity; truth and cognition in one; the united primordial parents; the Androgyne; the primaeval waters; darkness before creation; the restriction of the universe in the chaos of the waters before the coming of light; the potential before actualization. In funerary art Ouroboros represents immortality, eternity and wisdom. In many myths it encircles the whole world and is the circular course of the waters surrounding the earth. It can both support and maintain the world and injects death into life and life into death. Apparently immobile, it is yet perpetual motion, forever recoiling upon itself. In Orphic cosmology it encircles the Cosmic Egg. It is also called 'heracles' which identifies it with the solar passage; Macrobius associates it with the movement of the sun. The Alpha and Omega are often depicted with the Ouroboros. *Alchemic*: The unredeemed power of nature; latent power; the unformed *materia*; the *opus circulare* of chemical substances in the hermetic vessel. *Buddhist*: The wheel of *samsara*. *Egyptian*: The circle of the universe; the path of the sun god. *Greek*: 'All is one.' 'The All was from the beginning like an egg, with the serpent [*pneuma*] as the tight band or circle round it' (Epicurus). In Orphic symbolism it is the circle round the Cosmic Egg and is Aeon, the life-span of the universe. *Hindu*: The wheel of *samsara*. As latent energy Ouroboros shares the symbolism of KUNDALINI. q.v. *Sumero-Semitic*: The All One.

Oval As the lozenge it is the female life symbol; the vulva; the *vesica piscis*. It is used also as a halo encircling a sacred figure. See also NUMBERS, *Zero*.

Oven The feminine transforming power; the womb; birth. In Alchemy it is the Athanor, the 'body' of the psyche or soul of man in which the process of the Great Work takes place, the transmutation of the base matal, a process which symbolizes the development of self-mastery in unregenerate man. The spirit represents the fire.

Owl Ambivalent as the bird of wisdom and of darkness and death. *Amerindian*: Wisdom; divination. *Celtic*: Chthonic; 'the night hag'; the 'corpse bird'. *Chinese*: Evil; crime; death; horror; ungrateful children. On funeral urns it depicts death. *Christian*: Satan; the powers of darkness; solitude; mourning; desolation; bad news. The call of the owl is the 'song of death'. The owl was used to depict Jews who preferred the darkness to the light of the gospel. *Egyptian*: Death; night; coldness. *Graeco-Roman*: The screech owl symbolized wisdom and was sacred to Athene/Minerva. The owl was an attribute of

the Etruscan god of darkness and of Night. *Hebrew*: Blindness. *Hindu*: Emblem of Yama, god of the dead. *Japanese*: Death; ill omen. *Mexican*: Night; death.

Ox The ox can be symbolically interchangeable with the BULL (q.v.), in which case it is solar and fertility; but as the castrated ox it does not share the fertility symbolism and becomes lunar. It represents strength; patient toil; wealth; native power; sacrifice. *Celtic*: Symbol of Hu. *Chinese*: The ox takes the place of the bull in Spring and fertility symbolism and represents agriculture. It is the second of the twelve animals of the Terrestrial Branches. The white ox is contemplative wisdom in Chinese Buddhism. *Christian*: Patience; strength; the yoke of Christ; Christ as the true sacrifice; it is an attribute of St Luke who places emphasis on the sacrificial aspect of Christ's life in his gospel. The ox with the ass in nativity scenes is taken as depicting the Gentiles and Jews. The ox is an emblem of SS Blandina, Julietta, Leonard, Medard, Sylvester. *Graeco-Roman*: Agriculture; sacrifice. *Taoist*: Untamed animal nature, dangerous when undisciplined but powerfully useful when tamed. This symbolism is used in the Taoist and Ch'an Buddhist 'Ten Ox-herding Pictures', in which the ox is, at first, depicted as wholly black then, as the process of taming continues, the ox gradually becomes white and finally disappears completely as natural conditions are transcended.

Oyster The womb; the creative force of the feminine principle; birth and rebirth; initiation; the justice and law of cosmic life. In Chinese symbolism the oyster represents cosmic life; the power of the waters and 'the sacredness of the moon'; the yin power; fertility.

Padlock *Chinese*: Longevity (it locks to life); good health.

Pagoda An image of the Sacred Mountain, as world Centre and *axis mundi*. Its stories signify the degrees of ascent to the heavens while the decreasing size of the stories represents leading upwards to the infinite, illimitable space. It is suggested that the word is derived from the Italian 'pagoda', taken from the Persian, 'house of idols', or from the dagoba or STUPA (q.v.) as used in Theravada Buddhism.

Pairs The union of opposites in the world of manifestation; the male and female aspects, sun and moon, light and darkness, yin and yang etc. See also TWINS.

Pa Kua The eight complementary pairs of opposites, usually placed in a circle, the circumference of which symbolizes time and space. Each trigram in the Pa Kua represents a force in nature and there are four yin and four yang powers giving balance and harmony in the universe. The broken lines are yin and the whole lines yang.

☰ *K'ien*: Heaven; sky; active; power of the spirit; untiring strength; creative energy; causation; the all-penetrating male principle; the Father; the horse; the South.

☱ *Tui*: Collected Water; lakes; marshes; mists; clouds; absorption; impregnation; receptive wisdom; fertility; satisfaction; pleasure; inward-going intelligence; the goat; the South-east.

☲ *Li*: Fire; the sun; lightning; heat, penetrating zeal; the wisdom of devotion; purification; outward-going consciousness; brightness; elegance; the pheasant; the East.

☳ *Chen*: Thunder; quickening energy; power; will; impulse; movement; the dragon; the North-east.

☴ *Sun*: Wind; mind; the intellect; the breath of life; spirit; flexibility; penetration; wood; the cock; the South-west.

☵ *K'an*: Water; the moon; rain; rivers; the desire nature; emotions; instability; purification; imagination; difficulty; peril; the pig; the West.

☶ *Kan*: Mountains; physical nature; ascension; separateness; solitude; resting and arresting; the dog; the North-west.

☷ *K'un*: Earth; the passive, receptive aspect of the creative spirit; the moulding of primordial matter; the Mother; nourishment; the law; the ox; the North.

Palm Solar; exultation; righteousness; fame, as always growing erect; blessings; triumph; victory – 'The Palm, never shedding its foliage, is continually adorned with the same green. This power of the tree men think agreeable and fit for representing victory' (Plutarch). It is a Tree of Life and, as self-creative, it is equated with the Androgyne. As phallic it signifies virility and fertility, but if depicted with dates it is feminine: 'Thy stature is like to a palm-tree, thy breasts to clusters' (Canticles). Bearing good fruit in old age it symbolizes longevity and flourishing old age. *Arabian*: the Tree of Life. *Chinese*: Retirement; dignity; fecundity. *Christian*: The righteous who 'shall flourish like a palm tree'; immortality and, as such, is sometimes depicted with the phoenix; divine blessing; Christ's triumphal entry into Jerusalem; the martyr's triumph over death; Paradise. Palm branches signify glory; triumph; resurrection; victory over death and sin; it was a funerary emblem among the early Roman Christians, an attribute of one who had made the pilgrimage to the Holy Land, hence 'Palmer'. Emblem of St Paul the Hermit, who holds a palm in his hand, and numerous martyrs. Palm Sunday commemorates Christ's entry into Jerusalem. *Egyptian*: The tree of the calendar, producing a branch for each month. *Greek*: Emblem of Apollo at Delphi and Delos. *Hebrew*: The righteous man; emblem of Judea

The **ox** of immolation appears in an early Irish Gospel manuscript illumination of St Luke, whose symbol it is because of his emphasis on the sacrificial aspect of Christ's life.

On a 1st-century Roman coin, the **palm** celebrates the Roman victory over Judaea, here described as 'captive'.

The symbolism of this **palm** of victory over death incised on an early Christian tombstone is made explicit by the word 'victory' scratched beneath it in Latin written in Greek characters.

after the Exodus. *Sumero-Semitic*: A Tree of Life; emblem of the Phoenician Baal-Tamar, the Lord of the Palm, and of Astarte and the Assyro-Babylonian Ishtar.

Pansy *European*: Remembrance; meditation; thought. *Christian*: Emblem for Trinity Sunday.

Panther *Christian*: The panther was said to save people from the dragon or Evil One. As supposed to have sweet breath it typified the sweet influence of Christ. *Heraldic*: The panther is usually incensed and signifies fierceness; fury; impetuosity; remorselessness.

Paradise In most traditions Paradise is an enclosed garden, a garden-island or a 'Green Isle', notable exceptions being the Christian, where as the New Jerusalem it is a city, and the Celtic and Maori, where it is under the waters. It symbolizes primordial perfection and the Golden Age; the Cosmic Centre; pristine innocence; beatitude; perfect communion between man and God and all living things. It also represents the innermost soul, the abode of immortality; a place where time stands still; entry into primordial time, Great Time; the state in which heaven is so close to earth that it can be reached by climbing a tree, creeper, or mountain, or any axial symbol.
Paradise is always an enclosed space or surrounded by sea and is only open to the heavens. As God and man can communicate there, so man and animals live in perfect accord and speak the same language. In Zoroastrianism it is the Abode of Song. In all gardens of Paradise the two trees of Life and Knowledge, Immortality and Death, stand at the centre; from the roots of the Tree of Life flows a spring or fountain which gives rise to the four Rivers of Paradise, flowing to the four cardinal points and forming the vertical and horizontal arms of the cross.
Paradise Lost, or the Fall, symbolizes the descent from unity into duality and multiplicity in manifestation; the movement away from the centre of perfection and dispersal and disintegration in the world of multiplicity. Paradise Regained is the return to unity, to the spiritual centre, man's conquest of himself and regaining pristine innocence. Paradise Lost plunges man into time and darkness; Paradise Regained restores unity and ends time. Symbols of Paradise are the Centre; the enclosed and secret garden, having bird song and scented flowers; the rose garden; the Island of the Blessed; the Green Isle; Elysian Fields; the Promised Land; El Dorado; a cluster of pearls (Chinese), etc. The lost Paradise is guarded by monsters, dragons, or angels with flaming swords; to regain it entails great difficulties, trials and perils, which symbolize the arduous spiritual path of the journey back to the Centre.

Parasol See UMBRELLA.

Parrot Imitation; unintelligent repetition. *Chinese*: Brilliance; a warning to unfaithful wives. *Hindu*: An attribute of Kama, god of love. An oracular and rain-bringing bird. It had these qualities also in pre-Columbian America.

Parsley *European*: A mystic plant; the feminine principle. The crown of parsley was awarded to the victor at the Nemean games.

Partridge Fertility; fecundity. In Christianity it is ambivalent as representing both the truth of Christ and deceitfulness, theft and cunning (Jer. 17,11). It can also depict the Devil. Sacred to Aphrodite, the Cretan Zeus and the sun god Talos.

Paschal Taper *Christian*: Burning during the forty days from Easter to Ascension, it represents Christ's presence with the disciples for the forty days after His resurrection. Extinguished on Ascension Day it denotes the removal of Christ from the earth. It is also the light of the risen Christ and new life, and depicts the pillar of fire which guided the Israelites for forty years.

Passage The change from one plane to another, from this world to the next or the transcendent world. 'Difficult passage' symbolism is concerned with the passage from the profane to the sacred; the return to Paradise; gaining higher states of consciousness; transcending the pairs of opposites in the dualism and polarity of the manifest world. Paradox, as in itself transcending the limitations of the rational mind, is often employed in symbols of passage, such as the Strait Gate; the eye of the needle; the narrow or razor-edged path or bridge; the sword bridge; the ring in the jaws of a monster; passage between two millstones; the Symplegades; clashing rocks; the wall with no door; Scylla and Charybdis, etc. The symbolism of the ability to transcend time and space, day and night, is also used. The passage is impossible for the profane material body so can only be achieved at a spiritual level and in the 'timeless moment', also by means of ways not available to the physical senses. The physical is transcended by mind and spirit. It is the 'Way' of Taoism, Hinduism and Buddhism, the 'Strait Gate' of Christianity and the 'tariqah' of Islam. Rites of Passage are often based on an initial separation, followed by transition to a final state of unity. See also BRIDGE.

Passion *Christian*: Symbols of Christ's passion are the cross, ladder, sponge, seamless robe, dice, cock, spear, sword, pincers, hammer, nails, pillar and scourge, crown of thorns, reed, purple robe, basin and ewer, thirty pieces of silver, vinegar, rope, shroud, chalice, chains, red rose, blood-red poppy.

Peace The symbol of peace, par excellence, is the dove, or the dove with the olive branch. In Christianity the Virgin Mary is called the

Queen of Peace. With the North American Indians the CALUMET (q.v.) is the Pipe of Peace. The CORNUCOPIA (q.v.) can be associated with Peace as Plenty.

Peach *Buddhist*: With the citron and pomegranate, one of the Three Blessed Fruits. *Chinese*: Immortality; the Tree of Life; fairy fruit; Spring; youth; marriage; riches; longevity; good wishes. *Christian*: The fruit of salvation; peach with leaf attached, virtue of heart and tongue; the virtue of silence. *Egyptian*: Sacred to Athor and Harpocrates. *Japanese*: The Tree of Immortality. Peach blossom denotes Spring; feminine charm; marriage. *Taoist*: The Tree of Life in the Kun-lun Paradise, bestowing immortality and being the food of the Taoist genii or immortals. The peach with the phoenix is an emblem of Si Wang Mu, goddess of the Tree of Immortality and Queen of Heaven. Apotropaic: its stones are carved and used as amulets and talismans.

Peacock Solar; associated with Tree and Sun worship; also associated with the peony. It represents immortality, longevity, love. A natural symbol of the stars of the sky, hence of apotheosis and immortality. Since it becomes restless before rain it is associated with storms; its rain dance is also associated with the spiral. Worldliness, pride and vanity are comparatively modern attributes. *Buddhist*: Compassion; watchfulness. The peacock-feather fan is an attribute of Avalokitesvara, who is also Kwan-yin and Amitabha, as compassion. *Chinese*: Dignity; rank; beauty. Attribute of Kwan-yin and Si Wang Mu. The peacock feather was awarded to confer official rank for meritorious service and denoted imperial favour. Emblem of the Ming dynasty. *Christian*: Immortality; resurrection; the glorified soul, since it renewed its plumage and its flesh was believed to be incorruptible. The 'hundred eyes' are the all-seeing Church. It also symbolized the saints since its tail was like a nimbus. Surmounting an orb, it depicted rising above worldly things. The peacock's feather is an emblem of St Barbara. *Greek*: Solar; represents the bird-god Phaon, 'the Shiverer'. Originally an attribute of Pan, who yielded it to Hera as symbolizing the starry firmament; the Argus eyes were scattered over the tail by Hera. *Hindu*: Sometimes the mount of Brahma; also ridden by Lakshmi and by Skanda-Karttikeya, god of war; when ridden by Kama, god of love, it depicts impatient desire. The peacock is an emblem of Sarasvati, goddess of wisdom, music and poetry. *Iranian*: Peacocks standing on either side of the Tree of Life signify duality and man's dual nature. The peacock also denotes royalty and the Persian royal throne is the 'Peacock Throne'. *Islamic*: Light which 'saw Self as a peacock with its tail outspread'. The peacock's eye is associated with the Eye of the Heart. *Japanese*: The bodhisattva Kujaku-mayoo is always seated on a peacock. *Roman*: Juno's bird,

On the 12th-century porch of Great Rollington church, Oxfordshire, is this representation of **paradise** – a garden surrounded by water (symbolized by chevrons) and mythical beasts, decked with flowers and containing the all-enveloping serpent.

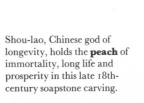

Shou-lao, Chinese god of longevity, holds the **peach** of immortality, long life and prosperity in this late 18th-century soapstone carving.

A Moorish textile from 12th-century Andalusia has woven into it duplicated confronting **peacocks** and the Arabic inscription, 'Perfect blessings!'

having the same significance as for Hera. An emblem of the Empress and the princesses.

Pear Hope; good health. *Chinese*: Longevity; justice; good government; good judgment. *Christian*: The love of Christ for mankind.

Pearl Lunar; the power of the waters; the essence of the moon and controller of tides; the embryo; cosmic life; the divine essence; the life-giving power of the Great Mother; the feminine principle of the ocean; the self-luminous; initiation; law in cosmic life; justice. The pearl was thought to be the result of lightning penetrating the oyster, hence it was regarded as the union of fire and water, both fecundating forces, and so denotes birth and rebirth; fertility. It also symbolizes innocence, purity, virginity, perfection, humility and a retiring nature.

The 'flaming pearl' (the union of fire and water) is the 'pearl of perfection' of the East. It is the Third Eye of Siva and Buddha, and is the crystallization of light; transcendent wisdom; spiritual enlightenment; spiritual consciousness. With the DRAGON (q.v.) of China it is suggested as either the 'night-shining pearl', the moon, which the dragon of light swallows, or as a roll of thunder from which the flame of lightning emerges, the pearl being belched forth by the dragon of the sky. It is depicted with dragons as masters of the waters and guardians of treasures. As the 'pearl of perfection' it is, with the dragon, the spiritual essence of the universe, also enlightenment; it signifies, too, the unfolding and development of man in the quest for enlightenment. The 'white pearl' is the 'treasure difficult to obtain'; the spirit; enlightenment; wisdom; the 'pearl of great price'. The seed pearl has the same symbolism as the 'flaming pearl' as the potentiality and unfolding of the flower of light. *Buddhist*: One of the Eight Treasures; the heart of Buddha, pure intentions; the Third Eye of Buddha, the 'flaming pearl' is the crystallization of light; transcendent wisdom; spiritual consciousness; the spiritual essence of the universe. *Chinese*: the yin, feminine principle; immortality; potentiality; good augury; genius in obscurity. As depicted with the dragon, see 'flaming pearl' and 'night-shining pearl' above. *Christian*: Salvation; Christ the Saviour; the Word of God; baptism; the hidden gnosis necessary for salvation, the 'pearl of great price', for which man must dive into the waters of baptism and encounter dangers. It is also virgin birth; purity; spiritual grace. *Gnostic*: The Fall and subsequent salvation. *Graeco-Roman*: Love and marriage, emblem of Aphrodite/Venus, the 'Lady of the Pearls', who rose from the waters. *Hindu*: The *urna*, the shining spot, the 'flaming pearl' on the forehead of Siva; the Third Eye; transcendent wisdom; the crystallization of light; spiritual consciousness; enlightenment. *Iranian*: The Saviour, giver of life, birth and death; longevity. *Islamic*: The Divine Word; heaven. *Sumero-Semitic*: The generative power of the waters. *Taoist*: 'The pearl of effulgence', the 'pearl of potentiality' and the 'night-shining pearl' are the yin powers of the waters and the lunar control of the waters with all their potentialities. The 'flaming pearl' symbolizes man's search for reality; spiritual unfolding; the experience of Light.

Pelican As the bird was thought to feed its young with its own blood it represented sacrifice, charity and piety. *Christian*: Christ's sacrifice; Christ as *nostro Pellicano* (Dante) who gave His blood for the sins of the many; the crucifixion; redemption through blood sacrifice; the Eucharist.

Pen *Christian*: Learning; the Evangelists; emblem of SS Augustine, Bernard and Thomas Aquinas. *Egyptian*: The pen with the staff depicts the awakening of the soul; attribute of Theut or Logios. *Islamic*: The reed pen, or calamus, symbolizes the universal intellect, the Essence, which writes destiny on the tablet of the *prima materia*; the unmanifest, on which the pen creates forms and destinies. The pen and book together are the active and creative act with the static creative substance and being. The pen is the first thing created of Light; it is also phallic.

Pentacle/Pentangle/Pentagram Symbolizes the figure of man with outstretched arms and legs; the integral personality; the human microcosm. Being endless, the pentacle takes on the significance, power and perfection of the circle. Its five points are spirit, air, fire, water, earth. With SALVS at the points it represents health and the five senses. Like the circle, it has the power of binding evil powers and elementals, hence it denotes good luck. In Christianity it stands for the five wounds of Christ and was the emblem of Sir Gawain, painted on his shield. In witchcraft the inverted pentacle depicts the Devil's Goat and the witch's foot. Inverted, it is also a sign of the reversal of man's true nature.

Peony *Chinese*: The yang principle (one of the few yang flowers); masculinity; light; glory; love; good fortune; riches; Spring; youth; happiness. It is the imperial flower, supposed to be untouched by any insect except the bee. It is often associated with the peacock. *Greek*: Healing. *Japanese*: Marriage; fertility; Spring; glory; riches; gaiety.

Persimmon In China, joy; in Japan, victory.

Pestle and Mortar Lunar; associated with the Great Mother, the mortar is the hollow and receptive, the feminine principle, in which the pestle crushes the elixir of life. In Chinese symbolism the hare in the moon holds a pestle and mortar in which it mixes the elixir of immortality. The pestle and mortar also signify the small factors which influence a situation or the events of life. Frequently depicted in the workshops of the Alchemist.

Phallus The masculine creative principle; the procreative, generative forces of nature and the human race; the function and potency of the Creator; the stream of life. An apotropaic symbol. Ithyphallic figures represent the imparting of life to man and nature; fertility; procreation; potency; they, too, are apotropaic. Phallic symbols are the *linga*, the Hindu aniconic representation of Siva as Creator; the pillar; obelisk; anything piercing or penetrating such as the sword, lance and arrow. But that which pierces also destroys, hence Siva as both creator and destroyer. In Celtic art the head surmounting a pillar is phallic, there being a traditional Celtic association between head and phallus, both being power and representing fertility; they can also be funerary and apotropaic. The phallus was used in Egyptian and Graeco-Roman cemeteries as a symbol of resurrection and renewal of life. It can be merely physical in its symbolism, as in the worship of Priapus, or be spiritual in significance, as in Hinduism.

Pheasant *Chinese*: Light; yang; virtue; prosperity; good fortune; beauty; emblem of the Emperor Yü. *Japanese*: Protection; maternal love.

Phoenix A universal symbol of resurrection and immortality, of death and rebirth by fire. It is a fabulous bird which dies by self-immolation. It remains dead for three days (the dark of the moon) and rises again from its own ashes on the third day; this is lunar symbolism, but the phoenix is universally symbolic of the sun as it is the 'fire bird' and signifies divine royalty, nobility and uniqueness. It also represents gentleness since it crushes nothing it alights on and feeds on no living thing, only dew. The phoenix is associated with the rose in all Gardens of Paradise. *Alchemic*: The consummation of the *magnum opus*; regeneration. *Aztec, Maya and Toltec*: Solar; blessings; happiness; it is the Quetzal, the companion of Quetzalcoatl. *Chinese*: The Feng-huang or Fung or Fum; the 'vermilion bird', the 'substance of flame'; it is one of the Four Spiritually Endowed, or Sacred, Creatures and like the dragon and *ky-lin*, with which it is always associated, it is both yin and yang. When it is the male *feng* it becomes yang, solar, the fire bird; but as the *huang* it is feminine, yin, and lunar. When portrayed with the dragon as a symbol of the Emperor, the phoenix becomes entirely feminine as the Empress, and together they represent both aspects of imperial power. In the feminine aspect the *huang* denotes beauty, delicacy of feeling and peace. It is also a bridal symbol signifying 'inseparable fellowship', not only for the married couple but for the complete yin-yang mutual interdependence in the

The celestial dragon on this early 18th-century Chinese vase is guarding the **pearl** of perfection, from which issues the lightning of consciousness.

A T'ang dynasty gold **phoenix** hair ornament lent its wearer the protection and majesty of the bird, one of the Four Sacred Creatures and a symbol of immortality, excellence and unique nobility.

universe in the realm of duality. Also, like the dragon and *ky-lin*, the phoenix is made up of various elements, typifying the entire cosmos: it has the head of a cock (the sun), the back of a swallow as the crescent moon, its wings are the wind, its tail represents trees and flowers, and its feet are the earth; it has five colours symbolizing the five virtues: 'Its colour delights the eye, its comb expresses righteousness, its tongue utters sincerity, its voice chants melody, its ear enjoys music, its heart conforms to regulations, its breast contains the treasures of literature and its spurs are powerful against transgressors' (from an ancient ritual). The appearance of a phoenix on any occasion was highly auspicious and signified peace and benevolent rule, or the appearance of a great Sage. A pair of phoenixes denoted the combination of Emperor and Sage. *Christian*: Resurrection; Christ consumed in the fires of the Passion and rising again on the third day; triumph over death; faith; constancy. *Egyptian*: Equated with the Bennu, the sun bird, as solar, resurrection and immortality and associated with Ra. It has been suggested as the helical rising of Sirius, which, in ancient times, preceded the rising of the Nile. *Japanese*: The sun; rectitude; fidelity; justice; obedience. *Roman*: The rebirth and perpetual existence of the Roman Empire; imperial apotheosis.

Phrygian Cap 'The cap of liberty'; freedom; nobility; a badge of liberty as, when freed, a slave assumed the cap. It is suggested also as the horn of the bull, and phallic. The conic or pyramidal cap appears on Osiris, on Ganymede, on the young Zeus, who is accompanied by a dog and eagle, and on the Dioscuri in Etruscan art.

Pig See SWINE.

Pigeon *Chinese*: Longevity; fidelity; Spring; lasciviousness. *Hindu*: Attribute of Yama, god of the dead. See also DOVE.

Pilgrim/Pilgrimage The pilgrim is one who follows a direct and purposeful path, as opposed to the aimless wanderer; he is the seeker after a goal and signifies aspiration after the sacred. Emblems of the pilgrim are: the staff and bowl or gourd; broad-brimmed hat; in Christian pilgrimage, the palm of the Palmer who had made the pilgrimage to the Holy Land; the ampulla, or flask, of the Canterbury pilgrim; the staff and scallop-shell of St James and the keys of St Peter for the pilgrimage to Rome. Pilgrimage symbolizes the journey back to Paradise or to the Centre; man, as a stranger in the world of manifestation, journeys back to his true home. All pilgrimage is made difficult, symbolizing the difficulty of regaining Paradise or finding spiritual enlightenment. Symbols of pilgrimage are those of ASCENSION and PASSAGE (qq.v.). Shrines and Sacred Mountains are the chief centres of pilgrimage.

Pillar The world axis; the vertical axis which both holds apart and joins Heaven and Earth, which both divides and unites them; a ritual world centre; an omphalos. Pillar and TREE (q.v.) symbolism are closely connected, and the pillar often symbolizes the Tree of Life. The pillar also represents stability, the concept of standing firm and, according to Philo, the idea of God who stands firm and is stability as opposed to human flux. It also raises the sacred or venerated above the profane or ordinary. A pillar of fire, or smoke, denotes the presence of a divinity. A broken pillar is death, mortality. A pillar surmounted by a human head indicates a terminus or boundary. Pillars surmounted by doves signify the Great Mother and especially the prophetic goddesses of Dodona. A pillar with a dolphin depicts the male and female powers combined; love. Irminsul, the Cosmic Pillar of the Saxons, was destroyed by Charlemagne.

Two pillars, often one black, one white, or a divided pillar, symbolize all bi-polarity; the dual aspect of the divinity or the bisexual or androgynous gods; the Tree of Life and the Tree of Knowledge or Death; the complementary opposites in manifest duality and their balance and tension in combined action. The right-hand pillar is white, masculine, while the left is black, feminine, symbolizing also time and space; spiritual and temporal power; the strong and the weak; tension and release; upward and downward movement; reason and faith; power and liberty; the will and the law, etc., also that every force postulates a resistance, every light a shade, every convex a concave. The two pillars also represent the support of Heaven and, therefore, form Heaven's Gate, the necessary way through which to enter the Temple or Church; this passing between two pillars typifies entry into new life, or another world, or eternity; it thus shares the door and gate symbolism. Twin pillars also portray the Celestial Twins (see TWINS) and are associated with the *dadophoroi* (see TORCH).

When there are three pillars, the central pillar symbolizes either equilibrium and the unifying force, or, if it has a crown at the top, it represents the most direct way to enlightenment or the Kingdom; but it is only possible to take this way when the two sides of the duad, good and evil, have been reconciled in the world and in oneself. Three pillars are also an aniconic symbol of the Great Mother, the lunar goddess and the three phases of the moon. They also represent wisdom, beauty, strength, or wisdom and power with goodness which unites them. Four pillars uphold the earth at the cardinal points. *Buddhist*: A fiery pillar is an aniconic representation of Buddha. *Chinese*: Uprightness; the way. The pillars of the imperial palace signify the support given by the princes to the Emperor. *Christian*: As Hebrew. *Egyptian*: The Djed pillar symbolized the resurrection of Osiris and his backbone as tree-axis, signifying stability. *Graeco-Roman*: An aniconic symbol of

Zeus/Jupiter. The two pillars are sacred to Zeus on Mount Lykaeos, and also denote the Dioscuri. Three pillars are the Great Goddess and the phases of the moon. *Hebrew*: The pillars of fire and smoke signified the presence of God, the sustaining power of God. The two pillars of Solomon's Temple were Boaz and Jachin, strength and stability, 'In Him is Strength' and 'The Stablisher', temporal and spiritual power, king and priest, throne and altar; one pillar could not sink and the other could not burn. In Qabalism the three pillars represent wisdom, strength and beauty. The pillar can be an aniconic representation of Jahveh and of Abraham. *Hindu*: In the temple the pillar surmounted by a crown is the architectural symbol of the highest point and is the most direct way of spiritual ascent, but is only possible for those who ascend from the centre, having overcome duality and being able to ascend from the darkness within to the light above. *Islamic*: 'The pillar of the just is the knowledge of God' (Qoran). The five pillars of Islam are the double testimony of faith; the canonical prayer five times daily; the fast of Ramadan; the tithe; the pilgrimage to Mecca. *Mithraic*: The twin pillars represent the *dadophoroi*, Cautes and Cautopates, the bull and the scorpion, light and darkness, etc. *Platonic*: Plato speaks of the luminous pillar of the heavens, surrounded by the eight spheres of different colours. *Sumero-Semitic*: The wooden pillar, or tree trunk, is an aniconic form of the Semitic Ashtoreth or Astarte. A pillar surmounted by a lion's head symbolizes Nergal and is solar; by a lance head, Marduk and solar; by a ram's head, Ea-Oannes. The pillar is the 'world spine' or axis. The three-pillar lunar symbolism appears in Phoenicia and particularly at Carthage. *Taoist*: The Tao, the way.

Pine Uprightness; straightness; vitality; fertility; strength of character; silence; solitude; phallic. As evergreen it signifies immortality. It was thought to preserve the body from corruption, hence its use for coffins and its presence in cemeteries; it is apotropaic. The pine cone is both flame-shaped and phallic, and represents the masculine creative force, fecundity and good luck. Bastius equates the pine cone with the spinning top as a vortex or whorl, i.e. the great generative forces. *Chinese*: Longevity; courage; faithfulness; constancy in adversity; emblem of Confucius. The pine is also depicted with the stork and the white stag. *Egyptian*: Emblem of Serapis when his cult developed in Egypt. *Greek*: Emblem of Zeus. The pine cone as phallic and fecundity was an attribute of Dionysos and surmounted his thyrsus; it was also an emblem of Artemis. As prophylactic it is associated with Aesculapius. *Japanese*: Longevity, and as such also appears with the stork and white stag. *Roman*: Emblem of Jupiter and of Venus; as the *pura arbor* it symbolizes virginity and is associated with Diana; it is also associated with Mithras.

On this candelabrum of the 1st millennium BC, the horse and the wheel, symbols here of earth and heaven, are joined by a **pillar** which keeps them simultaneously separate and united.

The **pine**-cone incense-burner on this ancient Nubian bronze shrine symbolizes the life-sustaining power and fertility of the gods to whose service and worship the incense was burned.

Semitic: The cone is a life symbol; fertility. The tree is sacred to the Phrygian Attis and his consort Cybele.

Pineapple Fertility; an emblem of Cybele; a pineapple surmounting a column is an attribute of Marduk.

Pipe Harmony; the pipes of Pan represent universal harmony in nature. Attribute of a satyr. See also CALUMET.

Pisces See ZODIAC.

Pitcher See VASE.

Plait Interdependence of relationship; continuity. The plait shares the symbolism of KNOTS (q.v.).

Plane Tree *Christian*: The all-covering love of Christ; charity; moral superiority. *Greek*: Learning; scholarship (academic discussions were held under a plane tree in Athens). *Iranian*: Magnificence; learning. *Minoan*: Sacred to the cult of the Cretan Zeus.

Planets Taken together, the major planets symbolize the mixture and interaction of all the essential forces of the universe and nature. The sun is the centre of the sphere of the universe, and Mars, Jupiter and Saturn are in the upper region, with Venus, Mercury and the Moon in the lower half. The planets, with the exception of the Sun, are higher in rank the further they are from the earth. In Islam each of the planets governs a climate.

Sun: Symbolized by the solar disk, sometimes with rays; the circle with the central point and innumerable variations of the disk and rayed circle; also by a chariot drawn by four white, or golden, horses, although the number of horses varies. The Sun is the attribute of all solar gods and the Archangel Michael. It represents the Centre; the heart; the centre of intuitive knowledge; the power of feeling and believing; the sensational and imaginative. Its colour is gold; metal, gold; day, Sunday; position, the zenith; age, young manhood; flower, chicory or sunspurge.

Moon: The crescent, or young woman in a chariot, holding a quiver, or huntress on foot with quiver and dogs. Symbolizes Time; movement; generation; the power of generation and conception; the vital spirit holding body and soul together; involuntary and instinctual action. All Queens of Heaven and Great Mothers are lunar. Colour, silver; metal, silver; day, Monday; position, nadir; age, infancy; flower, the peony.

Saturn: Originally the ruler of the Golden Age and the Seventh Heaven, now depicted as an old man holding a scythe; the destroyer; death and rebirth. As Cronos he is Time and Fate and holds the hourglass; sometimes he has a crow's head. God of the Earth, reason and intellect, the contemplative and rational; the principle of analytic thought in man; also concentration, contraction and sterility. Saturn also represents the dark spirit lying captive in matter and is associated with dragons, vipers, foxes, cats and mice and night birds. In Alchemy Saturn is the lead which, through transformation, attains the luminous state, that is gold. In Gnosticism he is depicted as both Father and Son, greybeard and youth. Colour, black; metal, lead; day, Saturday; position, North; age, old age; flower, asphodel, white heliotrope.

Jupiter: A seated, venerable figure, sometimes in a chariot, holding staff and spear. He is the Creator; the soul; limited space; the power of organization; decision; expression; expansion; intellectual will; the energetic and courageous; the air. Colour, blue, violet or orange; metal, tin; day, Thursday; position, the East; age, maturity; flower, agrimony.

Mars: An armed man, sometimes mounted on a horse, usually carries a banner or lance, but sometimes a sword or whip. Represents the positive, active and masculine; the passions; the passional and courageous; fire. Colour, red; metal, iron; day, Tuesday; position, South; age, manhood; flower, lambstongue, butterburr.

Venus: A woman in various forms, usually voluminously dressed, holding laurel. As morning or evening star she can be either solar or lunar and represents the uniting of the opposites; she follows the Moon and precedes the Sun; as the 'drawer of bow and thrower of javelins' she signifies the launching of the new moon on the sea of night and defends the moon against all monsters of darkness; she is the waters; feminine passivity; the passions; desires; the desiderative; the creative mother; synthesis; imagination. Colour, green, pale yellow or turquoise; metal, copper; position, West; day, Friday; age, adolescence; flower, white rose, vervain, all-heal.

Mercury: Young man wearing winged sandals and cap and carrying a caduceus, other emblems being the cock and ram. His sign combines the sun and moon and fiery and watery elements. He is the messenger; the awakener; rhythm; the god of trial and initiation; the mediator, bridging all contradictions and as his sign combines the opposites, so he embodies both male and female; he represents the interpretative; the power of expressing and interpreting sensation; analytical thought. In Alchemy he is the *quinta essentia*. Colour, purple or deep blue; metal, quicksilver; day, Wednesday; position, centre; age, youth; flower, valerian, hazel.

Uranus: Boundless space; the unmanifest; the will.

Neptune: The primordial ocean, the source of all things.

Beneficent planets are Jupiter and Venus; malefic are Saturn and Mars; ambivalent, Mercury. Masculine are Sun, Jupiter, Saturn, Mars; feminine, the Moon and Venus; Mercury

is androgynous. In Babylonian astrology
Marduk is assigned to Jupiter, Ishtar to Venus,
Nabu to Mercury, Ninib to Saturn, Nergal to
Mars. The Greek and Roman planets are
Cronos – Saturn; Ares or Heracles – Mars;
Aphrodite or Hera – Venus; Zeus – Jupiter;
Hermes or Apollo – Mercury. In Chinese
symbolism the Planets are Jupiter (suei-sing),
wood, the East; Mars (yong-ho), fire, the
South; Saturn (chen-sing), earth, the Centre;
Venus (t'ai-po) metal, the West; Mercury
(ch'en-sing), water, the North.

Plantain *Chinese*: Self-education (a student
who could not afford paper wrote on plantain
leaves). *Christian*: 'Way-bread', the path of
Christ.

Plants Like trees and flowers, plants symbolize
death and resurrection; the life-force; the cycle
of life. Plant and flower symbolism is closely
connected with the Great Mother, goddess of
the earth, of fertility and vegetation; it is also
associated with the fertility of the life-giving
waters; the sap-filled plant is motherhood.
Plants and trees are often regarded as mythical
ancestors and usually associated with the moon
cult. Plants or flowers which grow from the
spilled blood of a god or hero represent the
mystic union between man and plant and the
birth of life from death, life flowing from one
state to another, e.g. violets grew from the blood
of Attis; wheat and herbs from the body of
Osiris; the pomegranate from the blood of
Dionysos, anemones from the blood of Adonis
and red roses from the blood of Christ. In
Chinese symbolism the plant *Polyporus lucidus* is
the plant of immortality and is the food of the
Taoist genii or immortals.

Playing Cards See CARDS.

Plough/Ploughing The plough is an attribute
of gods and goddesses of agriculture, such as
Demeter, Triptolemos, Dionysos. To nomadic
people ploughing symbolizes the 'Fall' from the
state of perfection of primordial and paradisal
times. In Islam it represents low-mindedness,
vanity and impudence in a nation. Ploughing
signifies the breaking of the original *prima
materia* into the multiplicity of creation; the
opening of the earth to the influence of heaven;
man's mastery over the earth; fertility. The
plough is phallic and the ploughshare impregnates the earth; the furrow is feminine. In North
American Indian and other nomadic traditions
ploughing is evil and a violation of the body of
the Mother Earth.

Plum *Chinese*: Longevity; Winter; beauty;
purity; the recluse; pupils (unripe fruit). As
flowering in Winter it is strength; endurance;
triumph. The plum, bamboo and pine are the
'Three Friends of Winter'. *Christian*: The fruit
depicts independence; fidelity. *Japanese*: Plum

In a 14th-century Persian manuscript illumination,
an astrologer looks eagerly up at the dome of the
night sky, in which he sees nine signs of the principal
planets and stars.

Saturn governing Aquarius and Aries, hold the
sickle of agriculture and destruction and uses the
crutch of feeble old age though apparently strong in
body – altogether a symbol of the tension of saturnine
melancholy.

blossom is Spring triumphant over Winter; virtue and courage triumphant over difficulties; marriage; happiness. The tree is an emblem of the Samurai.

Plumage Power; strength; triumph. Plumes on warriors' helmets depict honour; triumph; defiance. *Aztec*: Celestial power; the soul. *Egyptian*: Ra, the sun, light and air. A single plume or feather is an attribute of the goddess Maat as truth and integrity. *Shamanistic*: Flight, ascent to heaven and communication with the spirit world. A bird-head or mask can be used instead of plumes or a feathered cloak. *Taoist*: Attribute of the priest, the 'feathered sage' or 'feathered visitor' who communicates with the next world. See also FEATHER.

Plumb rule In sacred architecture it symbolizes transcendent knowledge; the archetype controlling all works. It is also justice and rectitude. A Christian emblem of St Thomas.

Point See CENTRE.

Pole The 'pole of the earth' is the world axis, the cosmic Centre, the 'point quiescent'; it depicts stabilizing force and can take on the symbolism of the Tree of Life; it is also phallic, procreation and fecundity. In the Amerindian Sweat Lodge the bent pole of the vapour bath represents old age and the span of life from youth to old age. In Siberian and Shamanistic cults a pole can replace and symbolize the birch tree as a world axis and also uphold the welkin; it is fixed on the Pole Star and the firmament revolves round it. See also PILLAR.

Pole Star See STAR.

Pomegranate Immortality; multiplicity in unity; perennial fertility; fecundity; plenty. *Buddhist*: One of the Three Blessed Fruits, with the citrus and peach. *Chinese*: Abundance; fertility; posterity; numerous and virtuous offspring; a happy future. *Christian*: Eternal life; spiritual fecundity; the Church, the seeds being the numerous members. *Graeco-Roman*: Spring; rejuvenation; immortality; fertility; emblem of Hera/Juno and of Ceres and Persephone as the periodic return of Spring and fertility to the earth. It is also the plant which grew from the blood of Dionysos. *Hebrew*: Regeneration; fertility. The pomegranates with the bells on the priestly vestments represent fecundating thunder and lightning.

Poplar A tree of the waters. *Chinese*: Its leaves, differing in colour on either side, depict the yin-yang, the lunar and solar, and all dualities. *Graeco-Roman*: White poplar depicts the Elysian Fields and the black poplar Hades. The poplar is sacred to Sabazios and was carried in his rites; also an emblem of Zeus/Jupiter and of Heracles/Hercules, who wore a crown of poplar on his descent to Hades.

Poppy A symbol of the Great Mother as the One and the Many, the Mother and Maid; Night; sacred to all lunar and nocturnal deities; represents fertility; fecundity; oblivion; idleness. *Chinese*: Retirement; rest; beauty; success; but also as opium it is dissipation and evil. *Christian*: Sleep; ignorance; indifference. The blood-red poppy depicts the passion of Christ and the sleep of death. *Graeco-Roman* The period of the sleep and death of vegetation; emblem of Demeter/Ceres, Persephone, Venus, Hypnos and Morpheus.

Pot See CAULDRON.

Praying Mantis In China it represents pertinacity, greed; among the Bushmen it appears as a Trickster; in Greece it signified divination (*manteia*), and in Christianity it depicted prayer and adoration.

Pride Symbolized by the lion, eagle, peacock, mirror or a fallen rider. A solar quality.

Primrose In Europe the primrose typifies purity; youth; pertness; it is a Celtic fairy flower.

Prince/Princess The potential of royalty; the power and vigour of youthful royalty. The Prince is associated with the King as the fertility of his people and land. Winning the hand of a Princess, in myth and legend, is to aspire to the superior or highest state, a situation fraught with danger which can either kill the aspirant or raise him to a higher and more noble state, as in psychic and spiritual aspirations and quests.

Prow A phallic symbol; also an attribute of Tyche/Fortuna as Fate.

Prudence In Christian art the quality of prudence is usually depicted as a woman, sometimes double- or triple-headed, holding a mirror and serpent, or sieve, with Solomon at her feet.

Pumpkin The double pumpkin or gourd, like the hourglass, represents the upper and lower worlds. In Roman symbolism the pumpkin is stupidity, empty-headedness and madness. See also GOURD.

Putrefaction Dissolution and disintegration before reintegration and rebirth; the death of the body and release of the soul. Especially significant in Alchemy in the Great Work.

Pyramid A world Centre and *axis mundi* representing the primeval Sacred Mountain, which is often four-sided, such as Mount Meru. The apex of the pyramid symbolizes the highest spiritual, hierarchical and initiatory attainment; it also depicts fire, the flame, the solar masculine force, and is phallic. The pyramid with steps signifies the structure of the cosmos and the planes of consciousness; also the ascent of the sun in the firmament. Plato uses the pyramid to symbolize the earth element, with the cube as air, octahedron as fire, icosahedron as water and dodecahedron as ether. In Aztec symbolism the pryamid is the fifth sun of Quetzalcoatl.

Python The baleful power of darkness and of the feminine earth principle. Attribute of Apollo as the sun overcoming darkness, and as the serpent of wisdom.

Quail Associated with the night, but also with good luck and Spring; it has a phallic connotation and represents amorousness. *Chinese*: Courage; military zeal; Summer; also poverty (patched clothing). *Greek*: Spring; renewal of life; attribute and form of Asteria; connected with Zeus and Latona in Delos, hence with Apollo and Diana. *Hebrew*: Miraculous nourishment in the desert, but the food of wrath and lust. *Phoenician*: Sacrificed to Melkarth after his defeat of Typhon or Sephon as darkness. *Hindu*: The Asvins as day and night, light and darkness, revive the quail which has been swallowed by the wolf; i.e. the quail leaves in Winter but returns with the sun in Spring. *Roman*: Courage; victory in battle. *Russian*: In Russian folklore the quail and hare are the sun and moon found by the Dawn Maiden. Emblem of the sun, Spring and the Tsars. *Witchcraft*: The Devil's bird; diabolical powers; sorcery.

Quartz Australian aboriginal symbolism attributes to quartz the celestial power of light.

Quaternary See NUMBERS, *Four*.

Qubbah The Islamic Qubbah has the same symbolism of planes of existence as the STUPA, q.v.

Queen The feminine principle, equated with the Great Mother who is Queen of Heaven. In Alchemy she is quicksilver, with sulphur as the King. Her attributes are: the crown; crown of stars; turreted crown; crescent moon; stars; orb; sceptre; chalice; blue mantle. Her colour and metal is the lunar silver with the King as the solar gold. See also CHESS.

Quicksilver 'Steadfast water', symbolizing both the solid and fluid. It is the soul, the Queen, the feminine, fluid, volatile, cold principle which acts upon the masculine principle and so liberates it from its limitations of dryness and hardness. This is also the Tantric 'play' of the feminine and masculine which rouses to noble activity, illumination and power. The dissolving power of Quicksilver also represents the terrible aspect of the Great

For Laocoön and his sons, the **python** of Apollo, whose priest at Troy the father was, became the instrument of death, making possible the entry of the wooden horse into their city.

An amorous pair of **quails** form the body of this 18th-century Chinese wine vessel.

The 'White Rose' of alchemy, the **queen**, whose sceptred power is secondary to that of her consort and opposite, the king.

Mother, the poisonous aspect of the dragon or serpent, dissolution and death being necessary for, and leading to, rebirth and resurrection, hence the *aqua vitae*. Quicksilver is also the 'womb' of all metals. Together Sulphur and Quicksilver are the basic generative forces of the universe. As Mercury, Quicksilver contains all three basic astrological symbols, the crescent, circle and cross and the solar and lunar fire and water.

Quinary See NUMBERS, *Five*.

Quince A Greek symbol of fertility, the food of brides: the 'apple' of Dionysos and sacred to Venus.

Quincunx In the form of a cross it is the Cosmic Centre, the four cardinal points meeting at the fifth point, the Centre; it is the meeting point of Heaven and Earth.

Quintessence The quintessence of creatures under the Supreme Deity is the Lion among beasts; the Ox among cattle; the Eagle among birds; the Dolphin among fishes; Man among all.

Quiver The receptive feminine principle, with the arrow as the male; an attribute of Artemis and all hunters.

Rabbit A lunar animal, the rabbit and hare both live in the moon and are associated with Moon goddesses and Earth Mothers. In Aztec symbolism the Moon is a rabbit or hare. In China figures of white rabbits were made for the Moon Festival. The rabbit or hare is the TRICKSTER (q.v.) of the Indians of the eastern forests of America. Also symbolizes fecundity and lust, but wearing rabbit skins in rites denotes docility and humility before the Great Spirit. See also EASTER, HARE.

Radiance Pure spirituality; wisdom; sanctity; purity of heart; the supernatural. Symbolized by the sun's rays, radiate crowns, the nimbus, halo, aureole, mandorla.

Radii Identity with the Centre, the essential, with the circumference as the existential and analogous; radii also represent the alternating powers of active and passive generation; solar rays; equality: 'none is the last'. In the Wheel of Life the radii, or spokes, divide the circumference into periods in the cycle of manifestation. Four radii in a circle often depict the four rivers of Paradise and the quaternary. The figure also takes on the symbolism of the cross in the CIRCLE (q.v.).

Rain Divine blessing; revelation; the descent of the heavenly influences; beatitude; purification; fecundity; penetration, both as fertility and spiritual revelation; in this respect rain joins in the symbolism of the sun's rays and light. All sky gods fertilize the earth by rain. 'The rain, falling from the sky, impregnates the earth, so that she gives birth to plants and grain for man and beast' (Aeschylus).

Rainbow Transfiguration; heavenly glory; different states of consciousness; the meeting of Heaven and Earth; the bridge or boundary between this world and Paradise; the throne of the Sky God. The celestial serpent is also associated with the rainbow in that it, too, can be a bridge between one world and another. In French, African, Indian and Amerindian symbolism the rainbow is also a serpent which quenches its thirst in the sea. *African*: In some regions of Africa the celestial serpent is equated with the rainbow and is a guardian of treasures; or it encircles the earth. *Amerindian*: A ladder of access to the other world. *Buddhist*: The highest state attainable in the realm of *samsara* before the 'clear light' of Nirvana. *Chinese*: The sky dragon; the union of heaven and earth. *Christian*: Pardon; reconciliation between God and man; the throne of the Last Judgment. Christ, 'by whom we are protected from spiritual flood' (Dante). *Graeco-Roman*: The memorable sign to humans which Zeus printed on the clouds. The rainbow is sometimes depicted on the breastplate of Agamemnon as three serpents. It is the personification of Iris, winged messenger of the gods and especially of Zeus and Hera, or Jupiter and Juno. *Hindu*: The 'rainbow body' is the highest yogic state attainable in the realm of *samsara*; the rainbow is also the bow of Indra. *Islamic*: The rainbow has four colours, red, yellow, green, blue, corresponding to the four elements. *Scandinavian*: The bridge, Bifrost, the Tremulous Way, over to Asgard.

Ram Virility; the masculine generative force; creative energy; procreative power, hence its association with sun and sky gods as the renewal of solar energy. In the Zodiac the ram represents the renewed solar power of the spring of the year. The spiral of the ram's horns is used as a thunder symbol and can be connected with both sun gods and moon goddesses. The ram is pre-eminently a sacrificial animal. *Buddhist*: (Tibetan) The ram's head is the dorje Lak-pa. *Celtic*: Fertility; chthonic; an attribute of war gods as is also the ram-headed serpent associated with the horned god Cernunnos. *Christian*: Christ as leader of the flock; also as the sacrifice prefigured by the ram substituted for Isaac. *Egyptian*: Procreation; solar energy; creative heat; the renewal of solar energy in the year; the personification of Amon-Ra, 'Ra ... thou ram, mightiest of created things'. The ram-headed Khnemu later became Khnemu-Ra. The ram of Mendes is an attribute of Osiris. *Greek*: Sacred to Zeus/Sabazios as the ram god;

fertility; generative power. Sacred to Dionysos as generator; the ram of Mendes was sacred to Pan. In Cyprus the ram was associated with Aphrodite. The sign of Mars in the Zodiac. *Hindu*: Sacred to the Vedic fire god Agni; the sacred fire. *Islamic*: The sacrificial animal. *Scandinavian*: Thor's chariot is drawn by rams. *Sumero-Semitic*: A ram's head surmounting a column personifies Ea, Lord of the Ocean and Destiny. The Phoenician Baal/Hamon, as a sky and fertility god, is usually depicted with ram's horns on his head. Rashap is portrayed with ram's horns and his throne is supported by rams.

Rat A plague animal; death; decay; the underworld. *Chinese*: Meanness; timidity. The first of the symbolic animals of the Twelve Terrestrial Branches. *Christian*: Evil; emblem of St Fina. *Hindu*: Prudence; foresight. The rat is the steed of Ganesha, the vanquisher of obstacles, as successful endeavour.

Raven A talking bird, hence prophecy; otherwise ambivalent as either solar or the darkness of evil, as wisdom or the destruction of war. Ravens and wolves are often familiars of primitive gods of the dead. *Alchemic*: With the skull and grave, the raven is a symbol of the blackening and mortification, the *nigredo*, of the first stage of the lesser work and represents dying to the world, 'earth to earth'. *Amerindian*: The TRICKSTER (q.v.) of the eastern forest Indians. A culture hero and demiurge. *Celtic*: Associated with the wren in augury; the 'Blessed Raven' is an attribute of war and fertility goddesses. Morrigan is a raven goddess and Badb, the 'Raven of Battle', symbolizes war; bloodshed; panic; malevolence. The hero Bendegeit Bran has a raven attribute and Lugh has two magic ravens. When all black the raven is a bird of ill-omen, but with a white feather it becomes beneficent. *Chinese*: One of the symbolic animals of the Twelve Terrestrial Branches; it depicts power. A three-legged raven lives in the sun, denoting its three phases of rising, zenith and setting. *Christian*: The Devil, feeding on corruption; as pecking out eyes it is the Devil blinding sinners. The raven is a symbol of sin as opposed to the innocent soul of the white dove. The raven sent out from the Ark by Noah represents wandering, unrest and the unclean. In the symbolism of the Fall the raven often appears on the Tree of Knowledge from which Eve gathers the fruit. It also depicts solitude, hence the hermit saints, and is an emblem of SS Anthony Abbot, Benedict, Ida, Oswald, Paul the Hermit, Vincent. *Egyptian*: Destruction; malevolence. *Greek*: Longevity; sacred to Helios/Apollo; a messenger of the sun god; also an attribute of Athene, Cronos and Aesculapius. Invoked at weddings as fertility. In Orphic art the raven of death is depicted with the pine cone and torch of life and light. *Hebrew*: Carrion; the impure; mortification; destruction; deceit. *Mithraic*: The first grade of initiation; the servant of the sun. *Scandinavian*

The Egyptian god Khnemu, whose **ram** head symbolizes his fusion with the sun god, Ra.

The **quintessence** of alchemy is symbolized here by a fire-encircled eagle within the alchemist's flask.

For the Canadian Tsimshian Indians who made it, this ceremonial spoon with a **raven**'s head symbolized the ambivalent influence of that sly bird.

and Teutonic: Odin/Woden has two ravens on his shoulders, one, Hugin, 'thought' and the other, Munin, 'memory', who ranged everywhere and reported back all they had seen. The raven is an emblem of the Danes and Vikings.

Rays The sun; divine effulgence; divine favour; an emanation of the *nous*; the *corona radiata* is the 'hair of the sun god', the golden rays of Helios. A double halo of rays depicts the dual aspect of a divinity. Rays issuing from the shoulders of the Babylonian sun god Shamash and the Canaanite Shemesh denote the Sumero-Semitic sun god. The seventh ray of the sun is the path by which man passes from this world to the next and is the solar 'gate' or 'door'. Straight rays usually denote the light of the sun and undulating rays its heat. 'Descending rays ... indicate that the force of heaven resides in the rays which the sun sends down to earth' and rays rising were 'a sign that the power of the ascending rays brings to life everything which the earth produces' (Macrobius).

Reaping Death; mortality; castration. The Reaper is Death, usually depicted with a scythe, sickle, hourglass, and in the form of an old man or a skeleton; he is also Time and Cronos/Saturn.

Rebis The Philosophers' Stone of the Hermetic tradition and of Alchemy; it is the attainment of unity; the Androgyne; the reconciliation of all opposites; wholeness; enlightenment; regaining the Centre. The sun and moon, male and female, king and queen, sulphur and quicksilver, having undergone dissolution and the death of the *nigredo*, rise again as the *petra genetrix*, the perfection of the Hermaphrodite.

Red See COLOURS.

Reed/Rush Reeds or rushes symbolize recorded time. *Chinese*: Prosperous administration; their rapid growth depicts advancement. *Christian*: Christ's passion and death on the cross; humiliation; the faithful living by the waters of grace; emblem of St John the Baptist. *Egyptian*: Royalty; the fertilizing Nile. *Greek*: Emblem of Pan; music; harmony.

Reflection A reflection in water, a stream or glass depicts the temporal, phenomenal world. It can also symbolize truth. It is 'a moving image of eternity' (Plato).

Reindeer Sacred to the Scandinavian Great Mother Isa or Disa.

Reins The intelligence, will and guiding power of man, the driver or rider. See also CHARIOT.

Rending Rending and the rent garment symbolize an irrevocable decision or step; a break with the existing order or with a tradition; an attempt to break through to another plane; also penitence, anger and destroying wholeness.

Resin Incorruptibility; immortality. Trees producing resin share the same symbolism as evergreens. Like sap, resin was regarded as the soul substance of the tree; it was also called 'the tears of the Great Mother'. A source of fire, hence generation.

Resurrection Symbols are: the phoenix, lion, peacock, pelican, tree, serpent, rosemary, myrtle, box.

Rice Shares the symbolism of CORN (q.v.) in the West and, as an essential food, has a divine origin. It can be magic and provide supernatural nourishment, like manna, and can also replenish granaries miraculously. It is a symbol of abundance and divine provision and only had to be cultivated after the loss of Paradise and the separation of Heaven and Earth. Rice represents immortality; spiritual nourishment; primordial purity; glory; solar power; knowledge; abundance; happiness and fecundity which is its significance when thrown over brides at weddings. In Chinese Alchemy red rice is associated with cinnabar; with red sulphur in esoteric Islam and with sulphur in the Work in Hermeticism.

Right The right side is usually the solar, masculine, future, outward-going principle. In the West and in Christianity it is the side of honour. At the Last Judgment the sheep are on the right and the goats on the left; in crucifixion scenes the good thief is on the right, the bad on the left, or the Virgin Mary and the Church are on the right with St John or the Synagogue on the left. In Chinese symbolism the right is the yang, masculine, strength, but the left, yin, is the side of honour since strength tends to violence and thus to destruction and dissolution; only in time of war does the right become honourable. In Hinduism and Buddhism a sacred object must be passed on the left side, keeping the object on the right.

Ring Shares, to some extent, the symbolism of the circle as eternity, continuity, divinity, life. It also represents power; dignity; sovereignty; strength; protection; delegated power; completion; cyclic time. The ring is equated with the personality, and to bestow a ring is to transfer power, to plight a troth, to join the personalities. It is also a binding symbol: the wedding ring binds to a new state of union, completeness, fulfilment. An animal or monster's head holding a ring in its jaws depicts a guardian of the way; the open mouth is the gate of death and the ring is the way or 'strait gate' (see PASSAGE) or 'door of deliverance'; it is usually placed on doors as a knocker, or as the keystone of an arch, or as handles on urns, all symbols of entry or passage. *Chinese*: Eternity; the origin of all creation; authority; dignity. A complete ring is acceptance, favour; a broken ring is ambivalent as either rejection, disfavour, or as the two halves being kept as a contract or renewal of friendship. A ring sent by the Emperor was a summons to return to court; a half-ring signified banishment, exile. *Christian*: Eternity; union; spiritual marriage to the Church. Various rings denote the office of the wearer: the sapphire for cardinals and the bishop's ring signifying a bridegroom of the Church. A new Pope wears the Fisherman's Ring as an emblem of St Peter. The British Coronation Ring is 'the ensign of Kingly Dignity and Defence of the Catholic Faith'. Emblem of St Edward the Confessor. *Egyptian*: The origin of the symbol of the ring and the rod is unknown, but is suggested as an *axis mundi* or the revolving universe; the All; eternity. *Hindu*: The flame ring round Siva represents the cosmic cycle of creation and destruction. *Sumero-Semitic*: The ring, often a triple ring, is a divine attribute and worn by all gods; with the crown, sceptre and sickle it is a symbol of royalty.

Death the **Reaper** claims a soul in this vignette from a late 15th-century book of hours.

River The flux of the world in manifestation; the passage of life. The River of Life is the realm of the divinity, the macrocosm; the River of Death is manifest existence, the world of change, the microcosm. The 'return to the source', symbolized by the river flowing upstream, is the return to the pristine, paradisal state, to find enlightenment.

The mouth of the river shares the symbolism of the door or gate, giving access to another realm, to the ocean of unity. Usually, in rites of passage, or journeys from one state to another, the journey is from one bank to another, across the river of life or death, but if the journey is taken to the mouth of the river the banks become dangerous and must be avoided and the symbolism becomes that of the dangerous PASSAGE (q.v.).

The four Rivers of Paradise, flowing in the four cardinal directions, have their source in the spring, fountain or well at the foot of the Tree of Life, or from a rock beneath it, in the centre of Paradise; they symbolize creative power flowing from its unmanifest source into the manifest world to the extreme limit of the sea; that is, from the highest to the lowest plane. *Buddhist*: The flux of life. The Rivers of Paradise bring spiritual power and nourishment. The river of life must be traced back to its source to attain enlightenment. *Christian*: The four Rivers of Paradise, flowing from a single rock, represent the four Gospels flowing from Christ. *Greek*: Rivers are depicted as virile men with horns and long, flowing beards. *Hebrew (Qabalism)*: The rivers of life correspond to the Sephirotic Tree as bringing spiritual influences from the 'world on high' to the 'world below'. *Hindu*: The four Rivers of Paradise flow from the foot of the Tree of Life, on Mount Meru, towards the four cardinal points, forming the horizontal cross of the terrestrial world, related to the quaternary elements, the four phases of

In the centre of a Persian carpet of the 17th or 18th century, the four **rivers** of Paradise flow from a spring at the roots of the Tree of Life.

cyclic development, the four ages, or *yugas*, and the four sacrificial cups of the Vedas. The Hindu *amrita* is connected with the Vedic *soma* flowing from the Tree of Life. Rivers carved on doors of temples represent the purification of the devotee, ritual ablution; bathing in a sacred river confers ritual purification. *Iranian*: The River of Life flows from the Tree of Life and is associated with the flowing of the sacred *haoma*. *Scandinavian*: There are four rivers of milk flowing in Asgard. *Sumero-Semitic*: The four Rivers of Paradise form the four quarters of the earth, the four cardinal points and the seasons.

Robe *Chinese*: The imperial and official robes presented a symbolism of the entire universe, its perfection and the power of Heaven and the Emperor as its earthly representative; the symbols varied between the Taoist and the Buddhist, but the shape of the robe was also symbolic as the roundness of the sleeves depicted elegance of manners, the straightness of the seams signified incorruptibility in administering justice, the lower edge portrayed the horizontal position of the beam of the balance and firmness of will and calmness of heart. *Christian*: The purple robe depicts Christ's passion; the white robe, innocence, or the triumph of the spirit over the flesh; the seamless robe depicts the passion, also charity, unity. *Mithraic*: The robe of the *mystes*, or initiate, bore the signs of the Zodiac and in donning it the initiate became the god passing through the constellation.

Robin *Christian*: Death and resurrection. *Teutonic*: Sacred to Thor; a form of the storm-cloud bird.

Roc See FABULOUS BEASTS.

Rock Permanence; stability; reliability; rigidity; coldness and hardness. The Living Rock is man's primordial self. Dual rocks are a celestial doorway giving access to another realm (for clashing rocks see PASSAGE). *Christian*: Water gushing from the rock signifies the waters of baptism and salvation pouring from the Church. Christ is the rock, the source of living waters and the pure river of the Gospels. The rock is also strength, refuge, steadfastness; it is a symbol of St Peter. *Mithraic*: Mithra was born from a rock. See also STONE.

Rocking Carries the same significance as swinging; a fertility symbol. The rocking of a cradle, chair, etc., also represents life's ups and downs.

Rod Power; authority; dignity; an *axis mundi*; shares the symbolism of the STAFF (q.v.). The rod is an attribute of Aaron and all magicians; it has magic power and is able to resolve disputes; it is also carried by all divine messengers, such as Hermes/Mercury, and by the psychopomp conducting souls to the next world and to judgment. The blossoming, or sprouting, rod is the Cosmic Tree as the world axis. A rod emitting rays is an emblem of gods of thunder and lightning. The measuring rod is an attribute of Nemesis as retribution and a symbol of Time. The rod-and-line is associated with the solar Shamash and Marduk and sometimes with Ea as the architect of the universe. The rod of Moses, turned into a serpent and back again, parallels the alchemical *solve et coagula*. It appears in Islamic symbolism as the unregenerate soul turned into spiritual power.

Rood Screen *Christian*: Dividing the nave, the body, from the choir, heaven, the rood screen is the gate of death between the body of the Church and the entry into the heavenly state. The cross surmounting the screen symbolizes the death of Christ as the means of salvation and entering heaven. The screen also signifies the veil of the Ark of the Covenant. See also ICON.

Roof Shelter; protection; the feminine sheltering aspect.

Room The individual, with windows to the outside world and doors of passage to other realms. A totally enclosed room depicts virginity; it is also used in rites of initiation.

Rope Like the cord and all BONDS (q.v.), the rope both binds and limits yet provides the possibility of infinite extension and freedom; it can give access to heaven and is associated with rites of passage, hence with the ladder, bridge, tree, mountain, etc. The rope can also denote the serpent surrounding the earth or Cosmic Egg and the 'golden cord' of Homer. As a noose it can depict death or despair. *Australian aboriginal*: The medicine man produces the rope of access to other worlds from his own umbilical cord. *Bon-Bon*: In the pre-Buddhist religion of Tibet a rope connected heaven and earth, and the gods came down it to mix with men; after it was cut only souls could ascend by it to heaven; cutting the rope made man mortal. *Christian*: Christ's passion and betrayal. *Greek*: With the vase an attribute of Nemesis. *Hindu*: Gnosis is the invisible rope of ascent. The Indian rope trick symbolizes magic ascent to heaven, transcending earthly conditions, a decadent form of the invisible rope of spiritual ascent. *Sumero-Semitic*: The Accadian 'rope of the world' represents the waters surrounding the world, binding together heaven and earth. The Babylonian water god was often called the 'rope' or 'bond' of the universe. In Sumerian iconography a rope passing through a winged door depicts the bond of union between God and man, a mystic link.

Rosary The circle of wholeness and of time; perpetuity; endless duration; asceticism. *Buddhist*: The 108 beads represent the 108 Brahmins present at the birth of Buddha; the circle is the Wheel of the Law, also the Round of

Existence with the individual beads of manifestation strung upon it. *Christian*: The mystic rose
garden of the Virgin Mary; the 165 beads are
divided into five decades; each set of five
decades has its own 'mysteries' of the joys,
sorrows and glories of the Virgin Mary. The
large beads represent the *Pater Noster*, and a
Gloria, the small beads the *Ave Maria*. Attribute
of St Dominic. *Hindu*: The thread is the non-
manifest, the beads are the multiplicity of
manifestation and the circle is Time. The rosary
is an attribute of Brahma, Siva and Ganesha.
The rosary of Siva has thirty-two or sixty-four
berries of the Rudraksha tree, and usually
accompanies the figure of a Shaivite saint. Other
rosaries have 108 beads of Tulasi wood. *Islamic*:
The ninety-nine beads are the 'circular' number
and correspond to the Divine Names; the
hundredth bead, which is the Name of the
Essence, can be found only in Paradise.

Rose/Rosette A highly complex symbol; it is
ambivalent as both heavenly perfection and
earthly passion; the flower is both Time and
Eternity, life and death, fertility and virginity.
In the Occident the rose and lily occupy the
position of the lotus in the Orient and the mystic
rose closely parallels the symbolism of the lotus.
The rose is perfection; the pleroma; completion; the mystery of life; the heart-centre of
life; the unknown; beauty; grace; happiness,
but also voluptuousness; the passions and
associated with wine, sensuality and seduction.

In the symbolism of the heart the rose
occupies the central point of the cross, the point
of unity. As the flower of the feminine deities it is
love, life, creation, fertility, beauty and also
virginity. The evanescence of the rose represents
death, mortality and sorrow; its thorns signify
pain, blood and martyrdom. As funerary it
portrays eternal life, eternal Spring, resurrection.

The rose also typifies silence and secrecy, *sub
rosa*, a rose being hung, or depicted, in council
chambers to symbolize secrecy and discretion.
The golden rose denotes perfection; the red
rose, desire, passion, joy, beauty, consummation; it is the flower of Venus and the blood of
Adonis and of Christ; the white rose is the
'flower of light', innocence, virginity, spiritual
unfolding, charm; the red and white rose
together represent the union of fire and water,
the union of opposites; the blue rose is the
unattainable, the impossible.

The four-petalled rose depicts the four-
square division of the cosmos; the five-petalled
is the microcosm with the six-petalled as the
macrocosm. The rosette is the rose, or lotus,
seen from above. The 'Rose of the Winds' is
represented as a circle enclosing the double
cross, signifying the four cardinal and four
intermediate directions; it thus shares the
symbolism of the circle, the centre, the cross and
the radii of the solar wheel. The Rose Garden is
a Paradise symbol and is the place of the mystic
marriage, the union of opposites. *Alchemic*: The

The Chinese Imperial **robe** bore the symbols –
dragon, clouds, rainbow, waves, pearl – of the
prosperity, longevity and good luck which its wearer
would need to have and to exercise if he was to
achieve his role as mediator between earth and
heaven.

Lady with a **rosary**, by Aga Riza, court painter to
Shah Abbas I (1586–1629).

rose is wisdom and the *rosarium* the Work; it is also the rebirth of the spiritual after the death of the temporal. *Chinese*: Fragrance; sweetness in desolation; prosperity. The lotus carries the metaphysical symbolism. *Christian*: The flower of Paradise in its beauty, perfection and fragrance. The white rose is innocence, purity, chastity, the Virgin Mary; the red rose is charity and martyrdom and grew from the drops of Christ's blood on Calvary. A garland of roses is heavenly bliss and the Virgin Mary as the Rose of Heaven; the Rose of Sharon is the Church. The thorns of the rose are the sins of the Fall and the 'rose without thorns', or the Mystic Rose, is the Virgin Mary, exempt, by her Immaculate Conception in the womb of her mother, from the effects of sin. The golden rose is an emblem of the Pope and signifies special papal benediction. The rose is an emblem of SS Angelus, Cecilia, Dorothea of Cappadocia, Elizabeth of Hungary, Elizabeth of Portugal, Rosalia, Rose of Lima, Rose of Viterbo. *Egyptian*: Roses were sacred to Isis as symbolizing pure love freed from the carnal and were used in the mysteries of Isis and Osiris. The lotus carries other symbolism. *Graeco-Roman*: Love triumphant; joy; beauty; desire; emblem of Aphrodite/Venus. Roses were grown in Roman funerary gardens as symbols of resurrection and eternal Spring, or roses were brought at the Rosalia festival and scattered on the graves. The Roman Emperor wore a crown of roses. The red rose grew from the blood of Adonis and the rose is an emblem of Aurora, Helios, Dionysos and the Muses. *Hebrew* (*Qabalism*): The centre of the rose is the sun and the petals the infinite, but harmonious, diversities of Nature. The rose emanates from the Tree of Life. *Hindu*: The lotus parallels the symbolism of the Mystic Rose as a spiritual centre, especially in the chakras. *Islamic*: The rose symbolizes the blood of the Prophet, also his two sons, Hasan and Hosein, his two 'eyes' or 'roses'. In the Rose of Baghdad, the first circle represents the Law, the second the path, the third knowledge and the three together are Truth and the names of Allah. *Rosicrucian*: The Rose-cross is the Mystic Rose as wheel and cross; the rose is the divine light of the universe and the cross the temporal world of pain and sacrifice. The rose grows on the Tree of Life which implies regeneration and resurrection. The rose in the centre of the cross is the quaternary of the elements and the point of unity.

Rosemary *European*: Its enduring scent is equated with remembrance, constancy and devotion to memory. It is also funerary and sacred to Ares.

Rotundity As depicted in Oriental figures of Siva, Ho-tei and the Laughing Buddha, it represents attainment, high standing, importance. The rotundity of the Chinese god of wealth and the Hindu Ganesha depicts gluttony and, therefore, prosperity.

Round of Existence (The Wheel of Becoming). *Buddhist and Jain*: The circle symbolizes the round of all phenomenal existence, ceaseless change and becoming; the whole is held in the grip of Mara, or gShin-rje, Lord of Death. It is a diagrammatic representation of *samsara*, manifest life in all its phases between birth and death; a totality. At the centre are the three senseless creatures, the pig of greed and ignorance, the cock of carnal passion, the snake of anger, who, together, represent the qualities binding man to the world of senses, illusion, the essential nature of existence. Around the centre is a circle in which the left half depicts monks and laymen moving upwards to a happy rebirth and in the right half naked figures are descending to woeful rebirths. The six divisions of the next circle portray the possible destinations of man after death: at the top is the Highest Heavens, the right side the Titans and Gods, to the left humans; in the bottom half, to the right, are the unhappy spirits tormented by the senses, to the left is the realm of animals and, lowest of all, are the various hells of heat and cold. A figure of Buddha is present in every division to assist in ultimate salvation for all. The outer circle is divided into twelve pictures: a birth scene, depicting new life, growth and the process of becoming; a pregnant woman – the condition of becoming, the act of appropriation, perpetuating mortal life; a man picking fruit – appropriation leading to grasping at life, leading to desire; a drinking scene – desire as thirst for life, leading to the sense of feeling; a man with an arrow in his eye – the sense of feeling, leading to contact; a kiss – contact and the senses leading to the sphere of the senses; a house with many windows – the senses, leading to the existence of the personality; a ship on a journey – the personality, leading to the state of consciousness; a monkey picking fruit – consciousness, leading to elemental impulses; the potter and pots – shaping of the impulses, the condition of impulse being the absence of knowledge; a blind old woman – the absence of knowledge, the blindness of ignorance leading to death; a man carrying a corpse – death and suffering, leading to rebirth.

Round Table The circle of the table is that of the heavens, of perfection, wholeness, totality and a cosmic Centre; the Grail is the mystic centre; the twelve knights represent the signs of the Zodiac and the radii of the circle depict equality, 'none is the last'. In Christian symbolism of the Round Table the Seat Perilous is equated with that which was occupied by Judas Iscariot at the Last Supper. In Hindu symbolism the table, or wheel, is divided into twelve segments, the twelve months of the year, which correspond to the twelve Adityas, the 'shining ones'.

Rowan Wisdom; power against fairies and witchcraft. It is the Gallic Tree of Life. In

Scandinavian and Teutonic mythology it is sacred to Thor and Donar and provides power against sorcery.

Ruby See JEWELS.

Rudder Guidance; control; safety; an emblem of Tyche/Fortuna as Fate and of Abundance.

Rue The herb of the sun; the herb of grace; purification; virginity; apotropaic. In Hebrew symbolism it is repentance, and is also used as an apotropaic herb in ceremonies. In later times in Europe it became sadness as a homonym of rue. It is also an abortifacient.

Rule The perfection of the straight line; rectitude. See also *Plumb* Rule.

Sackcloth Mourning; repentance; humiliation.

Sacrifice The restoration of primordial unity, reuniting that which is scattered in manifestation. As all creation implies sacrifice it is the death-life, birth and rebirth cycle, so that sacrifice is equated with creation, and identifies man with aspects of the cosmos. It is also submission to divine guidance through reconciliation, offering the self to the will of God; expiation. Every place of sacrifice is an omphalos. Human sacrifice implied an atonement for *hubris*, the overweening pride of man, and a blood offering to the gods. Kings were sacrificed ritually as they were regarded as the bringers of fertility to the land as initiating irrigation works which brought the fertilizing and life-giving waters. When the king's fertility waned the land and the people also suffered, hence his sacrifice to the Earth Mother Goddess to restore virility in the new king. The sacrifice took place at the death of the old year, the time of the twelve days of chaos before the rebirth of the sun and the new year. Later a substitute or scapegoat was offered in place of the king. In the Vedic sacrificial ground the East represented the realm of the gods, the South the Ancestors, the West the Serpent, the North the People. In many mythologies and traditions the world was created from the parts of the sacrificial victim, as in Babylonian symbolism the world was made from the dismembered Tiamat, or, in Teutonic myth, from the Yinir. In animal sacrifice the head represents the dawn, the eye the sun, the breath the wind, the back the sky, the belly the air, the under-belly the earth. In sacrifice the sacrificer and sacrificed become one with each other and the universe, microcosm and macrocosm meet and attain unity.

Saffron In Europe it signifies disinterestedness; humility; renunciation; love; magic. It is the herb of the sun.

The symbol of the Qabalistic Rose Croix incorporates four **roses** as symbol of the perfection of quaternity.

One of the great wheels at the base of the temple of Konarak, symbols of the **round** of existence upon which even worship of the divine rests.

Isis as Fortuna, in a wall painting at Pompeii, holds the **rudder** of her control over the destiny of man.

Sagittarius See ZODIAC.

Sails The Spirit as breath or wind; the air; the winds. As an attribute of Fortune they signify inconstancy. In mediaeval Christian iconography sails can portray the Holy Spirit. They also typify fertility, pregnancy, increasing power, but, on the other hand, are related to the SHROUD (q.v.) and share some of its symbolism.

Salamander Usually depicted as a small, wingless lizard or dragon, sometimes as dog-like, leaping out of the flames which represent the element of fire. It is the animal of fire. The salamander was thought to be sexless, hence it was equated with chastity. In Christian symbolism it represents enduring faith and the righteous man who cannot be consumed by the fires of temptation. In Heraldry it depicts bravery and courage unquenched by the fires of affliction.

Salmon Phallic; fecundity. In Celtic symbolism it is wisdom; the foreknowledge of the gods; otherworld knowledge. Associated with Celtic sacred wells, it can take the place of the serpent as wisdom and contact with otherworld powers.

Salt Life; immortality; incorruptibility; permanence; fidelity; friendship; wisdom and knowledge (*sal sapientiae*); the soul. Later it also signified worth, piquancy and wit. *Alchemic*: Rectification; clarification; the fixed; the cubic stone; earthly nature; the body uniting the active and passive, spirit and soul. 'Wherever there is metal there are sulphur and quicksilver and salt; the three are Spirit, Soul and Body, the nature of metal and man. Salt is static and therefore the natural element in the ternary; salt is not merely the physical but also the "astral" body. Sulphur produces combustion, quicksilver evaporation, salt ... serves to "fix" the volatile spirit' (Valentinus). It is the principle of uninflammability and fixity and, mystically, the body of man. *Celtic*: The incorruptible Spirit, with earth as the corruptible body. *Christian*: The elect; divine wisdom; worth; purity; incorruptibility; discretion; superiority; strength (Mt. 5,13; Mk. 9,50; Col. 4,6). *Graeco-Roman*: Literary wit. Salt played an important part in sacrifices, and was also apotropaic, being placed on the lips of Roman infants of eight days to ward off evil spirits; this was probably the origin of offering salt to a Christian catechumen before baptism. Salt was used in holy water in some consecration ceremonies. *Hebrew*: Spiritual discernment.

Sand Instability; impermanence. In Islam sand signifies purity since it is used for ritual ablutions when no water is available.

Sandals The moon is 'the Goddess of the Brazen Sandals' and golden or brazen sandals depict the full moon. Winged sandals portray fleetness and are an attribute of the messenger gods, especially Hermes/Mercury. See also SHOE.

Sap The life-force; vitality; strength. Sap shares blood symbolism. The sap-filled plant signifies motherhood; to be full of sap is vitality and youthfulness and, by extension, 'sapless' is aged; 'sap-head' is youthful folly.

Sapphire See JEWELS.

Sarcophagus Shares the symbolism of the TOMB (q.v.) as an enclosed place and the enclosing feminine principle. It is also death and mortality.

Sardonyx See JEWELS.

Saturn See PLANETS.

Saturnalia The sinister aspect of Saturn; the winter solstice; the death of the old year and birth of the new, *dies natalis solis invicti*, the birthday of the unconquerable sun; the passage from chaos to cosmos; the suspension of time. The dead return during the twelve nights of the duration of the Saturnalia. It is also the time of the sacrifice of the old king, or his scapegoat, as waning fertility, and instigating the enthronement of the new king as virility. The twelve days of chaos symbolize the pattern of the coming months of the year. The period of chaos is governed by the Lord of Misrule, or the King of the Bean and Queen of the Pea. TRANSVESTISM (q.v.) is a feature of the time of chaos in Saturnalia, orgies, carnivals, etc. and signifies a form of return to chaos. Babylon held the twelve days of duel between Chaos and Cosmos; in Christianity these are the Twelve Days of Christmas.

Satyr Male spirits of profane nature; followers of the nature gods Silvanus, Faunus, Pan, Dionysos/Bacchus. They represent untamed nature, licence and lust, and have human heads with horns and goat beard, human hands and arms, but goats' bodies from the waist downwards. They may wear the crowns of ivy of Dionysos and can carry his thyrsos; other attributes are bunches of grapes, baskets of fruit, pitchers of wine, the cornucopia and the snake; their female counterparts in the Bacchanalia were the Maenads.

Saw The golden saw is the sun cleaving darkness; an emblem of the sun god Shamash. In Christianity the saw is an emblem of SS Euphemia and Simon Zelotes and, with the plane and hatchet, of St Joseph; it is also an emblem of Isaiah.

Scales The Scales of Justice represent balance; equality; justice; harmony; economy. In Christianity they are an emblem of the Archangel Michael. They are also the symbol of the sign Libra in the Zodiac and of the Greek Themis as law, order and truth. Scales of fish depict armour, protection and the god Ea-Oannes, Lord of the Deep; they are also worn by priestesses of the cults of the Great Mother, controller of the waters.

Scallop Shell See SHELLS.

Scalp Martial success. The scalp shares the head symbolism as containing the 'power' of the person; to capture the scalp is to capture its power.

Scapegoat Delegated guilt; escape from the consequences of sins; purging for sins; abolishing the past and its consequences by bearing the sins of others or of an entire community, thus freeing them. In the King-sacrifice (see SACRIFICE) a scapegoat later took the place of the king in the fertility sacrifice. In Christianity the scapegoat is a symbol of Christ as suffering for the sins of the world.

Scarab *Egyptian*: The sun; the path of the sun; self-creative power; Khepera, god of creation; resurrection; immortality; divine wisdom; ruling providence directing and regulating the productive powers of nature. Thought to be all males, the scarab also represented virility and the generative power of life. In Africa, in the Congo, it is a lunar symbol of eternal renewal.

Sceptre Divine or royal power; sovereignty; ministerial authority; phallic; the transmission of the life-force; the magic wand; it is an attribute of sky gods, monarchs and magicians. *Buddhist*: The diamond sceptre is the highest power; the Dharma; justice; authority; the seven positive and permanent virtues. See also DORJE. *Chinese*: Supreme authority; the *ju-i*; the power of faith, 'as you desire'; guards against the unexpected and points the way; an attribute of the god of learning and literature. *Christian*: Authority; an emblem of the Archangel Gabriel. *Egyptian*: Attribute of Osiris as judge of the dead. *Graeco-Roman*: An attribute of the sky god Zeus/Jupiter as supreme power, also of Juno and Cybele, and of a Roman consul. *Hindu*: The highest authority, the Dharma; an attribute of Indra as upholding the cosmic order and of Vasu upholding law and righteousness among men. See also VAJRA. *Japanese*: The *nyoi* depicts authority and is carried by abbots.

Scissors Ambivalent, a life-and-death symbol; it is both union, the two acting as one, and a severing, as cutting the thread of life. An attribute of the Fate Atropos who cut the thread of life.

Scorpio See ZODIAC.

Scorpion Death; destructive force; disaster; darkness. *Christian*: Evil; torment; treachery; Judas Iscariot. *Egyptian*: Attribute of Set in his

A maenad and a **satyr** play the flute and pipes in a bacchanalia recorded on a disk in the Roman Mildenhall Treasure.

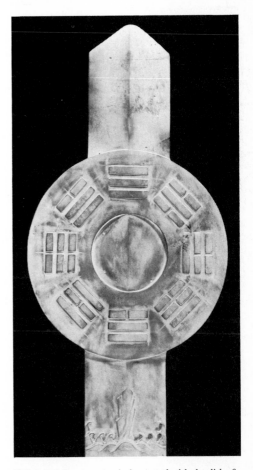

This jade Ming **sceptre** is decorated with the disk of heaven and, on its shaft, the rocks of earth: power must unite both.

typhonic aspect; also of Selk, or Selket, as protector of the dead. Seven scorpions accompanied Isis on her search for Osiris. *Hebrew*: Venom; death. *Mithraic*: The *dadophoroi*, with upwards- and downwards-held torches, are the Bull and the Scorpion as life and death, rising and setting sun, etc. *Sumero-Semitic*: Scorpions, or scorpion men, were guardians of the Gateway of the Sun, the Mountains of the East, and the Twin Gates. Scorpions were associated with Ishtar, or Nina, and were an attribute of the Phrygian Sabazius.

Scourge *Christian*: An emblem of Christ's passion and of St Ambrose.

Screen See ROOD SCREEN; VEIL.

Scroll Learning; knowledge; the unfolding of life and knowledge; the passing of time; the extent of a life; the scroll of the law; destiny. *Buddhist*: The unfolding of the Law; the scroll of the texts or *sutras*. *Chinese*: Longevity; scholarship. *Christian*: The Book of Life. The seven-sealed scroll which none can read shares the symbolism of the tablets of destiny. The scroll is an attribute of St James the Great, also associated with Isaiah, Jeremiah and the prophets. *Greek*: Attribute of Aesculapius as medical learning. *Egyptian*: Knowledge; associated with the papyrus as the emblem of Lower Egypt.

Scythe Death; time; the cutting off of life; an attribute of Cronos/Saturn and of the figures of the Reaper and Death. The scythe also symbolizes the harvest which, in turn, implies death and rebirth, the destructive and creative powers of the Great Mother. The form of the scythe is a union of the masculine, upright and cutting with the feminine as curved and reaping.

Sea See OCEAN.

Seal Authority; power; possession; individuality; also secrecy; virginity; conclusion.

Seal of Solomon See TRIANGLE.

Seamless Robe Wholeness; the integrated; the wholeness of a tradition; thus to rend the robe is to break with, or rupture, the tradition. In Christianity the seamless robe is a symbol of Christ's passion.

Sea Snail *Aztec*: The moon god, who appears and disappears; pregnancy; parturition, 'as the marine animal comes out of its shell, so is man born from the womb of his mother'.

Seasons The quaternary division of the year as Spring, Summer, Autumn, Winter, or, as in Egypt, the triple seasons of Sowing (Winter), Growing (Spring), Inundation (Summer). Groups of figures of the Seasons portray the recurring cycle of the ages. Spring: a child bearing garlands of flowers or carrying leaves, or a woman, or youth, wearing a crown of flowers, or carrying, or standing by, flowers; the animal of the Spring is the lamb; the zodiacal signs are Aries, Taurus, Gemini. Summer: a child, or woman, carrying a sheaf of corn, or crowned with a garland of corn; the animal is the lion or dragon, and the zodiacal signs are Cancer, Leo, Virgo. Autumn: a child, or woman, carrying bunches of grapes or a basket of fruit, or trodden grapes; the animal is the hare and the zodiacal signs Libra, Scorpio, Sagittarius. Winter: a child wrapped in a cloak, or an old man with white, frosty hair, holding a sickle, or with leafless trees; the animal is the salamander and the zodiacal signs are Capricorn, Aquarius, Pisces. In Chinese symbolism the Seasons represent orderliness, correctness and model behaviour, 'the seasons do not err'. They are portrayed by flowers: Spring, the cherry, peach and almond blossom; Summer, the lotus and peony (both solar); Autumn, red maple, convolvulus, chrysanthemum; Winter, plum blossom, bamboo and pine.

Sea Urchin *Celtic*: The 'serpent's egg', latent force; the seed; the life.

Seed Potentiality; latent power; the *semen virile*; the masculine principle. A symbol of the Centre, from which the Cosmic Tree grows. In Hinduism the seed is the Divine Spirit, Atman, at the centre of the being, the heart. The seed in the centre of the Hindu temple symbolizes Life and consciousness itself, *cit*.

Sephiroth In Qabalism the Ten Sephiroth are the principal aspects of God; his divine and infinite qualities and the spheres or emanations from the Ain Soph, usually symbolized by the Tree of Life. The first is the Monad, the First Cause, of which the other nine are composed of three trinities, each an image of the original trinity of male, female and uniting intelligence.

Seraphim Divine love; divine heat; the fervour of devotion, 'the fire of charity' (Dante). In Isaiah it is stated: 'Each had six wings; with twain he covered his face, with twain he covered his feet and with twain he did fly.' In Heraldry a seraph's head is depicted as that of a child, as purity, with three pairs of wings. The highest of the nine orders of angels.

Serpent A highly complex and universal symbol. The serpent and dragon are often interchangeable and in the Far East no distinction is made between them. The symbolism of the serpent is polyvalent: it can be male, female, or the self-created. As a killer it is death and destruction; as renewing its skin periodically it is life and resurrection; as coiled it is equated with the cycles of manifestation. It is solar and lunar, life and death, light and darkness, good and evil, wisdom and blind passion, healing and poison, preserver and destroyer, and both spiritual and physical rebirth. It is phallic, the procreative male force, 'the husband of all women', and the presence of a serpent is almost universally associated with pregnancy. It accompanies all female deities and the Great Mother, and is often depicted twining round them or held in their hands. Here it also takes on the feminine characteristics of the secret, enigmatic and intuitional; it is the unpredictable in that it appears and disappears suddenly.

The serpent was also believed to be androgynous and is the emblem of all self-creative divinities and represents the generative power of the earth. It is solar, chthonic, sexual, funerary and the manifestation of force at any level, a source of all potentialities both material and spiritual, and closely associated with the concepts of both life and death. Living underground, it is in touch with the underworld and has access to the powers, omniscience and magic possessed by the dead. The chthonic serpent manifests the aggressive powers of the gods of the underworld and darkness; it is universally an initiator and rejuvenator and 'master of the bowels of the earth'. When chthonic it is the enemy of the sun and all solar and spiritual powers and represents the dark forces in mankind. Here the positive and negative, light and darkness, are in conflict, as with Zeus and Typhon, Apollo and Python, Osiris and Set, the eagle and serpent, etc.

It also signifies primordial instinctual nature, the upsurging life-force, uncontrolled and undifferentiated; potential energy; animating spirit. It is a mediator between heaven and earth, earth and the underworld, and is associated with sky, earth and water and in particular with the Cosmic Tree. It is also the cloud-dragon of darkness and guards treasures.

The serpent can depict solar rays, the course of the sun, lightning and the force of the waters, and is an attribute of all river deities. It is knowledge; power; guile; subtlety; cunning; darkness; evil and corruption and the Tempter. 'It is fate itself, swift as disaster, deliberate as retribution, incomprehensible as destiny'.

Cosmologically the serpent is the primordial ocean from which all emerges and to which all returns, the primaeval undifferentiated chaos. It can also support and maintain the world, or encircle it as OUROBOROS (q.v.), the symbol of cyclic manifestation and reabsorption. The serpent which is visible is only a temporary manifestation of the causal, a-temporal Great Invisible Spirit, master of all natural forces and the vital spirit or principle. It is the god found in early cosmogonies which, later, gave way to more psychological and spiritual interpretations. Serpents, or dragons, are the guardians of the threshold, temples, treasures, esoteric knowledge and all lunar deities. They are producers of storms, controllers of the powers of the waters, encircling the waters, and are both water-confining and water-bringing. They are

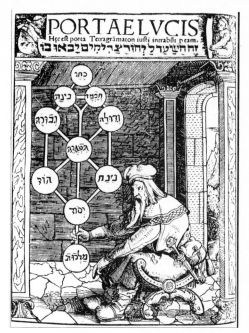

A 5th-century Qabalist treatise illustrates the tree of the **Sephiroth** as the 'Portal of Light: This is the doorway of the Tetragrammaton: the Just will enter through it.'

A T'ang pottery figurine of the zoomorphic man-**serpent**, a record of the Year of the Serpent, sixth in the Chinese cycle of the Twelve Terrestrial Animals.

invoked in all incantations of the dead who cross the waters of death.

As moving without legs or wings, the serpent symbolizes the all-pervading spirit; as penetrating crevices it is the inner nature of man, and conscience. It can also be a disguise of malefic powers, such as witches or magicians, depicting the evil and vicious aspect of nature. The *sol niger* is associated with the dark forces of the serpent. The Celestial Serpent, with the Chinese Azure Dragon, symbolizes the rainbow and both can form a bridge from this world to the next. A child playing with a snake depicts Paradise Regained, freedom from conflict and the end of the temporal world, having the same symbolism as the lion and lamb lying together.

The coiled, or knotted, serpent signifies the cycles of manifestation, also latent power, the dynamic, the potential, either for good or evil. Coiled round the egg, it is the incubation of the vital spirit; the Ouroboros, the encircling power of the waters round the earth. Coiled round the Tree or any axial symbol, it is the awakening of dynamic force; the genius of all growing things; the *anima mundi*; cyclic existence. Associated with the Tree of Life its aspect is beneficent, with the Tree of Knowledge it is malefic and the poison of the evil of the world of manifestation. Coiled round a woman, who is the Great Mother, the lunar goddess, the serpent is solar and together they represent the male-female relationship. The serpent, like the toad, is said to have a jewel in its head and possess treasures and magic rings.

When the eagle or stag appears with the serpent they are solar and manifest light with the serpent as darkness, the unmanifest and chthonic; together they are cosmic unity, totality; in conflict they portray duality, the pairs of opposites and the celestial and chthonic powers at war. The eagle is often depicted with the serpent in its talons, or the stag as trampling it underfoot, typifying the victory of good over evil, light over darkness, heavenly over earthly and spiritual over temporal powers. The fiery serpent is solar, purification, the transmuting and transcending of the earthly state. As a girdle or bracelet the serpent depicts the eternal revolution of the ages; succession; the cycle of dissolution and reintegration. Lozenges as ornaments on a serpent represent the phallic serpent and the female vulva as the solar-lunar, male-female unity, dualism and reintegration; the reconciliation of opposites; the androgyne. The ram-headed serpent is an attribute of all horned gods as generative power and fertility. Undulating serpents or dragons signify cosmic rhythm, or the power of the waters. Winged serpents or dragons are solar and typify the union of spirit and matter, the union of eagle and serpent and of all opposites; they also represent quickened understanding.

Two serpents together symbolize the opposites of dualism which are ultimately united. Entwining a tree or staff they are the spiral cycles of nature; the solstices; the two fundamental forces of winding and unwinding; the alchemical *solve et coagula*. On the CADUCEUS (q.v.) they represent the homeopathic powers of healing and poison, illness and health, 'nature can overcome nature'. Wound round each other they are Time and Fate, the two great binding powers. Two serpents or dragons biting each other's tails suggest that, although in seeming opposition, forces and things in the realm of duality actually spring from the same source and principle. The eggs of the reptile signify rebirth and its lidless eyes denote watchfulness, hence wisdom. The serpent often holds the fruit or herb of immortality. Sometimes the symbolism of the bull and ram are shared with the serpent as phallic, fertility and procreative power. The serpent as a rainbow which quenches its thirst in the sea occurs in French, African, Indian and Amerindian symbolism. *African*: A royal emblem; a vehicle of immortality; incarnations of the dead. The celestial serpent is also the rainbow and either encircles the earth, or is a guardian of treasures, or is a thunder spirit and associated with lightning. As a rainbow it quenches its thirst in the sea. The serpent can be a culture hero or mythical ancestor who gave man the forge and corn. It is connected with the waters and fecundity. The cult of the sacred python also occurs. *Alchemic*: The serpent on a pole is the fixation of the volatile quicksilver, the subjugation of the vital force. Passing through a circle it depicts the alchemical fusion. *Amerindian*: The thunder creature, lightning, the rain-bearer, the enemy of the Thunder Bird; lunar and magic power; the spear of the war gods. A symbol of eternity and a harbinger of death. The horned serpent is the water spirit, the fertilizing power of water. Snakes are mediators between men and the lower world. The Great Manitou takes the form of a serpent with horns with which it transfixes the Toad or Dark Manitou as evil. *Australian aboriginal*: The masculine principle; lightning. There is an association between the presence of a snake and pregnancy. *Aztec*: The plumed serpent, a combination of the Quetzal bird and the snake, is the sun; the spirit; the power of ascension; rain; wind; thunder and lightning; the primordial motion of wind and water; the breath of life; knowledge; the eastern region; it accompanies all rain and wind gods; it is phallic; eternal creation; unending time; an intermediary between God and man. It is the White God from whose black bowels the rain falls and is also an attribute of Quetzalcoatl and the Sky God of the Zodiac when it is solar, but it becomes lunar when the serpent represents the Earth Mother, the Snake Woman, Coatlicue, who wears a skirt of woven serpents. The snake can be a culture hero and mythical ancestor. A bird of prey grips the serpent god from whose blood mankind is born, symbolic of the dismemberment of original unity and the coming of multiplicity in the manifest world. *Buddhist*: At the centre of the Round of Existence the snake represents anger, with the pig as greed and ignorance and the cock as carnal passion, the three together signifying the sins which bind man to the world of illusion and the round, or wheel, of existence. The serpent is sometimes associated with Buddha who changed himself into a *naga* to heal the people in a time of disease and famine. *Celtic*: Associated with the healing waters and wells. The horned, or ram-headed, serpent which occurs frequently in Celtic and Gallic iconography represents Cernunnos, god of fertility and virility. The snake is an emblem of Bridgit as a Mother Goddess. A serpent-wreathed head is fertility and is apotropaic. *Chinese*: The serpent is seldom distinguished from the DRAGON (q.v.), but when it is it becomes negative, malevolent, destructive, deceitful and cunning and typifies sycophancy and is one of the five poisonous creatures. The brother and sister, Fo-hi and Niu-kua, are sometimes portrayed as two snakes with human heads, one of the rare animal-human combinations in Chinese symbolism. They are yin-yang and their symbolism is related to that of the caduceus. The snake is the sixth of the symbolic animals of the Twelve Terrestrial Branches. *Christian*: Ambivalent as both Christ as wisdom and raised on the Tree of Life as a sacrifice, and as the Devil in his chthonic aspect. The serpent, or dragon, is Satan, the Tempter, the enemy of God and the agent of the Fall; he represents the powers of evil; destruction; the grave; guile and craftiness; he is also the power of evil that man must overcome in himself. Dante equates the serpent with the damned, but entwining the Tree of Life it is wisdom and is beneficent, while with the Tree of Knowledge it becomes Lucifer and malefic. The serpent raised on the cross, or pole, is a prototype of Christ raised on the Tree of Life for the healing and salvation of the world; the serpent wound round the cross is sometimes portrayed with a woman's head to symbolize the Temptation; the serpent at the foot of the cross is evil, and in that position represents Christ's triumph over evil and the powers of darkness. In Christianity the serpent can change places with the dragon; like the Babylonian Tiamat, the Satan of Christianity is 'the great dragon . . . that old serpent, called the devil and Satan' (Rev. 12,9). The good serpent is seen in iconography rising from the chalice of St John. The evil serpent is Satan, the dragon of the Apocalypse. Tertullian says that Christians called Christ 'the Good Serpent'. The Virgin Mary crushes the head of the serpent of Eve instead of succumbing to him. *Egyptian*: The *uraeus*, the cobra, is supreme divine and royal wisdom and power; knowledge; gold. Apop, the coluber, as Set in his typhonic aspect, is the serpent of the mist, the 'demon of darkness', discord and destruction; also the baleful aspect of the scorching sun. Serpents at the side of the sun disk represent the goddesses who, as royal serpents, drove out the enemies of Ra, the sun god. Two serpents are Nous and Logos. The

A 19th-century South Indian sculpture shows a minor female deity with the **serpent** of creative energy issuing from her vulva.

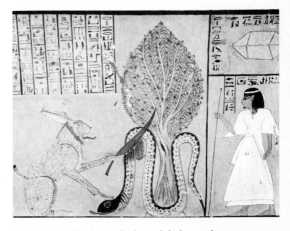

A cat, solar animal, attacks the undulating, and therefore watery, destructive, baleful and discordant **serpent** coiled round the Tree of Life in this Egyptian wall painting of the 14th century BC.

serpent with a lion's head is protection against evil. Buto, a snake goddess, takes the form of a cobra. The horned viper is an emblem of Cerastes. *Gnostic*: The author of divine gnosis. The winged serpent is Phanes, and, with a nimbus round it, depicts the Light of the World; knowledge and illumination. *Greek*: Wisdom; renewal of life; resurrection; healing and as such an attribute of Aesculapius, Hippocrates, Hermes and Hygieia; it is also an aspect of Aesculapius as saviour-healer. It is the life principle, and an *agathos daimon*; sometimes it is a theriomorph of Zeus/Ammon and other deities; sacred to Athene as wisdom and particularly to Apollo at Delphi as light slaying the python of darkness and of the deluge. Apollo not only frees the sun from the powers of darkness but liberates the soul in inspiration and the light of knowledge. The serpent is associated with saviour deities of the Mysteries and also represents the dead and dead heroes: the vital principle, or soul, left the body in the form of a snake, and souls of the dead can reincarnate as serpents. The snake is a symbol of Zeus Chthonios; it is also phallic and is sometimes depicted as wound round the egg as a symbol of vitality; it represents the passions vitalizing both the male and female principles. Women with hair of serpents, such as the Erinyes, Medusa and Graia, signify the powers of magic and enchantment, the wisdom and guile of the serpent. Two huge serpents, sent by the offended Apollo, crushed Laocoön and his two sons. The three serpents on the breastplate of Agamemnon are equated with the celestial serpent as the rainbow. Bacchantes carry serpents. *Hebrew*: Evil; temptation; sin; sexual passion; the souls of the damned in Sheol. The brazen serpent of Moses is homeopathic, 'like heals like'. Leviathan is a serpent of the deep. Jahveh launches 'the crooked serpent', lightning (Job 26,13). Qabalism depicts Adam Kadmon as a man holding an erect serpent by the neck. *Hindu*: The shakti; Nature; cosmic power; chaos; the amorphous; the non-manifest; the manifestation of the Vedic Agni, fire, the 'fierce serpent'; the dark serpent denotes the potentiality of fire. As Kaliya, vanquished by Krishna, who dances on its head, the serpent is evil. The cobra is a mount of Vishnu and as such is knowledge, wisdom and eternity. As the cosmic ocean Vishnu sleeps on the coiled serpent on the primordial waters, the oceanic, chaotic, unpolarized state before creation. His two *nagas*, with intertwined bodies, represent the already-fertilized waters and out of this union rises the Earth Goddess, symbol of both earth and waters. Ananta, the thousand-headed ruler of the serpents, is the 'endless', the infinite and fertility, whose coils encircle the basis of the world axis. Vritra, the imprisoner of the waters, is subterranean darkness which swallows the waters and causes drought; he, like Ahi 'the throttler', is a three-headed snake slain by Indra who releases the waters again with his thunderbolt. Entwined

serpents are chthonic. Two serpents with downward and upward movement represent the Divine Sleep and Divine Awakening in the nights and days of Brahma. The Naga and Nagina are serpent kings and queens or genii, often divinities in their own rights; they can be depicted as either fully human, or as snakes, or as humans with cobra heads and hoods, or with ordinary snakes' heads, or as human from the waist upwards and serpentine from the waist downwards. They frequently share the same symbolism as the Chinese Dragon as rain-givers and the life forces of the waters, fertility and rejuvenation. They are guardians of the threshold, of the door and of treasures, both material and spiritual, and of the waters of life; they are also protectors of cattle. As snake kings and queens they have their images under trees. To drive a stake through a serpent's head is to 'fix' it and at the foundation of a Hindu temple this is to imitate the primordial act of Soma, or Indra, in subduing chaos and creating order. A serpent sometimes entwines the lingam of Siva. With the elephant, tortoise, bull and crocodile, the serpent can be a supporter and maintainer of the world. See also KUNDALINI. *Inca*: The serpent and bird are the beneficent aspect of Quetzalcoatl. *Iranian*: An aspect of Ahriman or Angra Mainu, the Serpent of Darkness, the Liar. The Persian snake Azi-dahak is 'the throttler', enemy of the sun god. *Islamic*: Closely associated with life, the serpent is el-hayyah and life el-hyat and El-Hay, one of the chief names of God which signifies the vivifying, that which confers life, the life principle rather than the merely living; that which both animates and maintains, which imparts life and is the life-principle itself. *Japanese*: Personification and attribute of Susanoo, god of thunder and storms. *Manichean*: A symbol of Christ. *Maori*: Earthly wisdom; a swamp worker; irrigation and growth. *Minoan*: Snake symbolism is prominent in Crete and there seems some evidence that there was a pre-deistic serpent cult. The Great Goddess, protector of the household, is portrayed with snakes held in her hands and, later, serpents were also associated with the deities who succeeded her. On ancient coins the goddess is depicted enthroned under a tree and caressing the head of a snake; serpent and tree symbolism are closely connected. The snake is a symbol of fertility and is notable in the cult of Eileithyia, goddess of childbirth. The serpent seen by Polyides was carrying a herb which could restore life to the dead. The snake could be an incarnation of the dead, an ancestor, or a ghost, and on a grave mound the image of a serpent indicated the burial place of a hero and was a symbol of resurrection and immortality. Later the serpent represented Aesculapius, the physician-god. *Oceanic*: A creator of the world. The presence of a snake is associated with pregnancy. In some parts the Cosmic Serpent lives underground and will ultimately destroy the world. *Roman*: Serpents were associated with saviour divinities and fertility and healing deities such as Salus. The serpent is an attribute of Minerva as wisdom. *Scandinavian*: The serpent of Midgard encircles the world with the endless coils of the abyss of the ocean. The serpent Nidhogg, the 'Dread Biter', who lives as the root of the Yggdrasil, the Cosmic Tree, continually gnawing at it, represents the malevolent forces of the universe. *Sumero-Semitic*: The Babylonian Tiamat, 'the footless', the 'serpent of darkness', also depicted as a dragon, is chaos, the undifferentiated, the undivided, guile and wickedness, destroyed by Marduk as solar and light. The Assyrio-Babylonian Ea, as Lakhmu and Lakhamu, of the sea, are male and female serpents giving birth to the masculine and feminine principles of heaven and earth. Ishtar, as a Great Goddess, is portrayed with the serpent. The Phrygian Sabazios has a serpent as his chief attribute and in his cult the officiating priestess dropped a gold snake, as 'god through the bosom', through her robes to the ground. The corn goddess. Nidaba has serpents springing from her shoulders, and the snake is associated with both the Earth Goddess, of whom the serpent entwining a pole is a pictograph, and her Dying God son, who frequently has a serpent rising from each shoulder. The serpent set up on a pole and worshipped as a god of healing was an often recurring symbol in Canaan and Philistia. *Toltec*: The sun god looking out of a snake's jaws symbolizes the sky.

Shadow The negative principle as opposed to the positive of the sun. In some primitive tribes the shadow can represent the soul of the person; this also obtains in witchcraft and spells: care must be taken as to where the shadow falls, or not to pass into another person's shadow.

Shamrock The Arabian 'shamrakh' symbolizing the Persian Triads; it represents all triads; the Mystic Three; the sunwheel. It was adopted by Christianity as depicting the Trinity and is an emblem of St Patrick and Ireland.

Shaving See TONSURE.

Sheaf Unity; binding together; harvest; Autumn.

Shears Fate; death. See also SCISSORS.

Sheep Blind and unintelligent following; helplessness. *Chinese*: The retired life. The eighth of the symbolic animals of the Twelve Terrestrial Branches. *Christian*: The flock of Christ; the faithful; the Apostles.

Shells The feminine, watery principle; the universal matrix; birth; regeneration; life; love; marriage; fertility (a vulva analogy). Mollusc shells are symbols of the moon and virginity. For conch shell see CONCH. *Buddhist*: See CONCH. *Chinese*: The feminine, yin, principle, with jade as the yang; a good life in the next world; good fortune. *Christian*: The

The **serpent**, symbol of healing and therefore emblem of Aesculapius, on a 2nd-century Roman medallion.

St James the Greater, 'of Compostella', bears on his staff of pilgrimage the scallop **shell**, badge of the pilgrim who used it as a scoop for water and a plate for food, signifying his poverty and renunciation of worldly things.

In this Roman Christian sarcophagus panel two brothers are united, as they were in their birth, in the single **shell** of the life-giving female.

waters of baptism (shells are sometimes used for sprinkling the water); resurrection; funerary. The scallop shell denotes pilgrimage, originally to the shrine of St James at Compostella, later to any shrine; emblem of SS James the Great and Roch. *Graeco-Roman*: In funerary rites the shell signifies resurrection; it also indicates a journey across the sea; also sexual passion, the two halves being held closely together. Emblem of Aphrodite/Venus, 'born of the sea', who rides on a scallop shell, and of Boreas, the North wind. *Hindu*: The trumpet shell (*Turbinella pyrum*) is a symbol of Vishnu as the watery principle.

Shelter All symbols of shelter are associated with the Great Mother, the archetypal feminine, in her protective aspect, e.g. the cave, house, temple, city, village, wall, fence, gate, door, shield, tree, ship, cradle, etc.

Shepherd Leader and protector of any flock; a saviour; the shepherd is also a psychopomp, thus he is sometimes associated with the god of the dead who then has the crook and staff of the shepherd as an attribute. The Good Shepherd occurs in Sumerian, Iranian, Hebrew, Orphic, Hermetic, Pythagorean, Tibetan and Christian traditions. *Buddhist*: (Tibetan) Chenrezig, 'the All-merciful Good Shepherd', is incarnated in the Dalai Lama. *Christian*: Christ, the Good Shepherd; symbolizes his humanity and compassion, also the redemption of those gone astray. *Egyptian*: Ra is 'the Shepherd of all men'. Egyptian kings were shepherds of their flocks. *Greek*: Orpheus Boukolos, the Herdsman, is the Good Shepherd, his attribute being a ram, or kid, on the shoulder. Hermes Kriophorus, the ram-bearer, is a Good Shepherd. Pan is a herdsman and Hermes, or Mercury, is a shepherd of souls. *Hindu*: Siva is a herdsman and Krishna is associated with herdsmen and the young women who tended the cows. *Iranian*: Yima, the Good Shepherd, possessing the solar eye, holds the secret of immortality. *Islamic*: 'The divine glory is among the shepherds.' *Sumero-Semitic*: Tammuz, a lunar god and a shepherd, is the protector of flocks. The Phoenician Amynos and Magos taught herding to the people.

Shield Preservation; the sheltering, protecting feminine power. The shield is often an aniconic representation of a divinity or hero. The figure-of-eight shield was an attribute of the Egyptian Neith and was also found in the Minoan civilization. In Greece the shield was an emblem of Ares and of Athene, together with the aegis, as protection, which was worn while the shield was carried. The shield with the spear symbolized initiation of the *epheboi* into adulthood. An attribute of chastity personified.

Ship Ships, or boats, carry the sun and moon across the seas, and the earth is a boat floating on the primordial waters. Ships with horses'

heads and tails are solar and take the place of the sun chariot in symbolism. Female figure-heads are lunar, and the ship is then the sheltering aspect of the Great Mother, the womb, the cradle, the feminine vessel of transformation and a saviour and protector on the sea of life. As bearers of the sun and moon ships represent fecundity and the fertility of the waters; they also signify adventure; exploration; setting out on the sea of life, but also crossing the waters of death; in this connection ships share the bridge symbolism, and that of the Pontifex Maximus, in crossing from this world to the next. The ship of life, setting out on the waters of creation, has also an axial symbolism in that the mast is the *axis mundi* and shares the significance of the Tree of Life. *Buddhist*: The ship, or vessel, of the Law enables man to cross the ocean of existence and transmigrations to reach the other shore. *Celtic*: Attribute of Manannan, Lord of the Sea, whose ship went at his will without sails or oars. *Christian*: The Church, the Ark, the ship of salvation; safety from temptation. The cross is the mast of the ship. Emblem of SS Julian, Nicholas of Myra, Vincent. *Egyptian*: 'They believe that the sun and moon do not go in chariots, but sail about the world perpetually in boats – thus denoting their nourishment and generation from seminal moisture' (Plutarch). *Hindu*: 'A boat ... to bear mankind across to felicity' (*Rig Veda*). *Japanese*: The boat of the thunder god Kami-nari connects heaven and earth. *Roman*: Attribute of Janus as Pontifex Maximus. *Scandinavian*: Associated with the Vanir as fertility gods. The magic ship is an attribute of Freyja.

Shoe Ambivalent as authority and liberty, but also as the lowly and humble. The shoe denotes liberty and freedom since the slave went barefoot; also control, as the control of the shoe gives control of the person, hence the bride's shoe gives her into the possession of the bridegroom. Putting off shoes on entering a holy place represents leaving earthly contact outside, to enter in submissiveness and reverence, and to divest oneself of vice. In Hebrew symbolism the shoe is a thing of little value. In Christianity the shoemaker's tools are an emblem of St Crispin.

Shroud Death; funerary. Associated with Theseus and related to sail symbolism.

Sickle Mortality; death as the Reaper; attribute of Cronos/Saturn as Time and accompanies the figure of the skeleton, or old man, as Death. Cronos also has a sickle and hood as depicting the setting, or waning power of the Autumn sun. A Sumerian symbol of royalty. Often carried by Priapus as fertility; agricultural fertility.

Sieve Rain clouds and fecundity; also the act of purifying by sifting out the dross, hence to know oneself; criticism; conscience; selection; choice.

In Christianity it represents sifting out the unfaithful from the faithful, the baptism by wind. It is an attribute of the figure of Prudence. It is also the powers of acceptance or rejection by conscience. In Hinduism the sky is a sieve through which the *soma* juice is forced and then falls as fertilizing rain; it is also the discretionary bounty of the gods. In Orphic Mysteries the sieve was a purifier and was used symbolically as a cradle. In Egyptian symbolism it suggested selection of powers used. The sieve is a vehicle for witches.

Silver The moon; virginity; the feminine aspect with gold as the masculine; the Queen with the King as gold. *Alchemic*: The virginal state of the *prima materia*; Luna; 'the affections purified'. *Chinese*: Purity; brightness; the lunar yin. *Christian*: Chastity; purity; eloquence.

Siren Temptation; feminine seduction; deception; distraction of man from his true goal, luring him to temporal attractions and spiritual death; the soul caught in the lures of the sensual. Bird-sirens in Egypt were souls separated from the body; in Greek mythology they represented evil souls greedy for blood.

Sistrum The motion of the elements: 'The sistrum shows that whatever exists ought to be shaken and never cease from movement' (Plutarch). It is also said to represent the movement of angels' wings. Emblem of Isis as Queen of Heaven.

Skeleton Death; mortality; the swift passage of time and life. With the scythe and hourglass the skeleton depicts the Reaper, cutting off life; it can also symbolize the moon, the shades, the gods of the dead and is especially associated with Cronos/Saturn and with the Mayan god of death and the underworld. In Alchemy it represents the stage of putrefaction in the Work and is portrayed by the colour black. See also SKULL.

Skin Matter. The skin of a sacrificial animal, such as the bull or horse, or the fleece of a ram or sheep, represents the fat of the animal and, by extension, all life-sustaining produce; also progeny and longevity. To wear the skin is to take on the power or *mana* of the animal and puts the wearer in touch with the animals and their instinctual knowledge, as in Shamanism. Worn in initiation ceremonies, the skins depict the grades of initiation; rebirth; assurance of immortality. The black and white skins of animals or birds, worn in such rites, symbolize the two natures of man, also manifestation and the non-manifest. To slough the skin, as serpents do, is to put off the 'old man' and put on the new, to recover youth, to attain a higher state, immortality.

Skull The transitoriness of life; the vanity of worldly things; death; *memento mori*; the moon;

Christ as Good **Shepherd** in a 3rd-century Roman sculpture: an adaptation of a traditional symbol.

Xipe, the Aztec god of Spring, wears the **skin** of a sacrificed victim as his own, symbolizing the promise of rebirth and renovation in the annual return of Spring.

The **ship** of death incised on a Viking memorial stone emphasizes death as the end of one journey and the transitional passage to a new goal and beginning.

the shades; the dying sun; gods of the dead; time. The skull is, on the other hand, a symbol of the vital life-force contained in the head. The skull with the crossbones indicates death, the thigh also symbolizing a vital force, that of the loins; the flag carrying the skull and cross bones is an emblem of pirates. *Alchemic*: With the raven and the grave, the skull is a symbol of the blackening and mortification of the first stage of the Lesser Work, 'earth to earth', and signifies dying to the world; but it is also that which survives and so is used as a reminder of life and transmutation. *Buddhist*: (Tantric) The skull filled with blood symbolizes the renunciation of life. It is an emblem of Yama, god of the dead, and of Tara in her dark aspect. *Christian*: The vanity of worldly things; contemplation of death, hence an emblem of hermits. The skull with the cross is eternal life after Christ's death on Golgotha, the 'place of the skull', where Adam's skull was said to be buried. Emblem of SS Francis of Assisi, Jerome, Mary Magdalene, Paul. *Graeco-Roman*: Attribute of Cronos/Saturn as Time. *Hindu*: The skull filled with blood depicts renunciation of life; it is an attribute of Kali Durga. The skull also appears with Yama, as god of the dead, and with Siva and Kali as destroyers. *Mayan*: With the skeleton, the skull is a symbol of the god of death and the underworld.

Sky Transcendence; infinity; height; the Heavens; the realm of bliss; sovereignty; order in the universe. Sky gods are usually creators, omnipotent and omniscient, and symbolize cosmic rhythms. They are guardians of the law. Under a matriarchy, sky deities are usually feminine; occasionally the sky divinity is asexual. In Hindu symbolism the sky is the sieve, through which the *soma* juice is forced, falling as rain, fertilizing the land and accompanied by thunder and lightning.

Slug *Egyptian*: The origin of life, the semen, moisture.

Smith The Divine Smith is a Creator who fashions the earth and is the son and mediator of the Supreme Deity. His attributes are thunder and lightning, the hammer, tongs and anvil and he controls the power of fire. In Shamanism and Oceania the smith has a divine origin and there is an association between shamans, princes, heroes and smiths. The craft of the smith has a sacred and magical quality and he possesses initiatory secrets. The exception is in pastoral communities where the smith is despised and regarded as malevolent and the 'black' smith; his trade is considered unclean. The smith is often a culture hero or ancestor, notably in Africa, and he guards the altar or maintains the traditions of the society. Among the Balts a smith forged the sun and threw it into the sky. The Celestial Smith creates and organizes the world and imparts knowledge of the mysteries.

Smoke A column of smoke ascending from the opening in the roof of a temple, from a house, or the central opening of a tepee or yurt, is an *axis mundi*, the path of escape from time and space into the eternal and unconfined; it is temporal and spatial extension, the combination of fire and air; it also represents prayer ascending, an invitation to the deity to be present; it can also signify the soul ascending, purified by fire. In Christianity smoke is taken as suggesting the shortness of life and the vanity of fame, anger or wrath.

Snail As appearing and disappearing, the snail is lunar; its shell, from its form, is a natural symbol of the labyrinth, the spiral and the underground cavern. The sea-snail (buccinum) represents the androgyne as the dual principles of fire and water combined. The snail also signifies slowness and voluptuousness. In Christianity it denotes sloth, also sin as feeding on mud and slime.

Snake See SERPENT.

Sneeze A spontaneous expression of the life-principle which resides in the head; a manifestation of the soul; a disturbance of the soul or losing some of the life-force from the head; the confirmation of a prophecy.

Snow Coldness; frigidity. The melting of snow represents the softening of hardness of heart.

Snowdrop *European*: Purity; humility; hope. In Christianity it is an emblem of the Virgin Mary and the Candlemas.

Soil The Mother Earth; the matrix.

Solstice At the Winter Solstice the Great Mother, Queen of Heaven, gives birth to the Son of Light. 'The Virgin has given birth, the light grows' (*Death and Resurrection of Osiris*). The full moon is seen at its nadir and Virgo rises in the East. The *Janua coeli*, the Winter Solstice in Capricorn, is the 'door of the gods' and symbolizes ascent and the growing power of the sun. The Summer Solstice in Cancer, the *Janua inferni*, is the 'door of men' and is descent and the waning power of the sun.

Soma Is both a plant and a god, the incarnation of the Vedic god and sacred to his rites; it is also sacred to Indra and can be depicted as a bull, bird, embryo or giant. It symbolizes divine power and understanding; inspiration; the Nourisher of All Things. The sieve through which the *soma* juice is forced from the plant is the sky, the juice is the fertilizing rain, and the noise of its falling and its yellow colour are represented by thunder and lightning. It can also be depicted as a copper-coloured man, with a red pennant behind a three-wheeled chariot drawn by a pied antelope or ten white horses.

Son The double; the living image; the *alter ego*.

Soul Usually depicted as a bird taking flight. In Christian art it is sometimes portrayed as a young child emerging naked from the mouth, to signify new birth. In Egypt it is a bird, often with a human head and hands. In Greece, and elsewhere, the soul left the body in the form of a serpent.

South Represented by the noonday sun; fire; warmth; youth; Summer; the masculine principle, except in Egypt where it is darkness and the feminine element and the region of hell and the god Amset; also in India where the South is the night region and feminine. In China it was symbolized by the phoenix and the colour red. In Hebrew symbolism it is depicted as the winged lion.

Sow See SWINE.

Sowing The creative act; putting seed into the Earth Mother.

Space Sacred space is always a Cosmic Centre, as in the symbolism of temples, churches, tepees, lodges, etc. and is a place of meeting between heaven and earth where communication between the two becomes possible.

Spade Phallic; the masculine principle; sometimes an attribute of Saturn. Emblem of the Christian St Phocas.

Spark The vital principle; the soul; fire.

Sparrow *Christian*: Lowliness; insignificance; also lewdness and lechery. *Greek*: An attribute of Aphrodite. Identified with Lesbia. *Japanese*: Loyalty.

Spear A world axis symbol; the masculine principle; phallic; life-giving force; fertility; warlike prowess; the wand of the magician. Attribute of warriors and hunters. *Celtic*: With the sling, the spear is the 'long arm' of Lamfhada or Lug. *Chinese*: The insignia of various minor gods. *Christian*: An emblem of Christ's passion and an attribute of St Michael and of St Longinus, the centurion at the crucifixion. *Graeco-Roman*: The spear and shield of the *epheboi* symbolized initiation into adulthood, adult prowess. Attribute of Athene/Minerva and Ares/Mars. *Scandinavian*: The spear, Gunginr, forged by dwarfs and used by Odin, automatically found its mark.

Sphere Perfection; the total of all possibilities in the limited world; the primordial form containing the possibilities of all other forms; the Cosmic Egg; the abolition of time and space; eternity; the vault of heaven; the world; the soul; the *animus mundi* (Plato). The cyclic movement of renewal; revolution; the heavens. In Islamic symbolism the sphere is the Spirit, the primordial Light.

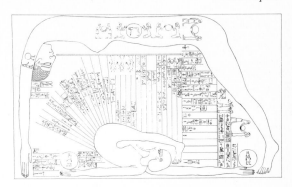

The Egyptian **sky** goddess Nut bends over the world of creation, ordering all things and creating them, while maintaining her position of transcendence.

The **soul** of St Stephen, first Christian martyr, is lifted by angels to heaven as it issues from his mouth. This sculpture of his death by stoning is on the façade of the Church of St Trophime at Arles.

Sphinx The mysterious; the enigmatic; power; Ra, god of the rising sun; wisdom; royal dignity; vigilance; strength. With the head of a man, or woman, body of a bull, feet of a lion and wings of an eagle, it represents the four elements and the combination of physical and intellectual power, the natural and the spiritual power incarnate in the Pharaoh. The androsphinx is human-headed and represents the union of intellectual and physical powers; the criosphinx has a ram's head and depicts silence; the hieracosphinx is falcon-headed and is solar; an all-lion-bodied sphinx, without wings, signifies power. The Theban sphinx is funerary, a protector of graves and denotes wanton destruction and is an enemy of mankind. The Greek sphinx is female-headed; the Minoan sphinx wears the 'lily crown'. The human-headed sphinx is also suggested as human spirit overcoming animal instincts.

Spider The Great Mother, in her terrible aspect as weaver of destiny, is sometimes depicted as a huge spider. All moon goddesses are spinners and weavers of Fate and the Cosmic Spider, the Great Spider, or the Great Weaver is also the Creator who spins the thread of life from its own substance and attaches all men to it itself by the thread of the umbilical cord and binds them to, or weaves them into, the web of the pattern of the world. The spider at the centre of its web also represents a world centre; it can also be either the sun surrounded by its rays, radiating in all directions, or the moon as the life-and-death cycle of the manifest world, or the year, weaving the web of time. *Amerindian*: The wind and thunder; protection from harm. *Christian*: The Devil ensnaring sinners; the miser bleeding the poor. A spider over a cup is an emblem of St Norbert. *Egyptian*: Attribute of Neith as a weaver of the world. *Greek*: Attribute of Athene as a weaver of the world and of Persephone, Harmonia and of the Fates, the Moirai, as spinners of destiny; form of Arachne. *Hindu and Buddhist*: The weaver of the web of illusion, *maya*, also the Creator as weaving the thread from its own substance. *Oceanic*: In some islands the Old Spider is the creator of the universe. *Roman*: Acumen; good fortune. *Scandinavian and Teutonic*: Holda and the Norns are spinners and weavers of destiny. *Sumero-Semitic*: Attribute of Ishtar and Atargatis as weavers of the world and of fate. See also SPINDLE; WEAVING; WEB.

Spindle/Spinning The spindle is an attribute of all Mother Goddesses, lunar goddesses and weavers of fate in their terrible aspect. All goddesses of destiny are spinners and weavers and are portrayed in their threefold lunar form and in groups of three as birth, life, death; past, present, future, etc. Of the three in the group two are usually good and helpful and one evil and cruel, the third being the breaker of the thread of life. The spinning whorls symbolize the revolutions of the universe, and spinning and weaving represent the feminine principle in its skills of weaving destiny and the veil of the world of illusion. Nereids have a golden spindle. Gaelic fairies spin and weave for favoured humans. See also SPIDER; WEAVING.

Spine The world axis; support; steadfastness. The Backbone of Osiris was set up after his dismemberment; this was the Egyptian *djed* symbol. Among the Ainu the spine is the seat of life and in the first created man the spine was made of supple willow wood. In Hinduism the spinal column is the passage of the awakened power of Kundalini which lies coiled and dormant as a serpent at the base of the spine. Symbols of the spine are any world axis, mountains, pillars, trees, horns, legs etc. Mount Meru is a world spine.

Spiral A highly complex symbol which has been used since paleolithic times and appears in pre-dynastic Egypt, Crete, Mycenae, Mesopotamia, India, China, Japan, pre-Columbian America, Europe, Scandinavia and Britain; it also appears in Oceania, but not in Hawaii. It variously represents both solar and lunar powers; the air; the waters; rolling thunder and lightning; it is also a vortex; the great creative force; emanation. As expanding and contracting it can depict the increase and decrease of the sun, or the waxing and waning of the moon and, by analogy, growth and expansion and death and contraction, winding and unwinding, birth and death. It can also signify continuity. It can portray the revolving heavens; the course of the sun; the cyclic seasons; the rotation of the earth. As the whirl of the air in thunder and storms and the movement of the waters, it denotes fertility and the dynamic aspect of things. As the whorl or vortex, Bastius equates it with the spinning top and the great generative forces. As the WHIRLWIND (q.v.) it is associated with the Chinese ascending dragon, and the spiral and whirlwind share the same symbolism especially as a manifestation of energy in nature. Spirals, or whorls, are associated with the spinning and weaving of the web of life and the veil of the Mother Goddess, controller of destiny and weaver of the veil of illusion. The spiral also shares the symbolism of the LABYRINTH (q.v.) and the danced, or walked, 'maze'. On the metaphysical plane it symbolizes the realms of existence, the various modalities of a being, and the wanderings of the soul in manifestation and its ultimate return to the Centre.

The double spiral ∽ ⌣ ⌢ ⌢ depicts the increase and decrease of solar or lunar powers as well as the alternating rhythms of evolution and involution, life and death, etc. It can also represent the two hemispheres; the two poles; day and night; all rhythms of nature; the yin and yang, shakta and shakti; the manifest and the unmanifest; also continuity between cycles. It typifies the androgyne and is connected with the caduceus symbolism of the two-way action, and with the *solve et coagula* of Alchemy. As thunder and lightning and rain-bearing clouds it is a fertility symbol. The spiral can also represent flame and fire, as in Celtic symbolism. In the Maori tradition it signifies the masculine principle and is phallic, though it is usually associated with the female vulva as the spiral of the seashell. In Crete and Mycenae the coiled tentacles of the octopus are connected with the spiral, thunder, rain and water. In China, Taoism and Buddhism sometimes portray the 'precious pearl', or 'dragon's ball' in spiral form; the double spiral takes on yin-yang symbolism.

The spiral is symbolized by all that is helical: snail shells, seashells, the ear, the tentacles of the octopus, animal horns, animals like the dog and cat that curl up, the coiled serpent, plants which grow in spiral form such as ivy, fir cones and the unfolding fronds of ferns. It is also associated with ears of gods and kings and with rain-bearing animals and reptiles and with the coiled and sleeping serpent Kundalini. Gods of the whirlwind or elements and movement such as Rudra and Pushan have their hair braided in spiral or shell form. The spiral is also connected with the navel as a centre of power and life.

Spire Aspiration heavenwards; also a phallic symbol. In Christianity it depicts God's finger pointing heavenwards.

Spittle The personality; the seal of good faith; an antidote against the evil eye; curative powers. To spit can also denote contempt.

Spleen Anger; ill-humour; melancholy. In Chinese symbolism it is one of the Eight Treasures, associated with the umbrella and the earth.

Spoon In Hindu ritual the sacrificial spoon is an attribute of Brahma and Agni.

Spring See WATERS; SEASONS.

Sprinkling A symbolic sequence of impregnation, conception, gestation, birth and baptism.

Square The earth, as opposed to the circle of the heavens; earthly existence; static perfection; immutability; integration; the quaternary under its static aspect; God manifest in creation; the totality of the Godhead, the three sides being its threefold aspect and the fourth totality. It also denotes honesty; straightforwardness; integrity; morality. It is the fixation of death as opposed to the dynamic circle of life and movement, while in architectural symbolism it represents the fixation of the buildings of agricultural and sedentary peoples in opposition to the dynamic and endlessly moving circular formation of nomadic tents and encampments. It represents limitation and therefore form. The square is the perfect type of

Oedipus's fateful encounter with the enigmatic **sphinx** – woman-headed, lion-bodied and eagle-winged – is recorded on an Attic dish.

To the American Indians, the **spider** on this disk of shell made it a protective amulet against danger from wind, rain and all those natural weather phenomena which might threaten the spider's own fragile web.

The apparently decorative **spirals** on this 16th-century Turkish bowl contract into their centres, echoing and strengthening the containing and protecting function of the object they embellish.

enclosure, e.g. gardens, cloisters, courtyards, etc., symbolizing permanence and stability. In sacred architecture it signifies transcendent knowledge; the archetype controlling all works. Four-square is a talismanic assurance of permanence and stability. Squaring the circle, or circling the square, is the transformation of spherical form, the sky, the heavens, into the rectangular form of the earth, and vice versa, in a sacred building, temple or church; it is the mystical union of the four elements; the attainment of unity in the return to primordial simplicity, the octagon, which often joins the square of the tower to the circle of the dome, being the halfway stage in squaring the circle. *Buddhist*: The square, or cube, at the base of a chörten, represents the earth level in the planes of existence. *Chinese*: The earth, the immovable, combined with the circle of heaven which revolves, the square and circle together (as in the old Chinese cash) are the union of yin and yang, earth and heaven, also symbolizing the perfectly balanced man. To 'act on the square' is the Confucian maxim: 'Do not unto others what you would not wish done to you.' The square with compass signifies order; propriety; the laws of virtue; paths of wisdom; the true guide. The square is the attribute of Niu-kua, whose brother holds the compass as depicting the female and male principles. *Graeco-Roman*: The square is a symbol of Aphrodite/Venus as the feminine reproductive power. *Hermetic*: A square standing on its base is stability, on its point movement, with the circle in the middle it is the *anima mundi*. *Hindu*: Foremost among the symbols of India, the square is the archetype and pattern of order in the universe, the standard of proportion and the perfect measure for man. It is the basis of the temple or any sacred centre and is balanced perfection of form; Purusha; essence; space; also the pairs of opposites; the four directions; the four castes, etc. The square and the circle are both ornaments of the dharma, the order of things in the cosmos and the world of man. The square at the base of a Stupa represents the earth plane. *Pythagorean*: The square symbolizes the soul.

Squirrel *Celtic*: With the bird, the squirrel is the emblem of the Irish goddess Medb. *Christian*: Avarice; greed. *Japanese*: Fertility; usually associated with the vine. *Scandinavian*: The 'Ratatosk' is a bringer of rain, water and snow. The squirrel in the Yggdrasil denotes spitefulness and mischief-making; it creates strife between the eagle and the serpent.

Staff Masculine power; authority; dignity; magic power; journeying; pilgrimage; it is also a solar and axial symbol. The staff, or crook, is an attribute of all Good Shepherds. *Buddhist*: Law and order; a symbol of Buddha's mace, i.e. his teaching. *Christian*: Christ as the Good Shepherd; pilgrimage. The staff with rings denotes episcopal power and authority; the staff born before high dignitaries depicts the dignity

of office; in the left hand the staff signifies cardinals, archbishops, bishops, abbots and abbesses. The staff of pilgrimage is an emblem of SS James the Great, John the Baptist, Jerome, Christopher, Philip the Apostle, Ursula. The budding staff is an emblem of SS Ethelreda and Joseph of Arimathaea. *Egyptian*: The staff and the flail are the chief attributes of Osiris as judge of the dead; the staff with the pen depicts the soul awakening and is an attribute of Theut or Logios. *Graeco-Roman*: The herald's staff, as the caduceus, is the chief attribute of Hermes/Mercury. *Hindu*: The three combined sticks of the staff of Vaishnava tradition symbolize the three realities or the three *gunas* constituting the phenomenal world, or the control of thought, word and deed of the saint or sage.

Stag Solar; renewal; creation; fire; the dawn; it is often associated with the Tree of Life. The stag at enmity with the chthonic serpent, like the warring eagle and serpent, represents the conflict of opposites, positive versus negative, light against darkness, etc. The stag trampling the serpent underfoot is the victory of spirit over matter, of good over evil. Following the hunted deer or stag often leads to symbolic situations, and the stag can also be a messenger of the gods or heavenly powers. Stags draw the vehicles of Father Time and Father Christmas. *Alchemic*: The stag with the unicorn depicts the dual nature of Mercurius, the philosophical mercury, the *nous*. *Celtic*: Solar; therapeutic; fertility; virility; the attribute of the warrior, the hunter god Cocidius and of Ossian and a form of the horned god Cernunnos. *Chinese*: Happiness; pecuniary gain. The white stag represents Shou-hsien, god of immortality. The dragon is called the 'celestial stag'. *Christian*: Piety; religious aspiration (Ps. 42); the soul thirsting after God; solitude; purity of life. As antagonistic to the serpent the stag portrays Christ, or the Christian, fighting against evil. Emblem of SS Adrian, Eustace, Eustachius, Ida, Felix, Julian the Hospitaller. The stag with a crucifix between its horns is an emblem of St Hubert. *Graeco-Roman*: An attribute of Artemis/Diana. *Hittite*: Important as the steed of the protective male deities. The God of Animals stands on a stag. *Japanese*: The dragon is the 'celestial stag'. *Mithraic*: The stag and bull together represent the moment of death. *Scandinavian*: The four stags of the Yggdrasil are the four winds. *Shamanistic*: The stag skin is frequently used in shamanistic rites (see SKIN). See also DEER. *Sumero-Semitic*: The fertility god was sometimes dressed as a stag for sacrifice. The stag's head is an emblem of Reshep.

Stairs ASCENSION (q.v.); transcendence; the change to a new ontological level. Spiral stairs depict the sun's movement; winding stairs symbolize the mysterious. The stairs of Solomon's Temple led to the Middle Chamber of the unknown future. Osiris is 'God of the

Stairs' leading to Heaven. See also LADDER; STEP.

Stake Christian symbol of torture or death by fire; emblem of SS Agnes and Dorothea.

Stallion In Iranian symbolism the stallion represents the solar power, fire, and is an attribute of the warrior class. It is an Aryan symbol of supremacy, solar, aggressive masculinity. After the Vedic period it was replaced by the lunar, erotic mare holding the fire of destruction at the end of the world.

Star The presence of a divinity; supremacy; the eternal; the undying; the highest attainment; an angelic messenger of a god; hope (as shining in darkness); the eyes of the night. Stars are attributes of all Queens of Heaven, who are often star-crowned. The star is pre-eminently the symbol of Ishtar, or Venus, as morning and evening star. The pole star marks the pivotal point in the sky and is thus the Gate of Heaven at night. It is a symbol of constancy and is pointed out as such in the Hindu marriage rites. In Egypt, the Pharaoh was, after death, identified with the Pole Star. The four-rayed star, later the Maltese Cross, is an aniconic form of Shamash as sun god and god of love and justice. The five-pointed star, upwards, is aspiration; light; the spiritual; education. Downwards, it is evil; witchcraft; black magic. The six-pointed star depicts the Creation and is also the Seal of Solomon. It is the combination of the masculine and feminine triangles and of fire and water (see TRIANGLE). The eight-pointed star in a circle is an aniconic form of Gula, consort of Shamash. *Aztec*: The morning star is the ascending, spiritual, masculine power of the sun and the evening star the descending, terrestrial, feminine power of the moon. *Chinese*: A star, or stars, with the sun and the moon depicts the spiritual wisdom of rulers. *Christian*: Divine guidance and favour; the birth of Christ; the Virgin Mary, as Queen of Heaven, wears a crown of stars, also as Stella Maris. The twelve stars are the twelve Tribes of Israel and the Apostles. Emblem of SS Athanasia, Bruno, Dominic, Humbert, Nicholas, Swidbert. *Egyptian*: Isis, as Queen of Heaven, wears a crown of stars. *Graeco-Roman*: According to Hesiod, the stars are the drops of blood of Ouranos. Venus is both the morning and evening star. Planetary gods are often depicted with a star on the forehead or overhead. *Islamic*: Divinity; supremacy. The star is depicted with the crescent. *Maori*: Guidance to the triumph of good over evil. *Mithraic*: The all-seeing eyes of Mithra. *Oceanic*: Stars are the children of the Mother Sun and Father Moon. *Sumero-Semitic*: Ishtar is the morning and evening star; she and Astarte are frequently depicted as star-crowned Queens of Heaven.

Starfish *European*: Stella Maris. Divine love; the inextinguishable power of love. In

The **stags** in a mosaic from the Lateran Basilica of St John drink from the renewing waters of life flowing from the base of the redeeming cross.

A 14th-century alchemical drawing of Pan-as-Mercury includes the **star** of achievement and completion in the background.

Christianity it is a symbol of the Holy Spirit; religion; charity; and of the Virgin Mary as Stella Maris.

Steam In the Amerindian ritual of the vapour bath, in the Sweat Lodge, it represents the whiteness, and sacred and life-giving power of the Spirit.

Stem The stem of a plant, like the trunk of a tree, symbolizes the manifest world, the middle world of the three, with the roots as the underworld and the branches, or flowers, as the heavens.

Steps ASCENSION (q.v.); grades in the hierarchical world and communication between these grades or levels; communion between heaven and earth; transcending profane space and entering sacred space. Steps up to an altar or throne symbolize the priest, king, or ruler, having the authority or mandate of heaven to ascend the steps leading to heaven. *Amerindian*: The months are the 'steps of the year'. *Buddhist*: The seven steps of Buddha represent the mounting of the seven cosmic stages, the seven planetary heavens, which is to transcend time and space, also to attain the centre in the seventh heaven, the highest state. *Egyptian*: Osiris is 'god of the stairs' leading to heaven; the nine steps up to his throne are the days of the ancient Egyptian week and the fourteen steps represent the days of the full growth of the moon. *Hindu*: The three steps, or strides, of Vishnu denote the three manifestations of light: the sun, lightning, fire; also the rising, zenith and setting sun; the earth, air and heaven; the three steps which gained control of the universe. *Mithraic*: The seven steps of different metals, corresponding to the major planets, are the seven grades of ascension of the initiate. *Parsee*: The three steps at an altar denote the three degrees of initiation. *Sumerian*: The steps up the Ziggurat, or Sacred Mountain, represent the seven heavens and were of different symbolic colours.

Stole *Christian*: The yoke of Christ; priestly power and dignity.

Stomach *Chinese*: One of the Eight Treasures, symbolized by the Sacred Jar.

Stone Stability; durability; reliability; immortality; imperishability; the eternal; cohesion; the indestructibility of the Supreme Reality. Static life. A stone, rock, mountain, tree, or grove, all of which are associated symbolically, can represent the cosmos in its entirety. Stones often accompany trees in sacred places, or stand alone to mark some sacred place or event; they are linked with the tree also in the sacred altar with the stone as the durable and enclosing and the tree as the changing and expanding. In primitive symbolism stones can give birth to people and have a life-giving potency, or people

can be turned into sacred stones. This is suggested as a lunar cult, symbolizing the moon as allied to both fertility and coldness, or with the frozen earth of Winter giving birth to Spring. Special stones have their own symbolism, such as jade, jewels and pearls; black stones, as the Ka'aba, the black stone of Cybele, black jade and pearls, are sometimes symbolic of the Cosmic Egg, or are an omphalos.

Tall, upright stones, columns and pillars are an *axis mundi*, which is also symbolized by the tree, or mountain, or tree on a mountain, or a column with a tree on it, and represent the supreme support of all things in the universe; they are also an omphalos, a fixed point or centre where man can regain Paradise, or find enlightenment. Conical stones and cairns share the symbolism of the upright stones and all can be phallic. Cubic stones signify stability and static perfection and are, as such, the foundation stones of sacred buildings. The stone of foundation is the rock on which the universe is founded, the keystone of the earth and the source of the waters of life, the rock which prevails against Hades and the powers of the underworld.

Spherical stones depict the moon, hence the feminine principle and all lunar goddesses. Uncarved stone is the *prima materia*, the feminine, and is associated with the male symbols of the chisel and all cutting instruments which shape, and give form to, the *prima materia*. The carved, or polished, stone denotes the character which has been worked upon and perfected.

A broken stone or column signifies death, disintegration or dismemberment. Heavy stones or rocks covering a well, spring or cave of treasure, hindering access to the waters of life which spring from the rock, symbolize the difficulties and necessary conditions which must be overcome or understood and fulfilled before the waters of life or the esoteric treasures of hidden knowledge can be found; sometimes the rock is miraculously struck to let the waters gush forth, or the cavern open. The stone AXE (q.v.) is an aniconic representation of divinity, or its supernatural power. The *lapis exilis* is the stone whose power restores the life of the phoenix and is related to, and sometimes called, the GRAIL (q.v.) and can confer perpetual youth on those who serve it. Thunder stones represent the power of thunder, lightning and storm, the power of that which cleaves and breaks.

Baetylic stones denote a place of indwelling divinity; an omphalos; the dwelling place of the sun spirit; dwellings of the spirits of the dead; the meeting place of heaven and earth; the sacred; holy ground. Baetyls are also prophetic stones, 'stones that speak', from which comes the voice of the divinity or oracle, such as the omphalos at Delphi. These stones have usually fallen from heaven and can be either the dwelling place of the divinity or its aniconic representation. In all nomadic and hunting tribes, stones are the 'bones of Mother Earth'.

African: (West). Blue stones are the power of the sky god. *Alchemic*: The hidden stone is the *prima materia*. The Philosophers' Stone, the Rebis, is the supreme quest, the 'double being' of the Hermetic Androgyne; the reconciliation of all opposites; the attainment of unity; regaining the Centre; perfection; absolute reality; the *petra genetrix*; the mover at will; spiritual, mental and moral wholeness in man; the liberated, unified Self; the *spiritus mundi* made visible. *Amerindian*: Stones are the bones of Mother Earth. *Arabic*: (Pre-Islamic). Stones were worshipped as aniconic images of Manat; stones and trees were extensively venerated. *Buddhist*: Black pebbles are evil deeds and white pebbles good deeds and are weighed in the judgment balance. *Celtic*: Rocking stones are prophetic. *Chinese*: Reliability; hardness. Stone chimes are a fertility symbol and are apotropaic. *Christian*: Sure foundations; indestructibility; St Peter as the foundation of the Church. Stones are also an emblem of SS Alphege and Stephen. *Egyptian*: Truth, 'the hard stones of Truth'; green stones signify youth and immortality. *Graeco-Roman*: 'The bones of Mother Earth' (Ovid). The black stone is a symbol of Cybele who, as goddess of the mountain, is also represented by a conical stone. The square stone is an attribute of Aphrodite/Venus. Stones are often associated with Cronos/Saturn and with the cult of Apollo, notably the omphalos at Delphi and the cubic altar at Delos. Hermes is a god of stones and can be represented by a cairn or heap of stones. *Hebrew*: The baetylic stone of Jacob was a meeting place of heaven and earth and of communication between them. The stones from the river Jobel were indestructible and formed the foundation of Jerusalem. The foundation stone of the Temple was the centre of the earth and supported the world. *Hindu*: Stone, as stability, is the basis of the temple and the altar. Conical stones, such as the *linga*, are an aniconic form of Siva as creator. *Islamic*: The black stone, the Ka'aba, is cubic and is an omphalos, a point of communion between God and man. *Japanese*: Stones and rocks are sacred objects in Shintoism. *Oceanic*: Rocks gave birth to all things in the world. *Sumero-Semitic*: Conical stones and pillars are the chief symbols and aniconic representations of Ashtoreth/Astarte and other Semitic deities.

Stork With the eagle and ibis, the stork is a destroyer of reptiles, in their baleful aspect, and is thus a solar bird; but, as an aquatic creature and a fisher, it is associated with the waters of creation. Children 'brought by the stork' are embryonic in the womb of Mother Earth and the creative waters and are found by the fishing storks. The stork also symbolizes the coming of Spring and new life and is a bird of good omen. *Chinese*: Longevity; happy and contented old age; filial piety, the recluse, dignified, aloof and secluded. *Christian*: Chastity; purity; piety; prudence; vigilance. As the harbinger of Spring it was used as a symbol of new life in the coming

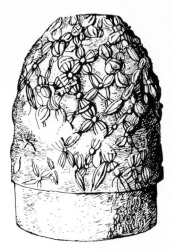

The Delphic 'navel of the world', the **stone** regarded as the durable, reliable and indestructible centre from which all the cosmos radiates and to which it refers back for stability and movement.

Among standing **stones**, the cromlech is usually taken as symbolizing the womb, in contrast to the phallic significance of the MENHIR. This one is in Malabar, South India.

of Christ and his Annunciation. *Egyptian*: Filial piety; the stork was thought to nourish its parents in old age. *Greek*: In the mysteries the stork goddess represented archetypal woman, the bringer of life, the nourisher. An attribute of Hera. *Roman*: Piety; filial devotion; an attribute of Juno.

Storm The creative power, the bringer of fertilizing rain. Thunder is the voice of the storm god and lightning brings fecundation and illumination.

Straightness The straight, or the 'bound', is the masculine, paternal, creative power as opposed to the circular, 'infinite', feminine maternal power.

Stranger The coming power of the future; the bringer of change; divine, or magic, power in disguise.

Straw Emptiness; unfruitfulness; death; weakness; worthlessness; the transitory.

Strawberry *Christian* The righteous man; the fruit of good works; fruits of the spirit. Accompanied by violets it signifies the humility of true righteousness.

Stream The flow of divine power, either of rays streaming from the sun or water from springs, fountains, vases, etc. Streams issuing from a vase, or from the body of a deity, depict the outpouring of the waters of divine munificence, life and fertility, like the four waters, or streams, of Paradise flowing from the Tree of Life. The stream is a symbol of self-nature in Buddhism. See also RIVER.

Stupa, Chörten The Doctrine; enlightenment; Nirvana. The square or cube at the base represents the earth, the various levels are the planes of existence, the circle of the dome is the heavens. It is also a symbol of the five *dhyani* Buddhas as aspects of the Absolute and the fivefold aspect of man (see NUMBERS, *Five*). The point, or spike, at the top of the dome is the world axis and a world centre, and the series of rings on it denote world soaring above world. The Islamic Qubbah has the same form and symbolism of the planes of existence.

Stylus See PEN.

Suckling New birth; adoption; charity. The Mother Goddess is often portrayed as suckling infants, or as having multiple breasts, as the great nourisher. In Christian art figures of Charity are depicted as nursing an infant, or sometimes with two children. Sucking can be both healthful and harmful as either the maternal nourishment, or the sucking out of the life-force.

Sulphur In Alchemy sulphur is the Spirit, 'non-burning fire'; the masculine, fiery principle; dryness; hardness; unification; rigid and theoretical knowledge. Sulphur 'fixes' the volatile QUICKSILVER (q.v.), but requires the interplay between the two generative forces as it remains limited and unfruitful until dissolved by quicksilver into living understanding, thus becoming freed from its limitations. Sulphur and quicksilver are the two basic generative forces of the universe, which, acting on each other, become volatile, the Spirit. In Christianity sulphur is associated with hell and the Devil. See also SALT.

Sun The supreme cosmic power; the all-seeing divinity and its power; theophany; motionless being; the heart of the cosmos; the centre of being and of intuitive knowledge; 'the intelligence of the world' (Macrobius); enlightenment; the eye of the world and the eye of the day; the unconquered; glory; splendour; justice; royalty. 'It is the visible image of Divine Goodness ... the Transcendent Archetype of Light' (Dionysius). 'There is no visible thing, in all the world, more worthy to serve as a symbol of God than the sun, which illuminates with visible life, first itself, then all the celestial and mundane bodies' (Dante). There is a traditional distinction between the visible and invisible, sensible and intelligible, outward and inward, suns.

In most traditions the Sun is the universal Father, with the Moon as Mother, with the notable exceptions of Amerindian, Maori, Teutonic, Oceanic and Japanese symbolism, where the Moon is the masculine and the Sun the feminine power. The sun and rain are the primary fertilizing forces, hence the bridegroom as sun and bride as moon goddess, the Sky Father and Earth Mother. As constantly rising and setting, and because its rays can be vivifying or destructive, the Sun symbolizes both life and death and the renewal of life through death. The Spring sun is the *sol invictus*. A solar disk with streams of water flowing from it represents the combination of sun and water, heat and moisture, as necessary to all life. The rayed sun and rayed heart share the same symbolism of the Centre as being the seat of illumination and intelligence. The sun in conflict with the serpent depicts light warring against darkness and heavenly against chthonic powers. The sun standing still is timelessness; the Eternal Now; the *nunc stans*; illumination; escape from time and the round of existence. The sun and moon together depict the male and female powers in conjunction.

Sun symbols are the revolving wheel, disk, circle with central point, radiate circle, swastika, rays whether straight or undulating representing both the light and heat of the sun, luminous chariots with sun gods driving white or golden horses, or crossing the world in solar ships, a radiant face, an eye, a bronze man, a spider at the centre of its web with the rays extending in all directions, solar birds and animals such as the eagle, hawk, swan, phoenix, cock, lion, ram, white or golden horse, winged or plumed serpent, the dragon of China. The white sun is associated with solar animals, but *sol niger* is connected with the serpent and chthonic powers. In hunting civilizations the sun is the Great Hunter. The sun is sometimes depicted as the fruit on the Tree of Life. When the solar deity is male the sun is represented by the right eye, when female by the left eye. 'Children of the Sun' are royal, incarnate gods. See also DISK. *African*: In some tribes the sun is feminine power, the Mother; among Bushmen it is the supreme deity. *Alchemic*: *Sol* is the intellect. *Sol* and *luna* are gold and silver, king and queen, soul and body, etc. *Sol niger* is the *prima materia*. The planetary sign of the sun, the circle with central dot, is a symbol of completion of the Great Work. *Amerindian*: The universal spirit, the heart of the sky. In some tribes the sun becomes the feminine principle, the Mother, in others the Sun and Moon are depicted as man and wife or brother and sister. The SUN DANCE (q.v.) is one of the most significant rituals. *Astrology*: Life; vitality; the incarnate character of the individual; the heart and its desires. *Aztec*: Pure spirit; the air; Quetzalcoatl; the eagle typifies the rising sun and heavenly aspect, and either the tiger or the falling eagle is the setting and earthly aspect. The plumed serpent is solar. Aztecs and Incas were 'children of the Sun'. *Buddhist*: The light of Buddha, the Sun Buddha. *Celtic*: The feminine power. *Chinese*: The yang, 'the Great Male Principle', the heavens; the eye of the day; the active force fertilizing the earth; power. The sun is one of the twelve symbols of power. Ten suns in a tree denote the end of a cycle. The cock and the three-legged 'red' raven live in the sun, the three legs representing the rising, noon and setting sun. *Christian*: God the Father, ruler and sustainer of the universe, radiating light and love; Christ 'the sun of righteousness'; the Logos; the divine essence in man. The sun and moon depicted with the crucifixion represent the two natures of Christ and the powers of Nature paying homage to the Lord of the Universe. The sun is the abode of the Archangel Michael, with the moon as that of Gabriel. St Thomas Aquinas is portrayed with the sun on his breast. *Egyptian*: The rising sun is Horus, with Ra as the zenith and Osiris as the setting sun. The right eye is the sun and the left the moon. Horus in conflict with Set as the serpent Apop is solar power warring with darkness. The winged sun disk is the solar power of Ra and Aton and renewal of life. *Greek*: The sun is the eye of Zeus. Apollo, as the sun, slays the python of darkness. In Orphism the sun is the 'Father of All', 'the great generator and nourisher of all things, ruler of the world'. The sun is the heart, with the moon as the liver of the universe. *Hebrew*: Divine will and guidance. *Hermetic*: 'The sun ... is the image of the Maker.' *Hindu*: 'The divine vivifier'; the eye of Varuna; Indra is solar and overcomes the dragon of chaos and darkness, Vritra. Siva is

A 9th-century BC cuneifom tablet records the re-foundation of the temple of the **sun** by the Babylonian ruler Nabu-apal-iddina, who sits in reverence beside the rayed disk symbolic of the sun's presence.

To the Aztecs, the rising **sun** was symbolized by the eagle. This example is from a Teotihuatecan fresco.

A rare representation, probably dating from the age of Constantine, of Christ as Helios the **sun**-god. The same attributes are seen as those given to Mithras and Sol – the prancing horses, billowing cloak, rays from the head.

also the sun whose rays are the creative Shakti bringing life to the world. The sun is the 'world door', the entrance to knowledge, immortality. The triple tree with three suns depicts the Trimurti. A tree with twelve suns denotes the Adityas, signs of the Zodiac and the months of the year. These twelve forms of the sun will appear simultaneously as one at the end of a cycle of manifestation. *Inca*: The sun was depicted as human in form, with the face as a radiant disk of gold and was 'the ancestor'. *Iranian*: The eye of Ormuzd. 'Whoso venerates the Sun that is immortal, brilliant, swift-horsed ... venerates Ormuzd, he venerates the Archangels, he venerates his own soul' (*The Nyaishes*). The winged sun disk also depicts Ormuzd or Ahura Mazda. *Islamic*: The eye of Allah, all-seeing, all-knowing. 'The sun is the reflection of the Sun beyond the veil' (Rumi). The heart of the universe and 'the sign of God in the heavens and earth'. *Japanese*: The sun is a lady and a snake divinity Amaterasu, 'she who possesses the great sun', born of Izanagi's left eye, and from whom the Mikado claims descent as the rising sun. The emblem of Japan. *Maori*: The sun and moon are the eyes of heaven. *Mithraic*: Mithra is a sun god. Sol, his quadriga and Cautes are usually depicted on the right with Luna and Cautopates on the left. *Oceanic*: The sun is most usually the Mother of All, with the moon as the Father and the stars as the children; in some parts the sun and moon are children of the first man and woman. The sun is 'the great eyeball'. *Platonic*: 'The author of visibility ... of generation and nourishment and growth' (Republic). The heat and light of the sun are creativity and wisdom. *Pythagorean*: The ten suns are cyclic perfection. *Scandinavian*: The eye of Odin/Woden, the all-seeing. The sun is depicted as the sun-snake. *Slav*: The sun god is depicted as a beautiful young man, or, sometimes, as born anew and dying each day; in Slav symbolism the sun and moon can change sexes. *Sumero-Semitic*: The sun gods Shamash and Asshur are represented by the winged sun disk. *Teutonic*: The sun is feminine and the Mother, with the moon as the Father. *Taoist*: The sun is yang and the great celestial power; the sun and moon together symbolize supernatural being, all radiance.

Sun Dance *Amerindian*: The regeneration of the sun and universal creation; union with the solar power. The ebb and flow of the dance denote the rising and setting of the sun and the phases of breathing and the heart-beat. A sun dance lodge is an *imago mundi*, the twenty-eight posts (four and seven are sacred numbers) depict the lunar month and each represents some particular thing in creation; the circle of the posts signifies the entire creation and the central tree is the sacred Centre.

Sunflower Worship; infatuation as slavishly following the sun; as constantly changing position it is unreliability and false riches. It is a Greek symbol of Clytie who turns into a sunflower when spurned by the sun god Apollo. It is an emblem of Daphne. In Mithraism it is an attribute of the sun god Mithra. In Chinese symbolism it represents longevity and has magical powers.

Swallow Hope; the coming of Spring; good fortune. *Chinese*: Daring; danger; fidelity; coming success; advantageous change. *Christian*: The Incarnation; resurrection; as returning with Spring it symbolizes new life. *Egyptian*: Sacred to Isis as the Great Mother. They are 'the imperishable northern stars' (*The Pyramid Text*) flying above the Tree of Life. *Graeco-Roman*: Sacred to Aphrodite/Venus. *Heraldic*: Depicted in Heraldry as the Martlet, Merlette or Merlot and symbolizes younger sons (as having no lands). *Japanese*: Unfaithfulness; but also domesticity and maternal care; associated with waves and willow trees in art. *Minoan*: Appears in Cretan art as associated with the Great Mother. *Sumero-Semitic*: Emblem and form of the goddess Nina as a Great Mother.

Swan Combining the two elements of air and water, the swan is the bird of life; the dawn of day; solar. It also signifies solitude and retreat and is the bird of the poet; its dying song is the poet's song; its whiteness is sincerity. The swan and goose are often symbolically interchangeable. *Celtic*: Swan deities are solar and beneficent; they possess the therapeutic powers of the sun and waters and are associated with the chariot of the sun and depict benevolence, love, purity; their music is magic. Swans with gold or silver chains round their necks are the supernatural appearance of divinities. *Chinese*: A yang, solar bird. *Christian*: The white swan is purity and grace and represents the Virgin Mary. Singing with its dying breath, it denotes martyrs and Christian resignation. Emblem of SS Cuthbert, Hugh, Ludger. *Graeco-Roman*: A form of Zeus/Jupiter as Leda's swan; amorousness; sacred to Aphrodite/Venus, also to Apollo as solar. A happy death. *Hindu*: Two swans together are 'that pair of swans who are Ham and Sa, dwelling in the mind of the Great, who subsist entirely on the honey of the blooming lotus of knowledge' (*Saundarya Lahari*). The Hamsa bird is carved on temples and symbolizes the perfect union towards which the celestial beings fly. Swans also represent inbreathing and outbreathing, breath and spirit. Brahma rides a swan, goose, or peacock, and the swan or goose is his emblem; it is the divine bird which laid on the waters the Cosmic Egg, the golden egg from which Brahma sprang. The Supreme Swan, the *paramahamsa*, is the universal ground, the Self.

Swastika One of the oldest and most complex of symbols, prehistoric and universal except for parts of Africa and Sumeria; found extensively in all Asia and in the pre-Aryan Indus Valley civilization, used widely by Jaina, Buddhists

and devotees of Vishnu; general in pre-
Columbian America, both North and South,
frequently used among the Hittites and found
on pottery in Cyprus and Troy, appeared
comparatively early in central, West and North
Europe, in Iceland, Lapland, Finland and pre-
Christian Ireland and Scotland and with the
Brigantes in England when it was associated
with the pagan Bridgit or Bride. The swastika
did not occur in Egypt until a few centuries BC
and not at all in Central Africa and Lower
Mesopotamia, but it has been suggested that the
four-faced Horus and other four-faced gods
were a swastika symbol, while Count Goblet
D'Alviella suggested that the swastika and the
crux ansata and the winged disk were basically
the same symbol and therefore mutually
exclusive and divided the ancient world into
two zones of symbolism, so that the swastika
predominated and in 'the whole Aryan world
except Persia, the *crux ansata* and the winged
circle never succeeded in establishing themselves in good earnest'. As an ancient symbol of
the Aryans it has been thought to be an aniconic
representation of their supreme divinity, the
Sun, and Dyaus, the sky god, and it is most
generally accepted as a sun symbol since it
frequently accompanies the solar disk. Its exact
symbolism, however, is unknown and it has
variously been suggested as the revolving sun;
the radiate wheel of the noon sun; the sun
chariot; the Pole and the revolution of the stars
round it; the four cardinal points; the four
quarters of the moon; the four winds and the
four seasons; a whirlwind movement; the
motion of revolving round the world; the
Centre; creative force in motion; the generation
of the cycles; the revolution of the wheel of life;
the cross as the four quarters over which the
solar power revolves converting it into a circle,
i.e. circling the square and squaring the circle;
the cross as the vertical and horizontal lines
depicting the spirit and matter and the four
grades of existence.

It is also suggested that the swastika is a
conventionalized human form of two arms and
legs, or the union of the male and female
principles; the dynamic and static; mobility
and immobility; harmony and balance; the two
complementary phases of movement, centrifugal and centripetal, inbreathing and outbreathing, going out from and returning to
the centre, beginning and end. Again, it is
suggested as a version of the labyrinth; of water
in movement; or a possible representation of
forked lightning, being a combination of the
two Z forms of lightning; or the two fire-sticks
and the whirling movement of the fire-wheel; or
the two bent sticks carried by the Vedic Queen
Arani to produce fire; or the Qabalistic Aleph,
symbolic of the primaeval motion of the Great
Breath whirling chaos into the creative centre;
or the Scandinavian sun-snake in double form.
Others think that the swastika was formed by
the crossing of the meander, or as a variation of
the Tau Cross. It has also been suggested as a

The Buddha on this 9th-century Sanskrit manuscript
bears on his breast the **swastika**, the seal of his heart
and symbol of the round of existence.

The **swastika** formed by four women and their hair
on this piece of Sumerian pottery of the 5th
millennium BC suggests the feminine generative
force.

symbol of submission and resignation as arms crossed on the breast in an attitude of submission.

The swastika appears with both gods and goddesses. Its being depicted with the feminine principle has led to suggestions that it represents the four lunar phases, but it is associated mainly with solar and generative symbols such as the lion, ram, deer, horse, birds, the lotus. It is found on altars, figures, vestments, urns, vases, utensils, pottery, weapons, shields, dresses, coins and spindle-whorls, where it is thought to depict the whirling movement of the spindle-drill. In all circumstances it is a symbol of good luck; good augury; good wishes; blessings; longevity; fecundity; health and life.

There are two forms of the swastika 卍卐 taken to symbolize the male and female, solar and lunar aspects; movement clockwise and anti-clockwise; also, possibly, the two hemispheres; the celestial and chthonic powers; the rising, vernal sun and the descending, autumnal sun. Evidence that the reversed swastika is feminine is given on the images of Artemis and Astarte, where it is depicted on the vulva triangle. In China the two swastikas are used as depicting the yin and yang forces. Interlaced swastikas, sometimes called 'Solomon's knots', symbolize divine inscrutability and infinity. The swastika which terminates the key symbol takes on key symbolism also. *Amerindian*: Good fortune; fertility; rain. *Buddhist*: The seal of Buddha's heart; the esoteric doctrine of Buddha; the Round of Existence. One of the Eight Auspicious Signs and appears on the footprint of Buddha. *Celtic*: Good luck; appears with thunder gods. *Chinese*: 'The accumulation of lucky signs of Ten Thousand Efficacies.' It is an early form of the character *fang* which denoted the four quarters of space and of the earth. Used as a border it depicts the *Wan tzu*, the Ten Thousand Things or Continuities, i.e. infinite duration without beginning or end, infinite renewal of life, perpetuity. It also symbolizes perfection; movement according to the law; longevity; blessing; good augury; good wishes. It is also the Thunder Scroll. The blue swastika denotes infinite celestial virtues; the red, infinite sacred virtues of the heart of Buddha; yellow, infinite prosperity; green, infinite virtues in agriculture. The clockwise swastika is yang, the anti-clockwise yin. *Christian*: The swastika appeared frequently as a symbol in the catacombs signifying Christ as the power of the world. In mediaeval times it was the gammadion, used to symbolize Christ as the cornerstone, also the four Evangelists, with Christ as the centre. *Gnostic*: A representation of Sitala, the Seventh Incarnation; also resignation. *Greek*: An attribute of Zeus as sky god and of Helios as solar; also appears with Hera, Ceres and Artemis. *Hindu*: The origin of the word Swastika – 'It is well.' Life; movement; happiness; good fortune. A symbol of the Vedic fire god and divine carpenter, Agni; the fire-sticks, the 'mystic double Arani'; also Dyaus,

the ancient Aryan sky god, later Indra; also associated with Brahma, Surya, Vishnu, Siva and with Ganesha as pathfinder and god of the crossroads. The swastika is sometimes used as a seal on jars of holy water from the Ganges. *Hittite*: Used extensively. *Iranian*: The swastika is not found in Zoroastrianism. *Islamic*: Among Asian Moslems the swastika denotes the four cardinal directions and control of the four seasons by angels, one at each point: West, the Recorder; South, Death; North, Life; East, The Announcer. *Jain*: The divine force, Creator of Heaven and Earth. The four arms represent the four grades of existence: protoplasmic life, plant and animal, human, celestial. With three circles above it denotes the Three Jewels of right belief, right knowledge, right conduct; with the crescent moon above it depicts the state of liberation, i.e. the waxing moon always growing fuller; with a single circle over the crescent it is the state of full consciousness, omniscience. *Japanese*: The heart of Buddha; good fortune; good wishes. *Manichean*: The swastika is the cross of the Manicheans and takes on all the symbolism of the cross. *Roman*: A symbol of Jupiter Tonans and Pluvius. *Scandinavian and Teutonic*: The battle axe or hammer of Thor as god of the air, thunder and lightning; good luck. In Lithuania it is talismanic and good luck and its Sanskrit name is used. The swastika is also found in Iceland. *Semitic*: It accompanies other solar symbols, but is also depicted as feminine generative power on the triangle of Astarte.

Swine The pig is a fertility symbol, hence prosperity, but also gluttony, greed, lust, anger and unbridled passion and the unclean. The sow is associated with the Great Mother and has a lunar, sky and fertility symbolism. *Amerindian*: A lunar and thunder animal and a rain-bearer. *Buddhist*: At the centre of the Round of Existence the pig represents ignorance and greed and is one of the three creatures depicting the sins which bind man to the world of illusion and the senses and rebirth. In Tibetan Buddhism the Diamond or Adamantine Sow is Vajravarahi, a Great Mother and Queen of Heaven. *Celtic*: The sow goddess, 'the Old White One', Keridwen, is the Great Mother, also Phaea, 'the Shining One' as the moon and fertility. The pig is an attribute of Manannan who provided supernatural food through his pigs which were killed and eaten and returned daily. *Chinese*: The pig signifies untamed nature, greedy and dirty naturally, but useful and fertilizing when tamed. *Christian*: Satan; gluttony; sensuality. Emblem of St Anthony Abbot who overcame the demon of gluttony. *Egyptian*: Sacred to Isis as the Great Mother and to Bes, but it can also be malefic as Set in his typhonic aspect. *Greek*: Swine were a symbol of Eleusis and were sacrificed to Ceres and Demeter as fertility goddesses. The sow is sacred to the Dictean Zeus, who was suckled by a sow. *Hebrew*: The unclean, a forbidden food. *Hindu*:

The Adamantine Sow, Vajravarahi, Queen of
Heaven, is the feminine aspect of Vishnu's third
incarnation as a boar, and is a source of life,
fertility. *Islamic*: The unclean, a forbidden food.
Oceanic: The sow is lunar and fertility. *Roman*:
Swine were sacrificed to Mars as god of
agriculture, also to Tellus and Ceres at harvest
time. *Sumero-Semitic*: An attribute of Rimmon,
of Tiamat and of the Great Mother goddesses.

Swinging Swinging and rocking are associated
with fertility rites and also symbolize 'life's ups
and downs'.

Sword Power; protection; authority; royalty; leadership; justice; courage; strength;
vigilance; physical extermination. It is also the
masculine principle, the active force, and is
phallic with the sheath as the receptive
feminine. On the metaphysical level the sword
is symbolic of discrimination; the penetrating
power of the intellect; spiritual decision; the
inviolability of the sacred. It possesses supernatural powers, either on the earth, under the
earth, or under the waters, and is associated
with giants and supernatural beings such as the
Lady of the Lake; it is also wielded by the
cosmic or solar Hero, conqueror of dragons and
demonic powers. As discernment it is a symbol
of the higher forms of knighthood, with the
lance as the lower form. The sword separates
and divides the body and soul, heaven and
earth, and the flaming sword separates man
from Paradise. The two-edged sword symbolizes the dual powers and inverse currents in
manifestation, creation and destruction, life and
death, powers which are contrary in appearance but complementary and one in
reality. The four swords of the sovereign at a
coronation are (1) the sword of state, (2) the
curtana or blunted sword of mercy, (3) spiritual
justice, (4) temporal justice. *Alchemic*: The
sword depicts purifying fire which kills and
revivifies as the penetrating spirit. *Buddhist*:
Discrimination which cuts ignorance at the
roots. 'As the sword cuts knots so should the
intellect pierce the deepest recesses of Buddhist
thought.' Manjusri, as wisdom, carries the
sword of discernment in his right hand. The
point of the sword of wisdom emits the light of
the indestructible *vajra*, destroying the hetero-
dox mind and driving away the enemies of
Dharma. *Celtic*: Attribute of the hero-king
Nuada; associated with the supernatural
underwater powers. The sword is the active
aspect of the will, with the crystal as the passive.
Chinese: Penetrating insight; a wave-shaped
sword represents a dragon swimming in the
waters. *Christian*: Christ's passion; martyrdom.
The flaming sword at each gate or corner
divides man from Paradise. The sword is an
emblem of the Archangel Michael and SS
Adrian, Agnes, Alban, Barbara, Euphemia,
Justinia, Martin, Paul, Peter, George of
Cappadocia, James of Compostella. *Greek*: The
sword of Damocles represents danger in the

God the Father, crowned Supreme Judge, wields his
sword of justice and authority in this scene of a Last
Judgement from an early 15th-century French book
of hours.

In many ancient cultures, the **swine** was a symbol of
the heavily fecund – but possibly devouring – Great
Mother; this 5th-millennium BC terracotta head of a
pig was probably a votive representation of the
goddess.

midst of seeming prosperity; ever-present danger; retribution. *Hindu*: The wooden sword of the Vedic sacrifice symbolizes lightning and has the same significance as the VAJRA (q.v.). The sword also represents the warlike nature of the *Asuras*. It is an attribute of the warrior caste. *Islamic*: The sword is symbolic of the Holy War of the believer against the infidel and of man against his own evil. *Japanese*: Courage; strength. It is one of the Three Treasures, with the mirror and jewel as truth and compassion. *Scandinavian*: An attribute of Freyr, his sword fought of its own accord. Surtr, the flame giant, wields a flaming sword. *Taoist*: Penetrating insight; victory over ignorance.

Sycamore 'Sycamore Fig' is the Egyptian Tree of Life, 'The Lady Sycamore', the 'wood of life'; it represents Nut, goddess of the heavens. Its fruit yields a milky substance so it is associated with the Mother Goddess, Hathor, as the cow and nourishment, generation, fertility and love. The tree is also connected with the many-breasted figure of Artemis of Ephesus, the fig of the sycamore being born on the stock of the tree, not on its branches.

Symplegades See PASSAGE.

T TAU CROSS, q.v.

Tabernacle *Hebrew*: A world centre; the heart of the world; the cosmos; the Holy of Holies; the abode of the Shekinah.

Table *Hebrew*: The Tables of the Law represent judgment and legislation. The Table of the Loaves, according to Philo, is the operation of grace for the realization of things terrestrial; Philo equates it with the twelve months of the year.

Tablet Destiny; the recording of past deeds and the future. The possession of tablets of destiny implies access to esoteric and magical knowledge in the hands of a god, king or priest. Plotinus equates the 'Guarded Tablet' with the universal soul. A funeral or ancestral tablet provides a resting place for the soul of the dead which would otherwise become lost, wandering and a malefic ghost. *Chinese*: Dignity; good omen. A tablet, with the grain of fertility, was conferred by the Emperor on his consort. A green jade tablet was used as a symbol of Spring at the Spring Festival and represented the East. A hammer-shaped tablet in the Emperor's hands depicts the Tablet of Power. The star Aldebaran was God of the Tablets. *Christian*: The Heavenly Tablets hold the future of mankind. The seven-sealed scroll which none can read signifies the Tablet of Destiny. *Graeco-Roman*: A tablet inscribed with the name of an enemy gave power over the person and was used

in spells and magic against him. In Orphic funeral rites tablets had initiatory formulae and invocations inscribed on them; these also gave control of the dead. The tablet, with the stylus, is an attribute of Calliope. *Hebrew*: The Tablets of the Law are the commands of God. *Hermetic*: The Emerald Tablet is a reflection of the macrocosm and microcosm: 'As above, so below.' The lowest corresponds to the highest; the basic unity of all things in the One. *Islamic*: The *prima materia* on which destiny and the divine plans are written. The 'Guarded Tablet' stretches from heaven to earth, making communication between them possible; made of pearl, its two surfaces of rubies and emeralds represent the Upper and Lower Waters, and, with ink, the Tablet symbolizes all possibilities in manifestation. *Sumero-Semitic*: The possession of the Tablets of Destiny confers omnipotence and magical powers and assists in overcoming the forces of chaos and evil; they helped Marduk to overcome Tiamat. Tablets are recorded fate; Nabu, the Sumerian scribe of the gods, keeps the Tablets of Fate. Aldebaran is the Star of the Tablet since his function was to write the decisions of the gods, taken at their vernal congress, on the Tablets of Fate.

Tail Balance, guidance, hence judgment and adjustment.

Talon See CLAW.

Tamarisk Manna was said to exude from the tamarisk tree. *Egyptian*: Sacred to Osiris, whose body was concealed in a tamarisk tree. *Sumero-Semitic*: Sacred to Tammuz and Anu. A Tree of Life. The tamarisk, with the date palm, was created in heaven.

Tambourine The shamanistic tympana or magic DRUM (q.v.). With the drum and cymbals the tambourine was used in ecstatic dancing and orgies; Maenads, or Bacchantes, following Dionysos, carry tambourines. Attribute of Heracles and Erato. In the cult of Cybele-Attis the initiate drank from the cymbal and ate from the tambourine.

Tarot The origin of the Tarot cards is unknown and the symbolism attributed to them varies widely. There are twenty-two major arcana or enigmas identified with the letters of the Hebrew alphabet, and they are said to form a symbolism of esoteric knowledge, philosophy and science which includes the whole of Man's spiritual and material experiences in the phenomenal world, also to trace the path of the initiate from ignorance to enlightenment. There are also fifty-six minor arcana, divided into four suits of court and numeral cards.

Tat *Egyptian*: The backbone of Osiris; the world axis; the Pole; stability; firmness; immutability; preservation.

Tau The T cross; life; the key to supreme power; phallic. It is also the cross of Mithraism and Thor's Hammer and, as a hammer, an attribute of thunder and smith gods. In Heraldry it is the Cross Potent. See also CROSS.

Taurus See ZODIAC.

Teeth Attack and defence; showing the teeth represents defence and enmity. In China teeth symbolized warfare. In some primitive initiation ceremonies a tooth was extracted and swallowed as a death and rebirth symbol, the teeth being the most enduring part of the body.

Temperance Depicted in Christian art as a woman with a sword, or two vases, with Scipio Africanus at her feet; other attributes are a clock or hourglass, bit and bridle, wine mixed with water, a windmill.

Temple An *imago mundi*; a microcosm; a spiritual world centre; the earthly counterpart of the heavenly archetype; the dwelling place of divinity on earth; the sheltering power of the Great Mother; the meeting place of the three worlds as having contact with heaven, the earth, the underworld and its waters; equilibrium. A temple is often symbolically the highest place in the land. Temples sometimes represent the cosmic structure and sometimes the religious relationship between gods and men. As the cosmic structure, the superimposed stages, or tiers, of the building are the horizontal, existential plane with its endless varieties and degrees of being; it is axial and a vertical bond between heaven and earth and earth and the underworld; the stages signify ascent towards the heavens and the spiritual ascent of the devotee; it is also an image of the Sacred Mountain. The central pillar of the temple is both the *axis mundi* and the Cosmic Tree.

The rock, or cave, temple symbolizes return to the centre, to nature, to man's primordial self, the living rock and the womb of rebirth. The triangular temple, supported by four pillars, depicts the triple form of the divinity presiding over the four elements as agents of creation and reproduction. The round temple represents the perfection of the circle or sphere and divine perfection. Hindu temples are constructed on the pattern of the universe and are images of the macrocosm and built as a MANDALA (q.v.). The square is the fundamental form of Hindu architecture, symbolizing order, stability and finality. There are three altars: at the East end the square fire altar represents the celestial world; the West-end fire altar is circular, depicting the terrestrial world; at the South end is the air-world and fire. The centre of the hearth is laid in the shape of a cross; the centre of the high altar is an omphalos, the innermost sanctuary; the central pillar, symbolizing the world axis and world tree, rises from the sanctuary of the seed, the womb. The area of the temple is divided into sixty-four squares, the

The **sycamore** (in the USA, the maple), to the ancient Egyptians the Tree of Life, was the emblem of Nut the sky goddess. This wall painting comes from a tomb of the 19th dynasty.

Four **tarot** card figures from the late 18th century, showing (top) the Juggler and the Clown, and (bottom) the Emperor and the Empress.

mandala, the cosmic plan. Heaven and earth meet at the gates, or doors, at the four cardinal points. The crown at the top of the central pillar represents divine glory, and the opening above it gives exit from the world heavenwards and entry to the celestial. The darkness inside the temple signifies man's need of light from outside himself, and that the temple is lit by the divinity.

The Temple of Jerusalem was an *imago mundi* and cosmic centre, a place of communion between God and Israel; it represented the beginning of cosmic time and was the dwelling-place or house of God on earth, a reflection of the Heavenly Tabernacle. According to Josephus the three parts of the Sanctuary denoted the three cosmic regions, the court, the lower regions, the sea; the Sanctuary, the earth; the Holy of Holies, Heaven. The Sumerian Temple, or ZIGGURAT (q.v.) was built in seven stages of ascent and descent and formed the vertical bond between heaven and earth and earth and the underworld and the waters, and the horizontal bond between the lands.

Ten Thousand Things In Chinese symbolism *wan*, as 10,000, is the uncountable, that is to say all existence in the phenomenal world, all creation which is the result of the interaction of the two primordial forces of yin and yang.

Ternary See NUMBERS, *Three*.

Terrestrial branches Twelve; see ZODIAC.

Tetraktys See NUMBERS, *Four*.

Tetramorphs 'The synthesis of the quaternary of elemental powers'. In Christianity the tetramorphs are Matthew, depicted as a man, or winged man, representing the human nature of Christ, the Incarnation; Mark, as a winged lion, roaring in the desert, preparing the way and depicting the royal dignity of Christ; Luke, a winged ox, or a calf, the sacrifice, the atonement and priesthood of Christ; John, an eagle, 'wings of an eagle hastening to lofty things ... one who can gaze on the sun' (Jerome), the Ascension and the divine nature of Christ.

The four Cherubim, sometimes portrayed as beings, sometimes as a mystical figure with four heads, man, lion, ox, eagle, are guardians of the four corners of the Throne of God and of the four corners of Paradise. They also represent the quaternary of elemental powers and wield the flaming swords of discrimination, guarding the entry to, and centre of, Paradise, inaccessible to unregenerate man. In Egypt the four Sons of Horus were depicted as one with a human head and three with animal heads. In Hinduism there are the four heads of Brahma.

Thigh The thigh is often used as a symbol of the phallus, hence creative power, procreation and strength. The skull and crossed thigh-bones represent the two vital sources of power, the head and the loins, of the person after death; they possess magical power, drawing away the life-force and are thus a symbol of death. In Egypt the thigh of the bull or hippopotamus is 'the phallic leg of Set'. Dionysos emerged from the thigh of Zeus.

Third Eye The Third Eye of Siva, or Buddha, the *urna*, the 'shining spot' or 'flaming pearl', in the centre of the forehead, symbolizes unity; balance; seeing things whole; deliverance from duality and the pairs of opposites; seeing *sub specie aeternitatis*; transcendent wisdom; the crystallization of light; spiritual consciousness; enlightenment. In no case is it a physical quality.

Thirst Longing; appetite; desire for experiencing life, either spiritual or material.

Thistle Defiance; austerity; vindictiveness; misanthropy. The food of asses. In Christian symbolism its thorns depict the passion of Christ, also sin, earthly sorrow and evil (Gen. 3); wickedness encroaching on virtue (Job 31). It is the emblem of Scotland as *Nemo me impune lacessit*.

Thorn Thorned plants, e.g. acanthus, acacia, rose, etc., symbolize the horns of the crescent moon; the thorn and the rose together depict the antithesis of pain and pleasure, suffering and joy. In Christianity the thorn denotes sin, sorrow, tribulation, and is an emblem of Christ's passion, the crown of thorns being a parody on the Roman Emperor's crown of roses. In Egypt the thorns of the acacia are an emblem of Neith.

Thread The thread of life; human destiny; fate, spun and woven by a divine power; unity; continuity; that which binds the universe together and from which the universe is woven; the sun, on which all things 'depend' and all life is threaded. The symbolism of the uniting thread applies to both the macrocosm and the events of man's individual life. The thread passing through the sphere of the pearl or precious stone is an *axis mundi*, and with the circular form of the bead depicts a cycle of manifestation. One of the most usual forms of thread symbolism as the thread of the world is the chaplet, rosary or garland. *Buddhist*: The Thread of the Teaching, or Discourse, is contained in the *sutras* and *tantras* and is the thread of wisdom running through the scriptures. *Hindu*: The thread is the Atman, the Inner Ruler; 'On me all things are strung as a row of pearls on a thread' (*Bhagavad Gita*). It is also the wind, i.e. the *pneuma*, 'the thread is the same as the wind' (*Upanishads*). The Thread of Brahma is the symbol of Mount Meru, the world axis, and in the human microcosm is the median canal. See also BONDS; CORD.

Threshing Floor A sacred place, separating the good from the dross; also representing the fertility of the earth. Its rotation signifies the movement of the universe, the sun, moon and planets.

Threshold Passage from the profane to the sacred, from outer profane space to inner sacred space; entering a new world. As a boundary symbol it is the line of meeting of the natural and supernatural; this is ritually defined in the ceremony of 'beating the bounds', redefining the realm of space in the same manner in which New Year ceremonies redefine time. Sinking in water, or entering a dark forest, or a door in a wall, are threshold symbols as entering the perilous unknown. Vestal goddesses of virginity are goddesses of the threshold, as are the Lares. Guardians of the threshold, who must be overcome before the sacred realm can be entered, are dragons, serpents, monsters, dogs, scorpion men, lions, etc. In the psychic and spiritual realm guardians prevent man from going too far or too fast and meeting or seeing more than he is capable of bearing in occult or esoteric knowledge.

Throne The seat of authority, knowledge and rule, both spiritual and temporal. The throne is raised on a dais as a world centre between heaven and earth. It also symbolizes the miraculously born who are portrayed on thrones of special symbolism, such as the dragon throne, the lotus, or the lion throne. The lap of the Great Mother, as Queen of Heaven, is symbolic of the throne. The throne implies a relationship between God and man or sovereign and subject. *Buddhist*: The Diamond Throne, the *vajrasana*, situated at the foot of the Tree of Knowledge, is the cosmic centre, the motionless point round which the world revolves, the place of illumination and enlightenment. Buddha is depicted as sitting on a Diamond, Lotus, or Lion Throne. The empty throne represents Buddha, his features being too glorious to be portrayed. The Throne of the Law is the teaching of Buddha and achieving Buddhahood. *Christian*: Episcopal and temporal dignity and rule; authority; jurisdiction. The Throne of God is of gold. The Virgin Mary is the Throne of Wisdom. See *Hebrew*, below. *Egyptian*: The Queen of Heaven, Isis, is 'the seat' and 'the throne' which is the lap of the Great Mother, the earth. The throne also depicts the divine and temporal rule of the Pharaoh. *Hebrew*: The throne of God, revealed to Ezekiel, is the 'Lower Throne' as God's dwelling place or 'house' on earth, in the Temple, a cosmic centre, with the Higher or Heavenly Throne of the New Jerusalem; it is supported by four living creatures with the faces of the lion, ox, eagle and man, the TETRAMORPHS. *Hindu*: The throne, like the temple, is based on the sacred square and its pairs of opposites; in the construction of the throne these are represented by order and chaos, knowledge and ignorance, sovereignty and anarchy. The positive values are depicted by the legs, as vertical, and the negative and

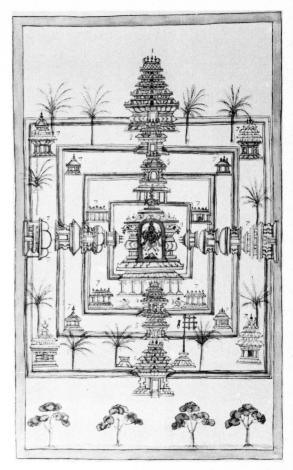

The plan of the **temple** at Conjeeveram indicates how the building has the form of a MANDALA, whose four gates lead to the centre where Vishnu, its patronal deity, resides.

An 18th-century Indian brass head of the goddess Durga, the Terrible Mother, whose **third eye** symbolizes her power to free men from the illusion of duality and imbalance.

horizontal by the shafts. The Diamond Throne symbolism is common to Hinduism and Buddhism. *Iranian*: The Persian royal throne is the Peacock Throne. *Islamic*: 'His throne was upon the water' (Qoran). The throne which encompasses the world is supported by eight angels. *Sumero-Semitic*: Both the authority and divine rule of the kings and the lap of the Great Mother, as the earth.

Thule The hyperborean, primordial spiritual centre; the 'point quiescent' (Aristotle); the point of meeting of heaven and earth. The Islands of the Blest; Paradise; The White Island; The White Mountain; The Green Island; The Island of Jewels; Avalon.

Thumb Power and transmission of power; the thumb upwards is beneficent power, good luck and good will; downwards it is the reverse. The pointed thumb and forefinger is phallic.

Thunder/Thunderbolts Thunder is the voice of the sky gods, with the thunderbolt as their weapon, the destroyer of serpents and spiritual enemies; divine anger; it is also an attribute of monarchs and magicians. Thunder, roaring like a bull, brings the fecundating rain and is associated with lunar changes. Rain coming only with thunder in some countries associates thunder with the fertilizing waters and the nourishing water from heaven. Rain which came with thunder was regarded as impregnated with power and was, therefore, more nutritive. 'The water often falls pregnant by thunder and their union is the cause of vital heat' (Plutarch).

The thunderbolt also symbolizes the sacred union of the fecundating sky god and the receptive earth mother; it is an attribute of all smith gods, such as Hephaestos, Vulcan, Thor. Symbols of thunder and attributes of all sky and storm gods are the hammer, drum, hatchet, lightning-axe, bull-roarer; the oak tree; rolling thunder is also represented by the dragon, the spiral and the flaming pearl. Thunder gods are often depicted with red hair. *Amerindian*: The Thunder Bird is the Universal Spirit, the Creator; the great forces of Nature, the dynamic sky power, also connected with the destructive forces of war, guardian of the sky-heaven approaches. The dog, serpent and pig are thunder animals as rain-bringers. *Buddhist*: The Tibetan DORJE (q.v.), the Chinese *ju-i* and the Japanese *nyoi* are the thunderbolt, or diamond mace, the 'adamantine', representing the divine force of the Doctrine; transcendental truth; enlightenment; it is the subduer of evil passions and desires. Of the Dhyani Buddhas, Amoghasiddhi carries a double thunderbolt and Akshobhya holds a single thunderbolt. 'The rolling of the Dharma thunder' is the spreading of the teaching of liberation for all living things. *Chinese*: The thunder god Lei-kung is depicted as a hideous blue-bodied man with wings and claws, his attributes are the drum, mallet and chisel. *Graeco-Roman*: Zeus/Jupiter, as sky god, wields a thunderbolt which can be either the weapon or the personification of the god; the thunderbolt is, with lightning, the 'sky-axe' of the Cyclops; the Brontes represented thunder and the Arges the thunderbolt. *Hindu*: The VAJRA (q.v.) is the thunderbolt of Indra and of Krishna; it is also the flash from the Third Eye of Siva and symbolizes divine force, cosmic intelligence, enlightenment, but, like lightning, it is both death-dealing and generative, and so represents the forces of both destruction and generation. The *vajra* has the same significance as the *dorje*, and both can be conventionalized in the shape of a flower, the fleur-de-lis form. *Japanese*: Thunder gods in Japan appear to denote the thunder both of the sky and of the underground volcano. Kami-nari is the god of rolling thunder, and thunder gods are associated with the ladder as a means of coming and going between heaven and earth. The thunderbolt surmounts the head, and is held in the hand, of Aizen-myoo, god of compassion, who uses it to subdue evil desires and passions. *Scandinavian and Teutonic*: Thor, the thunder god, holds his hammer, Mjölnir. Donar is a storm god. *Sumero-Semitic*: Adad, the storm god, rides a bull and holds thunderbolts; Marduk holds a thunderbolt, In Babylonian art the thunderbolt is associated with the bull.

Thyrsos A staff entwined with vine or ivy, or with a knot of ribbons, surmounted by a pine cone. It is a phallic symbol, the life-force, chiefly associated with Dionysos/Bacchus, but occurring also in Egypt, Phoenicia and among the Hebrews.

Tiara See CROWN.

Tide Reciprocity; balance in out-going and in-coming; opportunity. Associated with the outgoing soul at death: it was believed that the soul went out on the turning or ebb tide.

Tiger Ambivalent as both solar and lunar, creator and destroyer. When depicted as fighting with the serpent the tiger is celestial and solar power; in conflict with the lion, or eastern dragon, it is lunar, chthonic, malefic. It also symbolizes royalty; cruelty; strength; it can be a manifestation of the Earth Mother. *Alchemic*: In Chinese alchemy the tiger represents lead and bodily strength. *Aztec*: The western, setting sun; chthonic and earth powers. *Buddhist*: One of the Three Senseless Creatures of Chinese Buddhism as anger, with the monkey as grasping greed and the deer as love-sickness. *Chinese*: King of the Beasts and Lord of the Land Animals. When it is yang the tiger, in Chinese symbolism, takes the place of the lion in the West and depicts authority, courage, military prowess and the fierceness needed for protection. When in conflict with the yang celestial dragon, the tiger becomes yin as the earth; the two together represent the opposing forces of spirit and matter. The tiger is the third of the symbolic animals of the Twelve Terrestrial Branches and is the mark of military officers of the fourth class; it is also the emblem of gamblers. The god of wealth rides a tiger which is a guardian of money chests; the goddess of wind also rides a tiger. It is a guardian of graves and frightens away evil spirits. As being able to see in the dark it is chthonic; it is lunar as depicting the growing power of the new moon which is represented as a child escaping from a tiger's jaws – the child is 'the ancestor of the people', i.e. humanity, and the tiger depicts the powers of darkness from which the new moon, the light, escapes. The White Tiger is the western region, the season of Autumn and the element of metal, and it must always have its head to the South and tail to the North; the Blue Tiger is plant life, the East and Spring; the Red Tiger is fire, the South and Summer; the Black Tiger is water, the North and Winter; the Yellow Tiger is the Centre, the Sun, the Ruler. To 'ride a tiger' symbolizes to encounter and confront dangerous and elemental forces. *Egyptian*: An attribute of Set as the destroyer of Osiris and Set in his typhonic aspect. *Greek*: Tigers can be a substitute for the leopards drawing the chariot of Dionysos/Bacchus. *Heraldry*: The Tigre or Tyger represents fierceness and strength. *Hindu*: The emblem of the Kshatriyas, the royal and warrior caste. Durga, as destroyer, rides a tiger and Siva, as destroyer, sometimes wears a tiger skin. *Japanese*: Though mythical in Japan, it is used to denote courage and as an attribute of warrior heroes. *Shamanistic*: Superhuman powers; it is a messenger of the forest gods and is ridden by gods, immortals and exorcists.

Time The Creator and Devourer. 'Time has engendered everything that has been and will be' (*Bhagavad Gita*). 'Time, which in progressing, destroys the world' (*Upanishads*). It is also descent from, and return to, origins; it is a destructive force, but also the revealer of Truth. 'Once upon a time' symbolizes the Golden Age when all things were possible. The cessation of time is the break-through to enlightenment; eternity. The Black Kali depicts Time the Devourer, the pitiless destroyer. Black virgins represent the undifferentiated, the *prima materia*, the irrational, lunar, dark, feminine aspect of time. Symbols of time are the hourglass, clock, sickle, serpent, turning wheel, the circle as endless cycles but also cosmic completion, scythe, the Reaper, who is also Cronos/Saturn as Time. Lunar animals and symbols are also associated with time.

Tin The metal of Jupiter and the Zodiacal sign of Sagittarius.

Titans The forces of manifestation. In Buddhism they are depicted as supermen with the failings of warlikeness and ambition and envy which bring them to ultimate destruction.

A Hittite weather god holds the hammer of his **thunder** and the bolts of his lightning.

A frenzied maenad on a 6th-century BC Greek vase clutches a **thyrsos** while, with bared breast, she hurls herself into the transport of union with Dionysos/Bacchus.

Toad A lunar animal as belonging to the humid element. As appearing and disappearing it is both lunar and a symbol of resurrection. It can also depict evil, loathsomeness and death. Like the serpent the toad is said to have a jewel in its head. *Alchemic*: The dark side of nature, its lower, but fertile, dregs; earthly matter. 'Join the toad of the earth to the flying eagle and you will see in our art the Magisterium' (Avicenna). *Amerindian*: The Dark Manitou, the moon waters, the powers of darkness and evil overcome by the Great Manitou. *Celtic*: Often takes the place of the serpent as evil power. *Chinese*: The lunar, yin, principle; the unattainable; longevity; wealth and money-making. The three-legged toad lives in the moon, its three legs symbolizing the three lunar phases. *Christian*: The Devil; the toad enters into those possessed of the devil; avarice. *Greek*: An attribute of Sabazios. *Iranian*: Ahriman; evil; envy; greed; avarice, but also fertility. *Mexican*: The earth. The toad and toadstool represent the sacred mushroom giving enlightenment. *Oceanic*: Death. *Taoist*: An attribute of Hon Hsien-hsing. *Witchcraft*: A witch; good luck.

Tomb The womb of the earth and of the Earth Mother; the body imprisoning the soul. A symbol of the Mother Goddess as both death-dealing and sheltering; dying to the world. In Alchemy the grave, with the skull and the raven, represent the blackening and mortification of the first stage of the Lesser Work, it is 'earth to earth', dying to the world. Tombs were often the setting for ritual meals for the benefit of the dead on anniversaries and at seasons associated with death and resurrection, such as the New Year, Spring and Easter festivals.

Tongs An attribute, with the hammer and anvil, of all smith and thunder gods such as Hephaestos, Vulcan, Thor. Emblem of the Christian Bishop Eloi.

Tongue The voice of the deity; manifestation of a powerful voice; preaching; it has also a serpent and phallic symbolism. Fleshy tongues are often attributes of demons in Oriental art, and in mediaeval Christianity Satan frequently has a protruding fleshy tongue. Putting out the tongue, in the East, is symbolic of darkness-to-light, it has also an apotropaic significance and can be a form of greeting. The tongue protruding in animal representations is suggested as supplication for rain or water from the sky, vital to life and fertility. *Buddhist*: Buddha had a long tongue which 'recited sutras and disseminated knowledge concerning them'. *Chinese*: In China the tongue was associated with the antler as supernatural power. *Christian*: 'The tongue of an angel is called metaphorically the angel's power' (Aquinas). *Egyptian*: The extended tongue appears on the god Bes. *Greek*: In Greek art it is first a divine attribute then later a fearful device of the Gorgon. *Hindu*: 'Agni's tongue, the priestly voice, touches

heaven' (*Rig Veda*). Kali is usually depicted with protruding tongue. *Sumerian*: The Babylonian monster animals often have extended tongues.

Tonsure Shaving off the hair is symbolic of renunciation of the generative forces of nature; spiritual transformation; to be naked as a newborn babe; the ascetic life; entering the spiritual path of self-abnegation and renunciation of the world; consecration. Tonsure can also share the symbolism of the disk of the sun and of the crown and the dome. In Christianity it represents the crown of thorns as well as renunciation of the flesh.

Top Bastius says that the pine cone and the spinning top have the same symbolism of a vortex or spiral whorl, i.e. the great generative forces.

Topaz See JEWELS.

Torch Life; the flame of the life principle, the fire being phallic and the wood feminine, it is the divine male principle springing from the feminine tree, the soul-flame attached to the wood-matter, hence fecundating spiritual fire, illumination, intelligence, truth, immortality, also God who illumines the darkness and sees through all. The burning, or erect, torch depicts life; the extinguished, or downward-held, is death; or they can portray the rising and setting sun, light and darkness, etc. Torch-bearing at weddings and fertility rites denotes the generative power of fire. *Christian*: Christ as the Light of the World, also an emblem of his betrayal, and an emblem of SS Dioscurus, Dorothea; a dog with a torch in its mouth is an attribute of St Dominic. *Greek*: Life; the weapon of Heracles against the hydra; emblem of Eros and Venus as the fires of love, attribute of Demeter, Hecate, Persephone, Hephaestos. *Hebrew* (*Qabalism*): The torch of intelligence and the light of equilibrium. *Mithraic*: Torches are held upwards and downwards by the *dadophoroi*, Cautes and Cautopates, the Bull and the Scorpion, as life and death, the rising and setting sun, morning and evening, Spring and Winter, the lengthening and shortening of the days, etc. *Roman*: Funerary, illuminating the darkness of death and giving light in the world to come; attribute of Vulcan and Hercules. *Slav*: The rebirth of the sun, brought about by the sun god Svarog.

Tortoise The waters; the moon; the Earth Mother; the beginning of creation; time; immortality; fecundity; regeneration. The tortoise is frequently depicted as the support of the world as the beginning of creation and the all-sustaining. In China it possessed oracular powers. *Alchemic*: The tortoise represents the *massa confusa*. *Amerindian*: The Cosmic Tree grows out of the back of the tortoise. *Chinese*: One of the Four Spiritually Endowed, or sacred, Creatures, with the dragon, phoenix and *ky-lin*;

it represents the watery element, the yin principle, Winter, the northern region and the colour black, the colour of primordial chaos. The tortoise is also called the Black Warrior, and then becomes strength, endurance and longevity. The dragon and tortoise banner was carried by the imperial army as a symbol of indestructibility since both creatures survive a fight, the dragon being unable to crush the tortoise and the tortoise being unable to reach the dragon. The tortoise frequently appears with the crane as a longevity symbol. It supports the world, with its four feet as the four corners of the earth. *Christian*: Modesty in marriage; women living retired in their houses as the tortoise is in its shell, but appeared in early Christian art as evil in contrast to the cock of vigilance. *Egyptian*: Two tortoises appear with the sign of the Scales as the measure of the flood waters of the Nile. *Graeco-Roman*: The feminine principle, the fertility of the waters; an attribute of Aphrodite/Venus who rose from the sea; also an emblem of Hermes/Mercury. *Hindu*: Kasyapa, the North Star; the first living creature; the progenitor. An avatar of Vishnu, the Preserver; the power of the waters. The lower shell is the terrestrial world and the upper the celestial. The tortoise supports the elephant on whose back the world rests, the elephant being male and the tortoise female, representing the two creative powers. *Japanese*: The support of the abode of the Immortals and of the Cosmic Mountain. Longevity; good luck; support. Emblem of Kumpira, god of seafaring men and an attribute of the goddess Benten. *Mexican*: The Great Mother in her terrible aspect. *Sumerian*: Sacred to Ea-Oannes as Lord of the Great Deep. *Taoist*: Its shape symbolizes the Great Triad, or the entire cosmos, with the dome-shaped back as the sky, the body in the middle as the earth or as man, the mediator, and its under shell as the waters.

Totem/Totempole Representations of protective divinities, spirits or powers in Nature, or the protector of a particular tribe.

Touch To touch is to transfer power, as in the laying-on of hands. To touch wood is symbolic of grasping the Cosmic Tree, the *axis mundi*, the sacred centre and the place of sanctuary.

Tower Ascent, also vigilance; shares the symbolism of the LADDER (q.v.), and the round tower that of the PILLAR (q.v.). When the tower holds a virgin, princess, etc., it takes on the significance of the enclosed space or walled garden (see GARDEN). In Christianity this depicts the Virgin Mary, also called the Tower of Ivory, and the tower is also an emblem of St Barbara. The ivory tower symbolizes the inaccessible, also the feminine principle and virginity. The tower is ambivalent in its feminine sheltering and protective aspect, and masculine as a phallic symbol.

Liu-hai, a Taoist immortal, holds a three-legged **toad**, symbol of the moon and its changes, in this 18th-century Chinese porcelain.

Kali's outstretched **tongue** symbolizes her creative and destructive energy, always maintained in perfect equilibrium: she kills in order to create.

Transfiguration A manifestation of divinity or divine powers; the visible form of divinity. *Buddhist*: Buddha shed light for three miles around. *Christian*: The visible form of Christ's divine nature. *Hindu*: The manifestation of Krishna to Arjuna. *Iranian*: Zoroaster was transfigured in his mother's womb. *Shamanistic*: Illumination is the sign of supernatural powers.

Transformation The change of the hero or heroine from some imprisoning animal, bird, or other form, represents the release of the soul, usually after trials and tests, or the intervention of disinterested love, from the gross limits; limitations of the material world; or the inner transformation of man's lower nature.

Transvestism Symbolizes identity with the qualities of the original wearer; the return to primordial chaos. Orgies, the Saturnalia, the Twelve Days of Christmas, carnivals, 'fancy dress', all use transvestism as a symbol of the undifferentiated, primeval unity; it is also employed in the worship of androgynous deities such as Baal and Ashtoreth and Venus Mylitta. 'Hear us Baal! whether thou be a god or a goddess' (Arnobius). Transvestism is also found in Shamanism and in many initiation ceremonies where it can also imply loss of identity, i.e. death before rebirth. Wearing woman's clothing, or the mother's clothing, in initiation rites symbolizes the return to the womb.

Treasure The search for treasure has a twofold symbolism: either the search is for earthly treasure, such as gold or jewels, usually hidden in a cave or underground, the finding of which brings trials and tribulations and, where greed is the motive, leads to final disaster, or the search is for spiritual treasure, symbolizing esoteric knowledge or enlightenment, the search for the Centre, for lost Paradise, the Grail, etc., and the goal is guarded by monsters or dragons; this represents man's quest for, and discovery of, his own true nature. Generally supernatural aid is required in overcoming the trials and monsters, suffering and testing being necessary for spiritual attainment and man being insufficient in himself without divine guidance.

Tree The whole of manifestation; the synthesis of heaven, earth and water; dynamic life as opposed to the static life of the stone. Both an *imago mundi* and *axis mundi*, the 'Tree in the midst' joining the three worlds and making communication between them possible, also giving access to solar power; an omphalos; a world centre. The tree also symbolizes the feminine principle, the nourishing, sheltering, protecting, supporting aspect of the Great Mother, the matrix and the power of the inexhaustible and fertilizing waters she controls; trees are often depicted in the style of a female figure. Rooted in the depth of the earth, at the world centre, and in contact with the waters, the tree grows into the world of Time, adding rings to manifest its age, and its branches reach the heavens and eternity and also symbolize differentiation on the plane of manifestation.

An evergreen tree represents everlasting life, undying spirit, immortality. A deciduous tree is the world in constant renewal and regeneration, dying-to-live, resurrection, reproduction, the life principle. Both are a symbol of diversity in unity, the many branches rising from one root and returning again to unity in the potentiality of the seed of the fruit on those branches.

The Cosmic Tree is sometimes depicted as having its branches dividing and joining again, or by two trunks with one root and joining branches, indicating universal manifestation proceeding from unity to diversity and back to unity, the union of heaven and earth; or this can be portrayed by the 'linked tree' as two distinct trees joined by a single branch from which springs a shoot, signifying the unity of complementary principles, male and female, etc., or the Androgyne. Two reflected trees also share this symbolism.

As a world axis the tree is associated with the mountain and pillar and all that is axial. The tree, like the grove, mountain, stone and the waters, can, by itself, represent the cosmos in its entirety. The cosmic tree is often depicted as situated at the summit of a mountain; sometimes it is at the top of a pillar.

Symbols of the tree are the pillar, post, notched pole, a branch, etc., all of which are often accompanied by a serpent, bird, stars, fruit and various lunar animals. Trees bearing life-foods are always sacred, such as the vine, mulberry, peach, date, almond and sesame.

The Tree of Life and Tree of Knowledge grow in Paradise; the Tree of Life is at the centre and signifies regeneration, the return to the primordial state of perfection; it is the cosmic axis and is unitary, transcending good and evil, while the Tree of Knowledge is essentially dualistic with the knowledge of good and evil; it is associated, in many traditions, with the first man and his fall from the paradisal state, also with the lunar phases of decline and regeneration, death and resurrection. The Tree of Life also represents the beginning and end of a cycle; it has twelve fruits (or sometimes ten) which are forms of the sun and which will appear simultaneously at the end of the cycle as manifestations of the One. Immortality is obtained either by eating the fruit of the Tree of Life, as with the peach of immortality in the midst of the Taoist-Buddhist Western Paradise, or from drinking the liquid extracted from the tree, as the Iranian Haoma from the haoma tree. The Tree of Knowledge is often depicted as the vine, *in vino veritas*. Trees in Paradise which are laden with precious stones in place of flowers or fruit occur in Hindu, Sumerian, Chinese and Japanese Paradises. The Dying God is always killed on a tree. The Inverted Tree is a widespread symbol and is frequently a magic tree. The roots, in the air, represent the principle while its branches symbolize its unfolding in manifestation, inverse action, that which is on high descending below and that which is below ascending on high; it is the reflection of the celestial and terrestrial worlds in each other; it also indicates bringing knowledge back to its roots; or it can signify the sun spreading its rays over the earth and the power of the heavens extending downwards; illumination. In initiation ceremonies it denotes reversal, inversion, the death of the initiate; on funeral urns it depicts death.

The Sephirotic Tree is often inverted. The Tree of Light, or Heavenly Tree, which shines in the night, is the tree of rebirth, each soul being a candle, or lamp, on the tree, as with the Buddhist tree at feasts of the dead and the Christian Christmas Tree, the pine of Attis and of Dionysos, and the Teutonic fir tree of Woden, on which lights and luminous balls symbolize the sun, moon and stars in the branches of the Cosmic Tree. Presents on the tree were offerings to Dionysos and Attis, Atargatis and Cybele. Woden bestowed gifts on those who honoured his tree. The sacred bird often appears in the branches.

The Tree of Sweet Dew, or Singing Tree, is situated at the summit of the Sacred Mountain as the world axis. *A tree with a serpent*: the tree represents the *axis mundi* and the serpent coiled round it depicts the cycles of manifestation. The serpent, or dragon, guarding the tree signifies the difficulty of attaining wisdom; on the other hand the serpent may tempt the man, or woman, to obtain immortality, or knowledge, by getting the fruit of the tree for themselves and for him also. *Tree, stone and altar*: together they symbolize the microcosm, with the stone as the durable and everlasting, and the tree as the constantly changing and regenerating aspect. *Trees as oracles*: the tree can manifest the divinity, or be its mouthpiece, like the Oak of Dodona, the burning bush of Moses, or the sounds in the tops of the mulberry trees (2 Sam. 5). Trees with ten, or twelve, birds depict the solar cycle or, with three birds, the lunar phases. Tree-climbing symbolizes passage from one ontological plane to another; ascent to the gods, to heaven or to reality; attaining esoteric knowledge or gnosis by transcending the world. In Shamanism and in myth, poles, lianas, beanstalks or any climbing plant can also be scaled to reach other realms and obtain magical knowledge or powers. A twisted tree is magic or sacred in significance and can affect people for good or ill. *Alchemic*: The *prima materia*, both the origin and fruit of the Work. *Arabic*: The Zodiac is represented as a fruit tree of twelve branches, on which the stars are the fruits. *Australian aboriginal*: The World Tree supports the vault of heaven and the stars are lodged in its branches. The inverted tree is magic. *Buddhist*: The Fig, Pipal or Bo Tree (*Ficus religiosa*), under which Buddha attained enlightenment, is a Sacred Centre. The tree is a symbol of the Great Awakening; it is the Great Wisdom Tree, the

In this 13th-century BC Egyptian painting, a mother goddess distributes food and drink from the branches of a **tree** of life, into which she is incorporated and from which she is, in fact, inseparable.

The fourteen branches of this Indian bronze **tree** of life (15th century) open from a central stem, or axis, at whose centre is the lotus-sun, source of all life and endurance.

essence of Buddha. Its 'roots strike deep into stability ... whose flowers are moral acts ... which bears righteousness as its fruit' (*Buddhacarita*). *Celtic*: Various trees are sacred: the oak, beech, hazel, ash, yew; the Druidic oak and mistletoe represent the male and female powers. Esus appears with the willow tree. The Gaulish alder and yew are sacred, as are the Irish holly and yew, and the Gaelic rowan, which also has magical powers. Kentigern, or Mungo, is associated with the tree. *Chinese*: The Tree of Life is variously the peach, mulberry or plum, or the bamboo in Formosa and the Miao tribes. The Tree of Life, as the Tree of Sweet Dew, grows on the summit of the sacred mountain Kwan-lung as a world axis. The Year Tree has under its branches the twelve beasts of the constellations, the Symbolic Animals of the Twelve Terrestrial Branches. Trees with pairs of intertwining branches represent the union of pairs of opposites, or pairs of lovers. The sun with the tree ideogram denotes the close of day or, if the sun rests on the tree, the end of a cycle, the sun fallen to the roots of the tree denotes darkness; the tree with ten suns signifies the completion of a cycle. *Christian*: As putting forth both good and evil fruits, the tree is an image of man; as renewal through Christ's death on the cross it is resurrection. The tree of the cross was symbolically made from the wood of the Tree of Knowledge, so that salvation and life were fulfilled on the tree through which had come the Fall and death, the vanquisher vanquished. The cross is sometimes identified with the Tree in the Midst, the vertical axis of communication between heaven and earth. Mediaeval Christian symbolism has a Tree of the Living and Dead, bearing good and bad fruit on opposite sides and portraying good and evil deeds, with Christ as the trunk, the unifying Tree of Life, which is also depicted as the central of the three crosses on Calvary. The tree is an emblem of St Zenobius. *Egyptian*: The syca-more, the Tree of Life, has divine arms and is laden with gifts and water, as fertility, pours out of a vessel by it. Hathor can be portrayed as a tree giving nourishment and thus survival. The erica tree enclosed the coffin of Osiris. *Graeco-Roman*: The oak is primarily the tree of the sky god Zeus/Jupiter; the solar Apollo has the palm, laurel and olive. Artemis has various trees sacred to her: in Laconia she is called Karuatis, as the walnut tree; Artemis Soteira of Boia has the myrtle and it was from the myrtle that Adonis was born, and the Ephesian Artemis has the elm, oak and cedar. The vine is sacred to Dionysos/Bacchus, the olive to Heracles/Hercules, the plane to Helen of Sparta, the laurel to Daphne. The tree and pruning hook are attributes of Silvanus. *Hebrew* (*Qabalism*): The Tree of God symbolizes all creation, the manifest world. The Dew of Light emanates from the Tree of Life by which the dead are resurrected. The Sephirotic Tree has a right-and a left-hand column representing duality, but a middle column balances them and restores

unity. It is often inverted. 'The Tree of Life extends from above downwards and is the sun which illuminates all' (*Book of Zohar*). This tree has a vast symbolism of its own. The Hebrew Tree of Life grows in the middle of the Holy City. *Hindu*: The cosmos is a great tree with its roots in the underworld, its trunk in the world of man and the earth, and its branches in the heavens. 'Brahman was the wood, Brahman the tree from which they shaped heaven and earth' (*Taittiriya Brahmana*). It is the deity in its manifest aspect. The Cosmic Tree is sometimes shown as springing from the Cosmic Egg floating on the ocean of chaos. The Tree of Life is Aditi, the essence of individuality, while Diti, division, is the dualistic Tree of Knowledge, or Samsara, which Vishnu cuts down with his axe. The Adityas, the twelve signs of the Zodiac and the months of the year, are symbolized by the tree with twelve suns which will appear simultaneously at the end of the cycle as manifestations of the One. Two trees are sometimes depicted with trunks superimposed, the one being celestial and the other terrestrial, signifying that they are reflections of each other, 'two natures, one essence'. The triple tree with three suns represents the *Trimurti* (q.v.). The burning bush becomes the Cosmic Tree in the Vedic fire symbolism of Agni, who is also associated with the tree as the sacrificial pillar. On Mount Meru grown the tree Parajita which perfumes the whole world with its blossoms. In the Rig Veda the Asvattha tree is inverted. *Iranian*: The Cosmic Tree has seven branches, gold, silver, bronze, copper, tin, steel and 'a mixture of iron', representing the sevenfold history and the seven planets each governing a millennium. There is also the symbolism of the two trees, the white haoma, the celestial tree growing at the top of Mount Alborj, the sacred mountain and world axis, and the yellow tree which is terrestrial and a reflection of the haoma. The almond tree is also a Tree of Life. Zoroastrianism has the two trees – the Tree of the Solar Eagle, which sprang from the primordial ocean, and the Tree of All Seeds whose seeds are 'the germs of all living things'. *Islamic*: The Tree of Blessing which is neither East nor West, and therefore central, represents spiritual blessing and illumination, the light of Allah which illumines the earth. (The Tree, the olive, gives both nourishment and oil for lamps.) The inverted Tree of Happiness has its roots in the highest heaven and spreads its branches over the earth. From the Celestial Tree, the Tuba or Sidra, at the centre of Paradise, flow the four rivers of water, milk, honey and wine. The lote tree marks the impassable boundary. The Cosmic Tree grows at the top of the Cosmic Mountain and represents the whole universe. *Japanese*: The Tree of Life is the mythological Sa-ka-ti. The bonsai trees represent Nature in its austerity and wisdom. *Mexican*: The Cosmic Tree, the agave, the 'milk-yielding' cactus, with the falcon, is the power of the sun, or the liberation of the new moon. *Mithraic*: The Tree of Life is the pine. *Scandinavian*. The YGGDRASIL (q.v.) or ash is the Tree of Life and fountain of life. The tree, Laerad, grows outside Valhalla; on its branches the She-goat Heidrum browses and gives mead for the warriors to drink. *Shamanistic*: The birch, as the Tree of Life with seven branches, can be stylized as a seven-notched pole representing the seven planets and stages of ascent through the heavens; the branches are the starry vault. *Sumero-Semitic*: The Tree of Life symbolizes cosmic renovation; it has seven branches as the seven planets and heavens. The Babylonian Tree of Life, on which the universe revolves, has branches of lapis lazuli and bears wonderful fruit. The pine is sacred to the Phrygian Attis; the palm is the Tree of Life of Babylon, Phoenicia and Chaldea, while the vine is sacred to the Babylonian Siduri and is the Assyrian Tree of Life. The Accadian willow is sacred to the Accadian Zeus; the palm, pomegranate and cyprus are sacred Semitic trees. The Syrian Ashtoreth and Astarte can be symbolized by the aniconic tree trunk. *Taoist*: The peach is the Tree of Immortality. Trees with a pair of intertwining boughs, or with one common branch, signify the pairs of opposites, the yin and yang, in the unity of the Tao. *Teutonic*: The Tree of Life is the fir of Woden, or, later, the lime or linden. The fir later became the Christmas Tree.

Trefoil The Trinity; integration; equilibrium; also disintegration. It is also phallic as the male trinity and, as such, is symbolically interchangeable with the fig leaf.

Triad Triads are distinguished from Trinities in that the latter are a three-in-one while the members of Triads are distinct, such as the Astrological Sun-Moon-Venus, the Zoroastrian Fire-Light-Ether, and the Taoist Great Triad of Heaven-Man-Earth, the divine, the human and the natural, with man the mediator between the celestial and terrestrial. The Triad, like the Trinity, is often symbolized by a triangle, sometimes by a trident. In Taoism the tortoise, one of the four Spiritually Endowed Creatures, represents the Triad, with the upper shell as the dome of the heavens, the lower shell as the waters and the earth, and the central body as man. In triads of birth, life and death three goddesses are often represented as maiden, bride and hag, such as Persephone, Demeter and Hecate. They also depict the cyclic nature of the universe.

Triangle The threefold nature of the universe; heaven, earth, man; father, mother, child; man as body, soul and spirit; the mystic number three; the ternary; the first plane figure, hence the fundamental representation of surface; 'Surface is composed of triangles' (Plato); the equilateral triangle depicts completion.

The upward-pointing triangle is solar and symbolizes life, fire, flame, heat (here the

Giovanni da Modena has Christ crucified on the same **tree** from which Adam and Eve ate the fruit of the Fall, uniting in a single symbol both terminals of the mystery of the Redemption.

Gerolamo Dai Libri's *Virgin and Child with St Anne* shows its three personages sheltering in the shade of a **tree**, echo of the Tree of the Fall and portent of the Tree of the Cross.

horizontal line represents air), the masculine principle, the linga, the shakta, the spiritual world; it is also the trinity of love, truth and wisdom; it denotes royal splendour and is depicted as the colour red.

The downward-pointing triangle is lunar, the feminine principle, the matrix; the waters, cold, the natural world, the body, the yoni, the shakti; it symbolizes the Great Mother as genetrix. The horizontal line is the earth and its colour white. In mountain and cave symbolism the mountain is the masculine, upward-pointing triangle and the cave the feminine, downward-pointing.

The triangle in a circle depicts the plane of forms held within the circle of eternity. 'The area within this triangle is the common hearth of them all and is named "the Plain of Truth", in which the Reason, the forms and patterns of all things that have been, and that shall be, are stored up not to be disturbed; and Eternity dwells round them, from whence time, like a stream from a fountain, flows down upon the worlds' (Plutarch).

Three interlaced triangles denote the indissoluble unity of the three persons of the Trinity. The double triangle, the six-pointed star, the Seal of Solomon, the Mogun David, indicates that 'every true analogy must be applied inversely', 'as above so below'; it is the union of opposites, male and female, positive and negative, the upper triangle being white and the lower black; fire and water; evolution and involution; interpenetration, each being the image of the other; the hermaphrodite; the perfect balance of complementary forces; the androgynous aspect of the deity; man looking into his own nature; the twin forces of creativity; the synthesis of all elements with the upright triangle as the celestial nature and the inverted as the terrestrial, the whole representing universal man uniting the two as mediator. As the Seal of Solomon it is also the figure of the Preserver and gives spirit power over matter and is a ruler of genii. Two triangles lying horizontally and touching apex to apex are lunar, the waxing and waning moon; eternal return; death and life; dying and resurrecting. The point of touching is the dark of the moon and death. *Alchemy*: The two triangles are essence and substance, *forma* and *materia*, spirit and soul, sulphur and quicksilver, the stable and the volatile, spiritual power and bodily existence. Triangles depict the elements as: fire △; water ▽; air ◬; earth ▽. The two interlocking triangles are the union of the opposites which become 'fluid fire' or 'fiery water'. *Buddhist*: The pure flame and the Three Jewels of the Buddha, the Dharma and the Sangha. *Chinese*: The triangle with suspended swords signifies regeneration. *Christian*: The equilateral triangle, or the triangle formed by three interlacing circles, depicts the Trinity in unity and the equality of the three persons. The triangular halo is an attribute of God the Father. *Egyptian*: Represents the Triad. 'They

compare the perpendicular [of a right triangle] side to the male, the base to the female and the hypotenuse to the offspring of the two: Osiris as the beginning, Isis as the medium or receptacle, and Horus as the accomplishing' (Plutarch). The Hand of the Egyptians is the union of fire and water, male and female. A figure of three double triangles surrounded by concentric circles depicts the Khui, the Land of Spirits. *Greek*: The delta symbolizes the door of life, the feminine principle, fertility. *Hindu*: The upward and downward triangles are the shakta and shakti, the linga and yoni, or Siva and his shakti. *Pythagorean*: The equilateral triangle represents Athene as goddess of wisdom.

Trickster Appears in Amerindian, Chinese, Greek and Oceanic symbolism as the egoist, or the evolution of the Hero from the unconscious, chaotic and amoral to the conscious, integrated and responsible man. The Trickster also represents the life of the body which tends to cunning and stupid action and in this aspect shares the symbolism of the fool or jester in provoking laughter and exposing weakness; it is sometimes used as the villain to throw the Hero and the good into relief. Among the Red Indians it is symbolized by the Raven in North Pacific regions, the Coyote in the western mountains and the Rabbit or Hare in the eastern forests. The Scandinavian Loki is a Trickster.

Trident/Trisula Lightning; the thunderbolt; triple flame; the triple weapon of the heavens, air and water powers; the eternal. As the thunderbolt it is the weapon and attribute of all sky, thunder and storm gods; as the trident it is the emblem of all gods of the powers and fertility of the waters; it can also symbolize the heavenly Triad, also the past, present and future. *Buddhist*: The Trisula symbolizes the Three Jewels of the Buddha, the Dharma, the Sangha. It depicts the heaven of pure flame, also the destruction of the three root-poisons of anger, desire and sloth. It also represents the DORJE (q.v.). *Chinese*: Power; authority. *Christian*: Ambivalent as the three-in-one of the Trinity, in which context it also appears stylized in the fleur-de-lis. It is also the weapon of the Devil. *Graeco-Roman*: As the thunderbolt it is the weapon of the sky god Zeus/Jupiter; as the trident it is attribute of the sea god Poseidon/Neptune. *Hindu*: The Trisula as the VAJRA (q.v.) is the diamond sceptre of Indra as storm god and of Durga as destroyer. The trident is the weapon of Siva as creator, preserver, destroyer, and as past, present and future. It is also a fire symbol depicting the three aspects of Agni. *Minoan*: An emblem of sea-power, it appears at Knossos and Phaestos.

Trigrams *Chinese*: The Trigram is based on the symbolism of the yin-yang duad and the emergence of the reconciling third arising from the original pair. It also represents the three states of man as body, soul and spirit; the irrational emotions, the rational mind and the supra-rational intellect. See also PA KUA.

Trimurti The triple aspect of powers. In Hinduism it is Brahma as Creator, Vishnu as Preserver, Siva as Destroyer; but it is also Siva in his three aspects of Creator, Preserver, Destroyer, the unfolding, maintaining, concluding; or it can be portrayed as the Tortoise as Earth with the Great Mother in her terrible aspect with the symbols of flames and the death's-head, and the Great Mother in her beneficent aspect as the Lotus, Sophia, Tara, as wisdom and compassion. In Alchemy, in the Great Work, the tortoise is the *massa confusa*, the skull the *vas* of transformation, with the flower as the Self, wholeness.

Trinity Distinguished from the Triad as being a unity, three-in-one and one-in-three, symbolizing unity in diversity; the third uniting the opposites; the catalyst; 'The mean, acting as mediator, links the other two into a single complete order' (Proclus). *Buddhist*: The Triratna: the Buddha, Dharma, Sangha; also the Buddhas, the Sons of the Buddhas and the Dharmakaya. *Celtic*: There are numerous trinities, the three Bridgits are three-in-one as the lunar Great Mother, and the family, is three-in-one. *Christian*: Father, Son, Holy Spirit, or Mary, Joseph, Jesus. Symbols of the Trinity are the hand as the Father, the lamb the Son, and the dove the Holy Spirit; in colours these are represented by yellow, red and green and in qualities by Charity, Faith and Hope; other symbols are the triangle, three interlaced triangles or circles and the trefoil. *Egyptian*: Father, Mother, Son: Osiris, Isis, Horus. *Graeco-Roman*: Zeus, Poseidon, Hades; Jupiter, Neptune, Pluto; Sky, Ocean, Underworld. *Hebrew*: (*Qabalism*): The original Trinity of male-female and uniting intelligence. See SEPHIROTH. *Hindu*: The TRIMURTI (q.v.), also the threefold Brahman, the AUM, the imperishable Word. *Scandinavian and Teutonic*: Odin, Thor, Frigg; Woden, Donar, Frija. *Sumero-Semitic*: Anu, Ea, Bel; Sin, Shamash, Ishtar; Asshur, Anu, Hoa. In a trinity 'two thirds of him is God, one third of him is man' (*Gilgamesh*).

Tripitaka See BASKET, *Buddhism*.

Tripod The divine Triad; the rising, noon and setting sun; time as past, present and future.

Triquetra/Triskele/Fylfot The three-legged, or three-footed, or three-pronged symbol which largely shares the symbolism of the SWASTIKA (q.v.). It is the 'swift feet', probably solar movement, or the sun as rising, zenith and setting; it is also suggested as the lunar phases, renewal of life. Like the swastika it is a good luck symbol. It frequently appears with solar symbols and is seen on ancient coins of Aspendus in Pamphilia, on coins of Menecratia

Bellejambe's *Glorification of the Trinity* presents the Father in papal robes of authority, the Son as crucified redeemer, and the Spirit as un-earthly (and incorporeal) dove.

The **trident** of Siva, symbol of his threefold character as creator, preserver and destroyer, is reverenced and worshipped in an 18th-century painting from Rajasthan.

in Phrygia, on Celtic crosses where it is presumed to represent the Trinity and is a symbol of the sea god Manannan, and in Teutonic symbolism where it is connected with Thor. It is the emblem of Sicily and the Isle of Man.

Trisula See TRIDENT.

Trout *Celtic*: With the salmon, the trout is associated with sacred waters and wells and represents the foreknowledge of the gods, otherworld wisdom and knowledge.

Tug o' War The trial of strength between the gods of the sky and earth, or Zeus and other gods.

Tulip The Persian symbol of perfect love. Emblem of the Turkish House of Osman and of Holland.

Tumulus An artificial mountain which takes on the symbolism of the MOUNTAIN (q.v.) and is a world axis.

Turban Glory; the glory of the sun. *Hebrew*: The white turban of the Levite represented the full moon, the winding serpent of the moon god (Levi = serpent). *Islamic*: The crown or diadem; spiritual authority. The turban was also worn by Incas, Hittites, Babylonians and Egyptians. It is an essential attribute of the Sikhs.

Turkey The sacred bird of the Toltecs. The 'jewelled fowl', the food for ritual occasions, thanksgiving and festivals. The turkey, peacock and pheasant are associated with thunder and rain as they become restless before storms.

Turtle Longevity; slowness; lubricity. Phallic. *Amerindian*: The coward, braggart, sensualist, the earthly, Winter, the obscene or merely human. Its place can be taken symbolically by the leech. *Chinese*: Attribute of the god of examinations. *Egyptian*: Drought; an enemy of the sun god. *Maori*: The 'land-worker'; agriculture; success in harvest. For Turtle Dove see DOVE; see also TORTOISE.

Twelve See NUMBERS.

Twigs The barsom twigs of the Parsees, bound in a bundle, form 'the bundle of life', individual lives bound together in unity.

Twilight Uncertainty; ambivalence; the region between one state and another; a threshold symbol; the western light; the ending of life and the end of one cycle and beginning of another.

Twins Duality. The celestial and primaeval twins, the sons of the sun god, the two brothers, can represent the two sides of man's nature, the man of action and the man of thought, the ego and alter ego. Often they are at enmity, and one slays the other; they are then depicted as one light and one dark, symbolizing the sacrifice and sacrificer, day and night, light and darkness, heaven and earth, the manifest and the unmanifest, life and death, good and evil, the two hemispheres, polarity, the waxing and waning moon, etc. They can also be portrayed as twin circles or pillars. 'Helper' twins, such as the Asvins, the Dioscuri, the Scandinavian and Teutonic twin gods, protect from the elements. *African*: Usually an ill omen. *Amerindian*: The third stage of stabilization of man's development. Twins are often one good and one bad who fight together; the good survives, but the bad leaves traces of evil in the world. *Egyptian*: Osiris and Set are the twin powers of good and evil in conflict. Shu and Tefnut, twin lion deities, are the self-creative; Shu, space, is human-headed, wearing two or three feathers and holding the sky up with his hands; Tefnut, as rain goddess, is a lioness, or human with the head of a lioness. *Graeco-Roman*: The Dioscuri, Castor and Pollux, often depicted as one light and one dark, wear on their heads the domed caps which are the two halves of the Cosmic Egg from which they were born as sons of the sky god Zeus/Jupiter by Leda. Romulus and Remus are typical of twins at enmity. *Hebrew*: Cain and Abel, Jacob and Esau, are brothers at enmity and take on the conflicting-twin symbolism. *Hindu*: The Ashvins or Nasatyas, priests and physicians, are light and darkness, day and night, the morning and evening stars as sons of the sky god Dyaus; they drive a three-wheeled chariot, symbolic of the rising, noon and setting sun, or morning, noon and night; both are benevolent. *Manichean*: The Twin Spirit represents a kind of guardian angel. *Mithraic*: Twin male figures, the *dadophoroi*, with torches held upwards and downwards, are the rising and setting sun, life and death, etc. *Scandinavian and Teutonic*: Baldur and Loki are at enmity and are one good, one evil. The Teutonic twin forces are the Alci.

U The feminine receptive principle; the Great Mother; lunar; water; rain; the yoni.

Umbilical Cord The cord or thread by which the Great Weaver as Creator, or the Great Mother, binds or attaches man to the web of life and to his past, present and future (see SPIDER, WEAVING). The navel, or OMPHALOS (q.v.), is the world Centre and is symbolized by sacred stones, mountains, or any sacred centre.

Umbrella/Parasol The solar disk or wheel, its spokes are the rays of the sun and its haft the world axis; the canopy of the heavens; power, both temporal and spiritual; the shelter of the branches of the Cosmic Tree; as the parasol it is also warmth and protection. *Buddhist*: Protection; the state of Nirvana beyond concept and form. In Chinese Buddhism Viruhaka, or Mo-li hung, guardian of the South, has the umbrella of earthquakes, darkness and chaos; it is one of the Eight Treasures. *Chinese*: Dignity; high rank; protection; good luck. *Hindu*: Universal spiritual rule; royal dignity; protection. *Maya*: Royalty; dignity; rank; an attribute of Queen Moo.

Unicorn The lunar, feminine principle, with the lion as the male; chastity; purity; virginity; perfect good; virtue and strength of mind and body; incorruptibility. Having the two horns joined in one symbolizes the union of opposites and undivided sovereign power. Unicorns are sometimes depicted on either side of the Tree of Life as guardians. The conflict between the lion and the unicorn represents solar and lunar powers and the pairs of opposites. The unicorn is a 'water conner' and its horn can detect poison in water and render it harmless. *Alchemic*: The unicorn is quicksilver, with the lion as sulphur. *Chinese*: Often equated with the KY-LIN (q.v.), one of the Four Spiritually Endowed Creatures, it is the essence of the five elements; if it is depicted as white it is a lunar, yin, animal, but as the ky-lin it is a union of the yin and yang; it signifies gentleness, benevolence, good will, felicity, longevity, grandeur, wise administration, illustrious offspring. The horn of the unicorn is happy augury for the Emperor. To ride a ky-lin is to mount to fame. *Christian*: Christ, the 'horn of salvation'; the horn as an antidote to poison symbolizes Christ's power of destroying sin; the one horn indicates Christ and the Father as one, or Christ as the only son of God. As purity, feminine chastity and virginity, the unicorn is an emblem of the Virgin Mary and of all moral virtues. As a solitary it denotes monastic life; it is an emblem of SS Justina of Antioch and Justina of Padua. *Egyptian*: All moral virtues. *Graeco-Roman*: The lunar crescent. The unicorn is an attribute of all virgin, moon goddesses, especially of Artemis/Diana. *Hebrew*: Royalty; strength; power. *Heraldic*: It has the head and body of a horse, tail of a lion, legs and hoofs of a stag and a twisted horn in the centre of its forehead; it appears with the lion as lunar-solar powers. *Iranian*: Perfection; all moral virtues. *Sumero-Semitic*: Lunar; an attribute of virgin goddesses and appears with the Tree of Life. *Taoist*: One of the chief Taoist symbols, the essence of the five elements and virtues, as the ky-lin.

Union Symbols of union are all paired opposites; the complete circle; two interlocking circles; the double triangle; the androgyne; trees with interlocking branches; the horn of the unicorn; the yin-yang; the linga and yoni.

Uraeus *Egyptian*: Royalty; sovereignty; power; light; the powers of life and death; the power to rule; destruction of enemies; eye of Ra.

To the Aztecs, the **turtle** was a symbol of lubricious, bragging cowardice: hard on the outside, soft and slimy within.

On a 15th-century tapestry cushion-cover the **unicorn**, symbol of chastity and purity, lays its forelimbs submissively on the lady's lap.

Urim and Thummim On the ephod of the Jewish High Priest they symbolize lights and perfections.

Urn The feminine receptive and enclosing principle. Draped urns signify death. Urns with flames issuing from them depict resurrection, life out of death. Roman urns, used as voting receptacles, also represented fate. The urn is an emblem of Aquarius.

Urna See THIRD EYE.

Uzat/Utchat The Eye of Horus (see EYE); a charm against evil.

Vajra *Hindu-Buddhist*: The Thunderbolt or Diamond Sceptre, formed of two addorsed tridents of Siva as lightning and a rain-producer, wielded by Indra as temporal power and Agni as spiritual power. As the diamond it is the adamantine and depicts spiritual power; as the double vajra it is the thunderbolt and lightning and represents the forces of both destruction and fertilization, death-dealing and life-giving, the alternating and complementary forces of the universe. It is the Dragon-slayer's bolt, the shaft of light; progenitive power. It signifies compassionate activity. The stem is the world axis, extending between heaven and earth which are represented by the two ends, each the likeness of the other. The fourfold or crossed vajra also shares the symbolism of the wheel. The 'diamond' symbolizes the pure and indestructible and the man whom nothing can 'cut' or disturb. The vajrasana pose of Buddha depicts the state of eternal transcendence. See also DORJE.

Valerian *European*: Dissimulation; sacred to Hermes/Mercury.

Valley Life; fertility; cultivation; flocks; the sheltering feminine aspect. In Chinese symbolism the valley is the yin, shadowy state, with the mountain as the yang and sunny; the low and the high.

Vase The vase, water-pot and pitcher symbolize the cosmic waters; the Great Mother; the matrix; the feminine receptive principle; acceptance; fertility; the heart. The vase is frequently associated with the Tree of Life symbolism. A vase with flame issuing from it depicts the union of fire and water; a vase of wine signifies inspiration; a full vase, giving no sound, is the man of knowledge; a vase with flowers or boughs sprouting portrays the fertility of the waters; a flowing vase, usually in the hands of a divinity, symbolizes a beneficent female deity, or the Great Mother, pouring out the waters of life and fertility on the whole world; in the hands of a man the flowing vase denotes a libation to a divinity. For funerary vases see URN. *Buddhist*: One of the auspicious signs on the footprint of Buddha, denoting spiritual triumph and triumph over birth and death. *Celtic*: The healing waters; an attribute of mother goddesses. *Chinese*: Perpetual harmony; the vase of flowers is a Chinese-Buddhist symbol of harmony and longevity. The vase holding the waters of life is an attribute of Kwan-yin as compassion and fertility. *Christian*: A vase holding a lily denotes the Annunciation; an empty vase on a tomb depicts the soul gone from the body. A vase of ointment is an emblem of St Mary Magdalene. *Egyptian*: The heart; the waters; the matrix; the vivifying powers of nature; emblem of Osiris and Isis. *Graeco-Roman*: See URN. The wine-vessel of a satyr and an attribute of Hebe. *Hindu*: The power of shakti. *Sumero-Semitic*: An attribute of Great Mothers as the fertilizing powers of the waters. The vase is frequently depicted in scenes of pouring out libations to the deities. Anu was often symbolized by the overflowing vase of the waters of eternal life. *Zodiacal*: An attribute of Aquarius.

Vault The meeting place of heaven and earth; the entrance into eternal life; the sky. See also DOME.

Vegetation Unconscious life; death and resurrection; fertility; nourishment; abundance; inactivity; immobility.

Vehicles See CHARIOT.

Veil Darkness, the pre-dawn, pre-enlightened state, either cosmic or spiritual; darkness giving way to light; inscrutability; hidden or esoteric knowledge; secrecy; the illusion of the manifest world; ignorance; concealment; the darkness of mourning. But that which conceals can also reveal: direct and naked truth can be dangerous; thus the veil is also protective, both of the truth and the inquirer. The veil divides the Holy of Holies, the Highest Heaven, from the Holy Place, the temple or church on earth. The veil also represents submission to authority, hence the nun's and bride's veil, which also symbolizes sacrifice and death to the old life since the heads of sacrificial victims were often veiled and garlanded. Like hats and caps, the veil protects the inner life of the head where the life-power resides. It also obscures the personality and allows integration with others, as in ancient priesthood, and the deity worshipped was often veiled. Passing the veil denotes degrees of initiation and gaining esoteric knowledge. Blue veils indicate sky gods or goddesses. *Buddhist and Hindu*: The veil of illusion, *maya*, is the fabric from which the phenomenal world is woven; the obscuring of reality. *Christian*: Modesty; chastity; renunciation of the world; the division between Jews and Gentiles which was removed by Christ when the Veil of the Temple was rent in twain.

The rood screen is the veil of the Ark of the Covenant separating the Holy of Holies from the earthly body of the church. The cross on the altar is symbolically veiled during the period when Christ was in the tomb. *Egyptian*: The veil of Isis, the mysteries of the universe and creation, 'I am all that has been, and is, and shall be, and my veil no mortal man has yet lifted'. 'The veil is the universe which the goddess weaves' (Proclus). It is revelation, illumination and concealment. *Graeco-Roman*: An attribute of Hera/Juno. *Hebrew*: The Veil of the Temple and the Ark of the Covenant is the dividing place of the Holy of Holies, the Highest Heaven, from the Holy Place, the earth. Its four colours are the four elements: byssus, the earth; purple, the sea; red, fire; blue, the air. Moses veiled his face and its radiance when he spoke to the people of Israel. *Islamic*: The veil is of particular significance in Islamic spiritual symbolism; it represents veiled knowledge and revelation; revelation is the parting of the veil. The veil both reveals the Divine Nature and veils the Essence, and the Face of God is hidden by veils of light and darkness. Al Hallaj says that the veil is a curtain interposed between the seeker and his object. A veil separates the elite from the damned, believers from infidels. God speaks in revelation from behind a veil, and the Veil of the Name preserves the seeker from direct vision which would be too much for him to endure. The passional nature of man is 'veiled' nature since it does not see the light, but it is man, not God, who is veiled in this case. Mohammed, when portrayed, is often veiled. It is also shame and guilt. The Sufis say that seventy thousand veils separate Allah, the One Reality, from the world of matter and sense. *Sumero-Semitic*: The world of manifestation woven by the Great Goddess. The veil of Tamit at her temple was the palladium of Carthage. The shrine of Nabu, at Babylon, was veiled during the time of the descent of the Dying God into the underworld.

Venus See PLANETS.

Vertical The vertical is the essential and transcendent as opposed to the horizontal and existential plane; it represents height and aspiration towards the spiritual, and the vertical axis is the line of communication between the sacred and the profane, this world and the higher world.

Vervain/Verbena *Celtic*: The plant of magic, spells and enchantment. *Iranian*: The granter of wishes. *Roman*: Sacred to Mars and Venus; a wreath of verbena symbolizes marriage; protects against spells and enchantments.

Vesica Piscis An upright oval or ALMOND (q.v.) shape often surrounding a sacred figure; it is produced by two intersecting circles and is a basic figure in sacred geometry. See also MANDORLA.

In Islam, the Prophet and his family may not be depicted, so that the painter of this scene in which Fatima, Aisha and Um-Salma sit in conversation, showed them wearing the **veil**.

In this effigy of John Donne, carved by Nicholas Stone, the shrouded figure of the poet is standing on a funerary **urn**.

Vessels A universal feminine symbol, the womb of the Great Mother; shelter; protection; preservation; nourishment; fertility; it also represents inwardness and inner values. See also VASE. *Alchemy*: The hermetic vessel is the container of the opposites, the receiver and nourisher of that which is to be transformed. *Maya*: An overturned vessel is an attribute of Ixchel as goddess of the moon and of floods.

Vestments According to Josephus the Hebrew vestments represented: the linen, the earth; the cap of blue, the heavens and the sky; pomegranates, lightning; bells, thunder; the ephod, the universe made of the four elements; gold, the splendour of enlightenment; the breastplate, the world centre; the girdle, the ocean; the two sardonyxes on the shoulders, the sun and moon; the twelve stones, the twelve months and signs of the Zodiac; the crown of gold, the splendour which pleases God; the emerald, Spring; the ruby, Summer; the sapphire, Autumn, truth, sincerity, constancy and chastity; the diamond, Winter, the sun, light; the topaz, true love and friendship.

Victory Symbols of victory are the palm, crown, garlands, wreaths of laurel, ivy, myrtle, parsley, etc. (see WREATHS), the triumphal arch, wings. Four winged victories support the throne of Zeus.

Vigilance Symbols of vigilance are the cock (especially as a weather-vane), crane, goose, lion, dog and all guardian creatures such as serpents, dragons and monsters etc.

Vine/Vineyard Fecundity; life; a Tree of Life and in some traditions a Tree of Knowledge, in others it is sacred to Dying Gods. The fruitful vine represents fertility; passion; the wild vine denotes falseness and unfaithfulness. *Buddhist*: The entwining vine of covetousness and desire is to be cut at the roots. *Christian*: Christ is the True Vine and the disciples are the branches (John 15); it also depicts the Church and the faithful. Portrayed as a Tree of Life, with doves resting in the branches, it symbolizes souls resting in Christ and spiritual fruitfulness. The vine with corn signifies the Eucharist. *Egyptian*: Sacred to Osiris. *Graeco-Roman*: Pre-eminently the tree-symbol of Dionysos/Bacchus; sacred also to Apollo. *Hebrew*: The vine represents the Israelites as the chosen people; with the fig tree it depicts peace and plenty. *Sumero-Semitic*: Sacred to Tammuz and Baal; attribute of Geshtinanna, goddess of the vine.

Vinegar A jar of vinegar is an eastern symbol of life. In Alchemy antimonial vinegar represents conscience. In Christianity vinegar is a symbol of Christ's passion.

Violet Hidden virtue and beauty; modesty. In Christianity it depicts humility and the humility of the Son of God incarnate; the white violet is an emblem of the Virgin Mary and St Fina. In Greek mythology it is the flower of Io and Ares; violets grew from the blood of Attis.

Viper See SERPENT.

Virgin/Virginity The soul in its state of primordial innocence; inviolable purity; the pure and passive aspect; the inviolability of the sacred. Virginity is often associated with inviolability, as with vestal virgins, when violation was believed to weaken the magic power and hence the social structure. The virgin represents the feminine ideal and is the subject of the struggle, attainment and protection of the male Hero. The Black Virgin symbolizes the darkness of the undifferentiated, the Void, the *prima materia*; the colour black also represents the hidden and secret aspect of knowledge. As the dark, feminine aspect she is, particularly as Kali, Time, the destroyer, the irrational and the pitiless. As undifferentiated substance the Virgin is associated with the Mother, who is the manifest or differentiated universe.

Virgin Mother/Virgin Birth The virgin mother is the *prima materia*, the matrix, virgin earth, the bearer of light, transforming power; she is symbolized by the tree, flowers and fruits, particularly appearing as the corn goddess of the virgin shoots growing in February, the month of the Virgin Mother. Virgin goddesses are not necessarily *virgo intacta*, but 'unwed', i.e. free; their chief symbols are the moon and the serpent. Virgin birth is the union of the divine and the human, heaven and earth, which results in the birth of a god or superior being. It also symbolizes the birth of intelligence, or the higher faculties, in man. The Great Mother, Queen of Heaven, is a virgin and her son is born of the spirit or the will, or she is born of her own son, symbolizing original identity.

The Christian Virgin Mary is associated with a number of symbols: all enclosed places such as the walled garden, sealed fountain, the Ark, the living spring; also with the 'living bush', from the burning bush, a place of divine manifestation; the closed gate and the gate of heaven, the 'light cloud', pure and unattached from which blessing falls in spiritual rain; the untilled soil of Eden; the 'never extinguished lamp'; a bridge leading to heaven, a ladder by which Christ descended to earth; Star of the Sea, and many other attributes taken from the Song of Songs.

Virgo See ZODIAC.

Volute See SPIRAL.

Vulture Ambivalent as maternal solicitude, protection and shelter, and as death-dealing destruction and voracity. All vultures were thought to be female and symbolized the feminine principle with the hawk as the male;

they were said to combine 'the age of China, the sorcery of Egypt and the cunning of Arabia'. As a scavenger the vulture represented purification, a worker for good. In Egypt it represented the Mother Goddess, maternity and love, Isis having assumed the form of a vulture; it is purification and good works. Hathor is sometimes vulture-headed, and the bird is also associated with Mut, as an ideogram of her name, and she wears a vulture headdress, with Neith and Nekhebet. In Graeco-Roman mythology it is sacred to Apollo and is the steed of Cronos/Saturn.

Wall Symbol of the THRESHOLD (q.v.); passage from outer profane space to inner and sacred space; also symbolic of the sacred enclosure, which is both a protection and a limitation. City walls, 'the Great Round', represent the enclosing, sheltering feminine principle of the centre and the womb; round walls are often associated with the protection of the magic circle. The 'Great Wall' divides the cosmos from outer darkness. The wall of flame signifies both initiation and magic protection. The four walls of a rectilinear sacred building face the four celestial aspects. In Hindu sacred architecture the wall denotes stability and comprehensiveness. Wall paintings depict absolute knowledge. The 'wall with no door' shares the symbolism of the strait gate, clashing rocks, etc. See PASSAGE.

Wallet The feminine power of containing and a place of conservation, hence life and health; keeping that which is precious or valued. When it is associated with the bag it also suggests the conserving of personal actions to be held in testimony or on the day of Judgment. The wallet, with the staff, is an attribute of the pilgrim, whose 'scrip' is depicted hanging over the shoulder or from the staff; it is also an emblem of the almoner and merchant and of all messenger gods, particularly Hermes/Mercury, also of Priapus and of the Christian saints Judas, Matthew and Nicholas.

Walnut Shares with all nuts the symbolism of hidden wisdom, also fertility and longevity; the walnut was served at Greek and Roman weddings as such. It is also strength in adversity yet selfishness since nothing grows beneath it. The caryatids are nut nymphs.

Wand Power; conductor of supernatural force; an attribute of all magicians, shamans and medicine men. It is associated symbolically with the mace, sceptre, trident and crozier. The wand of Hypnos had the power of giving sleep and forgetfulness. The Gaelic 'white wand' of magic power was of yew; the Celtic magic wand was hazel.

Wanderer/Wandering The wanderer engages in aimless movement, as opposed to the

The sea-voyage of Dionysos, on a 6th-century BC Greek vase, with the god's **vine** as the mainmast of the ship.

The **vine** as a symbol of the Christian Eucharist carved into the capital of a pillar in the Spanish church of San Pedro de la Nave.

pilgrim who takes a direct and purposeful path. The wanderer is also symbolic of the knight's move in chess, where he is the knight errant or 'wanderer', who sets out on a journey or adventure not knowing where it may lead him. In Buddhism wandering symbolizes *samsara*, the condition of man caught in the cycle of birth and death until enlightenment and liberation are attained and the 'motionless' centre is reached.

War The process of disintegration and reintegration; abolishing disorder and establishing order out of chaos; the conflict between good and evil; the spiritual battle between good and evil in man's own nature; achieving unity. This is the battle, in Hinduism, of Krishna and Arjuna; in Islam it is the Holy War.

Warp See WEAVING.

Water The waters are the source of all potentialities in existence; the source and grave of all things in the universe; the undifferentiated; the unmanifest; the first form of matter, 'the liquid of the whole verification' (Plato). All waters are symbolic of the Great Mother and associated with birth, the feminine principle, the universal womb, the *prima materia*, the waters of fertility and refreshment and the fountain of life. Water is the liquid counterpart of light. The waters are also equated with the continual flux of the manifest world, with unconsciousness, forgetfulness; they always dissolve, abolish, purify, 'wash away' and regenerate; they are associated with the moisture and circulatory movement of blood and the sap of life as opposed to the dryness and static condition of death; they revivify and infuse new life, hence baptism by water or blood in initiatory religions in which the water or blood also washes away the old life and sanctifies the new. Immersion in water not only symbolizes the return to the primordial state of purity, death to the old life and rebirth into the new, but also the immersion of the soul in the manifest world. The waters of the Spring, or Fountain of Life, rise from the root of the Tree of Life in the centre of Paradise. As rain, water is the inseminating power of the sky god, fertility. As dew it is benediction and blessing, spiritual refreshment and the light of dawn.

To dive into the waters is to search for the secret of life, the ultimate mystery. To walk on waters is to transcend the conditions of the phenomenal world; all great Sages walk on waters. Running water is 'water of life' or 'living water'. Crossing waters is to change from one ontological state, or plane, to another; it is also separation as in crossing the sea or river of death, but, as water can be both the power of life and death, so it can also both divide and unite.

Water and fire are the two conflicting elements which will ultimately penetrate each other and unite; they represent all contraries in the elemental world. In a state of conflict they are the heat and moisture necessary for life, but 'burning water' is the union of opposites. Fire and water are also associated with the two great principles, the Sky Father and the Earth Mother, but the Sky Father can also represent the fecundating moisture of rain falling on the earth. Water with wine signifies the blending of the human and divine nature, or divinity mingled invisibly with humanity. In Christian art it depicts Temperance. Surrounding water, e.g. a moat, furrow, gutter, etc., is not merely defensive but the water makes the place within pure and encloses the sacred space. Water with clay is creation and also represents the potter as the shaper of the universe. Deep waters, e.g. seas, lakes, wells, are associated with the realm of the dead, or are the abode of supernatural beings and are closely connected with the Great Mother.

The Lower Waters are chaos, or the ever-changing manifest world, and the Higher Waters are the realm of the unifying waters; these are also connected with the Lesser and Greater Mysteries, and together they complete the One and mark the universal regeneration. Troubled waters depict the vicissitudes, illusion and vanity of life, 'the phantom flux of sensations and ideas'. Running water signifies life, the 'waters of life', the river, spring, or fountain of life, symbolized by the undulating line, or by the spiral or meander.

The waters, like the tree, grove, stone, mountain, can represent the cosmos in its entirety. Symbols of the life-giving, life-destroying, separating and uniting powers of the waters are often composite creatures, monsters or dragons, serpents, the falcon, lion, crocodile and whale, while the nourishing and fertilizing power is depicted in the cow, gazelle and, pre-eminently, the fish. Water is of great significance in magic rites. See also ELEMENTS. *Amerindian*: The flowing power of the Great Spirit. Water sprites are tempters to evil; they are seducers and signify change and decay and both the life-giving and life-taking aspects; they support the earth and are static as opposed to the dynamic sky aspect. *Aztec and Inca*: The waters are primaeval chaos. *Buddhist*: The perpetual flux of the manifest world. 'Crossing the stream' is frequently used as a symbol of passing through the world of illusion to attain enlightenment, Nirvana. Out of the primordial waters rose the stem of the great lotus, the world axis. *Celtic*: The waters, lakes, sacred wells, etc. have magical properties and are the dwelling place of supernatural beings, such as the Lady of the Lake; they also give access to the other world, and the powers of the waters represent other-world wisdom and the foreknowledge of the gods. Tir-nan-og, the Celtic Paradise, the land of the ever-young, is either beyond, or under, the waters or, like the Green Isle, surrounded by water. *Chinese*: The yin, lunar principle, symbolized by the trigram *K'an* (see PA KUA), with fire as the yang and solar power. Water denotes purity, the North region, and its symbol is the Black Tortoise, black being the colour of primordial chaos. *Christian*: The waters of regeneration; renewal; cleansing; sanctification; refreshment; baptism. A spring of water depicts Christ as the fountain of life; the fountain, or living spring also represents the Virgin Mary, who is also the waters as the womb of creation. Water mixed with wine is the passive acted upon by the Spirit, 'born of water and of the Spirit'. The mingling of the human and divine at the Incarnation. According to St Cyprian Christ is the wine and the water is the congregation as the body of Christ. In Christian art Temperance is depicted as water mixed with wine. Dew is benediction. *Egyptian*: Birth; regeneration; growth; the fecundation of the waters of the Nile, symbolized by the God Hapi who pours water from two pots. *Graeco-Roman*: Aphrodite/Venus rose from the waters; Poseidon/Neptune controls the power of the waters. The river Lethe is oblivion and the river Styx is crossed at death. *Hebrew*: 'The waters of the Torah' are the life-giving waters of the sacred law. The spring of water constantly available to the Israelites is wisdom, the Logos, according to Philo. At the creation 'the Spirit of God moved on the face of the waters'. *Hindu*: Agni is born of the waters and the earth and is the pillar supporting all existence. Varuna is controller of the waters. Vishnu sleeps on the waters, on the serpent, and from his navel grows a lotus enthroning Brahma, 'He who walks on the waters'. Lakshmi, 'she of the lotus', is also 'ocean-born'. *Iranian*: Apo, the water, is both solar and lunar power and the primordial ocean. *Islamic*: Water signifies mercy; gnosis; purification; life. As rain, or a spring, water is divine revelation of reality. It is also creation: 'From the water We made every living thing.' 'His throne was upon the waters' (Qoran). *Mandaean*: Water and wine represent the union of the Cosmic Father and Mother. *Maori*: Paradise is under the waters which symbolize primordial perfection. *Scandinavian and Teutonic*: The waters, in which dwelt the serpent of Midgard, encircled the earth, and the underworld was a place of mists. The Yggdrasil had its roots in the underworld and from them sprang the fountain Hvergelmir, the source of the rivers. *Sumero-Semitic*: Apsu, the primordial waters, existed in the beginning, with Tiamat as the sea and chaos. The serpents Lakhmu and Lakhamu were born of the waters. Marduk, as light, created the earth by overcoming Tiamat as chaos and the unmanifest. Ea-Oannes is Lord of the Deeps and 'God with the Streams' who can have a watering pot or water flowing from his arms and hands. *Taoist*: The strength of weakness; the power of adaptation and persistence; the fluidity of life as opposed to the rigidity of death. Water is the expression of the doctrine of *wu-wei* – giving at the point of resistance, it envelops and passes beyond it, ultimately wearing down even the hardest rock.

Waves As water in ceaseless movement, waves

Gustave Doré's lithograph of the **Wandering** Jew shows him passing through a cemetery while his shadow falls in the outline of Christ carrying the cross, the legendary cause of his exile.

A detail from a 12th-century Chinese painting with the **waves** of the sea drawn into a spiral of generation and flux.

denote vicissitude, change, illusion, vanity, agitation.

Wax Pliability; insincerity ('sincere' being 'without wax'). Wax, as fat, contains the life-substance, hence its use in magic and witchcraft to obtain power over people by means of images of wax.

Way See ASCENT; DESCENT; PASSAGE; PILGRIMAGE.

Weapons Power, often supernatural power; dominion; protection, also destruction. The appropriation of weapons symbolizes acquiring the powers of the vanquished. Playing with weapons is the triumph of love over war. Weapons of destruction in the hands of gods also symbolize liberation since they destroy ignorance and man's lower self to liberate consciousness and awareness.

Weaving The Primordial Weaver, the Great Weaver, is the creator of the universe, weaving on the loom of life the fate of all. All goddesses of Fate and Time are spinners and weavers. The weaver is also the Cosmic Spider and the thread of the Great Weaver is the umbilical cord which attaches man to his creator and his own destiny and by which he is woven into the world pattern and fabric.

The warp is the vertical plane, joining all degrees of existence; the qualitative essence of things; the immutable and unchanging; the *forma*; the masculine, active and direct; the light of the sun. The weft, or woof, is the horizontal; nature in time and space; the quantitative, causal and temporal; the variable and contingent; the human state; the *materia*, feminine and passive; the reflected light of the moon. The warp and weft in relationship form a cross at each thread, the crossing symbolizing the union of opposites, the male and female principles united. Alternating colours depict the dualistic but complementary forces of the universe. Night and Day are two sisters weaving the web of Time, the spatio-temporal fabric of cosmological creation. *Buddhist*: Weaving is the fabric of *samsara*, of illusion, of *maya*, of the conditioned, contingent and ever-changing existence. *Chinese*: The alternations of the yin and yang. 'The to-and-fro motion of the shuttle on the cosmic loom' (Chang-hung yang). *Christian*: The warp is the fundamental doctrine of the scriptures, the weft the commentaries on the doctrine. *Egyptian*: Neith, as a weaver of the world, has the spider as an attribute. *Graeco-Roman*: Athene/Minerva is a weaver of the world, as is Harmonia. The Fates, the Moirai, weave the web of destiny. *Hindu*: Brahma, the Supreme Principle, is 'That on which the worlds are woven as warp and weft' (*Upanishads*). Weaving is also the breath of life, and everything in the cosmos is connected by an invisible web. *Scandinavian and Teutonic*: Holda and the Norns are weavers of destiny. The Valkyries weave the web of victory with the warp of the intestines, raised on spears, into which they weave the red weft with arrows. *Sumero-Semitic*: Ishtar and Atargatis are weavers of the fabric of the world and of fate, and cut the thread of life. See also SPIDER; WEB.

Web The web of life, fate and time is woven by divine powers. The spider's web is a cosmic plan, with the radiation of the spatial components from the centre; the radii are the essential, with the circles as the existential and analogous. The spider in the centre of the web can represent the sun surrounded by its rays reaching in all directions, but it is also lunar as depicting the life and death cycle of the manifest world and the wheel of existence, with death at the centre. It also shares the symbolism of the labyrinth as the dangerous journey of the soul. In Hinduism and Buddhism it is the web of *maya*; in Christianity it denotes the snares of the world, of the Devil and human frailty, also the malice of evil-doers.

Weeping Grief; mourning. Ritual weeping was part of the ceremonies of the Dying God. Tammuz was the Lord of Weeping.

Weighing Souls are weighed at death as assessing merit and demerit. In Egyptian symbolism Osiris weighs the heart against the feather of truth. The same symbolism of being weighed in the balance is found in Hinduism and Christianity; in Islam the Archangel Gabriel is the 'soul weigher'.

Well The feminine principle; the womb of the Great Mother; the psyche. Having contact with the underworld, the well often contains magic waters with powers of healing and wish-fulfilling. A closed well depicts virginity. A well fed by a stream is the union of male and female. In Celtic mythology sacred wells give access to the other world and have magical properties and contain the healing waters. In Hebrew symbolism a well of fresh water denotes the Torah. In Christianity it represents salvation and purification. The well, spring, or fountain at the foot of the Tree of Life in Paradise gives rise to the Living Waters and the four rivers of Paradise.

West Autumn; the dying sun; middle age. The western direction is universally associated with dying, 'going west'. *Amerindian*: The home of the Thunderer. *Chinese*: Autumn; dryness; sorrow; the element metal, the colour white and the animal the White Tiger. *Egyptian*: The region of the hawk-headed god who symbolizes the West. *Hebrew*: Depicted by the winged man.

Whale The power of the cosmic waters, hence regeneration, both cosmic and individual; also the engulfing grave. The belly of the whale is both a place of death and rebirth, as in the Old Testament symbol of Jonah; being swallowed by the whale is entry into the darkness of death, and emerging from the whale, after the traditional period of the three days of the dark of the moon, is the emerging from the cavern of initiation into new life, resurrection. In Christianity the whale depicts the Devil, its jaws are the gates of hell and its belly is hell.

Wheat See CORN.

Wheel Solar power, the sun revolving in the heavens; the sun is the centre, with the spokes of the wheel as its rays. The wheel is an attribute of all sun gods and their earthly delegates as sun kings; it symbolizes universal dominion; the cycle of life; rebirth and renewal; nobility; mutability and change in the manifest world; it can also represent the world of manifestation, which is portrayed by the circumference as the limits of manifestation, with the centre, the point quiescent, the 'unmoved mover', as the cosmic centre which produces the radiation and power.

After death the judgement; the **weighing** of the soul. An altar frontal from Catalonia shows a soul being received into heaven in spite of attempts by two devils to falsify the verdict of the balance.

The wheel is also Time, Fate, or *Karma*, 'the wheel of fate that revolves relentlessly and unceasingly'. The circumference divided by radii depicts periods in cyclic manifestation. The rotation of the wheel of life, or ROUND OF EXISTENCE (q.v.), is cyclic rotation, change, becoming, dynamism. The wheel is associated with the lotus as the solar matrix and in particular with the Hindu *chakras*. The chariot wheel denotes sovereignty and authority. The winged wheel indicates extreme swiftness. The wheel-rolling ceremony symbolizes the sun moving across the heavens and is also taken to be a ritual encouragement of the sun at the winter solstice. *Buddhist*: The cosmos; the Wheel of the Law and of Truth; the Round of Existence; the symmetry and completeness of the Dharma; the dynamism of peaceful change; time; destiny; sovereignty. The Wheel of the Law and the Doctrine crushes illusion; its spokes are the spiritual faculties united at the centre, also the rays of light emanating from the Buddha, 'He who turns the Wheel of the Word and the Law', which started to revolve at his teaching at Sarnath. The wheel can be an aniconic representation of Buddha. The golden wheel is spiritual power. It is one of the Seven Treasures of the Universal Ruler and appears on the Footprint of Buddha as such. *Chinese*: As *Buddhist* and *Taoist*. *Christian*: Emblem of SS Catherine, Erasmus, Euphemia, Quentin. *Egyptian*: Man is fashioned on the potter's wheel of Khnemu, the Intellect. *Graeco-Roman*: The six-spoked wheel is an attribute of Zeus/Jupiter as sky god. The solar wheel depicts the sun chariot of Helios/Apollo and the wheel is also an emblem of Dionysos. The wheel of life, according to Proclus, is the cycle of generation, the wheel of Ixion. The wheel also symbolizes fate. *Hindu*: Unending, perfect completion; an attribute of Varuna and, later, of Vishnu. The wheel, stylized as the LOTUS (q.v.), depicts the CHAKRAS (q.v.). There is also the 'Wheel of the

The **wheel** of fortune in a 16th-century Italian fortune-telling book exemplifies the eternal round of good and bad luck, prosperity and poverty, stability and change.

Signs', the Zodiac, representing the revolution of the year, of time and life, all dependent on the sun. *Jain*: The eternally revolving wheel of Time. *Mithraic*: The sun revolving in the heavens. *Sumero-Semitic*: The wheel of life and the wheel of the sun are attributes of the sun gods Asshur, Shamash, Baal and of all war gods. *Taoist*: The phenomenal world. The wheel also represents the Sage, he who has attained the unmoving centre and who can move the wheel without himself being moved, i.e. *wu-wei*, 'non-action'.

Whip/Lash Authority; rule; government; domination; punishment; also a symbol of fecundity as a restorer of virile masculine power. The whip is associated with lightning and some storm gods and is also an attribute of the Great Mother in her terrible aspect. When the whip, or lash, and the crook appear together the whip represents cattle and the crook agriculture. In Egyptian symbolism Menat drives away evil spirits and care with the lash, which then becomes a symbol of happiness; this dual symbolism also obtained in China. The whip is an emblem of Menat, Osiris, Apollo, Dionysos, Cybele and the Erinyes. It is one of the symbols of Christ's passion and his cleansing of the Temple. Whipping was thought to stimulate fertility, not only male virility, and Roman brides were whipped; at the Lupercalia naked young men ran about whipping any women they met to ensure fertility. Fruit and nut trees were often whipped for the same reason.

Whirlpool The SPIRAL (q.v.) as the source of life and natural energy or magic. Hesiod says that Aphrodite rose from the whirling waters. In Hindu, Scandinavian and Gaelic mythology the whirlpool is regarded as a life-giving force. Zuñi myth has whirled water as a producer of life. Whirlpools connected with dragons are a centre of creative power in China and Japan. The Sumerian sea-serpent goddess is associated with the whirlpool. In Hinduism it 'encloses the embryo'.

Whirlwind Circular, solar and creative movement; ascent and descent. Whirlwinds were regarded as a manifestation of energy in nature, rising from a centre of power associated with gods, supernatural forces and entities who travel on whirlwinds, or speak from them. The whirlwind thus becomes a vehicle for the divinity: 'The Lord answered Job out of the whirlwind' (38,1; 40,6), and in Ezekiel's vision. A whirlwind could precede the fertilizing rain and so was connected with rain, wind and thunder deities. In China and Japan it was a thunder symbol associated with the ascending dragon. The Vedic Rudra, god of thunder and whirlwind, has hair braided in a spiral, and Pushan, lord of all things moving, has hair braided like a shell. In Egypt the whirlwind is an aspect of Typhon; in Amerindian symbolism it is the Great Spirit and its power. In witchcraft

it depicts the devil dancing with a witch and witches, wizards and evil spirits ride on whirlwinds. The whirlwind can also carry souls to the next world. It takes on the symbolism of the SPIRAL (q.v.).

White See COLOURS.

Whore In Alchemy the whore is the *prima materia*, the body sunk in darkness, the unredeemed.

Willow An enchanted tree, sacred to the Moon Goddess. The weeping willow depicts mourning, unhappy love, and is funerary. *Buddhist*: Meekness. *Celtic*: Associated with Esus who is portrayed as cutting down a willow tree. *Chinese*: Spring; femininity; meekness; grace and charm; artistic ability; parting. The willow is an attribute of Kwan-yin, who sprinkles the waters of life with a willow branch. A yin, lunar tree. *Christian*: Carried to represent palm on Palm Sunday. *Graeco-Roman*: Sacred to Europa; emblem of Artemis. *Hebrew*: Mourning – weeping by the willows of Babylon in exile. There is a day of willows at the Feast of Tabernacles. *Japanese*: Patience; perseverance. It is especially sacred among the Ainu since the spine of the first man was made of willow. *Sumero-Semitic*: An emblem of Tammuz; triumph; rejoicing; happiness. The willow is the Cosmic Tree of Accadia and was sacred to the Accadian Zeus. The withy is an emblem of Artemis and childbirth. *Taoist*: Strength in weakness; contrasted with the pine or oak, which resists the storm and is broken by it, the willow bends, gives way, springs back and survives.

Wind The Spirit; the vital breath of the universe; the power of the spirit in sustaining life and holding it together, hence the symbolic association of wind with cords, ropes, threads, etc. 'The rope of the wind ... The thread is the same as the wind' (*Upanishads*). The wind is also the intangible; transient; insubstantial; elusive. Winds are messengers of the gods and can indicate the presence of divinity, especially WHIRLWIND (q.v.). Wind and fire together represent the mountain and volcanic gods. In China *feng shui*, 'wind and water', is the science of finding favourable aspects. The Four Winds, associated with Aeon, are usually depicted as children, or childrens' heads, emerging from clouds, or as beardless men blowing or blowing horns. Wind is sometimes symbolized by wings or by the fan. Aeolus is god of winds and all instruments producing sound by wind.

Windmill Takes on WIND and AIR symbolism (q.v.); also represents harvesting and fertility. With the balance, it can be a symbol of Temperance in Christian iconography.

Wine The liquid of life; revelation; truth, *in vino veritas*; vitality; but it is also the blood of death

---

in sacrifice. Wine and blood are interchangeable symbols, except in Zoroastrianism. Wine can also be translated into fire. Wine, in sacraments, is wisdom drunk from the cup offered to the deity, or from the Grail, or the wine becomes the blood of the divinity, imparting spiritual or vital power to the initiate, or serving as a memorial to a sacrifice by the deity. Corn and wine together are both solar and divine nature; they also signify warmth and youth.

Wine and water are solar and lunar, fire and water, the two great powers of the universe; they also represent the blending of the divine and human natures, or divinity invisibly mingled with humanity. Wine and bread are the balanced product of man's work and skills in agriculture; also the masculine wine and feminine bread are the liquid and solid united, divinity and man united; the wine is the divine ecstasy and the bread the visible manifestation of the spirit which dies and rises again. Poured on the ground, wine is a libation to chthonic powers, or to the dead at funerary rites. Wine is often drunk ritually at weddings as a symbol of fertility.

In classical mythology wine is chiefly associated with Dionysos/Bacchus. Its powers of intoxication were regarded as manifesting divine possession. In Christianity the wine and bread of the sacrament symbolize the dual nature of Christ and are a memorial to his sacrifice. In Islam wine is the drink of the elect in Paradise, as contrasted with water for the faithful.

Wings Wings are almost entirely exclusive to Western and Middle East representations of divinities and supernatural beings. Far Eastern and Indian divine or supernatural beings, except for the Garuda, Cosmic Horse and Winged Dragon, do not share in wing symbolism. Wings are solar and depict divinity; spiritual nature; the moving, protecting and all-pervading power of the deity; the power to transcend the mundane world; the never-weary; the ubiquitous; the air; wind; spontaneous movement; the flight of time; the flight of thought; volition; mind; freedom; victory; swiftness.

Wings are attributes of swift messenger gods and denote the power of communication between gods and men. Outspread wings are divine protection, or the shrouding of the heavens from the fierce heat of the sun. The 'shadow of wings' is protection and trust. The winged sun, or DISK (q.v.), is the untiring journey of the sun across the firmament; the triumph of light over darkness; power from heaven; divinity. Winged deities are sun gods or gods of the Empyrean; but they are ambivalent as there are winged powers of evil and winged devils. Winged cap, sandals and caduceus indicate a messenger of the gods. The winged horse is solar and is ridden by heroes, or it is the Cosmic Horse. *Alchemic*: Absence of wings

On this Korean bottle (11th–13th centuries) the **willow** stands for the feminine virtue of patience in adversity. It is also the tree of Kwan-yin, goddess of mercy.

The outer wall of an Armenian church decorated with a seraph whose many-eyed six **wings** are a symbol of its supreme rank in the hierarchy of angels.

denotes the 'firm' nature of sulphur, wings depict the 'volatile' nature of quicksilver. *Buddhist*: Two wings represent wisdom and method. *Chinese*: The winged dragon is the celestial power, vital spirit (see DRAGON). The Cosmic Horse is winged and yang. Two birds together with only one wing each depict indissoluble unity, fidelity and a pair of lovers. *Christian*: Angels are winged as divine messengers or as having divine qualities. The Devil is often portrayed as having bat's wings. *Egyptian*: Neith is sometimes winged, but wings are rare in Egyptian iconography. *Graeco-Roman*: The four wings of Cronos, as the flight of time, are depicted as two spread and two resting, symbolizing perpetual movement and vigilance: 'rest in flight and flying while at rest'. Wings are also an attribute of Hypnos, who fanned people to sleep with his dark wings. Hermes/Mercury has the winged cap, sandals and caduceus of the messenger of the gods. Iris has wings as a messenger of Hera/Juno. The Roman Victory is winged. *Hebrew*: Archangels and angels, seraphim and cherubim, are winged. *Hindu*: The GARUDA (q.v.) is winged. *Iranian*: The winged disk is a symbol of Ahura Mazda or Ormuzd as light. *Islamic*: Eight angels support the throne which encompasses the world. *Mithraic*: The four winds and four seasons are represented by wings. *Shamanistic*: The winged horse is a psychopomp. Birds' wings, or feathered robes, symbolize communion between this world and the spirit world. *Sumero-Semitic*: The winged disk is a symbol, or direct representation, of the solar gods Shamash and Asshur. Four wings denote the four winds and seasons. The Semitic El has six wings or four wings, two at rest and two flying, having the same symbolism of vigilance and 'flying while resting and resting while flying' as Cronos.

Winnowing Separation; the sifting of the good from the bad. The mystic winnowing fan is associated with fertility rites.

Witch-Hazel Shares the symbolism of HAZEL (q.v.), but is also protection against fairies, witches and evil spirits. It is used in divination.

Wolf The earth; evil; the devouring; fierceness. Wolves and ravens are often familiars of primitive gods of the dead. *Alchemic*: The wolf, with the dog, is the dual nature of Mercurius, the philosophical mercury, the *nous*. *Aztec*: The howling wolf is the God of Dance. *Celtic*: A wolf swallows the sun, the Sky Father, at night. *Chinese*: Rapaciousness; cupidity. *Christian*: Evil; the Devil, the spoiler of the flock; the stiff-necked people (the wolf was believed to be unable to turn its neck); cruelty; craftiness; heresy. Emblem of St Francis of Assisi who tamed the wolf Gubbio. *Egyptian*: Attribute of Khenti Amenti and Upuaut. *Graeco-Roman*: Sacred to Ares/Mars as fierceness; also sacred to Apollo and Silvanus. A wolf nourished Romulus and Remus and is frequently depicted in

Roman art; it also denotes valour. *Hebrew*: Bloodthirstiness; cruelty; the persecuting spirit (Gen. 49, 17). *Hindu*: The Asvins rescue the quail of day from the wolf of night. *Scandinavian and Teutonic*: A bringer of victory; ridden by Odin/Woden. Fenris, the cosmic wolf, was a bringer of evil. *Witchcraft*: A mount of witches and warlocks; a form assumed as the werewolf.

Woman The Great Mother, the Great Goddess, the feminine principle symbolized by the moon, the earth and the waters; the instinctual powers as opposed to the masculine rational order. It is a highly complex symbolism as the Great Mother can be either beneficent and protective or malefic and destructive; she is both the pure spiritual guide and the siren and seducer, the virgin Queen of Heaven and the harpy and harlot, supreme wisdom and abysmal folly – the total complexity of nature.

The woman is symbolized by all that is lunar, receptive, protective, nourishing, passive, hollow or to be entered, sinuous, cavernous, diamond- or oval-shaped; the cave, walled garden, well, door, gate, cup, furrow, sheath, shield; also anything connected with the waters, the ship, shell, fish, pearl. The crescent moon, the reflected light of the moon, and the star are pre-eminently her attributes. In Chinese symbolism she is the yin; in Hinduism and Buddhism the shakti or Prakriti. In Indian art a beautiful woman depicts the beneficent aspect of Maya, the Great Mother, while the Black Kali, or Durga, represents the reverse. In Christian art the Church, the 'bride of Christ', is depicted as a woman holding a cross or chalice, or wearing a crown. A woman with veiled, or bandaged, eyes denoted the Jewish Synagogue. Figures of women were used to symbolize the virtues and vices and the seasons.

Womb The matrix; the Great Mother, the Earth Mother, hence 'the womb of the earth', with the cave as its chief symbol, and Dying Gods being born in a cave as emerging from the womb of the earth. The womb is also the unmanifest; the totality of all possibilities; plenitude. It is symbolized by the well and all waters and all that is enclosing, such as city walls, caskets, etc. In Alchemy the womb represents a mine, with the ores as the embryo; minerals are born of the earth, and man's function is to aid nature and hasten the birth.

Wood The wholeness of the primordial, paradisal state; that which gives shelter at birth and death in the cradle and the coffin; it also forms the marriage bed, the gallows cross and the ship of the dead, the lunar barque. Wood is the *prima materia* of the East, hence Christ as a carpenter; the carpenter uses tools symbolic of the divine power of bringing order out of chaos. In Hindu and Tibetan symbolism it is the *prima materia* out of which all things were shaped. 'Brahman was the wood, Brahman the tree from which they shaped heaven and earth' (*Taittiriya*

Brahmana). In Chinese symbolism wood represents Spring, the East and the colour blue or green. See also FOREST.

Woodpecker A prophetic bird; magic power; a guardian of kings and trees. In Graeco-Roman mythology it is sacred to Zeus/Jupiter, Ares/Mars, Silvanus, Tiora and Triptolemos; it guarded Romulus and Remus. The woodpecker is the Aryan bird of the storm cloud. In Christian symbolism it is the Devil and heresy undermining belief and human nature. To the proto-historic Amerindians it was a bird of war.

Word The Word, or Logos, is the sacred sound, the first element in the process of manifestation. Speech has creative force; the Central American Quetzalcoatl and Hurakan created the world by uttering the word 'Earth'. A Saviour is always the embodiment of the Word. In Hinduism and Buddhism the Word as the Dharma is the ineffable. See also OM.

Worm Death; dissolution; the earth. The serpent is sometimes called the 'great worm'.

Wormwood Bitterness; distress; torment; sacred to Ares/Mars.

Wreath Ambivalent as glory, victory, supremacy, dedication, holiness, and so placed on a sacred or venerated object, and as the *corona convivialis* denoting happiness, a happy fate and good luck, but also as the *corona funebris*, signifying death, and mourning and placed on a sacrifice. The bridal wreath represents the flowers of virginity, but also takes on the symbolism of the funeral wreath as dying to the old life and beginning the new. A wreath round a pillar indicates the course of the heavenly bodies round the sun. *Arabic*: A wreath of orange-blossom is fertility and marriage and worn by brides. *Chinese*: An olive wreath denotes literary merit and success. *Graeco-Roman*: A wreath of flowers is the diadem of Flora; of hawthorn or verbena, marriage; of oak leaves, the reward for saving life; a wreath of grass was awarded to a Roman military hero or saviour. Wreaths were awarded to the victors at the games: Olympian, wild olives; Isthmian, pine; Pythian, laurel; Nemean, parsley. The fennel wreath was worn at the rites of Sabazios. The Roman Emperor wore a wreath of roses.

Wren 'The little King', in the West it is often called the King of Birds; it can take the place of the dove as representing Spirit, but it can also denote a witch, in which case it becomes malefic. The wren is sacred to the Greek Triptolemos and the Celtic Taliesen. In Scotland it is the Lady of Heaven's Hen. It was extremely unlucky to kill a wren, but in England and France it was hunted at Christmas time, killed, hung on a pole, and taken round in procession and finally buried in a churchyard as associated with the death of the old year.

The twin **wolves** on a purse from the 7th-century ship burial at Sutton Hoo are protective animals of victorious magic.

An 11th-century American Indian shell disk is decorated with whirling **woodpeckers**, fierce symbols of war, depradation and sudden attack.

X A symbol of INVERSION (q.v.): 'Every true analogy must be applied inversely.' As the Roman number ten it takes on the perfection and completion of that number and, as the crux decussata, or cross saltire, it is in itself the perfect figure of completion and balance. The Romans used it as a boundary cross, hence it can symbolize a barrier. In Christianity it is the cross of St Andrew. It also shares the entire symbolism of the CROSS (q.v.).

Y As the fork, or furka, cross, Y depicts the figure of man; it was said by Pythagoras to be the emblem of human life, the foot being the innocence of the infant and the dividing arms the choice of the ways of good and evil in adult life; they are also the left and right hand paths, virtue and vice, the dividing ways and crossroads presided over by gods such as Ganesha and Janus. In Alchemy it represents the Rebis, the Androgyne. In Christianity it appears on vestments as the cross, and is also known as the Thieves of Calvary's cross.

Yarrow A specific against witchcraft. The Chinese sticks used in the *I Ching* guidance and divination are of yarrow, milfoil.

Year The Great Year represents a cycle of creation and destruction in the universe, or *aiones* of the Gnostics. It is a time of rebirth at which the world returns to the primordial state, an apocatastasis, the return of the Golden Age. See also NUMBERS, *Fifty*.

Yeast Fermentation, hence love. A specific against the plague.

Yellow See COLOURS.

Yew Funerary; mourning; sadness; but also a Celtic and Christian symbol of immortality. It is a Celtic magic wood and the White Wand was traditionally of yew.

Yggdrasil The Scandinavian Cosmic Tree, the Mighty Ash, the Ever Green, the fountain of life, eternal life and immortality. The gods met in council beneath its branches. Its roots were in the depth of the underworld, its trunk passed vertically through the waves, the earth and the world of men, thus uniting the three realms. The branches were the heavens and overshadowed Valhalla. From the roct rose the fountain Hvergelmir, the source of the rivers, the earthly time-stream. The root was constantly attacked by Nidhogg, the Dread Biter, representing the malevolent forces of the universe. Odin's charger browsed on the leaves, and in the boughs the eagle and serpent, as light and darkness, were in perpetual conflict. The squirrel, a mischief-maker, constantly created strife between the two powers. The four stags in the branches, as the four winds, also browsed on the leaves which were always renewed and the foliage was always green. The solar cock, as vigilance, was sometimes depicted on the branches. Odin sacrificed himself and hung for nine nights from the Yggdrasil: a rejuvenation sacrifice symbol.

Yin-yang The yin, depicted by the broken line — —, is the feminine principle and the yang, the unbroken line ——, is the masculine; together they symbolize all complementary opposites in the dualistic universe, in powers, qualities, human, animal and plant life. The yin must always come before the yang since it symbolizes primordial darkness before the yang light of creation.

The yin is also the primaeval waters, the passive, feminine, instinctive and intuitional nature, the soul, depth, contraction, the negative, the soft and pliable; it is symbolized by all that is dark and belonging to the humid principle, such as the colour black, the earth, the valley, trees, nocturnal animals and creatures that live in the waters or damp places and by most flowers.

The yang is the active principle, the spirit, rationalism, height, expansion, the positive, the hard and unyielding, and is depicted by all that is light, dry and high, such as the mountain, the heavens, all solar animals and birds. The fabulous animals, the dragon, phoenix and *ky-lin*, are all capable of embodying both the yin and yang qualities and signify the perfect interplay of the two powers or 'essences' in unity; this also applies to the lotus among flowers.

The yin-yang symbol, the *Ta ki*, depicts the perfect balance of the two great forces in the universe; each has within it the embryo of the other power, implying that there is no exclusively masculine or feminine nature, but that each contains the germ of the other and there is perpetual alternation. The two powers are contained within the circle of cyclic revolution and dynamism, of the totality. The whole forms the Cosmic Egg, the primordial Androgyne, the perfection of balance and harmony, the pure essence which is neither yet both. The two forces are held together in tension, but not in antagonism, as mutually interdependent partners; one in essence but two in manifestation.

Yoke Union; control; balance; discipline; obedience; slavery; humiliation; toil; patience. In Hinduism it is the Yoga, the origin of the word 'yoke', as the union of the human soul with the One, the final achievement of harmony and unity of being. In Christianity the yoke depicts the law of Christ. As associated with the ox it can represent sacrifice; agriculture and fertility.

Yoni Symbolized by U, it is the feminine, receptive, passive principle, with the linga as the masculine and active. It is also symbolized by all that is hollow, receptive or concave.

Yule From the Gallic 'gule', a wheel, Yule represents the wheel of the turning of the sun at the winter solstice, the death of the old year and birth of the new. Like the Saturnalia, it is the return of chaos and primordial darkness before the new year can be created and reborn. The dead return during the twelve nights of chaos, since the barriers between the worlds are down. Each of the twelve days forecasts the weather for the corresponding month of the coming year. It is also the festival of the Dying God, whose birthday is December 25, and who, as Tammuz, Attis and Dionysos, is symbolized by the aniconic log, ritually burned at the end of the old year, signifying the death of Winter and the rebirth of the power of the sun; the fire drives out death and, with its creative force, rekindles the solar power; it also burns out the old life of each person and creates the new, giving a fresh start at the new year; the ashes are scattered on the soil from which new life and the Spring will emerge. The Yule Log is of oak, the Cosmic Tree of the Druids. In other rituals of the Dying God it is the pine of Attis, Dionysos and Woden. The ivy wound round the log is the crown of Dionysos and the 'plant of Osiris'. Lights and luminous balls on the tree are the sun, moon and stars in the branches of the Cosmic Tree, or the lights can represent souls at the festivals of the dead. The tree of Attis and Dionysos was hung with presents as offerings to the gods, but the fir tree of Woden bestowed gifts on those who honoured his sacred tree.

December 25, the winter solstice, with the rebirth of the sun, has always been a significant celebration in solar worship. It was the *Dies natalis solis invicti* (Birthday of the Unconquered Sun) of Mithraism, when the powers of light triumphed over darkness. In Egypt the sun god was then reborn as Horus to Isis; in Alexandria it was also the birth of Osiris. In Babylon the constellation Virgo, sign of the Virgin Mother Goddess, gave birth to the sun. In Scandinavian myth Baldur appeared on the eve of December 25. The Christian celebration of midnight mass, centred round the crib, has lighted candles for Mary, the 'light-bearer'. The ancient ritual announcement, 'The Virgin has brought forth, light increases', has been heard in many places and many ages.

Yurt Like the Red Indian tepee, or any nomadic tent, the Mongolian yurt is a symbol of the cosmos in miniature. The floor is its base, with the central, rectangular sacred hearth arranged to represent the earth and the elements. The sides and the domed-shaped roof depict the sky and the central smoke-hole in the dome is the Sun Door and Gate of Heaven, symbolized by four, or eight, cross bracings in the wooden framework inside the hole.

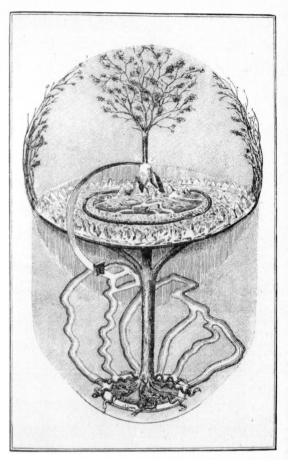

Yggdrasil, the world tree, grows from the nether world through the world of men and into the realm of the gods, uniting all three.

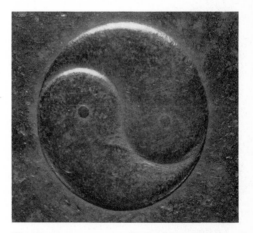

The **yin-yang**, supreme and indivisible symbol of integrity and the creative complementarity of opposites in all the universe, decorates a 17th-century Chinese ink tablet.

Z See ZIG-ZAG.

Zenith The peak; the highest; symbolized by all peaks, e.g. mountains, pyramids, spires, stupas, pillars and the central opening towards the sky in temples, sacred lodges, tepees, etc.

Zero See NUMBERS.

Ziggurat The Sumerian temple was built to symbolize the Sacred Mountain, dwelling place of divinity; it was a cosmic axis, a vertical bond between heaven and earth and the earth and the underworld and a horizontal bond between the lands. Built on seven levels, it represented the seven heavens and planes of existence, the seven planets and seven stages having seven metals and colours: 1. black as Saturn, lead; 2. red-brown, Jupiter, tin; 3. rose-red, Mars, iron; 4. gold, the Sun, gold; 5. white-gold, Venus, copper; 6. dark-blue, Mercury, quicksilver; 7. silver, the Moon, silver.

Zig-Zag Symbolizes lightning, fire from lightning and fecundity. It is an attribute of all storm gods. The Babylonian Adad holds a zig-zag or a bunch of three flames in his hand. The zig-zag shares the symbolism of the trident and the thunderbolt.

Zodiac A symbol of relationship in the universe, and of cyclic and seasonal transformation; it is the Wheel of Life; an archetype; the harmony of the Many and the One; the fall into the phenomenal world and salvation from it. Plato calls the twelve signs the 'gates of heaven'. Ptolemy says that the alternate signs are masculine and feminine, 'as the day is followed by the night, and as the male is coupled with the female', solar and lunar. The masculine signs are Aries, Gemini, Leo, Libra, Sagittarius, Aquarius, and the feminine are Taurus, Cancer, Virgo, Scorpio, Capricorn, Pisces.

Aries: Cardinal-fiery. The Ram, creative heat, the renewal of solar energy; the First Cause, the undifferentiated, the dawn. Its sphere of influence is the head; its flower the sage and water-milfoil; its stones the bloodstone as courage, endurance, longevity, wealth and the diamond as purity, fortitude, invincibility, strength, fearlessness.

Taurus: Fixed-earth. The Bull, solar, the creative resurgence of Spring, energy, fecundation, 'the bull of heaven'. It influences the throat; flowers are vervain and clover; stones, the sapphire as peace, illumination, divine favour, happiness, and the turquoise as courage and success.

Gemini: Mutable-air. The Twins, often one black, one white, as dualism, the negative and positive and all opposites, division, life and death, the dual nature of man, the necessary dualism inherent in manifestation. Influence the shoulders and arms; flowers are the wild gladiolus and holy vervain; the stone, agate as vigour, strength and success.

Cancer: Cardinal-water. A Crab, the moon, the waters, 'the gate from the Milky Way to manifestation' (Porphyry), the soul entering the world. It is the 'gate of men', the *Janua inferni* of the summer solstice and the declining power of the sun. It influences the chest and stomach; the flower is comfrey; stones, the moonstone as lunar, inspiration and love, and the pearl as power of the waters, purity and tears, the emerald as constancy and domestic happiness.

Leo: Fixed-fire. The Lion, the sun, that 'fierce lion', the all-seeing one, the will, the emotions, domination, creativity, magnanimity. Influences the heart, lungs and liver; the flower, cyclamen; stones, the topaz as solar and tourmaline as inspiration and friendship, and the sardonyx as brightness and courage.

Virgo: Mutable-earth. The Female, the Celestial Virgin, wisdom, associated with the Virgin Mother, the 'Spike of Corn' and is sometimes depicted as a woman holding an ear of corn, sometimes as a mermaid with a child in her arms. Influences the stomach and intestines; flower, calaminth; stones, the cornelian as concord and health, and jade as excellence, purity.

Libra: Cardinal-air. The Scales, or a woman holding the balance, equilibrium between the two natures of man, the natural and the spiritual. Influences the backbone and marrow; flower, the needle-plant or scorpion-tail; stones, the opal as foresight and friendship, and the lapis lazuli as courage, success, divine favour.

Scorpio: Fixed-water. The Scorpion, but can also be symbolized by the Eagle, Phoenix or Serpent, all of which are death and resurrection, death, mutilation and regeneration, symbols. Influences the kidneys and genitals; flower, artemisia and hound's-tongue; stones, carbuncle as prosperity and success, but also bloodshed, and the beryl as hope, youth and married love.

Sagittarius: Mutable-fire. The Archer, Centaur, Arrow. The whole man with his animal and spiritual nature. The bow and arrow symbolize power, its direction and control; the upward angle of the aim at 45° represents the perfect use of the force employed. Influences the thighs; flower, pimpernel; stone, the topaz as sagacity, divine favour, faithfulness, strength.

Capricorn: Cardinal-earth. The Goat, the Sea-goat of Ea and Varuna as the life-principle of the waters; can also be depicted as the crocodile, dolphin, or animals with fish-bodies, or as a sea-serpent. As half-goat, half-fish it is the dual nature of land and sea, height and depth; it

The snake-encircled body of Mithra, in this relief from Modena, is surrounded by the twelve signs of the **zodiac**, reading counter-clockwise from Taurus, the Bull.

is the winter solstice and the 'gate of the gods', the *Janua coeli*, the ascending power of the sun. It influences the knees; flower, sorrel and 'stinking tuscan' (smells like a goat); stones, jet, as sacred to Cybele and safe travel, also the black onyx as inspiration, strength, and the ruby as invulnerability and longevity.

Aquarius: Fixed-air. A figure pouring out water from an amphora, the Waterer, the waters of the creation of the world and of its destruction, cyclic death and renewal. Influences the legs; flower, buttercup, fennel and edderwort; stones, the garnet as health and devotion, and the zircon as wisdom and honour.

Pisces: Mutable-water. The Fishes, the two fishes pointing in opposite directions depict going and coming, past and future, the end of a cycle and the beginning of a new. Influences the legs; flower, birthwort and aristolochia; stone, amethyst as piety, resignation, humility.

The Arabian Zodiac is depicted as a fruit tree of twelve branches on which the stars are the fruits. The Egyptian Denderah has symbols of the northern constellations at the centre, surrounded by the signs of the Zodiac, but with Capricorn depicted as a goat with a fish's tail and the Scarabaeus replaces Cancer. The decantes support the outer circle on their raised arms and hands.

The Hindu Zodiac, the Wheel of the Signs, or the *Rasi chakra*, or evolutionary dance, has the sun chariot at the centre, surrounded by the planetary deities as Jupiter – Rahu and Ketu the dragon's head and tail; Mercury – the Buddha; Mars – Chandra or the moon; Saturn and Venus are depicted as Indian figures; the outer circle has the signs in the Egyptian order.

The Inca Zodiac agrees largely with the signs now in use; the inner circle has the signs for the twenty weekday names.

The Chinese Zodiac has the signs of the Twelve Terrestrial Branches (*chih*) as: the Rat, Ox, Tiger, Hare, Dragon, Snake, Horse, Goat, Monkey, Cock, Dog, Boar. These are the Beasts of the Constellations and are under the branches of the Year Tree; there are six wild and six domestic animals represented, six yin and six yang.

The Islamic Zodiac has six 'northern' (wet) and six 'southern' (dry) signs: Aries, Leo, Sagittarius – fire, hot, dry, East; Taurus, Virgo, Capricornus – earth, cold, dry, South; Gemini, Libra, Aquarius – air, hot, wet, West; Cancer, Scorpio, Pisces – water, cold, wet, North.

A 16th-century Iranian plate decorated with the signs of the **zodiac**; note how Virgo incorporates the eyes of the moon, female, ever-watchful.

❦

Glossary
Bibliography

❦

Glossary

alter ego, second self.

anima mundi, the world soul; the *materia* of the soul.

apocatastasis, the final restoration of the paradisal state; the Kingdom of God re-established on earth.

apotropaic, having the power of averting evil.

aqua vitae, the water of life; the quicksilver of the alchemist.

axis mundi, the world axis.

chthonic, pertaining to the underworld.

coincidentia oppositorum, the reconciliation of contraries; the identification of opposites.

corona convivialis, the festal crown, denoting happiness; *corona funebris*, the funeral crown, signifying death; *corona radiata*, the rayed crown or halo.

demiurge, in Platonic philosophy the creator of the world and man; in Gnosticism a creator below the Supreme God, sometimes suggested as imperfect and therefore letting in evil.

Dharma, The Law; the Truth.

dhyana, meditation; contemplation; an aspect of intellectual yoga.

epheboi, youths entering on initiation into adult society or cults.

fata morgana, a mirage; the deceptive.

femina alba, woman; the white, lunar, feminine principle; the white lily, the second stage of the Great Work in Alchemy.

feng shui, literally 'wind and water', the Chinese science of propitious aspects.

forma, the essential form or prototype.

gammadion, a figure comprising four capital Greek gammas set at right angles, thus forming a cross, fylfot or swastika.

hieros gamos, the sacred marriage between Sun and Moon, Priest and Priestess, King and Queen, etc., who unite to die and become the perfect androgyne.

homophone, having the same sound.

Iesous Hominum Salvator, Jesus Saviour of Men.

ignes fatui, will-o'-the wisps; marsh gas fires; the deceptive and falsely alluring.

imago mundi, world image.

in hac salus, literally, 'herein [find] well-being', or, probably, 'spiritual health'.

in hoc signo, 'in this sign', implying under the power of.

karma, literally, 'action'; in general the law that a given action produces a given result; the inescapable law of responsibility for one's actions and reaping their effects.

lapis exilis, the stone whose power restored life and conferred perpetual youth.

magnum opus, the Great Work, especially of Alchemy.

Manitou or Manito, the Universal Spirit among American Indians. The Supreme Deity or supernatural power among the Algonquins, Sioux and Iroquois.

massa confusa, the *prima materia*, the primordial chaotic state to be transformed in the Great Work.

maya, the illusion, through ignorance, that the world is a reality in itself.

memento mori, a reminder of the inevitability of death.

multum in parvo, literally, 'much in little'.

nigredo, the darkness of initiatory death; dissolution, the first stage of the Great Work in Alchemy.

nous, the intellect; the mind.

paradigm, an example; a pattern.

parthenogenic, self-reproducing; reproduction without sexual union.

petra genetrix, literally 'the mother rock'; it gives rise to the perfect androgyne.

pleroma, fullness, abundance; in Gnosticism the Divine Being and all aeons which emanate from it.

prima materia, Nature in her primordial state or substance; the primary substance of the world, containing the potentiality of all forms.

psychopomp, a conductor of souls to the place of the dead.

pudenda mulieris, the external female genital organs.

pura arbor, literally the 'essential or unspoiled tree', symbolizing virginity.

quinta essentia, Mercury in Alchemy; the central point of a cross or circle; the fifth point; the common ground of all four elements.

regressus ad uterum, regression to the pre-natal state.

samsara, the experiences of the world as the changing, contingent and unreal; the vicious circle of birth and death.

sistrum, a kind of rattle formed of metal rings and rods, used in connection with the worship of Isis in ancient Egypt.

sol invictus, literally, 'undefeated sun'; the rising power of the spring sun; *sol niger*, the 'black' sun, as opposed to the 'white' sun; symbolizes chthonic powers and the serpent.

solve et coagula, the two-way action, in Alchemy, of dissolution and coagulation, to divide and unite, dissolving the imperfect and crystallizing it in a newer and nobler form.

spiritus mundi, the world spirit; the vital and universal spirit.

sub specie aeternitatis, (see) from the viewpoint of the eternal.

sutras, Buddhist and Jain religious writings or scriptures, expressed in aphoristic style.

tantras, Hindu and Buddhist religious writings, instructing in the aim and method of union with the Divine.

tellus mater, the Earth Mother.

theriomorphism, taking the form of an animal.

Troy, It is suggested that Troy, Troja or Troia may be derived from the Celtic root *tro*, to turn – i.e. rapid revolution, to dance through a maze. Troy has also been compared with the Babylonian *tirani*, intestines.

vas, the vase; the matrix or uterus from which the philosophers' stone is born.

vesica piscis, an upright oval or almond-shape, often surrounding a sacred figure.

yuga, a phase of cyclic development; there are four yugas, the four ages of Gold, Silver, Bronze, Iron.

Bibliography

ABBOTT, J. *The Keys of Power: A Study in Indian Ritual and Belief*, 1932.

ALLCROFT, A. H. *The Circle and the Cross*, 1927.

ALLEN, Grant. *The Evolution of the Idea of God*, 1904

ALLEN, M. R. *Japanese Art Motives*, 1917.

ALLENDRY, René Félix. *Le Symbolisme des nombres*, 1948.

ALVIELLA, Goblet d'. *The Migration of Symbols*, 1894.

ANDRAE, W. *Die ionische Säule, Bauform oder Symbol?*, 1933.

APULEIUS. *The Golden Ass.*

Archaeologia, or Miscellaneous Tracts relating to Antiquity. Society of Antiquaries of London, XLVIII.

ASHE, Geoffrey. *All About King Arthur*, 1957. *The Quest of Arthur's Britain*, 1957. *From Caesar to Arthur*, 1960. *The Virgin*, 1976.

AYNSLEY, H. Murray. *Symbolism of East and West*, 1900.

BACHOFFEN, J. J. *Mutterrecht und Urreligion.* 1927.

BAILEY, H. *The Lost Language of Symbolism*, 1912.

BAKHTIAR, Laleh. *Sufi*, 1976.

BALL, Katherine. *Decorative Motives in Oriental Art*, 1927.

BANERJEE, P. *The Development of Hindu Iconography*, 1956.

BASHAM, A. L. *The Wonder that was India*, 1971.

BAYNES, C. F. *Change. Eight Lectures on the I Ching*, 1964.

BENTHALL, J., and POLHEMUS, T. (eds). *The Body as a Medium of Expression*, 1975.

BERNOULLI, Rudolf. Spiritual Development as Reflected in Alchemy, *Eranos Year Book*, 1960.

BEVAN, Edwyn. *Symbolism and Belief*, 1938.

BHARATI, Agehananda (Leopold Fischer). *The Tantric Tradition*, 1961.

BLACK ELK. See Neihardt, G. J.

BLINKENBERG, C. *The Thunder-weapon in Religions and Folklore*, 1911.

BLOUNT, G. *The Science of Symbols*, 1905.

BORD, Janet. *Mazes and Labyrinths of the World*, 1976.

BOWRA, C. M. .*The Heritage of Symbolism*, 1943. *The Greek Experience*, 1957.

BRANDON, S. G. F. *Religion in Ancient History*, 1973.

BRANSTON, Brian. *Gods of the North*, 1955. *The Lost Gods of England*, 1974.

BREASTED, James Henry. *Development of Religion and Thought in Ancient Egypt*, 1912.

BRELICH, A. *Vesta*, 1949.

BRIFFAULT, R. *The Mothers*, 1927.

BROMWICH, Rachael. *The Welsh Triads*, 1961.

BROWN, Joseph Epes. *The Sacred Pipe*, 1953. 'The Persistence of Essential Values Among North American Plains Indians', *Studies in Comparative Religion*, Autumn, 1969. 'The Unlikely Associates', *Studies in Comparative Religion*, Summer, 1970.

BROWN, Robert. 'On the Origin of the Signs of the Zodiac', *Archaeologia*, XLVII, 1883. 'Remarks on the Gryphon, Heraldic and Mythological', *Archaeologia*, XLVIII, 1885.

BUDGE, E. A. Wallis, *The Divine Origin of the Cult of the Herbalist*, 1928. *Amulets and Talismans*, 1930. *From Fetish to God in Ancient Egypt*, 1934.

BURCHARDT, Titus. 'Le Symbolisme du jeu des échecs', *Etudes Traditionelles*, Oct.–Nov. 1954. *Sacred Art in East and West*, 1967. *Alchemy*, 1967. 'The Heavenly Jerusalem and the Paradise of Vaikuntha', *Studies in Comparative Religion*, Winter, 1970.

BURLAND, Cottie Arthur. *North American Indian Mythology*, 1968.

BURROWS, Eric. 'Some Cosmological Patterns in Babylonian Religion', *The Labyrinth* (Ed. S. H. Hooke), 1935.

CAMMANN, Schuyler. 'Symbolism of the Cloud Collar Motif', *Art Bulletin of the College Art Association of America*, XXXIII, 1.

CAMPBELL, John Francis. *The Celtic Dragon Myth*, 1911.

CAMPBELL, Joseph. *The Hero with a Thousand Faces*, 1969.

CARPENTER, Edward. *Pagan and Christian Creeds. Their Origin and Meaning*, 1920.

CARR, H. G. *Flags of the World*, 1969.

CARUS, Paul. *Chinese Thought*, 1907.

CASE, P. F. *The Tarot*, 1947.

CHADWICK, Nora. *Celtic Britain*, 1964.

CHAMBERS, E. K. *Arthur of Britain*, 1927.

CHANDLER, Howard. 'On the Symbolic Use of Number in the "Divina Commedia" and Elsewhere', *Transactions of the Royal Society of Literature of the U.K.* 2nd Series, XXX, 1910.

CHAPLIN, Dorothea. *Matter, Myth and Spirit*, 1935.

CHARBONNEAU-LASSAY, L. *Le Bestiaire du Christ*, 1940.

CHATTERJI, Usha. 'Shakta and Shakti', *Studies in Comparative Religion*, Autumn, 1968.

CHEVALIER, Jean (Ed.) *Dictionnaire des Symboles*, 1973.

CHÖGYAM TRUNGPA. *Visual Dharma*, 1975.

CHU, W. K. and SHERRILL, W. A. *The Astrology of the I Ching*, 1976.

CHURCHWARD, A. *Signs and Symbols of Primordial Man*, 1913.

CIRLOT, J. E. *A Dictionary of Symbols*, 1962.

CLARK, R. T. R. *Myth and Symbol in Ancient*

Egypt, 1960.

COLLINS, A. H. *Symbolism of Animals and Birds in English Church Architecture*, 1913.

CONDER, Claud Reignier. *Syrian Stone-Lore: the Monumental History of Palestine*, 1886.

COOK, Arthur Bernard. *Zeus. A Study in Ancient Religion*, 1940.

COOK, Roger. *The Tree of Life*, 1974.

COOMARASWAMY, Ananda K. *Elements of Buddhist Iconography*, 1935. *The Transformation of Nature in Art*, 1956. 'Symplegades', *Studies and Essays in the History and Science of Learning*, 1946. *Time and Eternity*, 1947. *Art and Thought*, 1947. *Hinduism and Buddhism*, 1943. *Christian and Oriental Philosophy of Art*, 1956. *The Dance of Siva*, 1958. 'Khawaj Khadir and the Fountain of Life in the Tradition of Persian and Mughal Art', *Studies in Comparative Religion*, Autumn, 1970. 'The Symbolism of Archery', *Studies in Comparative Religion*, Spring, 1971.

CORY, William. *Ancient Fragments*, 1828.

CRAWLEY, A. E. *The Mystic Rose*, 1902.

CREEL, H. G. *Studies in Early Chinese Culture*, 1937.

CREUZER, F. G. *Symbolik und Mythologie der alten Völker*, 1836–42.

CROSS, F. L. (ed.). *The Oxford Dictionary of the Christian Church*, 1966.

CUMONT, Franz. *The Mysteries of Mithra*, 1903. *Astrology and Religion Among the Greeks and Romans*, 1912. *Recherches sur le symbolisme funéraire des romains*, 1942.

DABU, Dastur Kurshed S. *Message of Zarathushtra. A Manual of Zoroastrianism*, 1959.

DALE-GREEN, Patricia. *The Dog*, 1966.

DANIÉLOU, J. 'Le Symbolisme du temple de Jerusalem chez Philon et Josephe', *Le Symbolisme cosmique des monuments religieux*, 1957. *Primitive Christian Symbols*, 1964.

DAVIDSON, H. R. Ellis. *The Sword in Anglo-Saxon England*, 1962.

DAWSON, R. (ed.). *The Legacy of China*, 1964.

DEANE, J. B. *The Worship of the Serpent*, 1830.

DEEDES, C. N. 'The Labyrinths', *The Labyrinth* (ed. H. S. Hooke), 1935.

DEREN, Maya. *Divine Horsemen*, 1953.

DICKSON, L. E. *History of the Theory of Numbers*, 1919.

DOANE, T. W. *Bible Myths and their Parallels in Other Religions*, 1908.

DORESS, J. *The Secret Books of the Egyptian Gnostics*, 1960.

DORSEY, George A. 'The Arapaho Sun Dance', *Anthropological Series*, IV, 1895.

DORSON, R. M. (ed.). *Peasant Customs and Savage Myths*, 1968.

DROWER, E. S. *Water into Wine*, 1956.

DUCHESNE-GUILLEMIN, J. *The Western Response to Zoroaster*, 1958.

DUNBAR, H. Flanders. *Symbolism in Mediaeval Art*, 1929. *Symbolism in Mediaeval Thought and its Consummation in the Divine Comedy*, 1929.

EISLER, Robert. *Orpheus the Fisher*, 1921. *Orphisch-dionysische Mysterien-Gedanken in der christlichen Antike*, 1925.

ELIADE, Mircea. *The Myth of the Eternal Return*, 1954. *Le Symbolisme cosmique des monuments religieux*, 1957. *Patterns in Comparative Religion*, 1958. *The Sacred and the Profane*, 1961. *Images and Symbols*, 1961. *The Forge and the Crucible*, 1962. *Shamanism*, 1964. *The Two and the One*, 1965. *Myths, Dreams and Mysteries*, 1968.

ELWORTHY, F. T. *The Evil Eye*, 1895. *Horns of Honour*, 1900.

Eranos Yearbooks. *Ostwestliche Symbolik und Seelenführung*, 1934. *The Configuration and Cult of the Great Mother*, 1938. *Ancient Sun Cults and Light Symbolism*, 1943. *Zur Idee des Archetypischen*, 1945. *Man and Time*, 1951. *Spirit and Nature*, 1954. *The Mysteries*, 1955. *Spiritual Disciplines*, 1960.

EVANS, A. J. *Mycenaean Tree and Pillar Cult*, 1901.

EVANS-WENTZ, W. Y. *The Fairy Cult in Celtic Countries*, 1911. *Tibetan Yoga and Secret Doctrines*, 1958.

FAGAN, C. *The Symbolism of the Constellations*, 1962.

FARBRIDGE, M. H. *Studies in Biblical and Semitic Symbolism*, 1923.

FARNELL, L. R. *The Evolution of Religion*, 1905.

FARRER, Austin. *A Rebirth of Images*, 1949.

FERGUSON, G. W. *Signs and Symbols in Christian Art*, 1954.

FERGUSON, John. *Illustrated Encyclopaedia of Mysticism*, 1976.

FLETCHER, J. B. *Symbolism of the Divine Comedy*, 1921.

FORLONG, G. J. R. *Faiths of Man. Encyclopaedia of Religions*, 1964.

FOWLER, W. W. *The Roman Festivals*, 1899.

FRANKLAND, Edward. *The Bear in Britain*, 1944.

FRASER, T. T. (ed.). *The Voices of Time*, 1966.

FRAZER, J. G. *Adonis, Attis, Osiris*, 1906. *The Golden Bough*, 1911.

FREEMAN, Rosemary. *The English Emblem Books*, 1948.

GARSTANG, John. *The Land of the Hittites*, 1910. *The Hittite Empire*, 1929.

GELLING, Peter, and DAVIDSON, H. E. *The Chariot of the Sun*, 1969.

GILES, Herbert A. *History of Chinese Pictorial Art*, 1905.

GIVRY, Grillot de. *Witchcraft, Magic and Alchemy*, 1931.

GLEADOW, Rupert. *The Origin of the Zodiac*, 1968.

GLUECK, N. *Deities and Dolphins*, 1966.

GOLDSMITH, Elizabeth E. *Sacred Symbols in Art*, 1912. *Life Symbols as Related to Sex Symbolism*, 1924. *Ancient Pagan Symbols*, 1929.

GOODENOUGH, E. R. *Jewish Symbols in the Graeco-Roman Period*, 1953.

GOODYEAR, William H. *The Grammar of the Lotus*, 1891.

GOULD, S. Baring. *Strange Survivals*, 1892.

GOVINDA, Lama Anagarika. *Foundations of Tibetan Mysticism*, 1960.

GRABAR, André. *Christian Iconography*, 1969.

GRAVES, Robert. *The White Goddess*, 1952.

GREG, R. P. 'The Meaning and Origin of the Fylfot and Swastika', *Archaeologia*, XLVIII, 1885.

GRUBECH, V. *The Culture of the Teutons*, 1931.

GUÉNON, René. *Introduction to the Study of Hindu Doctrines*, 1945. *Man and His Becoming According to the Vedanta*, 1945. *L'Esotérisme de Dante*, 1949. *La Grande Triade*, 1957. *The Symbolism of the Cross*, 1958. *Symboles fondamentaux de la science sacrée*, 1962.

GUENTHER, H. V. *The Jewel Ornament of Liberation*, 1959.

GUILLAUME, Alfred. *The Legacy of Islam*, 1931.

HALL, James. *Dictionary of Subjects and Symbols in Art*, 1974.

HALLIDAY, W. R. *The Pagan Background of Early Christianity*, 1925.

HAMILTON, H. C. (trans.). *The Geography of Strabo*, 1912.

HARGRAVES, Catherine Perry. *A History of Playing Cards*, 1930.

HARRIS, J. Rendel. *The Cult of the Heavenly Twins*, 1906.

HARRISON, Jane. 'Bird and Pillar Worship in Connection with Ouranian Divinities', *Transactions of the Third International Congress for the History of Religions*, 1908. *Prolegomena to the Study of Greek Religion*, 1908. *Ancient Art and Ritual*, 1911. *Themis*, 1927.

HARRISON, Raymond. *The Measure of Life*, 1936.

HARTLAND, E. S. *The Science of Fairy Tales*, 1891.

HARTLEY, Christine. *The Western Mystery Tradition*, 1968.

HEINDEL, Max. *Ancient and Modern Initiation*, 1931.

HENDERSON, J. L., and OAKES, M. *The Wisdom of the Serpent*, 1963.

HENTZE, Carl. 'Cosmogonie du Monde dressé debout et du Monde, renversé, *Mythos et symboles lunaires*, 1932.

HESIOD. *Theogony*.

HIRST, Désirée. *Hidden Riches*, 1964.

HOCART, A. M. *Kingship*, 1931. *The Life-giving Myth*, 1952.

HOLIDAY, F. W. *The Dragon and the Disc*, 1973.

HOLMYARD, E. J. *Alchemy*, 1956.

HOOD, Sinclair. *The Minoans*, 1971.

HOOKE, S. H. (ed.). *The Labyrinth*, 1935. *Some Cosmological Patterns in Babylonian Religion*, 1935. *Myth and Ritual*, 1933. *Babylonian and Assyrian Religion*, 1953.

HOPPER, Vincent Foster. *Mediaeval Number Symbolism*, 1938.

HOWEY, M. Oldfield. *The Cat in the Mystery Religions and Magic*, 1956.

HULME, F. Edward. *Symbolism in Christian Art*, 1894.

HULTKRANTZ, Ake. 'Attitudes to Animals in Soshone Indian Religion', *Studies in Comparative Religion*, Spring, 1970.

HYAMS, E. and ORDISH, G. *The Last of the Incas*, 1963.

HYDE, James. 'The Under-thought of the "Elder Edda"', *Transactions of the Royal Society of Literature of the U.K.*, Second Series, XXX, 1910.

IAMBLICHUS. *On the Mysteries of the Egyptians, Chaldeans and Assyrians*.

INCE, R. *Dictionary of Religion and Religions*, 1935.

INMAN, Thomas. *Ancient Faiths Embodied in Ancient Names*, 1868. *Ancient Pagan and Modern Christian Symbolism*, 1869.

JACKSON, Wilfred. *Shells as Evidence of the Migration of Early Culture*, 1917.

JAMES, E. O. 'The Sources of Christian Ritual', *The Labyrinth*, ed. S. H. Hooke, 1935. *The Cult of the Mother Goddess*, 1959.

JAMES, T. G. H. *Myths and Legends of Ancient Egypt*, 1970.

JASTROW, M. *Die Religion Babyloniens und Assyriens*, 1902–12.

JENNINGS, Hargrave. *The Rosicrucians, Their Rites and Mysteries*, 1870. *The Obelisk. Notices of the Origin, Purpose and History of Obelisks*, 1877.

JENSEN, Hans. *Sign, Symbol and Script*, 1970.

JOHNSON, F. E. (ed.). *Religious Symbolism*, 1955.

JOHNSON, O. S. *A Study in Chinese Alchemy*, 1928.

JONES, Owen. *Grammar of Ornament*, 1856.

JOSEPH, B. L. *Elizabethan Acting*, 1964.

JOSEPHUS. *Antiquities*. Book XVIII.

JUNG, C. G. *Aion*, 1952. *Complex, Archetype, Symbol*, 1953. *Symbols of Transformation*, 1956.

KARSTEN, R. *The Civilization of the South American Indians*, 1926.

KENDRICK, T. D. *The Druids*, 1927.

KERÉNYI, Karl. *Labyrinth-Studien. Labyrinthos als linien reflex einer mythologischen Idee*, 1950. *Essays on a Science of Mythology*, 1950. *The Heroes of the Greeks*, 1959.

KING, C. W. *Antique Gems and Rings*, 1860. *The Gnostics and Their Remains*, 1864. *The Natural History of Precious Stones and of Precious Metals*, 1867.

KING, E. G. *Akkadian Genesis*, 1888.

KIRK, G. S. *Myth, its Meaning and Functions in Ancient and Other Cultures*, 1970.

KNIGHT, R P. *Le Culte de Priape*, 1866.

KNIGHT, W. F. Jackson. *Cumaean Gates. A Reference in the Sixth Aeneid to the Initiation Pattern*, 1936.

KOCH, Rudolf. *The Book of Signs*, 1930.

KOZMINSKY, Isadore. *The Magic and Science of Jewels and Stones*, 1922.

KRAMRISCH, Stella. *The Hindu Temple*, 1946.

KUNZ, G. F. *The Curious Lore of Precious Stones*, 1912. *The Magic of Jewels and Charms*, 1915. *The Book of the Pearl*, 1908.

LAJARD, Felix. *Le Culte de Mithra*, 1847. *Recherches sur le culte de Vénus*, 1854.

LANGDON, S. H. 'Semitic Mythology', *The Mythology of All Races*, 1931.

LANGER, Susanne K. *Philosophy of Reason, Rite and Art*, 1942.

LAROUSSE. *New Encyclopaedia of Mythology*, 1959.

LAUFER, Berthold. *Jade. A Study in Chinese Archaeology and Religion*, 1912.

LAYARD, J. *The Lady of the Hare*, 1944.

LEHNER, Ernst. *Symbols, Signs and Signets*, 1950. *Folklore and Symbolism of Flowers, Plants and Trees*, 1960.

LEISEGANG, H. 'The Mystery of the Serpent', *Eranos Yearbooks*, 1955.

LETHABY, W. R. *Architecture, Mysticism and Myth*, 1892.

LEWIS, H. Spencer, *The Rosicrucian Manual*, 1938.

LEWIS, R. M. *Behold the Sign. Ancient Symbolism,* 1912.

LINGS, Martin. 'The Qoranic Symbolism of Water', *Studies in Comparative Religion,* Summer, 1968. 'Old Lithuanian Songs', *Studies in Comparative Religion,* Winter, 1969. 'The Seven Deadly Sins', *Studies in Comparative Religion,* Winter, 1971.

LU K'UAN Yu. *Ch'an and Zen Teaching,* 1962.

LUM, Peter. *Fabulous Beasts,* 1952.

MacCULLOCH, J. A. *The Religion of the Ancient Celts,* 1911.

MACKENZIE, D. A. *Teutonic Myth and Legend,* 1912. *The Migration of Symbols,* 1926.

MACROBIUS. *Saturnalia.*

MASANI, Ruston. *The Religion of the Good Life,* 1954.

MATHERS, M. *The Kabbalah Unveiled,* 1957.

MATTHEWS, W. H. *Mazes and Labyrinths,* 1922.

McKAY, J. G. 'The Deer Cult and the Deer Goddess of the Ancient Caledonians', *Folklore: Transactions of the Folklore Society,* XLIII, 1932.

McNEILL, F. Marian. *The Silver Bough,* 1959.

MEAD, G. R. S. *Orpheus,* 1896. *Quests Old and New,* 1898. *Fragments of a Faith Forgotten,* 1931.

MEES, G. H. *The Revelation in the Wilderness,* 1951–4.

MILLS, J. *Sacred Symbology,* 1853.

MÖHLER, J. A. *Symbolik,* 1832.

MOULTON, J. H. *Early Zoroastrianism,* 1913.

MURRAY, Gilbert. *Five Stages of Greek Religion,* 1930.

MURRAY, H. J. R. *A History of Chess,* 1913.

MURTI, T. R. V. *The Central Philosophy of Buddhism,* 1955.

NASR, Seyyed Hossein. *An Introduction to Islamic Cosmological Doctrines,* 1964.

NEEDHAM, J. *Science and Civilization in China,* 1954–.

NEIHARDT, J. G. *Black Elk Speaks,* 1932.

NEUMANN, Erich. *The Great Mother,* 1955. *Amor and Psyche,* 1956.

NEWTON, John. *Origin of Triads and Trinities,* 1909.

NILSSON, M. P. *The Mycenaean Origin of Greek Mythology,* 1932. *Greek Popular Religion,* 1946.

NOTT, Stanley C. *Chinese Culture in the Arts,* 1946. *Chinese Jade,* 1962.

O'FLAHERTY, Wendy. *Origins of Evil in Hindu Mythology,* 1976.

OESTERLEY, W. O. E. 'The Cult of Sabazios', in S. H. Cooke (ed.), *The Labyrinth,* 1935.

OKAKURA-KAKUZO. *The Book of Tea,* 1919.

ONIONS, R. B. *The Origins of European Thought,* 1951.

OTTO, Walter F. *The Homeric Gods,* 1954.

OUSPENSKY, L. and LOSSKY, V. *The Meaning of Icons,* 1969.

PALLIS, Marco. *Peaks and Lamas,* 1940. *The Way and the Mountain,* 1961.

PAPUS. *The Tarot of the Bohemians,* 1910. *La Science des nombres,* 1934.

PAVITT, W. T. and K. *The Book of Talismans, Amulets and Zodiacal Gems,* 1914.

PERRY, W. J. *The Children of the Sun,* 1923.

PETRIE, W. M. Flinders. *The Gods of Ancient Egypt,* 1905. *Religious Life in Ancient Egypt,* 1932.

PETRUCCI, R. *La Philosophie de la nature dans l'art d'Extrême Orient,* 1910.

PETTAZZONI, R. *Essays on the History of Religions,* 1954.

PIGGOTT, Stuart. *Ancient Europe,* 1965. *The Druids,* 1975.

PIKE, E. Royston. *Encyclopaedia of Religion and Religions,* 1951.

PITT-RIVERS, G. *The Riddle of the Labarum,* 1956.

PLINY. *Natural History.*

PLUTARCH. *On the Cessation of Oracles.*

POWELL, T. G. E. *The Celts,* 1958.

PROCLUS. *The Sphere.*

PURCE, Jill. *The Mystic Spiral,* 1974.

QUINTILIAN. *Institutio Oratoria.*

RADIN, Paul. *The Story of the North American Indian,* 1928. *The Culture of Winnebago,* 1949. *The Trickster,* 1956. *The Road of Life and Death,* 1968.

RAGLAN, Lord. *The Temple and the House,* 1964.

RAINE, Kathleen. 'Traditional Symbolism in Kubla Khan', *Studies in Comparative Religion,* Summer, 1967.

RANSOME, Hilda M. *The Sacred Bee in Ancient Times and Folklore,* 1937.

READ, John. 'Alchemy and Alchemists', *Folklore, Transactions of the Folklore Society,* XLIII, 1933.

RÉAU, Louis. *Iconographie de l'art chrétien,* 1955.

REDGRAVE, Herbert Stanley. *Alchemy, Ancient and Modern,* 1922.

REES, Alwyn. *The Celtic Heritage,* 1974.

REINACH, S. *Cultes, mythes et religions,* 1908.

RHYS, J. *Studies in the Arthurian Legend,* 1891.

RIDLEY, M. R. (trans.). *Sir Gawain and the Green Knight,* 1962.

RINGGREN, H. and STROM, A. V. *Religions of Mankind,* 1967.

ROBERTSON, J. M. *Pagan Christs,* 1928.

ROHEIM, Géza. *Animism, Magic and the Divine King,* 1972.

ROSS, Anne. *Pagan Celtic Britain,* 1967.

ROUT, E. A. *Maori Symbolism,* 1926.

RULAND, Martin. *Lexicon of Alchemy,* 1892.

SAYCE, A. H. 'The Origin and Growth of Religion as Illustrated by the Religion of the Ancient Babylonians', Hibbert Lectures, 1887.

SCHLESINGER, M. *Geschichte des Symbols,* 1912.

SCHOLEM, G. G. *Major Trends in Jewish Mysticism,* 1955.

SCHUON, Frithjof. *L'Oeil du coeur,* 1950. *Spiritual Perspectives and Human Facts,* 1954. *Understanding Islam,* 1963. *Light on the Ancient Worlds,* 1965. *In the Tracks of Buddhism,* 1968. *Dimensions of Islam,* 1969.

SCHWAB, Gustav. *Gods and Heroes,* 1947.

SÉJOURNÉ, Laurette. *Burning Water,* 1958.

SEWARD, Barbara. *The Symbolic Rose,* 1954.

SEZNEC, Jean. *The Survival of the Pagan Gods,* 1953.

SHARKEY, John. *Celtic Mysteries,* 1975.

SHEPHERD, Odell. *The Lore of the Unicorn,* 1930.

SHORT, Ernest H. *The House of God. A History of Religious Architecture and Symbolism*, 1925.

SILBERER, H. *Problems of Mysticism and its Symbolism*, 1917.

SILCOCK, Arnold. *Introduction to Chinese Art and History*, 1936.

SILLAR, F. C. and MYLER, R. M. *The Symbolic Pig*, 1961.

SIMPSON, William. *The Buddhist Praying Wheel*, 1896.

SIRÉN, Osvald. *Gardens of China*, 1949.

SMITH, D. Howard. *Chinese Religions*, 1968.

SMITH, G. Elliot. *The Evolution of the Dragon*, 1919.

SNELLGROVE, David. *Buddhist Himalaya*, 1957. *Himalayan Pilgrimage*, 1961.

SPENCE, Lewis. *The Myth of the North American Indians*, 1914. *The Gods of Mexico*, 1923. *Myths and Legends of Ancient Egypt*, 1930. *British Fairy Origins*, 1946. *The Mysteries of Britain*, 1970.

SQUIRE, Charles. *The Mythology of the British Isles*, 1905. *Celtic Myth and Legend*, 1912.

STEWART, T. M. *Symbolism of the Gods of the Egyptians*, 1927.

STUART, J. *Ikons*, 1975.

SYKES, E. *Dictionary of Non-classical Mythology*, 1962.

SZEKELY, E. B. *The Teaching of the Essenes*, 1957.

TACITUS. *Germania*.

THIERENS, A. E. *The General Book of the Tarot*, 1928.

THOMAS, E. J. *The Life of Buddha*, 1975.

TIZAC, H. d'Ardenne de. *Les Animaux dans l'art chinois*, 1923.

TOLKOWSKY, S. *Hesperides. A History of the Culture and Use of Citrus Fruit*, 1938.

TOYNBEE, J. M. C. *Death and Burial in the Roman World*, 1971.

TREDWELL, W. R. *Chinese Art Motives*, 1915.

TUCCI, Giuseppe. *The Theory and Practice of the Mandala*, 1969.

TURVILLE-PETRIE, E. O. G. *Myth and Religion of the North*, 1964.

TWINING, L. *Symbols and Emblems of Early and Mediaeval Christian Art*, 1852.

URLIN, Ethel. *Festivals, Holy Days and Saints' Days*, 1915.

VAN BUREN, E. Douglas. *The Flowing Vase and the God with Streams*, 1933.

VAN GENNEP, Arnold. *The Rites of Passage*, 1959.

VAN MARLE, Raimond. *Iconographie de l'art profane au moyen-âge et à la renaissance*, 1931.

VERMASSEREN, M. J. *Mithras, the Secret God*, 1963.

VINYCOMB, John. *Fictitious and Symbolic Creatures in Art, with special reference to British Heraldry*, 1906.

VISSER, M. W. de. *The Dragon in China and Japan*, 1913.

VRIES, A. de. *Dictionary of Symbols and Images*, 1974.

WAITE, A. E. *The Book of the Holy Grail*, 1921. *The History of Magic*, 1930.

WALTHER, W. *Lehrbuch der Symbolik*, 1924.

WATTS, A. W. *Myth and Ritual in Christianity*, 1954.

WEBBER, F. R. *Church Symbolism*, 1927.

WEIGALL, Arthur. *The Paganism in Our Christianity* (n.d.).

WESTON, Jessie L. *The Quest of the Holy Grail*, 1913.

WESTROPP, H. M. and WAKE, C. S. *Primitive Symbolism as Illustrated in Phallic Worship*, 1885. *Ancient Symbol Worship in the Religions of Antiquity*, 1874.

WHEATLEY, Paul. *City as Symbol*, 1969.

WHITTICK, Arnold. *Symbols, Signs and their Meaning*, 1960.

WHYMANT, Neville. *A China Manual*, 1948.

WILKINS, Ethne. *The Rose-garden Game*, 1969.

WILLETTS, R. F. *Cretan Cults and Festivals*, 1962. *Everyday Life in Ancient Crete*, 1969.

WILLIAMS, C. A. S. *Outlines of Chinese Symbolism and Art Motives*, 1931.

WILSON, T. 'The Swastika', *Annual Report of the U.S. National Museum*, 1896.

WIND, Edgar. *Pagan Mysteries in the Renaissance*, 1968.

WISSLER, Clark. *The American Indian*, 1950.

WOODROFFE, John (Arthur Avalon). *Shakta and Shakti*, 1919. *The World as Power*, 1922–3. *The Serpent Power*, 1931.

WORNUM, Ralph N. *Analysis of Ornament*, 1877.

WOSEIN, Marie-Gabriele. *Sacred Dance*, 1974.

WRIGHT, A. R. *British Calendar Customs*, 1940.

YAP YONG and COTTERELL, A. *The Early Civilization of China*, 1975.

YETTS, W. Percival. *Symbolism in Chinese Art*, 1912.

ZAEHNER, R. C. *The Dawn and Twilight of Zoroastrianism*, 1961.

ZIMMER, Heinrich. *Myths and Symbols in Indian Art and Civilization*, 1946. *The King and the Corpse*, 1956.

208

Acknowledgments

The publisher's acknowledgements are due to the following institutions for permission to reproduce the illustrations on the pages mentioned:

Ankara Museum 173 *top*; Ashmolean Museum, Oxford 27 *centre*; Bewdley Museum, Worcs. 53 *bottom*; Biblioteca Apostolica Vaticana 29 *top*, 67 *bottom*; Biblioteca Estense, Modena 133 *bottom*; Biblioteca Marciana, Venice 41 *top*, 171 *top*; Biblioteca Mediceo-Laurenziana, Florence 159 *bottom*; Bibliothèque de l'Arsenal, Paris 137 *centre*; Bibliothèque Nationale, Paris 29 *bottom*, 91 *top*, 167 *top*, 189 *top*; Bodleian Library, Oxford 49 *bottom*, 133 *top*; British Library 19 *top*; British Museum, London 13 *centre*, 21 *centre*, 31 *top*, 37 *top*, 53 *top*, 57 *bottom*, 63 *bottom*, 89 *bottom*, 109 *top*, 111 *top* and *bottom*, 117 *bottom*, 123 *centre*, 135 *bottom*, 139 *top*, 145 *top*, 163 *top*, 165 *top*, 195 *top*; Cairo Museum 19 *centre*, 43 *bottom*, 131 *bottom*; Chester Beatty Library and Gallery of Oriental Art, Dublin 185 *top*; Delphi Museum 161 *top*; Field Museum of Natural History, Chicago 157 *centre*; Galleria Estense, Modena 199; Germanisches Nationalmuseum, Nuremberg 47 *bottom*; Government Museum, Madras 13 *bottom*; Gulbenkian Museum of Oriental Art, Durham 21 *top*, 27 *top*, 73 *top*, 127 *centre*, 145 *bottom*, 175 *top*; Haffenreffer Museum of Anthropology, Brown University 49 *top*; Instituto Nacional de Antropología e Historia, Mexico 153 *centre*, 183 *top*; Izmir Museum 25 *bottom*; Kupferstichkabinett, Berlin 23 *centre*; Louvre, Paris 35 *top*, 41 *bottom*, 59 *top*, 81 *top*, 107 *bottom*; Musée de l'Oeuvre Notre-Dame, Strasbourg 23 *top*; Musée Municipale, Douai 181 *top*; Musei Vaticani 39 *bottom*, 135 *top*, 153 *top*; Museo de Arte de Cataluña, Barcelona 191 *top*; Museo Laterano, Rome 151 *bottom*; Museum Antiker Kleinkunst, Munich 173 *bottom*; Museum of Fine Arts, Boston 141 *bottom*, 189 *bottom*; Museum of the American Indian, New York 21 *bottom*, 51 *top*, 85 *top*, 195 *bottom*; National Gallery, London 11 *top*, 55 *centre*, 179 *bottom*; National Gallery of Art, Washington D.C.: Kress Collection 151 *centre*; Nationalmuseet, Copenhagen 31 *bottom*, 33 *bottom*; National Museum of Korea 193 *top*; National Museum of Man, Ottawa 47 *centre*, 137 *bottom*; Ny Carlsberg Glyptothek, Copenhagen 137 *top*; Rheinisches Landesmuseum, Bonn 47 *top*; Royal Scottish Museum, Edinburgh 39 *top*, 45 *top*; Staatsbibliothek, Berlin 13 *top*; Stadtmuseum, Cologne 183 *bottom*; Statens Historiska Museum, Stockholm 23 *bottom*; Victoria and Albert Museum, London 33 *top*, 67 *top*, 77 *centre*, 79 *bottom*, 127 *bottom*, 129 *top*, 135 *centre*, 141 *top*, 157 *bottom*, 175 *bottom*; William Rockhill Nelson Gallery of Art, Kansas City 177 *bottom*.